D1090925

SOCIETY FOR NEW TESTAMENT STUDIES
*MONOGRAPH SERIES*



48

# MATTHEW AND PAUL

# Matthew and Paul

a comparison of ethical perspectives

ROGER MOHRLANG

Associate Professor of New Testament
Whitworth College
Spokane, Washington



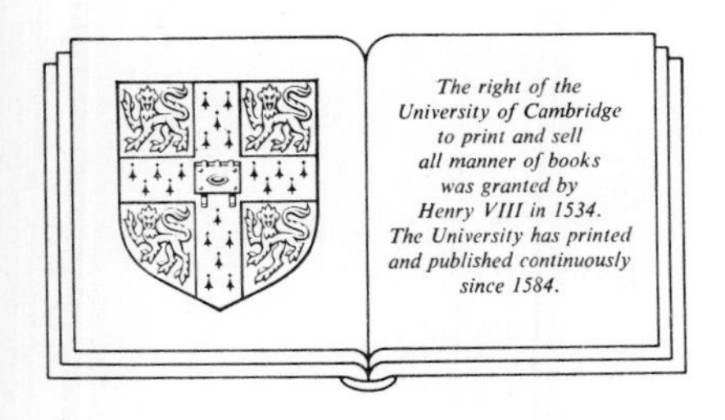

CAMBRIDGE UNIVERSITY PRESS

CAMBRIDGE
LONDON · NEW YORK · NEW ROCHELLE
MELBOURNE · SYDNEY

Published by the Press Syndicate of the University of Cambridge
The Pitt Building, Trumpington Street, Cambridge CB2 1RP
32 East 57th Street, New York, NY 10022, USA
296 Beaconsfield Parade, Middle Park, Melbourne 3206, Australia



First published 1984

Printed in Great Britain at
the University Press, Cambridge

Library of Congress catalogue card number: 83-10147

*British Library cataloguing in publication data*

Mohrlang, Roger
Matthew and Paul – (Society for New Testament Studies.
Monograph series; 48)
1. Matthew, *Saint* – Ethics 2. Paul of the Apostle, *Saint* – Ethics
I. Title II.Series
241 BS2545.E8

ISBN 0 521 25093 5

W.T.

*To Dot and Leslie*

## CONTENTS

# PREFACE

This study was conceived, strangely enough, under a thatch roof in a village in northeastern Nigeria, where I was working on the translation of the Higi New Testament from 1968 to 1974. It was given shape in the following years at Fuller Theological Seminary in Pasadena, under the tutelage of Dr Ralph P. Martin, and finally brought to birth at the University of Oxford in 1979, where it was presented in the form of a thesis to the Faculty of Theology for the degree of Doctor of Philosophy. This book has grown out of that thesis.

Of the countless people who have contributed, directly or indirectly, to the writing of this volume, two in particular are deserving of special acknowledgement. The Revd Canon J.L. Houlden, Lecturer in New Testament studies at King's College, London, whose stimulating little book, *Ethics and the New Testament*, first introduced me to the fascinating world of New Testament ethics when I was in seminary, did an excellent job of supervising my doctoral studies at Oxford, and the present work owes an immense amount to his wise guidance, inspiration and encouragement. To him I shall always be indebted. But it is my good wife Dot who deserves the greatest praise – not only for the countless hours she spent typing up various drafts of the manuscript and assisting with details, but also for remaining so cheerful and supportive throughout. (Who else would ever have so happily consented to continuing the proofreading of her husband's thesis only one hour after the birth of their first child?) For this and a thousand other things I bless her name – and the Lord we serve together. It is to these two good people that this book is dedicated, with my deepest gratitude.

I should also like to thank my friends and colleagues who read over and made useful suggestions on various chapters, especially Mr David J.A. Clines, the Revd Robert Morgan, and Dr F. Dale Bruner. Sincere thanks are also due the editors of the SNTS Monograph Series, Prof. R. McL. Wilson and Dr M.E. Thrall, and Miss Jane Hodgart of Cambridge University Press, for their many helpful comments and detailed suggestions;

and all those faithful servants of Bodley whose efforts made this research possible, yet whose labour commonly goes unthanked. Above all, *χάρις τῷ θεῷ διὰ Ἰησοῦ Χριστοῦ τοῦ κυρίου ἡμῶν.*

R.M.

*Whitworth College*

# ABBREVIATIONS

| | |
|---|---|
| AB | Anchor Bible |
| AGJU | Arbeiten zur Geschichte des antiken Judentums und des Urchristentums |
| *Amer.Jour.Theol.* | *American Journal of Theology* |
| Ana. Bib. | Analecta Biblica |
| *Ang.Theol.Rev.* | *Anglican Theological Review* |
| *Ann.Swed.Theol.Inst.* | *Annual of the Swedish Theological Institute* |
| ASNU | Acta Seminarii Neotestamentici Upsaliensis |
| ATANT | Abhandlungen zur Theologie des Alten und Neuen Testaments |
| ATD | Acta Theologica Danica |
| *Aus.Bib.Rev.* | *Australian Biblical Review* |
| BET | Beiträge zur Evangelischen Theologie |
| BHT | Beiträge zur Historischen Theologie |
| *Bib.Res.* | *Biblical Research* |
| *Bib.Theol.Bull.* | *Biblical Theology Bulletin* |
| *Bib.Trans.* | *Bible Translator* |
| *Bib.Zeit.* | *Biblische Zeitschrift* |
| *BJRL* | *Bulletin of the John Rylands Library of Manchester University* |
| BNTC | Black's New Testament Commentaries |
| BS | Biblische Studien |
| BU | Biblische Untersuchungen |
| BZNW | Beihefte zur Zeitschrift für die Neutestamentliche Wissenschaft |
| CB | Coniectanea Biblica |
| CBC | Cambridge Bible Commentary |
| *CBQ* | *Catholic Biblical Quarterly* |
| CGT | Cambridge Greek Testament |
| CGTC | Cambridge Greek Testament Commentary |
| CNT | Commentaire du Nouveau Testament |
| *Comm.Viat.* | *Communio Viatorum* |
| *Con.Theol.Mon.* | *Concordia Theological Monthly* |
| EB | Études Bibliques |
| EKKNT | Evangelisch-Katholischer Kommentar zum Neuen Testament |
| *Eph.Theol.Lov.* | *Ephemerides Theologicae Lovanienses* |

| | |
|---|---|
| *EpR* | *Epworth Review* |
| ET | English translation |
| *Ev.Theol.* | *Evangelische Theologie* |
| *ExT* | *Expository Times* |
| FRLANT | Forschungen zur Religion und Literatur des Alten und Neuen Testaments |
| GrNT | Grundrisse zum Neuen Testament |
| GTA | Göttinger Theologische Arbeiten |
| *Harv.Theol.Rev.* | *Harvard Theological Review* |
| *Hey.Jour.* | *Heythrop Journal* |
| *Hist.of Religs.* | *History of Religions* |
| HNT | Handbuch zum Neuen Testament |
| HTKNT | Herders Theologischer Kommentar zum Neuen Testament |
| HUT | Hermeneutische Untersuchungen zur Theologie |
| *IB* | *Interpreter's Bible* |
| ICC | International Critical Commentary |
| *IDB* | *Interpreter's Dictionary of the Bible* |
| *Interp.* | *Interpretation* |
| *JBL* | *Journal of Biblical Literature* |
| *JR* | *Journal of Religion* |
| *JSNT* | *Journal for the Study of the New Testament* |
| *JTS* | *Journal of Theological Studies* |
| KEKNT | Kritisch-exegetischer Kommentar über das Neue Testament |
| *Ker.u.Dog.* | *Kerygma und Dogma* |
| LHD | Library of History and Doctrine |
| *Luth.Qtr.* | *Lutheran Quarterly* |
| MarTS | Marburger Theologische Studien |
| *Mél.Sci.Rel.* | *Mélanges de Science Religieuse* |
| *Mish.*Ber. | *Mishnah* Berakoth |
| *Mish.*Men. | *Mishnah* Menahoth |
| *Mish.*Shab. | *Mishnah* Shabbath |
| MNTC | Moffatt New Testament Commentary |
| MünTS | Münchener Theologische Studien |
| NA | Neutestamentliche Abhandlungen |
| NCB | New Century Bible |
| NClB | New Clarendon Bible |
| *NIDNTT* | *New International Dictionary of New Testament Theology* |
| NLCNT | New London Commentary on the New Testament |
| *Nov.Test.* | *Novum Testamentum* |
| NTD | Das Neue Testament Deutsch |
| NTL | New Testament Library |
| *NTS* | *New Testament Studies* |
| NTSR | New Testament for Spiritual Reading |
| OBO | Orbis Biblicus et Orientalis |
| PNTC | Pelican New Testament Commentaries |
| *Rech.Sci.Rel.* | *Recherches de Science Religieuse* |

| | |
|---|---|
| *Rev.Bib.* | *Revue Biblique* |
| *Rev.Sci.Phil.Théol.* | *Revue des Sciences Philosophiques et Théologiques* |
| *Rev.Thom.* | *Revue Thomiste* |
| SANT | Studien zum Alten und Neuen Testament |
| SB | Stuttgarter Bibelstudien |
| S.-B. | Strack-Billerbeck |
| SBL | Society of Biblical Literature |
| SBM | Stuttgarter Biblische Monographien |
| SBT | Studies in Biblical Theology |
| SHAW | Sitzungsberichte der Heidelberger Akademie der Wissenschaften |
| SJLA | Studies in Judaism in Late Antiquity |
| *SJT* | *Scottish Journal of Theology* |
| SM | Sermon on the Mount |
| SNT | Supplements to Novum Testamentum |
| SNTS | Society for New Testament Studies |
| *SR* | *Studies in Religion/Sciences Religieuses* |
| Stud. and Docu. | Studies and Documents |
| *Stud.Theol.* | *Studia Theologica* |
| TBC | Torch Bible Commentaries |
| TD | Theologischen Dissertationen |
| *TDNT* | *Theological Dictionary of the New Testament* |
| *Theol.* | *Theology* |
| *Theol.Arbeiten* | *Theologische Arbeiten* |
| *Theol.Stud.* | *Theological Studies* |
| *Theol.u.Glaube* | *Theologie und Glaube* |
| *Theol.Zeit.* | *Theologische Zeitschrift* |
| THNT | Theologischer Handkommentar zum Neuen Testament |
| TICP | Travaux de l'Institut Catholique de Paris |
| TNTC | Tyndale New Testament Commentaries |
| *Tri.Theol.Zeit.* | *Trierer Theologische Zeitschrift* |
| TU | Texte und Untersuchungen zur Geschichte der altchristlichen Literatur |
| *Tyn.Bull.* | *Tyndale Bulletin* |
| *Un. Sem.Qtr.Rev.* | *Union Seminary Quarterly Review* |
| UNT | Untersuchungen zum Neuen Testament |
| VIKJ | Veröffentlichungen aus dem Institut Kirche und Judentum |
| WC | Westminster Commentaries |
| WCB | World Christian Books |
| WMANT | Wissenschaftliche Monographien zum Alten und Neuen Testament |
| *Z.Ev.Eth.* | *Zeitschrift für Evangelische Ethik* |
| *ZNW* | *Zeitschrift für die Neutestamentliche Wissenschaft* |
| *ZST* | *Zeitschrift für Systematische Theologie* |
| *ZThK* | *Zeitschrift für Theologie und Kirche* |

# INTRODUCTION

Contemporary New Testament scholarship reflects the current trend in literary criticism to see works as 'integrated wholes', and the body of a writer's work as 'a totality proceeding from a single mind'.[1] Redaction-critical studies in particular have therefore focused attention as never before on the theological perspectives of the New Testament writers themselves, in an attempt to understand how these may have shaped their writings. As a result, there is a growing appreciation of the importance of understanding the individual writers' thought, and a renewed interest in comparing their viewpoints.

The writings of Matthew[2] and Paul are of special interest in this regard, because of the different positions they seem to take with respect to the Jewish law – a matter that would appear to have far-reaching implications not only for their own views of the Christian life (and those of the communities they represent), but also for Christian theology and ethics more generally. These two writers therefore provide a useful point of focus for the larger question of unity and diversity in the New Testament as a whole.

This particular study is an attempt to compare the two writers' views on ethics. Its concern is not so much with the specific content of their moral teachings (though that inevitably enters in), as with the overall structure of their ethical thought. The aim is to analyse the most important factors underlying their ethics, to see how these basic elements relate to one another and to their theological views more generally, and then to compare their perspectives.

Special attention is given to the motivation of ethics, for here we expect to find important clues to their understanding of the relationship between theology and ethics. Though rarely exploited, motivational considerations represent a crucial point of interaction between belief and behaviour, and thus provide a useful point of entry into the writers' thinking.

The chapters are therefore structured around five topics of major importance to the motivation of ethics in their writings: law, reward and punishment, relationship to Christ and the role of grace, love, and inner forces. Under each of these heads we examine first Matthew, then Paul, and then essay a comparison of their thought. A brief concluding chapter attempts to synthesize the results, highlight the chief conclusions, and identify the key factors underlying their differences.

The study centres on an analysis of the text itself. Accordingly, and to avoid interruption in the flow of the argument, most of the critical interaction with New Testament scholarship is relegated to the notes. In addition, it should be noted that the investigation covers the whole of the text, and not merely the so-called 'ethical sections';[3] implicit as well as explicit elements must be taken into account if one is to gain a truly comprehensive understanding of the writers' thought.

### *Presuppositions*

The following are major assumptions and critical judgements underlying this study.

#### 1. Matthew

(1) Concerning Matthew's written sources, Mark is regarded as the only identifiable source upon which we may safely rely. In spite of its traditional acceptance, no assumptions are made about the author's use of a hypothetical Q document;[4] accordingly, consideration of Luke is left largely to the side.[5] Matthew's attitude toward Mark appears to be one of respect generally, though he clearly regards it as inadequate in certain respects, and feels the freedom to alter it according to his own understanding.

(2) The analysis is to a certain extent not dependent on any particular view of sources; for I assume that, by and large, the final form of the Gospel, as interpreted tradition – irrespective of its derivation – reflects the understanding of Matthew himself. Though there are some difficulties in maintaining this view consistently for every detail of the Gospel, it is taken as a working assumption – and a reasonable one, in view of the freedom the evangelist displays at so many points in adjusting the Marcan tradition to his own viewpoint. (What applies to Mark presumably holds for any other source as well.) We expect the author's own perspective to be most clearly revealed, of course, at those points that diverge most sharply from the Marcan account; and here a redaction-critical approach (employed judiciously[6]) proves to be useful. But unlike Windisch,[7] we need not take these to be the *only* points that manifest Matthew's perspective. One can learn both from what he adjusts and from what he retains in the tradition.[8] In other words, following Houlden,[9] I make the simple assumption

that, from whatever source he derives it, Matthew subscribes to what he writes – just as Paul does. Whatever else it is, then – and I certainly do not wish to belittle the importance of the underlying tradition or to over-emphasize the evangelist's own creativity – the Gospel may be viewed as representative of the thought of Matthew himself (but not necessarily the totality of his thought).

(3) Behind the writing of such an ecclesiological Gospel is assumed the presence of a community with which the evangelist identifies, and whose understanding and traditions are mirrored in what he writes[10] – though this does not imply that the final result does not reflect Matthew's own shaping. Whether this 'community' consists of a single congregation or several remains an open question; in any event, it is assumed that the particular emphases arising out of the evangelist's selective reworking of the traditional material bear at least in part directly on the immediate needs and problems of this community[11] – though the intended audience for the Gospel may be of a much wider scope, of course. Thus, Matthew may be considered as much a 'pastor' as Paul.[12]

(4) Though a large degree of coherence is expected,[13] neither absolute consistency nor a totally systematized viewpoint is demanded.[14] It is considered more reasonable to allow for certain discrepancies on the part of a single redactor than to account for the apparent self-contradictions[15] by positing multiple redactors – the final one of whom at least must then be charged with inconsistency in any case.

## 2. Paul

(1) With regard to Paul, the following letters are accepted as authentic: Romans; 1, 2 Corinthians; Galatians; Philippians; Colossians; 1,2 Thessalonians; Philemon.[16] Note that Colossians and 2 Thessalonians are retained as probably genuine[17] (their inclusion does little to change the essential picture in any case[18]); but Ephesians and the Pastorals are excluded as at least questionable. The portrait Luke paints of Paul in Acts differs sufficiently from Paul's own writings (at least with regard to ethics) to be likewise excluded from consideration;[19] occasional points of comparison, however, are noted.

(2) In general, questions concerning the integrity of the epistles have little bearing on the work, for virtually the whole of the accepted corpus may still be taken as Paul's own writing and therefore reflecting his own thought.[20]

(3) The fact that each of Paul's letters is historically and contextually conditioned, and must therefore be understood first of all in the light of

its own *Sitz im Leben* (a point correctly emphasized in many recent Pauline studies[21]), in no way negates the validity of searching for an underlying ethical (or theological) structure – though it certainly complicates that task and raises a valid caution against generalizing without taking due consideration of all the possible factors shaping Paul's statements in context.[22] The motivation of ethics, for example, though certainly determined in part by his assessment of the specific problems and communities being addressed, may not unreasonably be assumed to reflect more basic elements in the overall structure of his thought also.

(4) Several recent works notwithstanding, within the span of the accepted corpus I see no conclusive evidence of any major development in Paul's thought,[23] in either theology or ethics – though there are clearly differences of emphasis and presentation reflecting the different situations being addressed in the various letters. Indeed, it is the failure to take these different issues sufficiently into account that underlies many of the recent (and unnecessary) postulations of a 'progression' in Paul's thinking.[24] Further, the very difficulty of dating Galatians and the prison epistles with any degree of certainty itself renders suspect most attempts to trace such a development.[25]

(5) As with Matthew, so for Paul neither absolute consistency nor a totally systematized viewpoint is demanded; but a large measure of overall coherence is expected.[26]

(6) In distinction from some other analyses, rather than attempting to define one primary starting-point or all-embracing 'centre' of Paul's thought (whether it be eschatology, anthropology, justification by faith, the question of Jews and gentiles, participation in Christ, etc.[27]) – a problematic approach that is fundamentally inadequate to deal with the full range of the apostle's thought and its complexities[28] – I prefer to adopt a more pluralistic approach, and to think in terms of a number of different strands, any one or more of which may be dominant and formative at any given point in his argumentation. Clearly, however, some are more central than others – e.g. the conviction of God's grace in Christ, which Paul brings to bear on a wide variety of issues.

(7) Finally, for both writers I recognize the importance of attempting to distinguish between those sanctions that are of primary importance and those that function in a secondary way, as reinforcement and support.[29] At the same time, however, even the secondary considerations reflect something of the writer's thought (though perhaps on a different level), and therefore also reveal aspects of the underlying ethical construct.

### *Brief Survey of Previous Work*

Up till now, relatively little detailed comparative study has been done on the overall ethical perspectives of these two writers – or indeed, of any of the New Testament writers. Considerable research has been done, of course, on various aspects of their ethical thought individually, and much of this may be found summarized in recent major works on New Testament theology. Several major works on New Testament ethics are also available,[30] but on the whole they are rather disappointing, with few reflecting a sufficiently critical methodology to be of much use for comparative purposes. Of them all, J.L. Houlden's *Ethics and the New Testament*, though brief, is by far the most stimulating and fruitful – and has provided both the foundation and the approach for the present study itself.

Most of the earlier work on ethics in Matthew's Gospel centred on the Sermon on the Mount,[31] which was all too often treated independently of the rest of the Gospel. More recent investigations have dealt with characteristic themes of the Gospel as a whole – e.g. law, authority, righteousness, obedience and judgement.[32] In addition, since the Second World War numerous attempts have been made to identify the *Sitz im Leben* behind the Gospel,[33] and many of these include useful analyses of major ethical motifs. There is no single study, however, that provides a truly comprehensive account of Matthew's ethical viewpoint; perhaps the writings of G. Barth, Blair, and Strecker come closest to doing so.

Considerably more research, of course, has been done on Paul's thought than Matthew's. In addition to countless articles and volumes written on various aspects of Pauline theology and ethics, there is a large number of substantial works that set out to provide a comprehensive view of his thought as a whole, several of which are concerned primarily with his ethics.[34] There are also a number of Pauline studies devoted specifically to motivational considerations[35] – though many include analyses that, for one reason or another, are less than fully satisfactory. Overall, for depth of perception and analysis, the most significant major works are probably those of Bultmann, Furnish, Ridderbos, E.P. Sanders, and Beker.[36]

Though there have been few thorough comparative studies of Matthew and Paul, there have been numerous attempts to compare Jesus and Paul;[37] and to the extent that such works draw upon Matthean materials, they serve indirectly to illumine our understanding of the relation between Matthew and Paul. But, on the whole, they are of limited value.

Comparative work on the two writers themselves has blossomed only since the advent of redaction criticism; unfortunately, much of it has been done largely in passing. For the most part, attention has focused on some aspect of the question of law and grace ( often centred on the concept of righteousness), the most obvious and significant point of comparison.[38] A few writers have devoted major sections to Matthew and Paul individually and/or to a comparison of their perspectives, or certain aspects of them. Of these, the most illuminating and useful analyses are those of Windisch, McArthur, Hill, Campenhausen, Wendland, Houlden, and Furnish;[39] the most provocative, those of W.D. Davies and Goulder.[40]

Though many of these comparative studies yield fruitful insights, none provides a really comprehensive comparison of the two writers' ethical thought; most are of much more limited scope. In addition, a good number lack either balance or precision and accuracy, and consequently present a somewhat distorted picture – with some emphasizing their similarities, others their differences. The resulting impression is quite confused: while some see Matthew and Paul in intimate accord, others see them in profound disagreement; on this issue scholarly opinion is widely divergent. What is required, then, if a clearer, more accurate understanding of their relative ethical perspectives is to be gained, is a more thorough analysis of the structures of thought underlying their ethics,[41] and a closer, more careful comparison of the patterns that emerge – with a more precise description of the exact points of similarity and difference than has heretofore been achieved. This study is devoted to that end.

# 1

# LAW

For religious Jews in the early Christian era, the Mosaic law was the authoritative expression of God's will and absolutely central to all of life. As such, it functioned both as the basis of ethical obligation and as the definitive proclamation of what constituted morally upright behaviour. Ethical living was accordingly understood largely in terms of compliance with the law. As in any moral system based on legal considerations, authority, obedience and judgement were key concepts in the overall structure, and heavily coloured the Jewish view of life.

In view of the fact that both Matthew and Paul appear to reflect Jewish backgrounds,[1] it is appropriate to begin our study by investigating the extent to which traditional legal concepts have shaped their ethics. To what extent do the two writers view the Christian life within the framework of the law, and to what degree do they think of ethical behaviour as motivated by a sense of 'law'? How has their understanding of Christ modified their conception of the law and its role in the Christian's life? As this whole question is of fundamental importance for our understanding of their moral perspectives, especial attention will be devoted to it.

## 1. *Matthew*

The importance in Matthew's thinking of the whole question of the law[2] and its place in the Christian community is clear from the prominent place he gives to Jesus' discussion of the issue in 5.17–48. But when we inquire more specifically into Matthew's understanding of the law, we find ourselves confronted by a problem of considerable complexity. For side by side lie statements that appear to assert both the continuing validity of the law and its abrogation, that express both rigorously conservative and radically progressive interpretations. How do we reconcile such seemingly disparate statements?[3]

## 1.1 The Law Affirmed

We look first at the evidence in the text that suggests Matthew views the law as still valid for the Christian community.

### *5.17–19: the law*

Apart from the evangelist's tendency to think in terms of legal concepts,[4] the primary evidence for this belief is the programmatic passage 5.17–19. The passage is of crucial importance for the understanding of law in the Gospel, but notoriously difficult to interpret. As it has already been discussed in detail numerous times,[5] I shall simply highlight some of the key issues.

Much of the discussion centres on the meaning of *πληρῶσαι* in 5.17: in what way does Matthew view Jesus as 'fulfilling' the law? On this point, there is considerable divergence of opinion and no consensus at all.[6] At least four distinct senses have been proposed for the term in this context, with regard to the law: (1) to obey or carry out the demands of the law;[7] (2) to affirm or validate the law;[8] (3) to explicate or live out the deeper meaning and intent of the law;[9] (4) to complete or bring to pass the ultimate goal of the law[10] – an interpretation that is sometimes taken to imply that some or all of the precepts of the law are now set aside as no longer applicable.[11] The latter interpretation would give *πληρῶσαι* the same meaning in relation to both 'the law' and 'the prophets' (which, however, are probably not to be treated separately[12]), but from other considerations is the one least likely to represent the writer's intention. Matthew uses the term *πληρῶσαι* elsewhere[13] in both this sense[14] and the first sense (3.15);[15] but the larger context of 5.21–48 and those passages that emphasize the priority of love (7.12; 9.13; 12.7; 22.40) suggest the third sense, while the antithesis of *πληρῶσαι* to *καταλῦσαι* in the immediate context argues for the second. In the light of the various possibilities, some understandably opt for a broader, more comprehensive interpretation of the term.[16] In any case, with such lack of consensus, it is certain that our understanding of Matthew's view of the law cannot be based on a clear and agreed exegesis of *πληρῶσαι* in 5.17.

The interpretation of 5.17–19 is further complicated by confusion regarding the history of the tradition lying behind it, and the extent to which these *logia* do or do not represent Matthew's own understanding.[17] The wide divergence of opinion on this matter points up the extreme difficulty of attempting to distinguish tradition and redaction in non-paralleled passages such as these, and supports the conviction that it is preferable to treat such passages as wholes, as interpreted tradition reflecting in its entirety the writer's own understanding and viewpoint.[18] And with regard to 5.17–19, no matter what the precise nuance of πληρῶσαι or the exact details of the tradition-history lying behind the text, the point of the passage as a whole, as it now stands in the Gospel, can only be that *the entire law remains valid* and demands strict obedience from the Christian community.[19] This in turn precludes any antinomian implications of πληρῶσαι in 5.17.

Those who deny this conclusion on the basis of statements made elsewhere in the Gospel sometimes point to the temporal qualification added in 5.18*c* (ἕως ἂν πάντα γένηται), which some take as a reference to the fulfilment of the law in the life, death, resurrection and/or teachings of Jesus or the early Church[20] – in the third or fourth sense of πληρῶσαι above. But in the immediate context of 5.18–19, it is more likely that this clause merely reiterates the sense of 5.18*a*, which affirms either the eternal validity of the law (as popularly understood),[21] or (more probably, in view of 24.34f) its validity until the Eschaton.[22] In either case, it must be understood in the traditional Jewish sense.[23] Similarly, those who claim that 'these commandments' in 5.19 refers to Jesus' teachings that follow in 5.21 – 7.12,[24] and not to the commandments of the law spoken of in 5.18, can do so only by ignoring the plain meaning of the expression in the more immediate context of 5.17–19. It can only be concluded, then, that the passage as a whole is to be understood as an affirmation of the continuing validity of the entire law for Christian disciples – right down to the least jot and tittle. But whether the point of view represented in this assertion is consistent with the rest of the Gospel is a quite different question.

Matthew's belief that the law is binding upon the Christian community is evidenced also in his redaction of Marcan pericopes dealing with legal questions. At a number of points where Mark seems to portray Jesus in sharp disagreement with the law, Matthew reduces the sharpness of the disagreement or otherwise colours it so as to avoid the implication that the law is no longer authoritative and binding.[25] Consider the following passages:

*12.1–8, 9–14: the sabbath*[26]

It has long puzzled scholars that one of the few Marcan pericopes omitted by Matthew should be the first Marcan account of Jesus' healing on the sabbath (Mk. 1.23–8), with its otherwise significant reference to Jesus' authority (a key Matthean motif).[27] But the omission of this pericope, together with its introductory reference to the sabbath (Mk. 1.21; cf. verse 29), has the effect of separating the following stories of Jesus' healing of

Peter's mother-in-law and the crowd (Mt. 8.14–15*, 16–17*[28]) from any awkward reference to the sabbath at all.[29] Further, it is significant that when Matthew does at last deal with the thorny issue of Jesus' apparent violations of the sabbath law, it is only after he has first laid the groundwork by making explicit both Jesus' affirmation of the abiding authority of the law (5.17–19) and his radical yet humanitarian interpretation of it (5.20–48; cf. 7.12; 9.13). The shifting of the two major pericopes dealing with Jesus' sabbath 'violations' back to chapter 12 would seem to be an attempt by the evangelist to remove them from the embarrassing position of prominence they hold in Mark's Gospel (Mk. 2.23–8; 3.1–6). It is also noteworthy that Matthew has prefaced the two pericopes with 11.28–30, which – apparently in contrast to the burdensome tyranny of Pharisaic legalism – speaks of Jesus' 'easy yoke' and 'light burden', and thus functions as an interpretative principle in its own right for what follows.[30]

Within the first pericope (12.1–8), Matthew's addition of ἐπείνασαν (12.1) may be intended either to show that the disciples had a reason for breaking the sabbath,[31] or to bring their situation more into line with that of David, who, with his companions, was 'hungry' and 'ate' (12.3f);[32] or it may simply be an attempt to make explicit what is already implicit in the passage, with its underlying concern for the priority of human needs (12.7).[33] Undoubtedly more significant is the evangelist's insertion into the argument of a precedent from the Torah itself (12.5; cf. Num. 28.9–10) as legal support, in good rabbinic *qal waḥomer* fashion.[34] Here the law itself is seen to allow for one commandment to take precedence over another. Also important is Matthew's careful omission of Mark's sharp statement, 'The sabbath was made for man, not man for the sabbath', while retaining the following expression of Jesus' lordship over the sabbath (12.8*). Our overall impression, then, is that while Matthew makes allowance for Jesus' authoritative interpretation of the law with its emphasis on compassion (12.7), he is careful to avoid leaving the impression that the general law of the sabbath itself is in any way invalidated.[35] For Matthew, 'Jesus performs the radical action, yet the Law remains inviolate'.[36] Some see Jesus portrayed here as a 'special dispensation'-giver with regard to the sabbath law, exercising his Messianic prerogative to 'bind' and to 'loose';[37] but it is preferable to take it simply as a matter of the true interpretation and use of the law. Matthew's point is that 'the law and the prophets' themselves allow for precisely such an interpretation.

In the second pericope (12.9–14), the Matthean reformulation (12.10) turns the focus away from the healing itself to the more general question of the legality of healing on the sabbath. Again the evangelist depicts Jesus as entering into *qal waḥomer* argumentation (12.11) to defend his action:

if a sheep, then surely a person.[38] And again he sharpens the emphasis on the overriding importance of showing mercy (12.11f). The key point, expressed in Mark as a question, is converted by Matthew into a declaration that serves as a forceful conclusion to Jesus' argument: 'So *it is lawful* to do good on the sabbath' (12.12). Here again we see Matthew's legal orientation: though the focus is on the expression of compassion, it is viewed within the framework of the law.[39] Taking the two pericopes together, then, it seems likely that Matthew views the Christian community as still under obligation to maintain the general sabbath law, though not in the same strict and rigid sense as Pharisaic Judaism.[40] In particular, generous allowance is to be made for the expression of care for those in need on the sabbath.[41] Matthew's insertion of *μηδὲ σαββάτῳ* in the eschatological discourse (24.20) is taken by the vast majority of scholars as confirmation of his sabbatarianism – though to understand this as an instance of sabbath legalism raises serious problems that force us to consider alternative interpretations as well.[42]

*15.1–20: ritual uncleanness*[43]

Apart from the heightening of anti-Pharisaic bias (15.12–14), omission of the explanation of Jewish customs, improvements in the flow of the argument made by reordering,[44] and careful revision of Mark's thirteen vices to bring them more into line with the second half of the Decalogue (15.19; cf. 19.18),[45] the primary alteration of this pericope of any real significance is Matthew's omission of the key Marcan comment, *καθαρίζων πάντα τὰ βρώματα* (Mk. 7.19). While this could be taken simply as an insignificant skipping-over of an intruding Marcan parenthesis,[46] it is more likely an indication of Matthew's reluctance to portray Jesus as breaking with the whole system of Jewish food laws. The slight alteration of 'nothing' (Mk. 7.15) to 'not what ...' (Mt. 15.11) may well be a further indication of the same tendency.[47] Here Matthew eliminates those Marcan elements that conflict most sharply with the dietary laws,[48] and shifts the focus instead to the nature of true defilement (cf. 15.20). In so doing, he probably reveals his own reluctance (and the reluctance of his community) to abandon the dietary laws as a whole.[49] The primary point of the pericope, however, is taken over directly from Mark without a qualm, for it serves Matthew's purposes admirably: namely, that real defilement is an inward matter, a matter of the heart, and not one of mere dirtiness, as with the Pharisees.

Taken by itself, this pericope might suggest that Matthew's Jesus is set in opposition to the oral tradition in general (15.3, 6, 9*);[50] but in the context of the Gospel as a whole (cf. 23.2f, 23), the opposition must be understood as directed rather against those points of the tradition that either conflict with or ignore the more basic demands of the law (cf. also 9.10–13).[51] As we shall see later, the scribal tradition appears to retain its fundamental authority in Matthew's thinking generally.[52] The evangelist's omission of Mk. 7.13*b*, 'And many such things you do', supports Houlden's view that 'Matthew, unwilling to divest the tradition of its authority, confines himself to condemning obvious abuse.'[53]

*19.3–9: divorce*

The omission of Mark's reference to the possibility of a wife divorcing her husband (Mk. 10.12) is generally taken as another sign of Matthew's Jewish background.[54] The significance of other alterations, however – most of which are relatively slight – is somewhat disputed. Matthew's addition of *κατὰ πᾶσαν αἰτίαν* to the initial question (19.3) is seen by several scholars as having the effect of moving the discussion closer to the form of a rabbinic-style debate on the legal grounds of divorce;[55] but it may simply be an attempt by the evangelist to anticipate the exception phrase that follows, *μὴ ἐπὶ πορνείᾳ* (19.9; cf. 5.32). Though various interpretations of the latter phrase have been put forward,[56] it is still most likely that Matthew intends the phrase to be taken in the broader sense of illicit sexual relations more generally – in which case it may be an indication that he inclines to the Shammaitic position on legal questions, and therefore favours a strict line in general;[57] but this view has been recently challenged, and not without reason.[58] In any case, here is one point at which Matthew is less strict than Mark. The primary effect of Matthew's reordering of the pericope is to improve the flow of the argument and to focus on the priority of the Genesis provision rather than the Mosaic concession.[59] W.D. Davies sees possible significance also in the fact that in Matthew it is the Pharisees, and not Jesus, who initiate the question about the Mosaic ruling: 'The Matthaean Christ does not himself initiate a comparison which might suggest opposition to Moses, or rather criticism of him, whereas the Marcan Christ has no such scruples.'[60] In any event, Moses' word is here viewed primarily as concession and not as legislation, just as in Mark. The overall thrust of the account may therefore be interpreted not as an abrogation of Torah, but as an intensification of its demands, just as with 5.31–2.[61]

*22.34–40: the great commandment*

In this pericope (which will be discussed more fully later[62]), Mark's question, 'Which commandment is the first of all?' (Mk. 12.28), posed by a *γραμματεύς*, is converted by Matthew into 'Teacher, which is the great commandment in the law?' (Mt. 22.36), set in the mouth of a *νομικός*.[63] Small though the change may be, its effect is reinforced by Matthew's redaction of the concluding statement of Jesus' response to read, 'On these two commandments depend all the law and the prophets' (22.40; cf. 7.12). The whole question is tied much more closely by Matthew to the law.[64]

Most of the other redactional instances cited occasionally as evidence of the evangelist's nomistic tendencies carry no real weight and tell us little about his understanding of the law.[65] For example, the assertion that Matthew prefers law 'of God' to law 'of Moses'[66] cannot be maintained, because the few references in question are better explained on literary than theological grounds. (The alteration of 'Moses' to 'God' in 15.4 simply brings it into line with the neighbouring references to 'the commandment of God' and 'the word of God' (15.3, 6); and his redaction of Mk. 12.26 in Mt. 22.31f is simply an example of the normal Matthean tendency to abbreviate and clarify a somewhat awkward and roundabout Marcan construction.) Similarly, Matthew's alteration of *ἀγαθέ* to *ἀγαθόν* in 19.16 ('what good deed must I do ...?' – which eliminates a difficult Marcan reference that appears to deny Jesus' essential goodness) and the redactional addition in 19.17 ('If you would enter life, keep the commandments') do little more than make explicit what is already implicit in Mark. There may, however, be some significance to be seen in Matthew's inclusion of references to Jesus' 'teaching in their synagogues' in 4.23 and 9.35.

### *Scribes and oral tradition*

Related to a certain preoccupation with the question of what is 'lawful' (12.2*, 4, 10, 12; 14.4; 19.3; 22.17*; 27.6) is Matthew's interest in the whole question of interpreting and applying the law. The question naturally arises, then, how Matthew views the teachings of the traditional interpreters of the law, the scribes. Generally, like the Pharisees (with whom most of them are identified), they come in for heavy denunciation in the Gospel; but there are two significant references that seem to imply that the evangelist does not wish to deny the validity and authority of the scribal system as a whole. In 23.2f, the disciples are instructed to 'practise and observe' whatever the scribes and Pharisees teach – but not what they *do* – because of their role as the acknowledged expounders of the Mosaic law (*ἐπὶ τῆς Μωϋσέως καθέδρας ἐκάθισαν*).[67] And in 23.23, while their hypocrisy and misplaced priorities are strongly denounced because of their neglect of *τὰ βαρύτερα τοῦ νόμου*, their observance of such fine points of the tradition as tithing mint, dill and cummin is nonetheless affirmed – the clearest endorsement in the Gospel of at least some elements of the oral tradition.[68]

This immediately raises questions about the common assertion that Matthew draws a sharp dichotomy between written Torah and oral tradition, and presents Jesus in unrelieved opposition to the latter;[69] Matthew knows no such sharp distinction between the two. But in view of the way these two references seem to conflict with attitudes to scribal teaching expressed elsewhere in the Gospel (15.1–20; 23.4ff; cf. 7.29; 16.11f), they are treated by many scholars merely as *logia* carried over by Matthew from earlier tradition, which in their original, literal sense at least, do not represent his own understanding at all.[70] Many prefer to regard them as of negligible significance in view of the polemical context in which they are set, which focuses primary attention not so much on the teaching of the scribes and Pharisees as on their hypocrisy in practice.[71] Others are simply baffled by such conflicting tendencies in the data.[72] But it is significant that Matthew *has* included these statements in his Gospel; and to regard them simply as examples of the integrity with which he treats the tradition that has been handed down to him, even when it conflicts with his own view, does less than justice to the freedom he obviously feels to adjust it elsewhere. Accordingly, although these two references obviously cannot be isolated as evidence of Matthew's blanket approval of scribal teaching *tout entier*,[73] I judge that their presence in the text is very likely a hint of his basic respect for the scribal function of interpreting the Mosaic law, and an acknowledgement of the need for oral tradition in general;[74] he knows that the law always requires interpretation.[75] On the whole, it is not the function of the scribes that is disputed – nor oral tradition *per se* – but the spirit and priorities of their teaching (16.11f must be understood in this sense) and the hypocrisy of their lives in practice.[76] The Gospel does not simply reject the authority of those who 'sit on Moses' seat' over the Christian community (cf. 23.2f), but it does call the community to a critical evaluation of their lives and – yes, even of their teachings, at least to the extent they conflict with the deeper principles of the Torah itself (as elucidated by Jesus). But having said this, we must acknowledge that on the face of it, 23.2f at least does stand in some degree of tension with certain other statements in the Gospel, and Matthew has done little to clarify how the different emphases are to be reconciled – if indeed they are fully reconciled in his own thinking.[77] Nonetheless, in his implicit recognition of the need for authoritative interpretation and application of the law, he stands at one with the scribes and Pharisees.

Matthew's basic respect for the role of scribes may perhaps also be seen in his reduction of the number of negative Marcan references to them, and in his tendency to substitute other terms at those points.[78] More significant still are two texts that appear to speak of the presence of scribes in the

Christian community itself (13.52; 23.34).[79] The first of these may simply be a reference to converted Jewish scribes,[80] and is not unreasonably taken by some to be a self-designation of the writer of the Gospel himself.[81] The second, however, distinctly raises the possibility of there being a separate order of Christian scribes[82] – though we cannot be certain. (In any case, γραμματεύς is not simply a Matthean term for disciples in general.[83]) These references would seem to imply that there are some men who function as scribes in the Christian community.

If so, what is their role and authority in the church, and how does it differ from that of the Pharisaic scribes? Without question, they are more than simple copyists;[84] and the reference to 'new and ... old' in 13.52 would seem to imply that their interpretation and teaching draw on both Jewish and Christian traditions. W.D. Davies comments, 'Such scribes, we may presume, would exercise their function both in relation to the words of Jesus, as the new interpretation of the Law of Moses, and with the latter itself.'[85] What is not clear, however, is the precise relation between Christian and Jewish scribes with regard to the authority of their teaching for Matthew's Jewish–Christian[86] community – many of whom are undoubtedly already steeped in Jewish scribal traditions. It seems likely that the Matthean church is at that point of overlap, when the authority of Jewish scribes as interpreters of the Mosaic law is still recognized in principle, but when Christian scribes are beginning to replace them as the acknowledged teachers and authoritative interpreters within the church.[87]

There are definite differences between the two, however: unlike the Jewish scribes, no Christian scribe is ever to be called either ῥαββί or καθηγητής (23.7f, 10);[88] that role is reserved strictly for Jesus himself, the supreme διδάσκαλος. The ultimate authority to interpret Torah belongs to him, not to Christian scribes; their authority is derived from and subordinate to his (28.18; cf. 16.19),[89] and their interpretation and teaching are governed by his. Christian scribes are thus concerned not merely with the interpretation of Torah, but with the teachings of Jesus himself (cf. 28.19f) and with *his* interpretation of Torah; the focus has shifted somewhat. Inevitably they deal directly with the law of Moses also; but their understanding of its demands is now shaped in large measure by Jesus' own interpretation.

Finally, what of the two references to 'binding' and 'loosing' (16.19; 18.18)? Is either of these, as many understand them to be, a reference to the authority of Christian scribes to interpret the Torah or the tradition of Jesus' sayings?[90] While such an understanding is perhaps possible, it is more probable that both texts refer to the exercise of discipline in the church; the second in particular can hardly be interpreted otherwise.[91]

Matthew's wide knowledge and frequent use of Old Testament Scripture is one of the strongest pieces of evidence for the claim that he himself is a converted scribe. Scriptural citations are adduced not only to demonstrate that Jesus' life is the fulfilment of prophecy,[92] but also to justify Jesus' interpretation of the law when it deviates from accepted Pharisaic practice (e.g. 9.13; 12.5–7).[93] The evangelist not only takes over and sharpens Mark's picture of Jesus as a skilled interpreter of Scripture,[94] he also presents him as one whose own life is entirely governed by perfect obedience to 'what is written' (4.4, 7, 10; cf. 3.15). Jesus too lives 'by every word that proceeds from the mouth of God' – and this confirms that, for Matthew, the Torah is not simply prophetic, but remains valid as instruction.[95]

*Antinomianism*

At a few points, the Gospel speaks explicitly against *ἀνομία*.[96] The charge appears to be directed in one case against the scribes and Pharisees (23.28), and thrice against some within the Christian community itself (7.23; 13.41; 24.11f). However, in no case does the context demand that *ἀνομία* should be understood literally in relation to the question of law[97] – as its application to the Pharisees may suggest in itself. In every instance the reference is sufficiently general to allow for the various translations adopted, for example, by the RSV: 'evil-doing', 'iniquity', 'wickedness'. *Ἀνομία*, then, is probably best taken in a broader moral sense,[98] as the antithesis of Matthew's *δικαιοσύνη*, and not identified with the concept of antinomianism (in the narrow, more literal sense) against which he battles in 5.17–19. In other words, there is no sure evidence that the writer's use of the term *ἀνομία* tells us anything about his view of the law – other, perhaps, than his preference for legal vocabulary (which in itself may be significant).

The question remains, however, against whom is Matthew fighting in 5.17–19? That the passage is directed against an antinomian position or charge of some kind (in the more literal sense of the word) is virtually certain; but is it directed against a part of the Christian community itself,[99] or intended as a response to those levelling this charge at the community from the outside?[100] Moule argues forcibly for the latter position, claiming that 5.17–20 is better understood as 'a defence against anti-Christian Pharisaic allegations that Christianity lowered moral standards, than as an attack on antinomianism within the Church'.[101] Such an interpretation is attractive because it fits in well with the general conflict with Pharisaic Judaism portrayed throughout the Gospel. Those who incline to the former position often see the passage directed against the ones viewed as guilty of *ἀνομία* in 7.23; 13.41; 24.11f. Accordingly, the finger is frequently pointed to the false prophets of 7.15, 22; 24.11f[102] – though 7.22 concerns not just prophets, but charismatics more generally,[103] and the link between false prophets and *ἀνομία* in 24.11f is very tenuous indeed.[104] Further, there is no consensus on just who these false prophets are.[105] But the weakest part of this particular proposal remains the assumption that *ἀνομία* is to be understood in a strictly nomistic sense, and therefore equated with Matthew's antinomian concern in 5.17–19.[106]

The other viable interpretation is to see 5.17–19 directed against some form or distortion of Paulinism with which the Matthean community has come into contact.[107] The evangelist's critical reference to those who mouth the words *κύριε κύριε* could perhaps be adduced as evidence of this. The usual suggestion of Syria as the location for the writing of the Gospel fits in acceptably with this interpretation, for it then becomes probable (assuming a later date for Matthew than Paul) that Matthew and his community would have at least some contact with gentile Christians and churches who have absorbed aspects of Paul's teaching, and therefore be familiar with the theological position of the apostle.[108] This, however, remains no more than an hypothesis; there is no further evidence to confirm it.[109]

I conclude, then, that it is impossible to identify precisely the direction from which the antinomian threat or charge is seen to come;[110] the two most likely possibilities are that it derives either from Pharisaic libel aimed at the community from the outside, or from some expression of Pauline influence within the Christian community itself.

### *The law and entering the kingdom*

To what extent does Matthew portray the observance of the law as essential for gaining entrance to the kingdom of heaven? E.P. Sanders has argued that for late Judaism as a whole, obedience to the law is viewed within the context and framework of the more fundamental concept of God's covenant, and that (contrary to popular opinion) '*obedience maintains one's position in the covenant, but it does not earn God's grace as such*'.[111] The kingdom of heaven is attained not by righteous deeds *per se*, but by God's mercy; obedience to the law is the necessary condition for remaining within that mercy. If this concept of 'covenantal nomism' was pervasive in Palestinian Judaism in the early Christian era, as Sanders presumes,[112] then we may not unreasonably expect it to lie behind the Jewish–Christian writing of Matthew as well. And when we turn to the Gospel, this is precisely what we find: a strong demand for obedience to the law, set within the context of an underlying structure of grace and the framework of the new covenant of God's salvation and forgiveness in Jesus (1.21; 26.28).

Though the emphasis is clearly on the demand for obedience, nowhere does the Gospel state that it is by obeying the law that one enters the kingdom; what it seems to imply rather is that if one does *not* obey the law, one will *not* enter the kingdom. The surprising thing, given the concern over antinomianism, is that it nowhere states this explicitly. There is, of course, the sanctioned demand for deeper *δικαιοσύνη* in 5.20, characterized in the antitheses by radical obedience to the fundamental intent of the law and implicitly linked to the rigorous statements of 5.17–19. Similarly, the promise of safety from judgement for those who obey Jesus' words (7.24) is certainly to be understood in the light of both Jesus' affirmation of the law (5.17–19) and his authoritative interpretation of it (5.21–48).[113] Explicit references to the point, however, are difficult to find. Matthew's redactional insertion in Jesus' response to the question of the young man in 19.16f, 'If you would enter life, keep the commandments', though it appears on first glance to be significant, in reality only makes explicit what is already implicit in Mark, as we have already noted. Besides, the endorsement of the law in this passage functions largely as a mere preface to Jesus' own more radical demands that follow, which give the true conditions for gaining life in this pericope.[114] The reference to the exclusion from the kingdom of all those characterized by *ἀνομία* (7.23) likewise says little to the point, in view of the non-nomistic sense of *ἀνομία* probably assumed. Nowhere, then, does Matthew come right out and say that one must observe the law in order to enter the kingdom and obtain eternal life. Most probably, this is because it is such a fundamental tenet of the Matthean community that he simply takes it for granted;[115] but perhaps it is just worth inquiring if there might be something else behind it. There is, for example, the enigmatic reference in 5.19, where whoever denies the validity of the entire law is said not to be excluded from the kingdom, as in rabbinic literature,[116] but merely to be 'least' (ἐλάχιστος) in the kingdom[117] – a remarkable statement for Matthew. Might it be that the evangelist feels compelled to recognize that there are some in the Christian community who deny the validity of the law, yet must be considered authentic disciples of Christ; and that, although regarded as second-rate citizens, they cannot be denied entrance to the kingdom on the basis of their antinomian position alone?[118] Could it be that, although wanting to affirm the full validity of the law for his own community, he is nonetheless reluctant to insist on the observance of every jot and tittle as a prerequisite for entering the kingdom in view of the number of Christians who adhere to a more Pauline position – some of whom may be within the circle of his own community? (We have no idea of the full extent to which Matthew's community itself is confused or split over the question.) All this is sheer speculation, of course; but there may be factors other than the obvious hidden behind the evangelist's failure to state explicitly the absolute necessity of observing the law as a condition for entering the kingdom.

The overall conclusion, then, is that, for Matthew, the law in its entirety remains a valid and authoritative expression of the will of God for the Christian community, and all of life is viewed from this perspective.[119]

## 1.2 The Law Interpreted

### *5.21–48: the antitheses*[120]

There is much in the Gospel, however, that differs sharply from the traditional understanding and observance of the law, and which in some cases even appears to deny the law itself. The antitheses are a prime example of this. The claim is occasionally made that at least some of them express not the continuing validity of the law, but rather its abrogation. Accordingly, numerous and varied attempts have been made to distinguish between those antitheses that surpass or transcend the law and those that abrogate it[121] – and in some cases, we must frankly acknowledge that the actual effect of an antithesis *is* to annul a precept of Torah.[122] But as Daube and W.D. Davies point out, from Matthew's perspective the basic purpose of the antitheses as a whole is not to break with the law, but to call for heightened obedience to its deepest intent: 'The point is that in none of the antitheses is there an intention to annul the provisions of the Law but only to carry them to their ultimate meaning.'[123] Here the evangelist declares that the kind of righteousness the law requires is of a much deeper level than that of mere legal conformity. His objective, then, especially in view of the programmatic 5.17–19,[124] is to portray Jesus not in conflict with the law, but as demanding radical obedience to its deepest demands, to the ultimate will of God (7.21; 12.50; 21.31) – in disposition as well as deed.[125] Indeed, it is only this radical kind of obedience that constitutes the deeper *δικαιοσύνη* without which, Matthew's Jesus declares, one cannot enter the kingdom at all. (Hence 5.20 is rightly viewed as a heading for the whole section.[126])

Numerous attempts have also been made to demonstrate that the antitheses are directed specifically against oral tradition;[127] but these likewise prove inadequate to account for the data. The first five antitheses all refer directly to commandments in the written Torah itself, and the sixth has no obvious rabbinic parallels.[128] Further, as we have already suggested, Matthew knows no sharp and absolute distinction between written Torah and oral tradition (cf. 23.2f, 23); his is not a Sadducean viewpoint.[129] Nevertheless, it is true that the brunt of Jesus' criticism in the Gospel as a whole is directed not against the law itself, but against the prevailing interpretation and practice of it[130] – especially as expressed in the lives and teachings of the scribes and Pharisees; and in view of 5.20, that thought is present here as well.

*Anti-Pharisaic polemic*

Criticism of the Pharisees[131] occurs throughout the Gospel, but is most prominent in their numerous confrontations with Jesus (many of which are taken over from Mark, but further sharpened by Matthew[132]) and in the much expanded diatribe of chapter 23.[133] In spite of the apparent approval of their teaching in 23.2f, 23, Matthew's redactional additions in 16.11f make it clear that the disciples are to regard the Pharisees and their teaching with a wary eye;[134] for they are 'blind guides' (15.14; cf. 23.16, 17, 19, 24, 26),[135] hypocrites who preach, but do not practise (23.3ff).[136] Focusing on external compliance rather than true inward obedience (23.25ff), their lives are governed by outward forms and motivated by pride and the desire for recognition (23.5). In their concern for the minutiae of the tradition, they have overlooked *τὰ βαρύτερα τοῦ νόμου* (23.23f). Legalists in the strictest sense, they have little genuine compassion and concern for others (9.13; 12.7; 23.4, 13, 23; 27.6); indeed, they are a positive hindrance to those who sincerely want to gain the kingdom (23.13). In the end, relying on their status as 'children of Abraham', they reject both the message and the messengers of God (23.34). The Gospel bitterly denounces their hypocrisy, their legalistic spirit, their focus on mere externals, and their lack of true compassion. Whether the picture it draws is accurate and fairly represents the Pharisees as a whole, is quite beside the point.[137] (Matthew's outlook and horizon are undoubtedly essentially local and parochial.) What is important is that it is clearly Pharisaic interpretation and practice of the law that Matthew is here concerned to combat, and from which he wishes to protect the Christian community.[138]

Accordingly, much of Jesus' ethical teaching is set explicitly or implicitly in contrast with the lives and teachings of the Pharisees.[139] The qualities praised in the beatitudes (humility, meekness, mercy, inward purity and the seeking of true righteousness), for example, are the antitheses of those that characterize the Pharisees (cf. 9.13; 12.7, 11f, 34, 39; 15.3, 8; 16.4; 21.43f; 23.4, 5ff, 13, 23f, 25f, 27f). So are the marks of true inner piety spoken of in 6.1–8, 16–18, which are explicitly contrasted with the pompous show of the 'hypocrites' in the synagogues (6.2, 5,

16; cf. 7.5). W.D. Davies sees additional contrasts implicit in 5.14–16; 7.1ff, 15–21 (cf. 23.2f, 4, 14; 15.14).[140] The whole function of the antitheses is to illustrate a kind of *δικαιοσύνη* and obedience to the will of God that is at once more radical and more inward than that of the Pharisees (5.20).[141] And yet, at the same time, Matthew can speak of Jesus' teaching as an 'easy yoke' and 'light burden' (11.28–30) – a reference that itself stands in stark contrast to the 'heavy burdens, hard to bear' of Pharisaic legalism (23.4).[142] Smith summarizes the evangelist's view of the Pharisaic attitude to the law well: 'Despite or because of its scrupulosity, its fulfilment of the Law was inadequate ... Its legalism made man's duty towards God at once too heavy and too light a burden. If it encumbered the devout with a load of legal minutiae, it made the way easy for the formalist and the hypocrite.'[143] I conclude, then, that though Matthew appears to maintain respect for the rabbinic system and oral tradition as a whole, he is highly critical of the Pharisees themselves – with regard both to their own observance of the law and to the spirit and balance of their teachings.[144]

Though full discussion of this issue will be reserved for later, the point at which the teaching of Jesus differs most sharply from that of the Pharisees is in the priority he gives to the love commandment in the interpretation and application of the law.[145] This is seen most notably in his citation of Hos. 6.6 at two key points of dispute with the Pharisees (9.13; 12.7; cf. 21.31f). The first of these, which portrays Jesus eating with 'sinners', seems to stand in some tension with the strict line taken on food laws generally;[146] but this may be an example of the way the love commandment takes precedence in Matthew's thinking over strictly legalistic regulations when the two conflict.[147] As the most important ethical commandment of the law (22.36ff), the love commandment both defines the moral essence of the law (7.12; 22.40; cf. 19.19) and provides the critical principle by which the individual commandments of the law and tradition are to be read, interpreted and evaluated.[148] This strong emphasis on love does not nullify the concern for the observance of specific regulations and precepts,[149] but it does imply a definite shift in focus and the establishment of a distinct order of priorities. For Matthew, then, the formal understanding of the law as a uniform code of rules, every detail of which is supposedly equally important, is clearly abandoned (cf. 23.23).[150]

### 1.3 Matthew's Dual Concern

We come back, then, to the question with which we began: how do we reconcile the seemingly contradictory elements in Matthew's view of the law? As we have seen, side by side lie statements that appear to express both rigorously conservative and radically progressive interpretations: the law is upheld in its entirety, but the priority given to the love commandment effectively allows for the breaking of one commandment for the sake of another; the teaching of the scribes is endorsed as the authoritative pronouncement of those who 'sit on Moses' seat', yet is criticized as perverse. Can such divergent elements be integrated into a consistent whole?

There are several possibilities open to us, and each has its adherents: we may (1) treat the contradictory elements as different but equally viable strands of Christian tradition faithfully retained by the author eclectically;[151] (2) regard one as tradition, the other as redaction – with the latter representing the author's true viewpoint;[152] (3) consider them as the results of separate redactions representing different viewpoints;[153] (4) treat one as of negligible importance in its context, and give priority to the other;[154] (5) consider both as viewpoints of a single author, held in either reconcilable or irreconcilable tension: if the former, attempts may be made to explain them in terms of their contexts, as addressed to different issues;[155] if the latter, they may be assumed to represent some degree of inconsistency in the thought of the writer himself.[156] In reality, of course, variants and combinations of the above options are possible, and various possibilities may be applied to different points of conflict.

Without attempting even to begin to deal with the complexities and intricacies of each of these proposed solutions, I would suggest that by far the greater part of Matthew's divergent statements regarding the law (regardless of their derivation) may be viewed as the work of a single writer waging battle on two fronts: on the one side, against some unspecified antinomian threat or charge; and on the other, against the misplaced priorities of the Pharisees. With regard to the former, he defends the abiding validity of the entire law; with regard to the latter, he emphasizes the right interpretation of the law – even though this leads him at times to contradict not only parts of the scribal tradition but also individual commandments of Torah itself.[157] It is Matthew's dual citizenship in two communities that makes such a combination possible: as a Jew, he cannot conceive of denying either the validity of the law or the basic authority and need of scribal interpretation; but as a Christian, he recognizes that it is Jesus' interpretation of the law that is supremely authoritative, and that sits in judgement upon all others.[158] The existing tensions, then, probably reflect both the divergent affinities of Matthew's Jewish–Christian community and the fact that Matthew has only imperfectly integrated the various elements into one coherent whole.

Suggs attempts to reconcile the divergent strands by viewing Matthew's Jesus himself as Torah-incarnate (cf. 11.28–30), thus eliminating any distinction between Jesus' words and the words of Torah: 'For Matthew, there is no inconsistency ... because he appeals *always* to the Torah even when he appears to contradict it. For him, Jesus is Wisdom-Torah.'[159] Alternatively, and perhaps preferably, one could say that, for Matthew, there is no distinction between Jesus' words and the words of Torah, not because he is Torah-incarnate, but because as Messiah, Lord and Son of God, his words bear the authority of the One who gave Torah;[160] Torah and Jesus both demand obedience because the authority of God himself stands behind their proclamation of the will of God. Suggs' point is well taken, however, that the evangelist apparently perceives little inconsistency or contradiction between the two.

### 1.4 Matthew's Jesus and the Law

This brings us to the question, what is the place of Matthew's Jesus in this matter? In view of the nature of the antitheses especially, it is frequently claimed that Matthew portrays Jesus as a new lawgiver, a 'new Moses', and that the Sermon on the Mount functions in Matthew's theology as a new law.[161] Often this claim is tied to the early tradition, revitalized by Bacon, that the evangelist intentionally structures the five discourses of his Gospel to parallel the five books of the Pentateuch; but as Banks and others have amply demonstrated, such an assertion lacks true foundation.[162] In support of this understanding of Jesus, however, various attempts have been made to trace the motifs of a 'new Moses' and a 'new law' in Jewish Messianic expectations of the time, and to relate these to the Gospel; but there appears to be no conclusive evidence that such a belief was ever prominent or widespread at the time.[163] Indeed, such expectations as there were appear to be rather late and quite varied,[164] and often represent little more than the esoteric speculations of small but learned minorities.[165] Similarly, when we turn to the Gospel, though we find a number of parallels between the lives of Jesus and Moses,[166] the motif is certainly not a dominant or exclusive one; and nowhere does the evangelist ever refer to Jesus explicitly in Mosaic terms. In general, there is little evidence to suggest that Matthew thinks of Jesus as a 'second Moses';[167] and as W.D. Davies correctly concludes, this forbids any predominantly Mosaic approach to the Sermon on the Mount.[168]

Likewise, taking the Gospel as a whole, it is quite misleading to speak of Jesus' teachings as a 'new law' – at least in the strict sense of the word, as a collection of legal regulations.[169] Neither the form nor the content justifies such a designation. Similarly, those who interpret Matthew's formulation of Jesus' teachings primarily in terms of Christian halakoth[170] tend to overestimate the halakic element in the Gospel, and fail to recognize the vast difference between the bulk of Jesus' teachings and genuine rabbinic halakoth. Jesus' teachings in the Sermon, for instance, are fundamentally neither casuistic in formulation nor legalistic in content; they do not function merely as a body of legal rulings intended to define in detail what constitutes morally acceptable behaviour. In general they lack the comprehensive specificity of halakah and its preoccupation with the letter of the law. Further, many of his demands are of such an all-embracing, inward nature, that they simply cannot be 'kept' in the way that laws are commonly kept; nor can one's response to them be measured, evaluated, and judged in the same way as one's obedience or disobedience to legal regulations. On the whole, then, the teachings in the Sermon cannot be codified and made to fit into a halakic framework.[171] In the words of T.W. Manson, Jesus' teaching is 'a compass rather than an ordnance map ... the object is to give direction rather than directions'.[172]

True, certain of Matthew's formulations are susceptible of halakic interpretation, especially in chapter 18;[173] and these may well be signs of at least the initial stages of a developing Christian casuistry, as several have suggested.[174] In fact, from one perspective this is precisely what we would expect, in view of the seemingly legal orientation of Matthew's community and the active role of scribes in it (13.52). But it is quite inaccurate to speak of the Gospel as a whole as written from a halakic viewpoint; Matthew provides us with no comprehensive, detailed system of rabbinic-like halakoth for the living of the Christian life. Indeed, this in itself may substantiate the conviction that Matthew's community is content to abide by the Torah and the traditional rabbinic halakoth on most points. In any case, it certainly argues against any full-blown view of Jesus' teachings as a *nova lex*, at least in the strict sense.

It is significant that the writer nowhere explicitly refers to Jesus' teachings in terms of 'law'; as *ἐντολαί*, yes – but as *νόμος*, no. For Matthew, the 'law' is still the law of Moses; it has lost none of its authority. To claim for Jesus' teachings the status of 'new law' would be to deny his assertion of the validity of the old (5.17ff). And to summarize the Sermon as a 'law of love' misses the central point.[175] This is not to deny that Matthew portrays Jesus' teaching in terms of authoritative demand – and that in the most absolute, all-inclusive sense;[176] indeed, from this point of view one could say that Jesus' teaching does function as a kind of law to the evangelist.[177] But in no way does it replace Torah as 'the law' in Matthew's thinking.

The crucial point is this: Matthew presents Jesus not as a new lawgiver, but as the giver of a new interpretation of the law. Matthew's Jesus is the great expounder and interpreter of Torah.[178] His teaching is not a new law in itself, but the authoritative interpretation of the old law – the Messianic interpretation, which reveals the true nature of the will of God.[179] Sharply set over against the strictly legalistic interpretation of Pharisaic Judaism, Jesus' interpretation focuses not on the letter of the law, but on radical obedience to its deepest intent; above all, it stresses the priority to be given to the love commandment as the most important commandment of the law, and its key principle of interpretation. From this perspective we can agree with the main thrust of J.T. Sanders' statement, that Matthew 'endorses a *Christian casuistry* in which the command to love provides in each case the direction in which one moves when attempting to derive the particular guide for conduct from the Torah'[180] – though, strictly speaking, to regard this as 'casuistry' is almost a contradiction in terms. Thus, the evangelist's affirmation of the validity of the law in every detail (5.17–19) must be evaluated in light of his understanding of Jesus' interpretation of it.

And yet, Jesus is much more to Matthew than just the authoritative interpreter of Torah (as, for example, the Teacher of Righteousness is to the Qumran community); he is *Lord*, the Messiah, the Son of God. (Note that he is properly addressed not as ῥαββί or διδάσκαλε, but as κύριε.[181]) As such, his words carry every bit as much authority for Matthew as do those of the law itself (7.24–9; 28.18); indeed, it is his authority that is prominent in the Gospel, even more than that of Torah.[182] Without in any way denying the authority of the law or the tradition, the centre of Matthew's focus has shifted away from the law to Jesus himself. Kilpatrick is correct: 'The central position that Judaism gave to the Law, the Gospel gives to Jesus.'[183] We must be careful, then, not to overestimate the prominence of the law in Matthew's Gospel;[184] the disciple's life centres not merely on submission to the law, or even to Jesus' interpretation of the law – though that is an important part of it, and everything is viewed within that framework – but on obedience to Jesus himself as Lord.[185] To be a disciple is therefore to be a δοῦλος of Jesus (10.24f).

### 1.5 Matthew's View of the Christian Life

What kind of picture, then, do we get of the Christian life in Matthew's Gospel? Clearly, it is life lived within the framework of the law, under the authority of both Torah and the scribal tradition (5.17–19; 23.2f, 23); the emphasis, however, is not simply on compliance with the letter of the law, but on heartfelt obedience to the law at the deepest level, radical obedience. It is a difficult and demanding life – so much so that the evangelist can even write: 'the gate is narrow and the way is hard, that leads to life, and those who find it are few' (7.14).

And yet, paradoxically, Matthew speaks of Jesus' yoke as 'easy' and his burden as 'light', and 'rest' is promised to those weary labourers who take it up (11.28–30).[186] The implication is that Jesus' compassion-oriented teaching, even with its emphasis on radical obedience to the deepest intent of the law, is easier to bear than the intolerable burden of Pharisaic legalism (23.4)[187] – perhaps partly because Christian obedience is exercised in the supportive company of Jesus himself (18.20; 28.20).[188]

But the disciple still lives under a 'yoke' nonetheless – there is no escape from that; and even though the yoke is described as 'easy', the demand is still for perfection (5.48).[189] The fact that Jesus' teachings in the Sermon centre on inner attitudes and obedience to the spirit of the law rather than the letter, makes the life of the disciple no less strenuous. Rules and regulations still have their place in ordering the details of daily life, of course; but the disciple must now be governed on a deeper level by an all-inclusive commitment to doing the will of God. The resulting view of the Christian life is in one sense less harsh; but in another sense, it is even more demanding.[190] Compared with the stern strictness of the Pharisees, Matthew's Jesus is experienced as 'gentle and lowly in heart' (11.29); yet when it comes to accountability in judgement, some may still find him a 'hard man' (25.24).

## 2. *Paul*

When we come to Paul's view of the law,[191] we encounter the same kind of seemingly contradictory statements that we find in Matthew. On the one hand Paul writes as if Christ is 'the end of the law' (*τέλος νόμου*: Rom. 10.4);[192] yet in the same letter he insists the law is not done away with but 'upheld' (*νόμον ἱστάνομεν*: Rom. 3.31). He can speak of the 'curse' of the law (*κατάρας τοῦ νόμου*: Gal. 3.13), yet still see it as 'holy' (*ἅγιος*), and its commandment as *ἁγία καὶ δικαία καὶ ἀγαθή* (Rom. 7.12). Again, how do we reconcile such ostensibly divergent statements? It is a perplexing problem that has engaged the attention of a good number of biblical scholars lately.[193] The recent trend to explain the phenomena in terms of a development in Paul's thought from Galatians to Romans,[194] however, is a basically unsatisfactory solution that fails to take adequate account of (1) the extent to which Paul's statements in Galatians are accentuated and sharpened by his polemic; (2) the different aspects of the law in focus in the divergent statements; and (3) the uncertainties of assigning a pre-Romans date to Galatians – for which there is still no conclusive evidence.[195] It is a case of overdifferentiation that, as Hahn points out, overlooks the fundamental 'inner unity' of Paul's concept of law in the two letters.[196] But how, then, do these different statements fit together in his thinking?

### 2.1 The 'End' of the Law

We begin by asking in what sense Paul thinks of Christ as *τέλος νόμου*. If we take *τέλος* in the sense of 'termination', it would appear there are at least three ways in which the law is viewed as essentially ended in Christ.

*As a way of 'righteousness'*

In Rom. 10.4, Christ is declared to be the end of the law *εἰς δικαιοσύνην*,[197] i.e. as a means of salvation or a way of finding acceptance with God – a theme that is developed in Romans and Galatians especially. As this motif is central to virtually every major study of Pauline theology, I shall do little more than summarize the main points here, and focus rather on those aspects more relevant to ethics.

Opinions vary widely as to how the apostle came to his radical views;[198] but whatever the reasons, Paul is now absolutely convinced that one's standing with God is secured not by obedience to the law, but by faith in Christ *χωρὶς νόμου* (Rom. 3.21ff, 28, 30; 4.16; 10.4, 9ff; Gal. 2.16; 3.6, 8, 11, 18, 22, 25f; cf. Rom. 1.17; 5.20; Gal. 3.2, 5, 14; 4.5ff, 19). In fact, it is only by 'dying' to reliance on one's obedience to the law that one truly comes to 'live' by faith (Gal. 2.19). Here righteousness is no longer conceived in terms of obedience to the law, but as the free gift of God for those who believe (Rom. 1.17; Gal. 5.5); Christ himself is now viewed as the believer's righteousness (1 Cor. 1.30; 2 Cor. 5.21). These two different views of *δικαιοσύνη* are sharply contrasted by Paul at several points (e.g. Rom. 9.30–2; 10.3ff; Phil. 3.9f). In his understanding, the whole system of law – at least as popularly understood – centres on the concept of 'work' and 'wages' (Rom. 4.4; cf. Gal. 3.2f, 12); and this, he argues, is the antithesis of God's way of 'faith', which depends rather on his free gift of grace (Rom. 4.14; 5.15–21; 6.23; 9.11; 11.6; Gal. 2.20f; 3.11f).[199] The former, reliant on the 'flesh' (Gal. 3.3), panders to selfish pride; the latter engenders true humility (Rom. 3.27). They are two entirely different ways of approaching God, he insists, and only one is valid (cf. Gal. 4.21ff). Given the nature of both God and humanity, there is simply no way that a legal system can give life (Gal. 3.21). What Paul disputes here is the apparently popular conception of the law as a means of salvation, not the more sophisticated understanding of its learned interpreters;[200] he is writing not so much to convince knowledgeable Jews, as to keep gentile converts from being persuaded by Judaizing propagandists.[201]

In defending his thesis, Paul analyses in some depth the basic inadequacy of the law.[202] The primary problem, he maintains, is that no one can fully measure up to its exacting standards. Viewed as a means of salvation, the law demands the absolute and entire obedience of those who live under its rule (Gal. 3.10); but this is rendered frankly impossible by the tyrannical power of sin (Rom. 3.9, 10, 23). From the viewpoint of the law, the whole world stands guilty before the judgement of God (Rom. 3.19), for no one is – or ever can be, in his own strength – fully obedient to its demands (Rom. 11.32).[203] Thus, all who rely on their obedience to the law for their standing with God rely on a false hope, and stand unknowingly under a curse (Gal. 3.10).

But because the issue is of such central importance to those of Jewish background, Paul is pressed to deal with the obvious questions, Why then the law? What is its function? And how does it relate to Christ? And here it may be said that, in general – looking at it retrospectively from the viewpoint of the cross – he assigns a largely negative, preparatory function to the law.[204] The original basis of the Hebrew people's relationship with God, he points out, was God's own promise of grace; the law was only added later (Gal. 3.15–18; cf. Rom. 4.10ff) – and even then it was obviously secondary, for it was transmitted not directly by God, but only indirectly through angels (Gal. 3.19).[205] And why was it given at all? 'Because of transgressions', he claims (Gal. 3.19), and then goes on to argue the tautology that without the law there can be no transgression (Rom. 4.15; 5.13), nor sense of transgression (Rom. 7.7ff); indeed, apart from the law sin is 'dead' (Rom. 7.8ff). The law therefore brings about an awareness of sin by exposing its nature as transgression against the commandments of God (Rom. 7.7ff, 13; cf. 3.20; 5.20). But more than that, it sharpens this awareness by arousing and stimulating the very thing it forbids (Rom. 7.5, 7ff; 1 Cor. 15.56)! Not that the law itself is evil, Paul emphasizes (and here he checks himself); on the contrary, the law is *ἅγιος* – and the commandment *ἁγία καὶ δικαία καὶ ἀγαθή* (Rom. 7.12; cf. 7.7, 16) – for it does come (at least indirectly) from God. The problem lies rather in the nature of sin (Rom. 7.13ff, 17–20), which uses the holy demands of the law to exploit the weakness of human *σάρξ* (Rom. 7.7ff, 11; 8.3); for the *σάρξ* -dominated person is simply unable to comply with the authoritative demands of the law of God (Rom. 8.7). The result is that the law, in itself holy and good, nonetheless functions as an instrument of death in the hands of sin (Rom. 7.11). Paul extends the metaphor to speak even of the law itself as a written code that 'kills' (2 Cor. 3.6), and of the service of the law as *ἡ διακονία τοῦ θανάτου* (2 Cor. 3.7; cf. 3.9). Here, even though he formally describes it as 'holy', Paul cannot conceal his conception of it as an enemy.[206] Confronting humans with the harsh demands of God, the law offers no answer to the problem of sin other than to condemn it (Rom. 4.15).[207] The purpose of the law in Paul's apologetic, then, is not only to manifest the moral demands of God and make transgression of them legally punishable, but also to make people aware of their own disobedience and inability to fulfil them, and therefore to sharpen their sensitivity to their own sin and guilt. In this sense the apostle can even say: 'Law came in, to increase the trespass' (*ἵνα πλεονάσῃ τὸ παράπτωμα*: Rom. 5.20)[208] – a most remarkable view of the Torah! He thus argues that the law has a largely preparatory function for the gospel of Christ, the message of grace. Its role is likened to that of a *παιδαγωγός* (Gal. 3.23ff), useful in the early stages of a child's development for disciplined instruction, training and restraint,[209] but no longer required once the child becomes fully grown. The law functions merely as a parenthesis in God's dealing with humankind (2 Cor. 3.7ff, 11; Gal. 3.19; cf. 2 Cor. 5.17), and is of a strictly secondary nature. But, Paul is quick to add, in no way does this overthrow the law (Rom. 3.31): far from denying its validity, the doctrine of justification by faith upholds and affirms both the absolute demand of the law and its true role in God's scheme of things; and, he claims, it confirms and fulfils the basic teaching of the law itself (Rom. 4).[210]

Paul's strongest words are reserved for those who insist that Christians must be circumcised and observe the law in order to be saved. With vitriolic contempt, he castigates them as 'dogs', 'evil-workers', 'those who mutilate the flesh' (Phil. 3.2), and even wishes they would go on to castrate themselves (Gal. 5.12)! The sharpness of his polemic against these troublemakers inevitably colours the whole tone of his critique of the law.[211] Such heresy, he insists, not only leads into bondage (Gal. 2.4), it denies the very basis of salvation in Christ (Gal. 2.21). Christians who submit to Judaizing influence and revert to circumcision and legal observances place themselves under obligation to obey the whole system of law, and thereby cut themselves off from God's grace in Christ (Gal. 5.2–4; cf. 2.18; 3.10); the two are mutually exclusive. It is this that makes the whole matter of law so serious to the apostle: at bottom it is a theological and not simply an ethical issue.[212]

### *As a legal code*

Secondly, and related to the above, at least for gentile Christians the law no longer functions as legislation comprehensively ordering the specific details of daily life. (Note the absence of any reference to scribes in the list of church positions in 1 Cor. 12.27ff.) Christian behaviour is not determined by a multitude of rules and regulations.

In Paul's thinking, part of the problem of life under the law, at least as popularly conceived, is its orientation toward mere external compliance; his focus is rather on the need for response from the heart. Thus, against Jewish legalists he insists that the real meaning of circumcision is an inward matter: 'He is a Jew who is one inwardly (*ἐν τῷ κρυπτῷ*), and real circumcision is a matter of the heart, spiritual and not literal (*ἐν πνεύματι οὐ γράμματι*)' (Rom. 2.29; cf. Phil. 3.3; Col. 2.11); mere circumcision in itself is of absolutely no value (Gal. 6.15f). Paul knows that truly doing the will of God is not a matter of mere legal compliance, but demands a radical, all-inclusive kind of response motivated on a much deeper level, activated by the Spirit from within one's heart (2 Cor. 3.3). He therefore sharply contrasts life 'under the old written code' with 'the new life of the Spirit' (Rom. 7.6). It is a significant shift of perspective with regard to the dynamics of the Christian life.

Accordingly, nowhere do we find Paul encouraging his readers to observe any of the cultic–ritual laws prescribed in Torah, as a general practice. On the contrary, he commonly discourages them from doing so, on theological grounds (at least when he is addressing non-Jewish Christians[213]), and on one occasion roundly condemns some who apparently do observe them (Gal. 4.10).[214] For Paul, ritual observances (whether Jewish or pagan) are of no significance for the Christian; believers are not bound by legalistic regulations 'in questions of food and drink or with regard to a festival or a new moon or a sabbath' (Col. 2.16). Such matters are mere human formulations, and Christians live their lives on an entirely different plane. And so he chides the Colossians: 'why do you live as if you still belonged to the world? Why do you submit to regulations, "Do not handle, Do not taste, Do not touch" ... according to human precepts and doctrines?' (Col. 2.20ff). Such rules and regulations, he declares, are but faint shadows of reality – which is Christ himself (Col. 2.16f). Besides, though observance of such prescriptions may give the outward impression of piety, it has no power to effect genuine virtue at the deepest levels of the believer's life (Col. 2.23[215]). And so, Paul insists, Christians are freed from a life ordered by legalistic precepts (cf. Gal. 2.4); and with regard to Jewish legalism especially, they must take pains to ensure that they remain that way (Gal. 4.31 – 5.1).

At several points, the apostle appears to be concerned especially with the Christian's response to traditional food regulations, either Jewish or pagan (e.g. Rom. 14.1ff; 1 Cor. 8.1ff; 10.23ff; Col. 2.16ff; cf. Gal. 2.11ff).[216] Though the various passages relate to somewhat different issues (only Gal. 2.11ff can with certainty be said to deal specifically with Jewish laws), Paul makes it quite clear that in no case need the

Christian feel bound by any such regulations. 'Nothing', he argues, 'is unclean (κοινόν) in itself' (Rom. 14.14); Christians may freely eat anything without fear of contamination because ' "the earth is the Lord's, and everything in it" ' (1 Cor. 10.25–7). Eating in itself, or not eating, cannot affect one's relationship with God (1 Cor. 8.8) – unless it is done in worship of idols (1 Cor. 10.21); for 'the kingdom of God is not food and drink ...' (Rom. 14.17f). All that really matters is Christ (Col. 2.17, 20–3). Thus, as a general principle Paul discourages the observance of food laws because of their theological implications.[217]

In Rom. 14, however, where he apparently sees less danger of major theological principles being violated, Paul makes greater allowance for individual difference of opinion within the Christian community itself, at least on the questions of vegetarianism and the observance of special days. Here he encourages Christians to be tolerant of their 'weaker' brothers and sisters who have scruples about eating meat,[218] and not to criticize those who keep holy days (14.2ff, 5). In these cases at least, Paul recognizes that the observance of certain ritual laws may for some be a valid form of Christian worship (14.6ff); and that, he implies, is the most important criterion in this context (cf. 1 Cor. 10.31) – i.e. it is still *theological* considerations that are decisive.

There are times, however, when *ethical* factors come more into play, and demand certain adjustments in general principles. Thus, for example, even though they themselves may have no compulsions about it, Christians are to restrain themselves from eating commonly prohibited items in the company of those who would be offended by their doing so (Rom. 14.13–23; 1 Cor. 8.10–13; 10.28f, 32).[219] For even though in principle nothing is *κοινόν*, it is *κοινόν* for anyone whose conscience considers it so (Rom. 14.14, 23). The overriding principle is that the Christian must at all costs avoid offending others (*ἀπρόσκοποι ... γίνεσθε*: 1 Cor. 10.32), whether they be Jews, Greeks, or other Christians – though there are times when theological considerations take precedence even over this (cf. Gal. 2.11ff).

In any case, here we see Christian behaviour governed not by legal prescriptions, but by quite other principles: conscience (Rom. 14.23; 1 Cor. 8.12; 10.28f), consideration for others (Rom. 14.13ff; 15.1ff; 1 Cor. 8.9–13; 10.24, 28f, 32f), and commitment to Christ as Lord (Rom. 14.6ff; cf. 1 Cor. 8.12; 10.31) – and it is these underlying motives that Paul is primarily concerned to stress. In principle, he largely concurs with the popular opinion of the Corinthians that *πάντα ἔξεστιν* (1 Cor. 6.12; 10.23)[220] – i.e. that the Christian is a totally free person (cf. 1 Cor. 8.9; 9.1), not bound by formal legalities; but for Paul, Christian freedom is always subordinated to the higher ethical principle of consideration for the welfare of others (1 Cor. 6.12; 10.23; Gal. 5.13).

*As the power of sin*

Thirdly, we may say that the law is no longer experienced as the enslaving 'power of sin' (1 Cor. 15.56) in the Christian life. Because believers are no longer 'under law' but 'under grace', sin can no longer rule their lives with quite the same free hand it once had (Rom. 6.14). In a somewhat loose analogy to the breaking of the marriage bond by the death of one of the partners, Paul declares that Christians are now 'dead' to that which held them captive,[221] discharged from the law (Rom. 7.4, 6), because 'the law of the Spirit of life in Christ Jesus' has set them free from 'the law of sin and death' (Rom. 8.2; cf. Gal. 5.18).[222] What is in particular focus in these texts is the freedom the believer now enjoys from the authority and power of the law as a régime that makes sin compulsive. The Christian is no longer a *δοῦλος* but a *υἱός* (Gal. 4.7) – one who no longer lives under bondage to the law (cf. Gal. 4.1–10, 24f;[223] Rom. 8.15), but in the liberating power of the Spirit (Rom. 8.15, 21; 2 Cor. 3.17; Gal. 2.4f; 4.4–7). In this sense, the Spirit may be said effectively to replace sin and the law as the dynamic force in the believer's life.[224]

Paradoxically, now that the Christian is emancipated from the tyrannical power of the law, at last he is able truly to fulfil its demands (Rom. 8.4)[225] – something he could never do under the law itself! Indeed, argues Paul, only as one is liberated from the grasp of the law can one's life begin to yield real 'fruit' for God (Rom. 7.4) – which for him is always 'the fruit of the Spirit' (Gal. 5.22f); and against such 'there is no law' (Gal. 5.23). A life fully opened to the Spirit takes on a quality that quite transcends the demands of the law. In Paul's view, then, the true *καρπὸς δικαιοσύνης* (in an ethical sense) comes only through Jesus Christ (Phil. 1.11), not through the law; the law is a power that inhibits ethical living.

What, then, do we make of Rom. 7.14–25? If indeed the Christian is freed from the control of the law (Rom. 6.14; 7.4) and thereby enabled to meet its deepest moral demands (Rom. 8.4), how do we understand these despairing words of Paul about his apparent total inability to do what is right in view of the indomitable power of sin in his *σάρξ*?[226] To begin with, there seems to be good reason for assuming that the apostle is writing here not primarily of his own experience, but of the plight of people more generally.[227] Further, the passage is best interpreted as a description of the experience not of believers, but of those without Christ.[228] Those who disagree point to the *πνεῦμα–σάρξ* conflict in Gal. 5.17 and argue that nowhere else in Paul's writings do we gain the impression that he experienced conflict and despair over the demands of the law in his pre-Christian days; on the contrary, he emphatically declares that with regard to righteousness according to the law he was blameless (*ἄμεμπτος*: Phil. 3.6; cf. Gal. 1.13f).[229] Such an argument, however, is susceptible of criticism at a number of points: (1) it fails to discern the basic difference between the conflicts depicted in Rom. 7.14–25 and Gal. 5.17;[230] (2) it assumes that the two brief references in Phil. 3.6 and Gal. 1.13f are sufficient in themselves to demonstrate that Paul's pre-Christian experience was free from conflict with regard to the law – thereby overlooking the fact that both texts are set in polemical contexts directed to quite other issues; (3) it typically assumes that behind 7.14–25 must lie Paul's own experience[231] – though it is more likely simply a well-thought-out and carefully articulated analysis of the human plight from a later Christian perspective in an attempt to expose the law's weakness; (4) it ignores the fact that, apart from a shift in tense (necessitated by 7.14*a* and continued naturally), there is no indication of any sharp break with the immediately preceding context, which explicitly describes the situation of a person under the law; (5) in some cases it reads too much into the arrangement of the concluding elements in 7.25;[232] and (6) it sharply conflicts with Paul's description of the believer's life elsewhere as no longer helpless before the enslaving power of sin and the law, but liberated from its rule by the new life of the Spirit (Rom. 6.14; 7.4–6; 8.2ff; Gal. 5. 18).[233] This in fact is precisely the point of the larger context in which the passage is set (Rom. 7.4ff; 8.1ff) and by which it must be interpreted. It is this clear contrast with the immediately following context that most clearly marks 7.14–25 as describing the conflict not of the Christian, but of a person living helplessly under the power of law;[234] for it is not the possibility of sinning that is here being discussed, but the *impossibility of not sinning*. The picture of one who is a 'slave' of sin (*πεπραμένος ὑπὸ τὴν ἁμαρτίαν*: Rom. 7.14), totally unable to do what is good because he is held 'captive to the law of sin' (Rom. 7.23), is not at all the picture generally painted of the Christian life by Paul. I conclude, then, that if the passage is seen not to fit well with the two brief references Paul makes to his own pre-Christian experience of the law, it fits even less well with the unequivocal statements he makes elsewhere about the new life of the Christian as one freed from the power of the law.

### 2.2 The Moral Function of the Law

But this is not to say that the law has absolutely no function or validity in Paul's ethics. The very fact that he says the *σάρξ* -oriented person 'does not submit to God's law' (Rom. 8.7) implies in itself that he thinks of the Spirit-governed person as in some way doing so. But in what sense? This Paul nowhere spells out precisely.

A number of statements in his letters, however, suggest that he makes some kind of distinction in his thinking between the ritual and moral aspects of the law[235] – though the distinction is nowhere explicitly formulated. Although the former are clearly considered as abrogated (at least for gentile believers), the latter seem to be implicitly viewed as still valid: 'For neither circumcision counts for anything nor uncircumcision, but keeping the commandments of God' (1 Cor. 7.19).[236] Here 'the commandments of God' must refer primarily to the moral and not to the ritual demands of the law.[237] It is the moral aspects of the law that are probably also in focus in Paul's statement, 'the law is holy, and the commandment is holy and just and good' (Rom. 7.12).[238] Further, the fact that the commands of the second half of the Decalogue are cited at least three times (Rom. 2.21f; 7.7; 13.8ff) without any sense of denigration, is itself a tacit acknowledgement of the validity of their teachings – and at least in the latter case, of their authority as well.[239] There are several indications, then, that in its *moral* demands, the law remains an authoritative revelation of God's will for the Christian community in Paul's thinking,[240] and therefore functions as a (largely unspoken) criterion for defining ethical behaviour. His understanding of 'sin' almost certainly reflects this.

There is a definite shift of focus however. No longer is it the individual commandments of the law that are determinative, but rather the love commandment; for this, in Paul's view, essentially summarizes and fulfils the moral demands of Torah (Rom. 13.8–10; cf. Gal. 5.14).[241] From the context and from what we have already learned, it is clear that the phrase 'and any other commandment' in the first passage (Rom. 13.9) must refer primarily to the moral commandments; there is no way that the love commandment, directed as it is to the neighbour, can be viewed as the essence of the ritual and ceremonial aspects of the law.

Summing up, then, we may say that there are at least three ways in which Christ explicitly spells the end of the law, according to Paul: (1) as a means of salvation; (2) as a comprehensive body of rules governing the details of daily life and behaviour; and (3) as a power that gives sin its authority. In these respects the law has no jurisdiction over Christians (Rom. 6.14ff; 7.1–6; 8.2ff). But as *moral* demand, the law remains implicitly a valid expression of the will of God – though the focus has now clearly shifted away from the individual laws themselves to the all-embracing principle of love that sums up and fulfils the law. So though the ethical standards of the law are maintained, Paul sees the Christian life governed not so much by its various precepts as by a single basic principle on a much deeper level. The role of the Mosaic law in the motivation of Pauline ethics, then, is more implicit than explicit.

### 2.3 'Legal' Tendencies in Paul's Ethics

But what of the concept of law more generally? At a number of points, for example, Paul's parenesis consists simply of commands. Is this in itself not evidence of a certain legal bent, a basically authoritarian mentality? There are a number of elements in his writing that could be so interpreted.

Käsemann, for instance, finds in the epistles numerous *Sätze heiligen Rechtes*, i.e. (usually) apodictically or casuistically formulated statements attached to a strong threat or decree of judgement (e.g. 1 Cor. 3.17; 14.38; 16.22; Gal. 1.9; cf. 1 Cor. 5.3ff; Rom. 2.12; 2 Cor. 9.6). Here, he asserts, we see Paul's ethical statements plainly motivated by the divine law of *jus talionis*.[242] J.T. Sanders concurs, and suggests that this reveals a side of Paul's ethics that is both arbitrary and absolute, and not at all based on the 'indicative' of justification, as is normally the case with his imperatives.[243]

Paul's appeals to ethical commands of the Lord (e.g. 1 Cor. 7.10; 9.14; 14.37)[244] are often viewed in much the same way. They stand out strikingly because of the way the apostle contrasts them so sharply with his own advice in 1 Cor. 7.10, 12, 25. This would seem to suggest that, what Paul does know of the commands of the Lord, he views as the final authority, sufficient in themselves to motivate ethical behaviour without further appeal.[245]

He also lays down rules and regulations for the conduct of church life on the basis of his own authority (e.g. 1 Cor. 7.17; 11.16, 34; 14.34f; 2 Thess. 2.15; 3.10, 12),[246] and insists on obedience to them (2 Cor. 10.6; 2 Thess. 3.6, 14; cf. 1 Cor. 14.38; 2 Cor. 2.9; 7.15; Phil. 2.12; 2 Thess. 3.4; Phm. 21). Further, as a minister of Christ, he speaks of his authority as deriving from the Lord himself (2 Cor. 10.8; 13.10);[247] indeed, it is Christ, he declares, that is speaking through him (2 Cor. 13.3). That his instructions can be very authoritarian and demanding may perhaps be inferred from the statement of his opponents that 'his letters are weighty and strong' (*βαρεῖαι καὶ ἰσχυραί*: 2 Cor. 10.10), and from his own acknowledgement that in some things he writes 'very boldly' (*τολμηρότερον*: Rom. 15.15). It is an indisputable fact that Paul freely gives orders and expects them to be obeyed.

How do we interpret these seemingly authoritarian statements in view of the assertions he makes elsewhere about the negative character and function of law? Some conclude that the apostle is frankly inconsistent, or that he wavers unpredictably between the two positions. Schoeps, for example, sees Paul as totally inconsistent: having radically rejected the law, he nonetheless proceeds to express virtually the whole of his parenesis in terms of law: 'In fact, all Paul's exhortations ... are in the last resort but illustrations ... of the principle: "The law is holy and the commandment is holy and just and good."'[248] J.T. Sanders' view is more qualified: 'He seems to intend that all action should be grounded in the basic principle of doing the good to one's fellow man; yet, when confronted with an actual event calling for some kind of ethical direction, he has a tendency to forget that ground rule and to rule arbitrarily, i.e., by direct revelation from the Lord.'[249] Thus Sanders sees Paul's inconsistency at its greatest when he is confronted with immediate moral dilemmas.[250] Houlden, however, suggests it is most prominent when his focus shifts away from the present to the future:

> When Paul considers the idea of lawfulness in the context of the status already conferred upon the Christian, then freedom is the keynote (Gal. v, 1) and 'all things are lawful' ...; but when he takes the long-term view, then the idea of lawfulness in effect reasserts itself, and lists of forbidden kinds of behaviour are supplied.[251]

Houlden also sees traces of Paul's inconsistency in more peripheral areas:

> In other words, as Paul's ethics spread out towards the edges, especially when he turns to questions on which it would be hard to see the bearing of central beliefs and where perhaps the best a man can do is to rationalize his prejudices or intuitive convictions, he makes use of principles which are not easily worked into the central logic of his teaching.[252]

Others, however, interpret the data as a mark not of Paul's inconsistency, but of the degree to which his world-view and ethics are influenced by his rabbinic background. Some even claim that, as a Christian, Paul remains essentially a Pharisee in both mentality and practice. Among those who hold this view is W.D. Davies, who insists, 'the Apostle was, in short, a Rabbi become Christian and was therefore primarily governed both in life and thought by Pharisaic concepts ... Moreover, Paul observed the Law, and that in the pharisaic manner, throughout his life.'[253] Ellison's understanding is similar: even in his work among gentiles, Paul himself remains fully within the law, continuing to observe it as a Pharisee.[254] From such a viewpoint, legal tendencies in the apostle's thinking present no problem at all; indeed, it is the non-legal aspects that require explanation!

Davies even suggests that the centrality of legal concepts in Paul's thought confirms that for him Christ is lawgiver as well as redeemer.[255] In fact, the references he makes to the commands of the Lord are sufficient, Davies claims, to establish the strong probability that Paul knows an authoritative collection of dominical sayings that include ethical teachings, and that it is this to which he refers when he speaks of the 'law of Christ'.[256] Jesus not only replaces the Jewish Torah, he assumes the significance of a 'new Torah'.[257] The fact that life 'in Christ' replaces life 'under the law' in no way diminishes the concept of Torah, for now the indwelling Christ becomes a law written on the heart.[258] In Davies' thinking, even the Spirit functions as a kind of law to Paul, spontaneous though it be.[259] He thus argues that the concept of Torah is fully as integral to Pauline Christianity as to Judaism, and that it is only because of Paul's gentile interests and his conflict with the Judaizers that the 'law of Christ' is not more emphasized in his writings.[260] In no way, he claims, are Paul's legal tendencies 'a mere overhang from a pre-Pauline Jewish–Christian legalism unrelated to the essentials of Paul's thought';[261] rather they form the very core of it. For Davies, then, Paul is the great *Tanna* of the gentiles.[262]

But here we must draw the line, and challenge a number of the above assertions. Though there certainly are elements of authoritarianism in Paul's writing, quite in keeping with the character of his background and his sense of vocation (and perhaps his personality also), their importance in the structure of his ethics must not be exaggerated. The apostle's conception of ethical motivation is not fundamentally a 'legal' one.

That there are *Sätze heiligen Rechtes* in his writing, for example, goes without question; but as Käsemann himself acknowledges,[263] their occurrence is quite limited – and they certainly do not play a dominant role in the motivation of ethics.[264] The emphasis of Käsemann and Sanders on the importance of the concept of 'holy law' in Paul's thought, then, presents a somewhat distorted picture.[265]

Similarly, at only three points does Paul appeal directly to commands of the Lord to motivate ethics (1 Cor. 7.10; 9.14; 14.37); and even here it is clear that he regards them not so much as legal decrees demanding strict obedience, as authoritative principles to be applied in the light of circumstances – for he obviously feels the freedom to qualify them himself (1 Cor. 7.10f; 9.14f).[266] It cannot be true, then, that the collected traditions of Jesus' teachings function as the primary basis of Christian morality for

Paul – else we would have many more explicit references to them than we actually do.[267]

As for the rules and regulations he lays down for the conduct of church life, these do not, for the most part, bear the absolute authority and implicit threat of divine judgement that are generally associated with 'law' or a decree of the Lord, and do not carry the weight of either. Bearing little more than Paul's own authority in most cases, and expressing largely his own convictions about correct conduct, they function rather more like practical guidelines, the kind of rules that are necessary for the orderly functioning of any community – even one under the active working of the Spirit.[268] They are especially prominent in 1 Corinthians, where Paul deals with a number of specific church problems. The few instances of appeal to the higher authority of Christ also occur in the Corinthian correspondence, and must be interpreted in the light of his peculiar tensions with that community.

Apart from the infrequent appeal to a direct command of the Lord, it is at those points where Paul confronts cases of obvious vice or anticipates resistance that his instructions come closest to taking on the nature of 'law' (cf. 1 Cor. 5.3ff; 2 Cor. 10.6; 2 Thess. 3.12, 14);[269] here his authoritarian tendencies emerge most sharply. Generally he prefers to appeal rather than to command; but when gentler methods seem likely to prove ineffective, Paul has no hesitations about 'laying down the law'.[270] The usefulness of this tougher approach, however, appears to be limited in his thinking to the negative function of curbing vice or imposing restraint on unacceptable behaviour (cf. Gal. 3.23; note the similar function of the law in Rom. 13.9f); he makes little use of it to arouse *good* behaviour. For Paul, the appeal to authority is a relatively ineffective means of evoking truly ethical living on a deep level. Nonetheless, the very fact that he does resort to it at times is an implicit acknowledgement in itself of the value and indeed necessity in his thinking of motivating ethics by authority and demand, at least in certain well-defined contexts.

Here, if anywhere, the apostle renders himself guilty of inconsistency. For at this point his own practice reveals that he does not, after all, have quite such an entirely negative view of the function of law as some of his statements about the Torah might suggest (Rom. 5.20; 7.5f, 7ff; 1 Cor. 15.56). But even then, he is careful to insist that the problem lies not with the law itself – which is holy, just, good and indeed *πνευματικός* (Rom. 7.7, 12, 14) – but rather with the nature of sin and the weakness of human *σάρξ* (Rom. 7.7–25).

Those who charge Paul with thoroughgoing inconsistency often fail to distinguish between the different functions of the law in focus in his seemingly contradictory statements. His negative assertions regarding the salvific and regulatory functions of the law, for example, nowhere invalidate his tacit affirmation of its moral function. His general agreement with the saying, 'all things are lawful' (which, it should be noted, stands in a very specific context and is immediately qualified by other moral considerations), is certainly not intended to be an endorsement of the kind of behaviour he elsewhere cites as strictly prohibited; freedom from the law (Gal. 5.1) is never taken by him to mean freedom from the moral demands of the law. It is a question of the aspect of law in focus. Such statements become 'contradictions' only when considered apart from their contexts. Nor is it accurate to say that the concept of 'lawfulness' or forbidden behaviour arises in his mind primarily when he looks toward the End;[271] it arises rather whenever he focuses on particular vices which break with demands of the moral law (cf. the vice lists in 1 Cor. 6.9f; Gal. 5.19ff; Col. 3.5f), and which therefore have eschatological consequences. That is, looking toward the End is the result, not the cause, of the awareness of forbidden behaviour. And as for J.T. Sanders' charge that Paul's use of authoritative decrees contradicts his basic intention that 'all action should be grounded in the basic principle of doing the good to one's fellow man',[272] this represents a misunderstanding of the apostle's recognition that people with different attitudes require different sanctions to motivate; i.e. the ideal is not always possible. This is not to say that Paul is nowhere inconsistent; it is simply to suggest that at least some of the charges of inconsistency levelled against him lack real foundation and accuracy.

Further, that Paul's thought and writing reflect traces of his Pharisaic background is inevitable.[273] But that Paul the Christian continues to observe the traditional practices of the Jewish law as a Pharisee is beyond belief[274] – at least if we restrict ourselves to his own writings (Acts presents a slightly different picture: cf. 18.18; 21.26). An important passage in 1 Cor. 9 makes it clear that when he does follow Jewish traditions, it is largely for missionary purposes:

> To the Jews I became as a Jew, in order to win Jews; to those under the law I became as one under the law – though not being myself under the law – that I might win those under the law. To those outside the law I became as one outside the law (*ὡς ἄνομος*) – not being without law toward God but under the law of Christ (*μὴ ὢν ἄνομος θεοῦ ἀλλ' ἔννομος Χριστοῦ*) – that I might win those outside the law ... I have become all things to all men, that I might by all means save some (1 Cor. 9.20f).[275]

Note that here Paul expressly regards himself as not being 'under the law'. There is nothing in his writings to suggest that his ordinary daily life and conduct are governed by legal regulations halakic-style, nor is such a perspective reflected in his ethical teaching.

Nor is there warrant for W.D. Davies' emphasis on the role of Christ as a new lawgiver in Paul's thought, and on his teachings as a new Torah.[276] Indeed, as we have seen, it is unlikely that the apostle has first-hand acquaintance with any substantial body of fixed ethical tradition viewed as deriving from Jesus.[277] It is not primarily in his role as 'lawgiver' that Paul locates Christ's significance for ethics.

What then does Paul mean by the 'law of Christ' (Gal. 6.2; 1 Cor. 9.21)? Though the precise denotation is nowhere specified, it is most naturally interpreted in context as a reference to Jesus' emphasis on the love commandment as the controlling rule of life and ethics: 'Bear one another's burdens, and so fulfil the law of Christ' (Gal. 6.2).[278] This, if anything, is what Paul understands to be the essence of Jesus' moral demand. Given his infrequent references to Jesus' teachings, the 'law of Christ' cannot be viewed as an authoritative collection of dominical sayings or Christian halakoth; it is 'law' in a quite different sense.[279]

I conclude, then, that it is important not to overestimate the 'legal' dimension of Paul's thought, but to recognize both its limits and the factors determining its manifestation – i.e. his implicit conviction of the abiding validity of the *moral* demands of the law, and the usefulness in certain circumstances (e.g. when confronted with obvious vice or anticipated recalcitrance) of motivating ethical behaviour by authority and decree. On the whole, therefore, we may say that the concept of law plays a secondary and not a primary role in the structure of Paul's ethics. While traditional Jewish legal concepts form the basic substructure of his thought and the backdrop for his radical understanding of Christ, his view of the Christian life is not fundamentally a 'legal' one.[280]

### 2.4 The Law and Ethical Obligation

What then becomes of the sense of obligation underlying ethics? John Knox claims that Paul's invalidation of the law entirely cuts away the ground from under any sense of ethical obligation whatever: 'For law in some sense is the necessary presupposition of obligation.'[281] Paul's emphasis on justification by faith *χωρὶς νόμου* therefore renders completely valid the charge of antinomianism against him, according to Knox.[282] Convinced that the apostle has undermined the 'moral seriousness and strenuous moral effort' that are 'the necessary presuppositions of any goodness it may be given one to have', he concludes: 'I should say that Paul went too far ... when he denied the continuing validity and the absolute indispensability of the law itself.'[283]

But, as observed above,[284] Paul does *not* reject the law *in toto* and for all purposes, and it is this that lies at the heart of Knox's misunderstanding. In failing to distinguish the various functions of the law in focus, he fails to realize that Paul's negation of the soteriological and regulatory aspects of the law in no way denies the validity of its *moral* demands in his thinking. And in limiting his concern to the issue of law, Knox fails to recognize the extent to which Paul understands moral obligation to be based on grounds other than that of law. In these respects at least, Knox's critique is oversimplified and fails to appreciate the complexity of Paul's thought.[285]

But if the moral demands of the law remain valid, and Scripture continues to be regarded in this sense as an authoritative expression of the will of God (cf. Rom. 15.4; 1 Cor. 9.8ff; 10.11), why does Paul make such little explicit use of it in the motivation of ethics? Though he frequently cites it (especially in a prophetic sense) in support of his statements in other contexts,[286] very rarely does he base his moral injunctions on it – even when its decrees are directly applicable and would be the easiest means of reinforcing his statements and evoking response.[287] Perhaps the most convincing evidence of this is the absence of scriptural citations to support ethical statements in the whole of Philippians, Colossians, 1 and 2 Thessalonians, and Philemon – and the fact that even the love commandment is only infrequently cited. Further, on those relatively few occasions when he does appeal to Scripture in the context of ethics, rarely does it function as the primary and decisive point of appeal; it tends rather to operate on a secondary level, as confirmation, support and background explanation to help the argument along (e.g. Rom. 12.19, 20; 14.11; 1 Cor. 5.13; 9.8ff; 10.25–7; 14.34).[288] Why is this so?

The most important reason would seem to be Paul's desire to encourage a sense of ethical obligation based on deeper principles than that of mere obedience to the demands of law. At a number of points, for example, his writing implies that the kind of moral response he hopes for is one specifically *not* based on mere submission to external authority, but arising freely from the heart and motivated by more positive factors (e.g. 2 Cor. 9.5, 7; Phm. 14). His preference is to appeal for ethical response rather than to command it (Phm. 8, 9; cf. 2 Cor. 8.8: 'I say this not as a command ...');[289] whenever possible, therefore, he shies away from the use of flat, unreasoned prohibition in favour of reasoned argumentation (see e.g. 1 Cor. 7.25–38; 11.1–16 – though in the latter case the reasoning is rather forced and arbitrary).[290] On the whole, then, it is clear that

Paul wants to arouse a deeper, more internalized moral response and sense of ethical obligation than that based on mere submission to the demands of law.[291]

### 3. *Comparison of Matthew and Paul*

As a result of their common Jewish background,[292] there are certain fundamental points of similarity in the two writers. Both see themselves as upholding the law (though in different senses: Mt. 5.17–19; Rom. 3.31). Both express the conviction (explicit in Matthew, more implicit in Paul) that the basic moral demands of the law, typified by the second half of the Decalogue (Mt. 15.19; 19.18f; Rom. 13.9), remain a valid expression of God's will for the Christian community. And both, accordingly, see life in terms of obedience and judgement (though the emphasis differs). In these respects the basic presuppositions of Jewish morality are taken as axiomatic.[293]

As Christians, however, both writers have broken with certain elements of the traditional understanding and practice of the law – though in different ways and to different extents. This may be reflected in the fact that both seem to be concerned with the threat or charge of antinomianism (in some form or other: Mt. 5.17–19; 1 Cor. 6.12; 10.23),[294] which may at least partially derive from or be associated with the critical position they themselves have adopted. For as a result of their understanding of Jesus, both have come to a critical evaluation of the law that entails the effective abrogation of at least some of its precepts because of the priority given to the love commandment as the epitome of the law. Both writers have come to realize that true righteousness, real doing of the will of God, is much more than mere formal observance of the letter of the law, that it is an internal as well as an external matter – though Matthew draws out the implications more fully, while Paul focuses rather on the background issues and the underlying theological structure. But the most important fact is that, for both, it is the person of Jesus that is now central; he replaces the law as the primary focus and centre of concern. It is *his* words, authority and significance that are now of ultimate importance, not simply those of the law. The whole question of the law and Jesus' relationship to it, however, and the implications of this for the Christian community, are matters of serious concern to both writers, and issues to which both give priority.

The viewpoints of Matthew and Paul on this question, however, are markedly different; for at bottom, their understandings of the role of the law in the Church are radically divergent.[295] Matthew, whose writing reflects the perspective of a church predominantly Jewish in background and outlook,[296] views the Christian community as still under the jurisdiction of the Mosaic law (albeit as now interpreted by Jesus); while Paul, whose mission is directed outward to the non-Jewish world, sees the life of the Christian community as no longer fundamentally ordered by the law at all. For Matthew, the entire law remains authoritative, right down to the least jot and tittle, and the question of what is 'lawful' (including the whole matter of authoritative interpretation) is still vitally important;[297] but for Paul, the law – at least as a religious system and a means of coming to God – is now superseded by Christ, and the question of legal authority has ceased to be of central concern. For the evangelist, therefore, the rules and regulations of Torah and the scribal tradition continue to play an important part in ordering the details of daily life; for the apostle, apart from their more general moral and prophetic functions, they are largely irrelevant. Faced with the threat or charge of antinomianism, Matthew argues strongly that the whole law is valid and authoritative for the Christian community; while Paul, countering Judaizing pressures on his non-Jewish congregations, argues even more strongly that it is *not* – at least in its salvific and regulatory functions.[298] Matthew's view of the Christian life, then, retains more of a legal flavour than Paul's; and, on this basis, Paul would probably see at least some of the statements in the Sermon on the Mount (especially 5.17–19) not as of a piece with his own thought, but as a *fauler Kompromiss*.[299]

In general, Matthew maintains a more positive view of the nature and function of the law than Paul, who in defence of his thoroughgoing theology of grace is more concerned to expose its inherent weakness than to justify its validity. Paul argues that it is hopeless to attempt to fulfil the demands of the law (at least in one's own strength), and all who base their relationship with God on their hopes of doing so are doomed. The law can never be viewed as the key to moral living, he asserts, because it only arouses and stimulates the very sin it forbids; indeed, it is the very authority of the law that gives sin its teeth – and that is precisely its purpose, claims Paul. So the law, holy and good in its own right, effectively becomes an enemy; it functions as an instrument not of life, but of death – the antithesis of the gospel of Christ. Thus, Paul sets the whole system of law in sharp contrast with that of grace and faith in Christ, the one based (at least as popularly understood) on a mentality of reward for human effort, the other on God's free gift and the power of the Spirit. To revert to the former is to cut oneself off from the grace of the latter; for only in the latter can one find salvation and truly fulfil the moral demands of God.

Such a negative view of the law, it can only be concluded, would be entirely foreign and unacceptable to Matthew, who assumes not only that it is right and good to obey the law in detail – indeed, *not* to do so is to render oneself 'least' in the kingdom (Mt. 5.19) – but also (apparently) that it is quite within the range of human capability to do so. His would seem to be a traditional Jewish view: 'The commandment was given to be obeyed, and the implication is that man can obey it.'[300] The hopeless picture of despair painted by Paul in Rom. 7.14–25 is probably not one that Matthew would recognize or endorse at all, for there is nothing to suggest that he shares Paul's concept of the law as an enslaving power, as the 'power of sin'. Nor does Matthew share Paul's view of a sharp dichotomy between law and grace, or law and faith, with one based on human effort and the other on divine gift; for him, the two are entirely compatible concepts. The Christian finds salvation and grace within, not outside, the context of the law. Whereas for Paul God's grace is manifest in the fact that Christ explicitly replaces the law as the way of salvation, becoming the believer's righteousness himself, for Matthew God's grace in Christ is viewed from within the framework of the law, and experienced at least partly in the life of deeper righteousness made possible by Jesus' true interpretation of it.

So it appears that Matthew's community is encouraged to continue its observance of at least certain elements of Jewish ritual law, while on several occasions Paul's churches are explicitly discouraged from doing so. Though our evidence on this point is too fragmentary to allow for conclusive generalizations, it would seem that Matthew is more reluctant than Paul to abandon such traditional practices as observance of the sabbath law[301] and the dietary regulations, at least in principle; and he clearly implies that there is still a need for authoritative scribal interpretation of Torah to define the nature and limits of acceptable practice. Paul, on the other hand, has little use for scribes (1 Cor. 1.20), and frankly castigates those who hanker after the teachings of the Mosaic law as 'unillumined' or 'veiled' in their understanding (2 Cor. 3.14–16). Though Matthew's focus is no longer primarily on the observance of the ritual–ceremonial law itself, he says nothing that would discourage its practice in general – though now, of course, it must be set in the light of the fundamental priorities of Jesus' teaching. Paul, however, appears to have adopted a strictly pragmatic view, observing it only when it is practically useful to his ministry to do so (1 Cor. 9.20ff; cf. Acts 21.20–6). Thus, though both writers are interested in the question of food restrictions, the positions they seem to adopt on the issue are quite different.[302] Matthew's silence on the question of circumcision is probably best taken as an indication that the writer and his community simply assume its continued validity, and not (as Goulder proposes[303]) that the whole matter has been discussed and settled a generation earlier. And if this is so, such a silence may suggest that it is not a Pauline position that the evangelist is combatting, especially in view of the possible presence of gentiles in the Matthean community; but arguments from silence remain inconclusive. In any case, of the two writers it is undoubtedly Matthew who makes greater allowance for combining the 'new' with the 'old'.

This basic difference of perspective is reflected in their conceptions of *δικαιοσύνη*.[304] Matthew understands it in traditional Jewish terms, i.e. in terms of obedience to the law; for him it is a strictly ethical concept. Paul, however, conceives of it largely apart from the law: for him it is primarily a gift of God, not the result of human effort, and made effective in one's life by the work of the Spirit within. Both writers recognize the need for a radical kind of righteousness that functions on a far deeper level than mere compliance with the letter of the law; but whereas the evangelist sees it attained by thoroughgoing and determined obedience to the deepest intent of the law, the apostle views it as possible only if one is freed from the law to live by faith in the power of the Spirit. For both it is Christ that makes real righteousness possible; but their perceptions of how this happens are quite different.[305]

Neither is a legalist in the narrow sense of the term.[306] Both, for example, give priority to the love commandment as the most important point of the law;[307] but there is a subtle difference in their treatment of it. For Matthew, it is understood within the context and framework of the law; i.e. it is viewed essentially as a commandment to be obeyed, indeed as the greatest commandment of the law. As such, it functions also as the primary principle for interpreting and applying the law, and therefore as the determinative criterion at points of conflict – which effectively allows for the breaking of one commandment for the sake of another. But for Paul, as the essence and fulfilment of the law the love commandment essentially *replaces* the law as the working principle of life (Gal. 5.6).[308]

Thus, even though Matthew sees Jesus' yoke as 'easy' and his burden as 'light', his view of the Christian life still calls for radical submission to the demands of the law; while Paul thinks of the Christian life as fundamentally no longer under the law at all. So the two writers offer quite different answers to the basic question of how to live a moral life: for Matthew, the answer lies in the direction of obedience to the law; for Paul, it lies in being freed from the law to experience the new life of the Spirit. Whereas Matthew perceives the human problem to lie in the inadequate interpretation of and obedience to the law, Paul perceives it to lie in the attempt to follow the way of law at all.[309]

What may be concluded, then, about the relationship of law and obligation in their ethics? To what extent do the two writers ground their ethical injunctions in the concept of law? If by 'law' we mean Torah, neither Matthew nor Paul makes any extensive appeal explicitly to this – and this is somewhat surprising, especially for Matthew. In part, this may reflect the fact that the evangelist simply takes it for granted that the life of the Christian community is governed by the dictates of Torah (as 5.17–19 makes perfectly clear); it may also reflect the fact that it is now the authority of Jesus and his teachings that are central to Matthew's focus, not that of the law *per se*. However, if we take 'law' in the broader, more general sense of authoritative command or demand, that is a different question. Both writers make use of 'law' in this sense to motivate ethics, though again, in different ways and to different extents.[310] Though both Matthew and Paul attribute ultimate authority to the words of Jesus as Lord,[311] Paul's appeal to them is infrequent and of only secondary importance in his writing, while Matthew's is frequent and of primary importance in his (though here, obviously, the difference in genre is an important factor). For Matthew, the demand for obedience to Jesus' teachings appears central. Paul, however, generally prefers to encourage a kind of moral response that is motivated at a much deeper level than that of mere compulsion or sense of obedience, and thus at a number of points distinctly shies away from an authoritarian approach. But when it comes to restraining clear-cut cases of obvious sin or potential obduracy (i.e. when harsher measures seem called for), he feels absolutely no compunction about 'laying down the law' and spelling out the consequences of such behaviour explicitly. On the whole, however, it is his conviction that truly *good* behaviour cannot be simply legislated, but must arise out of the heart on other grounds. Precisely here, then, is the limit in Paul's mind of the validity of 'law' as a motivating factor for ethics. Matthew, on the other hand, seems implicitly to place greater confidence in the power of authoritative command both to suppress the bad and to evoke the good. For him, the very fact that something is commanded by the Lord (or by the law) – with the implicit threat of judgement that bears – is apparently sufficient in itself to motivate moral behaviour.

All in all, though both have their points of inconsistency, it is perhaps accurate to say that Paul's thoroughgoing critique of the law represents a more fully thought-out and consistent position than Matthew's. The latter, it would appear, wants to have his cake and eat it too: as a Jew, he is careful to emphasize the validity of the law right down to the least jot and tittle – and the authority of traditional scribal interpretation also, at least as a general principle; but as a Christian he realizes that Jesus' teaching transcends the authority and at least some of the specific rulings of both. The resulting synthesis inevitably reflects a certain amount of tension and disparity; but there is no sure evidence that Matthew himself is aware of it.[312] Consequently, it is difficult to integrate perfectly the various statements in his Gospel concerning the law; in the end, they must be understood and interpreted individually in light of the evangelist's different concerns. Paul's inconsistency, however, lies rather in his seeming denial of the value of certain principles at work in the Jewish law, which he himself puts to good use (albeit in a limited sense) in his own parenesis – namely, the value in certain contexts of motivating ethics by authority and decree. Though numerous statements denying the validity of the law (e.g. Rom. 6.14; 7.4, 6; 1 Cor. 10.23; Gal. 5.1) appear to conflict with Paul's own tacit acceptance of its moral demands, these cannot be regarded as flat contradictions if the particular aspect of law in focus in the individual contexts is taken into account. In general, many of the statements that give rise to a sense of inconsistency (in both writers) occur in polemical contexts, and must be interpreted accordingly.

Clearly, any attempt to understand the different positions of the two writers must take into account both the different constituencies of their churches and the different fronts on which they fight;[313] but it must also take into account the basic difference of perspective of the writers themselves (and the traditions and experiences that have shaped their understanding). For when all is said and done, it can only be concluded that Matthew's viewpoint is closer to that of traditional Judaism, while Paul's represents a more radical break with it.[314] Though Jewish concepts lie in the background of Paul's thought, Christian reformulations clearly dominate the foreground. For both writers, however, it is the figure of Jesus and their understanding of him that is central and ultimately determinative.

## 2

# REWARD AND PUNISHMENT

Having looked at the ethics of Matthew and Paul from the viewpoint of law, we now shift our attention to the different but related question of recompense. Of what significance are the concepts of reward and punishment, especially eschatological[1] reward and punishment, in their overall moral perspectives? To what extent do the two writers seek to motivate ethical behaviour by either enticement or threat? The results of the analysis in this chapter should correlate, at least to some degree, with those of the preceding one, as the two issues are related.

## 1. *Matthew*

As we might expect of one whose outlook is so strongly shaped by legal perspectives, Matthew has more material relating to rewards and punishment than any of the other evangelists.[2] The idea of recompense, especially eschatological recompense, pervades the Gospel and functions significantly in the evangelist's motivation of ethical behaviour.

### 1.1 Eschatological Recompense and Ethical Motivation

Matthew writes with an eye to the kingdom. For him, the hope of gaining entrance to the kingdom of heaven is of central importance, and bears directly upon the whole matter of ethics. This is what lies behind the demand for deeper righteousness in the Gospel (5.20; cf. 6.33). Thus, the initial summaries of the preaching of both John the Baptist and Jesus are programmatic for the teaching that follows in the Sermon on the Mount: 'Repent, for the kingdom of heaven is at hand' (ἤγγικεν: 3.2; 4.17*; cf. 10.7). The evangelist makes it clear that a radical change of heart and life is essential if one is to gain the kingdom. The prominence of the concept in Matthew's thinking is seen in the beatitudes especially, which are significantly placed at the very beginning of the Sermon (5.3–12); here it is the promise of the kingdom, above all else, to which appeal is made for a moral life. The beatitudes thus plunge the reader directly into the heart of the Sermon, identifying both its major concern (a life of deeper righteousness) and the eschatological issue hanging in the balance. For Matthew, it is God's kingdom and righteousness that are to be pursued above all else (6.33), and the former cannot be had without the latter.

But it is the negative side of this issue that Matthew is most concerned to stress, i.e. the danger of failing to attain the kingdom, and the fearful prospect of judgement that implies. This, in fact (judging from the context of 3.6–12 and the evangelist's general emphasis), is probably what underlies the call to repentance in 3.2 and 4.17*, even though what is formally expressed is the more positive consideration of the nearness of the kingdom. Indeed, it is probably the threat of judgement that underlies the warnings about not achieving the kingdom (5.20; 18.3).[3] For Matthew, eschatological judgement is a corollary of the coming of the kingdom, and references to the latter therefore often indirectly express the threat of the former. In general, it is the threat of judgement and loss of the kingdom that serves as the dominant motivating force for ethics throughout the Gospel.[4]

The tone is set very early, in the strong element of judgement attributed by the evangelist to the preaching of John the Baptist (3.7–10), the latter part of which is repeated almost verbatim by Jesus in 7.19. Here Matthew makes it clear at the outset that judgement is executed on the basis of the presence or absence of 'fruits of repentance' (*καρπὸν ἄξιον τῆς μετανοίας*), a point implied also in the threefold emphasis on the expectation of 'fruit' in the parable of the wicked husbandmen (21.34, 41, 43). Against the background of the unrepentant Pharisees especially, Matthew sets the fiery picture of Jesus as a judge who stands ready to separate the 'wheat' from the 'chaff', and to burn the 'chaff' with unquenchable fire (3.11f; cf. 13.30);[5] and it is the fruits of *μετάνοια* that distinguish the 'wheat' from the 'chaff'.

The threat of eschatological judgement pervades the whole of the Sermon on the Mount, where it reinforces the demand for radical obedience to the law and the real doing of the will of God. The strong appeals to judgement in the antitheses, for example, are all intended to back up the stringent demand for deeper righteousness in 5.20 – without which, Matthew claims, one shall not enter the kingdom at all. Here the threat of judgement is cited even against such specific behaviour as the expression of anger or abuse toward one's brother (5.22; cf. verses 25f[6]) and the lustful look (5.28ff); the seriousness with which the evangelist takes the matter is seen in his references to *γέεννα* especially (5.22, 29, 30; cf. 18.8f*).[7] At other points, the threat of judgement is less explicit, but present nonetheless implicitly (cf. 5.13, 19, 25f, 31f, 34; 6.12, 14f). The theme returns toward the end of the Sermon, where passing judgement on others (in a condemnatory sense) is prohibited on the grounds that it renders one liable to the judgement of God being passed on oneself (7.1f). The Sermon concludes with a series of strict warnings backed by eschatological threats that remind the reader that: (1) to follow the easy way taken by the majority is to follow the way that leads to destruction (7. 13f); (2) only those who seriously apply themselves to doing the will of God will gain entrance to the kingdom (7.21; cf. 21.28–32); and (3) only those who build their lives on the firm rock of obedience to Jesus' teaching will in the end stand unmoved in the storm of judgement (7.24–7).[8] From beginning to end, it is the promise of eschatological reward and (even more) the threat of eschatological loss and judgement that function as the primary sanctions behind the ethical teachings of the Sermon.[9] Here Matthew's free and unabashed use of the threat of judgement attests his conviction of its value in inciting the Christian community to live up to the high moral standards of Jesus.

His emphasis on judgement is seen in passages outside the Sermon also. In the vast majority of cases they occur in Matthew's own material or redaction (e.g. 8.12, 29; 10.15, 26–8; 11.20–4; 12.41–2; 13.42, 50; 18.3, 10; 22.13; 24.51; 25.30), and not merely in extracts taken over from Mark. Of all the evangelists, it is Matthew who most expressly portrays the Son of Man himself as Judge (cf. 13.30, 37–42; 25.31–46; note especially the redactional additions 3.12; 16.27), and who paints the torments of eschatological judgement most vividly. Thus, it is Matthew who most explicitly describes the Judgement in terms of fire (Mt. 3.10–12; 5.22; 7.19; 13.40–2, 50; 18.8–9; 25.41)[10] and *γέεννα* as a place of 'outer darkness' where 'men will weep and gnash their teeth' (cf. 8.12; 13.42, 50; 22.13; 24.51; 25.30).[11] For vivid details, there is nothing quite comparable to this in his description of the delights of the kingdom (cf. 5.12; 19.28f; 22.2–4; 25.10, 21, 23, 34; 26.29*). The overall impression one gains, then, is that the fear of judgement is a major element in Matthew's thought, and plays a crucial role in his ethics (cf. 10.26–8).

There are a number of references to the future coming of the Son of Man that function in a very similar way as ethical sanctions.[12] With regard to the time of his coming, the evangelist's statements are somewhat ambiguous: several texts reflect a strong view of imminence (10.23; 16.28*; 24.34*; cf. 3.2, 10; 4.17*; 10.7),[13] but others seem to acknowledge the fact of delay (24.14, 48; 25.5, 19; cf. 24.36; 28.19f).[14] In any case, when Matthew appeals to the Parousia as a sanction for ethics, it is not so much its imminence *per se* that is in view as the fact of its certainty and unexpectedness.[15] This is precisely the point of the warnings in the references to the flood (24.37–9), the men in the field and the women at the mill (24.40–2), the thief and the householder (24.43–4), and the ten virgins (25.1–13); it is implicit also in the parable of the wicked servant (24.48–51). The message proclaimed in all of these passages is: 'be ready; for the Son of man is coming at an hour you do not expect' (24.44; cf. verse 42; 25.13). Thus, the allusions to the delay of the Parousia, far from removing the issue to the background, only reinforce the warning to the Christian community to be prepared and ready for its coming.[16] Those who fail to heed the warning will share the fate of the hypocrites in the place where people weep and gnash their teeth (24.51; 25.30). The fundamental sanction underlying these warnings, of course, is the threat of judgement associated with the Parousia (cf. the parable of the talents: 25.14–30); and being 'ready' is viewed above all as a matter of how one lives in relation to the demands of God upon one's life, i.e. whether one is *πιστός* and *δίκαιος*[17] (cf. 24.45–51; 25.14–30, 37, 46). Generally speaking, the appeal to the Parousia functions, like the threat of judgement, as a sanction reinforcing the demand for deeper righteousness. In Matthew's thinking, then, the fact that the Parousia is near in no way negates either the importance of moral living or the need for ethical instruction; on the contrary, it accentuates the urgency of both.

It is significant that Matthew speaks of reward and punishment chiefly in eschatological terms. This may be seen in the beatitudes, for example, where (as already noted) the various promises of reward – addressed in some cases specifically to those who suffer in this world – are all generally understood to be eschatological and not this-worldly in nature (cf. 5.3, 5, 10, 12).[18] Matthew's version of Jesus' promise to those who have given up much to follow him is also significant: the Marcan references to specific rewards in this life are all eliminated, and as a result the entire focus is shifted to the future (19.27–9; cf. Mk. 10.30).[19] Though not all of his references to reward are unequivocally eschatological in nature,[20] it seems that the evangelist generally conceives of reward as something to be received in the future kingdom, when the humble will be exalted (23.12; cf. 18.4), and those who are 'last' will become 'first' (19.30*; 20.16; note in this regard the distinction between the 'least' and the 'greatest' in the kingdom itself: 5.19; 18.4; cf. 11.11). For him, life in this world would seem to be a time of humiliation and suffering (cf. 5.3–12, 38–42, 43–8; 8.20; 25.35f); vindication and reward await the future (cf. 5.3–12; 25.34).[21] So for Matthew, disciples live with their eyes fixed not on the things of this world (6.19–21, 24f, 33), but on what lies beyond – the kingdom and the End. They lay up for themselves treasures in heaven (to be accumulated against the Day of Judgement), not upon earth (6.19f; cf. 19.21). They are prepared to suffer hardship in this world, because they know that reward awaits them in the kingdom; and of all the evangelists, it is Matthew who most strongly emphasizes these rewards (5.3–12, 46; 10. 41–2; 19.28–9; 25.21, 23, 34).[22]

The evangelist conceives of the final Judgement as recompense not only for what one is, but for what one does. Matthew's redaction of Mk. 8.38 makes it explicit that when the Son of Man returns, he will repay every person *κατὰ τὴν πρᾶξιν αὐτοῦ* (16.27); and this is precisely what is depicted in the parable of the talents (25.14–30). Similarly, in the account of the final Judgement in 25.31–46, the *δίκαιοι* are defined (at least formally) by their acts of mercy, and the 'cursed' by the absence of theirs;[23] and it is on this basis that judgement is meted out. In the context of a warning against blasphemy, the focus shifts from deeds to words, but the basic principle remains the same: 'by your words you will be justified (*δικαιωθήσῃ*) and by your words you will be condemned (*καταδικασθήσῃ*)' (12.37); here blasphemous words constitute the evil act. It is a traditional Jewish view of judgement, based on works, as recompense for how one lives. It is not surprising, then, to find an emphasis in the Gospel on *doing* the will of God (cf. 7.21). But we must remember that, in Matthew, what one *does* is always a reflection of what one *is*; i.e. the question of behaviour can never be separated from that of inner character (cf. 7.16–20; 12.33–5). The tree is always identified by its fruit.

### 1.2 Matthew's Concept of Reciprocity

Underlying this emphasis on judgement is a strong sense of reciprocity that seems to colour the whole of Matthew's thinking about ethics and one's relationship to God, in which God's response to an individual is seen to be of the same kind or degree as that expressed by the individual to others. To some extent this contradicts his description of God as one who 'makes his sun rise on the evil and on the good, and sends rain on the just and on the unjust' (5.45). But the point of this appeal to God's beneficence, it must be remembered, is to justify a particular attitude that disciples are called upon to adopt in relation to those who oppose them; it is not a general principle of grace upon which one may presume. More commonly, it is the concepts of reciprocity and recompense that dominate the evangelist's writing and provide the basis for his ethics. Thus, for example, his appeal for mercy is grounded in the promise of God's reciprocal mercy (5.7), and the full expression of the latter is made dependent on the manifestation of the former (6.12, 14f).[24] Like Luke (6.36), Matthew can also appeal to God's mercy as a model (cf. the parable of the wicked servant: 18.23–35, especially verses 32f); but it is the threat of God's reciprocal action that is especially stressed (cf. 18.35). This, in fact, is precisely why judgement of others is to be avoided: *ἐν ᾧ γὰρ κρίματι κρίνετε κριθήσεσθε* (7.1f); and in the immediately following statement (taken over from Mark), the underlying principle is enunciated explicitly: *ἐν ᾧ μέτρῳ μετρεῖτε μετρηθήσεται ὑμῖν* (7.2) – a 'tit for tat' kind of *jus talionis* (cf. 13.12; 25.29). Consequently, with regard to hospitality shown to Jesus' servants, to receive a prophet is to receive a prophet's reward (*μισθὸν προφήτου*), and to receive a righteous man is to receive a righteous man's reward (*μισθὸν δικαίου*: 10.41; cf. verses 40–2).[25] The same principle is also at work (though indirectly) in the statement about the 'first' being 'last' and the 'last', 'first' (19.30; 20.16; cf. 5.3–12; 23.12). And though it lies outside the realm of ethics, the same would also seem to be true of 10.32f, where acknowledgement or denial of Jesus before others is said to evoke a similar response to the person concerned by Jesus before his Father in heaven.[26] In all these cases, Matthew speaks of a reciprocal response on God's part, similar in kind or measure to the attitude or behaviour shown by the disciple to others. Thus, though the *jus talionis* is strictly ruled out as a basis for interpersonal relationships (5.38ff), it apparently continues to function in Matthew's thinking on the level of the disciple's relationship with God.[27]

In passing, it may be noted that several of Jesus' responses to requests for healing also appear to reflect a certain element of reciprocity. In addition to taking over (though with characteristic abbreviation) those Marcan passages that portray Jesus' healing as a reward-like response to the expression of faith (9.22*; 14.36*), Matthew rephrases a number of Jesus' responses to emphasize that his healing is specifically 'according to' (*ὡς, κατά*) the person's faith (8.13; 9.29; 15.28).[28] This link in the evangelist's thinking between the strength of one's faith and Jesus' response is mirrored in the references that expressly associate *ὀλιγοπιστία* or unbelief with his non-response (13.58; 14.31; 17.19f; note, however, that in the latter pericope even the smallest measure of faith contains the promise of an 'impossible' yield). Certainly these passages reflect the evangelist's concern to strengthen the *ὀλιγοπιστία* of the Christian community by underscoring the dichotomy between faith and unbelief or doubt; but they also leave us wondering whether *πίστις* functions in Matthew's thought somewhat like an act of righteousness that evokes its own reward. In any case, here Jesus' response is represented as being in measure to the confidence of one's expectations – and this may give us some idea of the extent to which the concept of reciprocity pervades the evangelist's thinking.

In summary, then, it may be said that the concept of divine recompense (especially eschatological recompense) is deeply embedded in Matthew's thought, and heavily colours his perception of the Christian life. In a certain sense, his ethics may be viewed as teleological ethics: everything is done with a view to its consequences (cf. 5.44f, 46; 6.1–6, 16–18), especially the eschatological consequences; for ultimately God judges people on the basis of how they live, in relation both to one another and to his demands upon them. In part, this recompense mentality is the natural outcome of a view of the Christian life as one lived under the law; but it would also seem to reflect the writer's conviction of the power of threat and enticement to motivate ethical behaviour. For Matthew, life focuses on the End (which is expected in the not-too-distant future), and there are therefore no weightier sanctions than the promise of eschatological reward and (especially) the threat of eschatological retribution; the two function simultaneously and complementarily in his writing, but the primary emphasis is clearly on the latter.[29]

### 1.3 Clues to the *Sitz im Leben*

If we look carefully at the particular groups against which the threats of judgement are most sharply directed, we find certain possible clues to the *Sitz im Leben* of the Gospel. Unrepentant Jews, for example, are condemned much more in Matthew than they are in either Mark or Luke.[30] Although originally destined to inherit the kingdom, they are now doomed to the place of torment (8.12); and it is against them that the strong words of judgement in 10.15, 11.20–4 and 12.41 (cf. verse 45) are specifically directed. Here it is because of their refusal to repent at the message of Jesus and his disciples that judgement is decreed. The same point underlies the parable of the wicked husbandmen (21.33–46; cf. 3.10) and the reference in the parable of the great supper to the destruction of the city because of the people's rejection of the king's invitation (22.1–8)[31] – though it is against the religious leaders specifically that these two parables appear to be primarily directed (21.45; cf. verse 23; 22.15f). Indirectly, of course, these passages carry threatening overtones for the ethical life of the Christian community as well; but it is against Jewish unrepentance that they are principally aimed.

On the whole, it is the Jewish religious leaders (the Pharisees and scribes especially[32]) who suffer the brunt of Jesus' condemnation. The scathing words of John the Baptist against them in 3.7–12 set the tone for the entire book – yet this is one of the few pericopes in which the possibility of repentance at least remains open to them. In the vast majority of cases, Matthew gives the impression that they are utterly beyond the pale of repentance, simply condemned (15.13f), with an absolutely miserable death awaiting them (21.41, 43).[33] Thus, the Gospel declares that they will never be forgiven, 'either in this age or in the age to come' (12.31f); even the tax-collectors and the harlots (who every good Jew knows will be condemned in the Judgement) precede them into the kingdom (21.31). Here again, what is primarily in focus is their rejection of Jesus and his message (cf. 23.34ff).

In chapter 23, however, the moral grounds of their condemnation are enunciated: they are denounced as hypocritical (23.3ff, 13, 15, 23, 25, 27, 29; cf. 6.2, 5, 16), vain and egocentric (23.5ff; cf. 6.2, 5, 16), misleading (23.13ff), religiously undiscerning (23.16ff), and concerned only with externals (23.23ff) – all because they are inwardly corrupt (23.25ff; cf. 12.34–7). Matthew's Jesus concludes, 'You serpents, you brood of vipers, how are you to escape being sentenced to hell?' (23.33). Here the link between moral behaviour and eschatological recompense is more explicit; and at this point the overtones for the ethical life of the Christian community become more pronounced. It is in this light that the evangelist warns his community that unless their righteousness exceeds that of the scribes and Pharisees, neither will *they* enter the kingdom of heaven (5.20). In any case, Matthew's accentuation and sharpening of the judgement motif against unrepentant Jews and their religious leaders in particular clearly suggests that his community has broken with the synagogue,[34] and undoubtedly expresses some of the strong feelings arising out of the resulting conflict.

A number of the threats of judgement, however, are directed against the followers of Jesus themselves – in particular, against those who to all outward appearances seem to be true disciples and yet are not. Again the emphasis on judgement is stronger than it is in the other synoptics – a fact that suggests that the writer clearly intends such passages to serve as warnings to the Christian community. In 7.21ff, for example, Matthew's Jesus makes it clear that not everyone who confesses him as Lord will enter the kingdom of heaven, but only those who truly do the will of the heavenly Father (cf. 5.20); even enthusiasts manifesting charismatic gifts and power may at the End find themselves excluded on this basis as *ἐργαζόμενοι τὴν ἀνομίαν* (7.22f). And those 'wolves in sheep's clothing' who have made their way into the community as *ψευδοπροφῆται* (7.15; cf. 24.11, 24) – though their precise identity is nowhere defined[35] – come in for special judgement (7.19). Here there may be intimations of internal tensions in Matthew's own community. Two parables in particular, that of the tares (13.24–30, 36–43) and that of the net (13.47–50), leave us with the distinct impression that he is aware of writing to a mixed audience whose final sorting-out will be fully revealed only at the Judgement (cf. 18.17f);[36] and this impression is strengthened by the fact that those against whom judgement is decreed in the parables of the Parousia (24.45–51; 25.1–13; 25.14–30) are spoken of as *δοῦλοι* (24.48–50; 25.14, 26, 30) who know their master is returning (24. 48; 25.14f, 18; cf. 25.1, 6f), and who call him *κύριε* (25.11, 24) and know they are ultimately responsible to him (25.18, 24f). Those who are condemned in these passages are spoken of as 'worthless servants'; but they are 'servants' nonetheless, not total outsiders. The various threats of judgement in the above passages, then – many of which are worded in the strongest possible terms – may be interpreted as intended for those in the Christian community whose attitude and behaviour fail to measure up to the demanding standards of deeper righteousness and wholehearted obedience to which the disciple is called. These are the ones who come to the wedding feast without the proper garment, whose fate is to be 'bound hand and foot, and cast into outer darkness', to weep and gnash their teeth (22.11, 13).[37] Bornkamm rightly concludes that for Matthew, the community of disciples – at least as presently constituted – 'is not a collection of the elect and eternally secure, but a mixed body which has to face the separation between the good and the evil at the final judgement'.[38] For such a mixed community as this, the evangelist apparently considers it necessary to emphasize both the stringency of Jesus' demands and the eschatological consequences of failing to measure up to them.

More than once Matthew brings in the promise of reward (10.42; cf. 25.34–40) and the threat of punishment (18.6, 10; cf. verse 14; 25.41–5) specifically in connexion with the treatment of Jesus' disciples. The references in 10.42 and 25.31–46 seem to concern the treatment accorded them by those primarily outside the community;[39] but the warning in 18.6ff appears to be directed against some within the mixed community itself (note again the reference in 7.15 to false prophets as 'wolves in sheep's clothing'). In any case, these passages probably express Matthew's concern for the welfare of Jesus' 'little ones' (*οἱ μικροί*) in their life and mission in the world (cf. also 10.14f, 40ff; 18.6, 10); and the strong use of the recompense sanction in this context would seem to reflect his conviction that God himself is watching over them and will ultimately vindicate them. Thus in 25. 31–46 an act of kindness or neglect shown to a disciple in need[40] is interpreted as an act of kindness or neglect shown to Jesus himself, for which judgement will be meted out accordingly on that Day.

The strong threat of judgement in the Gospel, then, probably reflects not only the recompense-oriented mentality of Matthew himself, but also the particular *Sitz im Leben* in which he writes. Set within the context of an apocalyptic expectation of the soon-coming End, and directed to a community that would seem to be experiencing both harassment from the outside and a certain degree of turmoil and moral slothfulness on the inside, the evangelist's emphasis on judgement is very likely intended both to fortify and encourage Jesus' 'little ones' in their relations with the non-believing Jewish community around them (by assuring them of God's ultimate justice), and to warn the mixed community itself of the dangers of moral laxity and negligence. Matthew's Jesus is a preacher of strict righteousness, and the threat of eschatological judgement is the strongest and most effective means that the evangelist knows of reinforcing his stringent demands for a life of absolute obedience. It is these factors that probably lie behind his decision to emphasize the threat of judgement rather than the element of grace – which, though not absent, remains rather more in the background.[41]

## 2. *Paul*

Paul's writings also reflect a certain recompense mentality, arising primarily out of his Jewish background and moral presuppositions. But in his case, the appeal to divine recompense as a sanction (whether positive or negative) is conditioned by other theological and psychological considerations, and it is important to distinguish which aspect of judgement is in focus. On the whole, he prefers to motivate Christian behaviour by more worthy considerations than those of mere reward and punishment; but he is enough of a pragmatist to resort to baser motives when the occasion demands it.

### 2.1 Justification by Faith and Judgement by Works

The fundamental nature of the principle of eschatological recompense in the background of Paul's thought is evident in Rom. 1–3, an extended passage that serves as foundation for the entire theological construct that follows. Building on the traditional Jewish conviction that God judges and punishes people for their moral failures (Rom. 1.18, 24–32; 2.2f, 5f, 9, 12, 16; 3.6), Paul argues that, on this basis, the whole world stands guilty before God, deserving of his retribution (Rom. 3.9–20, 23). For those who live outside of God's grace in Christ, therefore, the threat of eschatological judgement is real. Hence Paul speaks openly of the condemnation of those who refuse to believe the 'truth' but enjoy 'unrighteousness' (2

Thess. 2.12), those who have no knowledge or love of God, and no concern to obey the gospel of Christ (2 Thess. 1.8–9; cf. 1 Cor. 16.22[42]). The opponents of the gospel, the 'enemies of the cross of Christ', are especially cited as those who shall be punished on that Day (Gal. 5.10; Phil. 1.28; 3.18f; 1 Thess. 2.16; 2 Thess. 1.6; cf. Gal. 1.8f). In the context of a discourse on election, Paul goes even so far as to speak of those who are not in Christ as 'vessels of wrath (*σκεύη ὀργῆς*)[43] made for destruction' (Rom. 9.22) – the implication seemingly being that God himself, as the fearful Sovereign who chooses to have mercy on some and harden others, and whose purposes men dare not question (Rom. 9.6–24), has ordained them so (cf. Rom. 9.20ff).[44]

Sharply to be distinguished from these, however, are the 'vessels of mercy (*σκεύη ἐλέους*) ... prepared beforehand for glory' (Rom. 9.23) – believers, who by God's grace stand justified, with a righteousness accorded them by God himself (Rom. 4.5–8, 22–5; 5.1, 9, 17; 8.30; 1 Cor. 6.9–11). As those who are 'chosen from the beginning to be saved' (2 Thess. 2.13), 'destined ... [not] for wrath, but to obtain salvation' (1 Thess. 5.9), Christians (generally speaking in Paul's thinking) stand secure in God's love; Jesus Christ himself will keep them guiltless to the end (*ἀνέγκλητοι*: 1 Cor. 1.8; cf. 1.30). Deliverance, rest and relief will be their portion on that Day when God comes to inflict wrath and vengeance on their tormentors (1 Thess. 1.10; 2 Thess. 1.6–10). Thus, on the whole Paul draws a sharp line between those who are within God's grace and those who are outside it; and the threat of eschatological retribution applies largely to the latter, not the former. Grace supersedes recompense as the active principle by which the believing community lives (Rom. 5.15–21). There is no danger of condemnation (*κατάκριμα*), claims Paul, for those who are securely 'in Christ' (Rom. 8.1; cf. 5.1).

But unfortunately, it is not quite as simple as all this. For when the focus of Paul's thought shifts to the more practical matters of ethics, and especially to particular moral problems in the churches, the warnings of judgement reappear – this time directed to the *Christian* community. Consider, for example, the threat of judgement inherent in Paul's words against falling into idolatry, sexual immorality and complaining (1 Cor. 10.5–12, 22);[45] the sharp warning of the Lord's vengeance upon (presumably sexual) wrongdoing (1 Thess. 4.6); the threat of destruction for anyone who destroys God's 'temple' (1 Cor. 3.16f);[46] and the more general reminders of God's recompense upon the wrongdoer (Col. 3.25), and upon the one who 'sows to his own flesh' (Gal. 6.7f;[47] cf. 2 Cor. 9.6). The threat of judgement may also be present (though less explicitly) in the various exhortations to live *ἐν φόβῳ θεοῦ* (2 Cor. 7.1; cf. 6.17f; Phil.

2.12;[48] Col. 3.22; 4.1), and in Paul's expressed desire that the Christian communities should be found 'blameless' at the Parousia (*ἀπρόσκοποι*: Phil. 1.9f;[49] *ἄμεμπτοι*: 1 Thess. 3.12f; *ἀμέμπτως*: 1 Thess. 5.23). Whoever disregards God's demands for holy living, Paul insists, disregards God himself (1 Thess. 4.7f); and the clear implication is that in so doing one courts judgement upon oneself. These and numerous other references to God's judgement suggest that the concept of eschatological recompense continues to provide the basic frame of reference for the apostle's view of life, even in relation to the Christian community; and though it is often not clear whether the threatened judgement is conceived in present or eschatological terms (and if the latter, in what sense), the references are clearly sufficient to bring into question the certainty with which he seems to assert the believer's security elsewhere.

When directed to the believing community, the threat of judgement is enunciated most strongly when Paul focuses on those forms of behaviour most unsuited to the life of a Christian, i.e. obvious vices.[50] On at least three different occasions Paul reinforces his lists of morally unacceptable behaviour with the threat of unalloyed eschatological recompense, the harshest sanction he knows: 'Do you not know that the unrighteous (*ἄδικοι*) will not inherit the kingdom of God?' (1 Cor. 6.9f);[51] 'I warn you ... that those who do such things shall not inherit the kingdom of God' (Gal. 5.21); 'On account of these the wrath of God is coming' (Col. 3.5f).[52] In the context of a *theological* discourse, Paul asserts triumphantly that there is 'no condemnation for those who are in Christ Jesus' (Rom. 8.1); but when the focus shifts to *moral* issues, his warnings seem to imply that members of the Christian community whose lives are characterized by vices such as these face the danger of eschatological doom.[53] Here we see the strength of his conviction that certain kinds of behaviour are simply incompatible with life in Christ, and therefore, generally speaking, mark one who is outside the realm of God's grace.

It is evident, then, that Paul's general conviction of the believer's eschatological security in Christ does not, in his thinking, preclude the use of the threat of judgement as a sanction for ethics when it is required. Grace does not exclude personal accountability. Indeed, at more than one point Paul writes as if Christians have to face a final judgement much as everyone else: 'For we shall all stand before the judgement seat of God ... So each of us shall give account of himself to God' (Rom. 14.10, 12; cf. 1 Cor. 4.5); 'For we must all appear before the judgement seat of Christ,[54] so that each one may receive good or evil, according to what he has done in the body' (2 Cor. 5.10; cf. Rom. 2.6–16, esp. verse 6). One certainly cannot say, then, that for the believer 'nothing is ultimately at stake ... in his choices and deeds'.[55]

Unfortunately, Paul nowhere makes clear precisely how these passages (the latter of which speaks explicitly of a judgement by works[56]) are to be reconciled with the statements he makes elsewhere about the believer's justification by faith *apart* from works (Rom. 3.21–8; 4.1–25; Gal. 2.15 – 5.6).[57] That he seems able to hold both principles simultaneously without any great sense of contradiction is clear; and as E.P. Sanders observes, such a position is quite in keeping with the traditional Jewish synthesis of the concepts of salvation by grace and judgement by works.[58] But the crucial question remains: in what sense is he able to do it? Is it a matter of holding two largely incompatible principles concurrently (as Houlden seems to suggest[59]), or do the two integrate more fully (as Sanders implies[60]) – and if so, how? To deal fully with all the complexities of this most vexing of Pauline problems would carry us well beyond the scope of this study;[61] at least part of the solution, however, lies in distinguishing more precisely than is commonly done the various aspects of judgement in focus in the different references.

## 2.2 Different Aspects of Judgement

In general, when Paul speaks of judgement in relation to the Christian community, he speaks of it in both eschatological and non-eschatological terms; and on the eschatological level he thinks of it in two quite different senses, one having to do with ultimate condemnation, the other with rewards and the loss of them for Christians in the new age.

On the eschatological level, of those references which warn of ultimate condemnation, a number refer to the danger of Christians falling away from their firm standing in Christ, and therefore away from their secure position in God's grace; i.e. at bottom they reflect theological rather than simply ethical concerns. This is the case, for example, with those passages which stress that salvation is dependent on maintaining a firm grip on one's faith (1 Cor. 15.1f; Col. 1.22f; cf. 1.28; 2.18f; Rom. 11.20–2; Phil. 2.16), and those that warn of the danger of reverting to the law (Gal. 4.21–30; 5.2–4). Others, however, seem to be concerned more directly with the moral life itself – as, for example, those which speak of exclusion from the kingdom for those whose lives are characterized by vice (1 Cor. 6.9f; Gal. 5.19ff; Col. 3.5f), and those which relate the consequences of sin more generally: 'sin ... leads to death ... The end of those things is death ... For the wages of sin is death ... To set the mind on the flesh is death ... for if you live according to the flesh you will die' (Rom. 6.16, 21, 23; 8.6, 13; cf. 7.5, 9–11, 13) – all of which are set in clear contrast to the life of obedience, life 'in the Spirit', which leads to eternal life. And though in these contexts Paul frequently reaffirms his confidence in his readers that *they* are not living in the way of sin and death (Rom. 6.14, 17, 22; 7.4ff; 8.9ff, 15; 1 Cor. 6.11; Col. 3.3f, 7, 9f, 12),[62] nonetheless the constant reminder of the eschatological consequences functions implicitly as a goad prodding them to take the matter of ethical living with the utmost seriousness.

Because ethical living is the mark of one who has 'died with Christ' and lives 'in Christ' (Rom. 6.2ff; 7.4; 8.1ff; 2 Cor. 5.17), these references also implicitly call upon believers to live in a way that would confirm their own standing in Christ. What appears on the surface to be a straightforward sanction for ethics, therefore, may well have theological overtones on a deeper level. In reality, Pauline theology and ethics cannot be divorced;[63] just as one cannot properly speak of being in Christ apart from an ethical life (especially in view of the role of the Spirit: Rom. 8.9), so it is moral living that confirms (or denies) one's status in Christ. For Paul, imputed righteousness cannot be separated from *realized* righteousness; the lack of the latter brings into question the former. Or to put it somewhat differently: though moral living in itself does not earn salvation, the *lack* of moral living may exclude one from it.[64] Believers are under a certain continual obligation, therefore, to confirm their calling and election by the obedient response of their lives, and thereby to demonstrate that they remain safely within the circle of God's kindness. The seriousness with which Paul takes this matter is reflected in 1 Cor. 9.24–7 especially. So beneath the generally buoyant motif of the eschatological certainty of the Christian's future, there runs a darker undercurrent of foreboding and threat – the warning of the danger of ultimate rejection and judgement in the midst of expectant hope.

Certain of Paul's references to eschatological judgement, however, are to be understood in a different sense: i.e. not in terms of the loss of salvation, but in terms of reward or the loss of it for believers in the new age. And here if anywhere the element of merit enters most strongly into his thinking. The clearest example of this is found in 1 Cor. 3; after enunciating the principle that 'each shall receive his wages (*μισθός*) according to his labour (*κόπος*)' (1 Cor. 3.8), he goes on to speak of a judgement of 'fire' that awaits Christians on that Day:

> ... and the fire will test (*δοκιμάσει*) what sort of work each one has done. If the work which any man has built on the foundation [Jesus Christ] survives, he will receive a reward (*μισθός*). If any man's work is burned up, he will suffer loss (*ζημιωθήσεται*), though he himself will be saved, but only as through fire (1 Cor. 3.12–15).[65]

Though it is leaders in the church that are primarily in focus in the immediate context, in all probability the judgement that Paul envisages here extends to every servant of Christ, and thus may not unreasonably be generalized to include the entire Christian community. In any case, the final statement (3.15) makes it clear that in this passage, judgement in the sense of condemnation or doom is excluded (here all are saved); it is a question rather of reward or loss of reward for believers in the new age.[66] What these rewards are is nowhere specified, but clearly they cannot be identified in this context with eternal life itself (nor the loss of reward with the loss of life: 3.15). It is an entirely different aspect of judgement that is in view, oriented specifically to Christians safe within God's grace.

This two-level concern with eschatological judgement is reflected in the various statements Paul makes about his own life. On the one hand, though he sometimes writes as if he is reasonably assured of his own salvation and confident that when he dies he will be with Christ (2 Cor. 5.8; Phil. 1.21, 23), he also seems keenly aware of the danger of slipping away from God's grace and the peril of being finally rejected should he do so ('lest ... I myself should be disqualified': 1 Cor. 9.26f).[67] The latter passage is better understood as an example of earnestness to be imitated (cf. 1 Cor. 9.24f; 10.1ff; 11.1) than as an expression of fearful uncertainty on Paul's part;[68] but it does reflect something of the seriousness with which he views the moral life in regard to one's relationship with God, and the resolve with which one must seek to remain secure in God's grace, in his thinking. This same determination may be seen in Phil. 3.8–14, though again the context (3.15, 17) would suggest that the passage is to be interpreted primarily as a model for imitation.[69] In any event, it is clear that neither the principle of justification by faith nor the truth of election eliminates the need for constant vigilance and serious striving in order to attain the ultimate goal.[70]

The fact that Paul anticipates receiving *μισθός* for his own labour as a servant of Christ (1 Cor. 3.8) is confirmation of his belief that Christians will be recompensed in the new age for their life and work on earth (cf. 1 Cor. 3.12–15). But neither is this a matter to be taken lightly; for it is still the judgement of God, and Paul is clearly aware that he will be held responsible in it both for the ministry that has been committed into his hand and the quality of his life more generally (1 Cor. 4.1–5[71]).

Thus, it is apparent that the apostle thinks of judgement on an eschatological level in two quite different senses: (1) as threat of ultimate condemnation, for unbelievers and those who either theologically or morally fall away from their secure position in God's grace in Christ (in which case 'faith' becomes meaningless and the concept of justification by faith therefore irrelevant); and (2) as the expectation of reward or loss of reward in the new age for those who remain securely within that grace. In a few cases, notably Rom. 14.12 and 2 Cor. 5.10 (the latter especially is a crucial text), the wording is so general that it is impossible to tell with certainty precisely which aspect of judgement Paul has in mind – though the strong element of merit in 2 Cor. 5.10 would suggest it fits best into his overall structure if interpreted in the second sense[72] (otherwise one could hardly avoid the conclusion that he advocates two incompatible doctrines simultaneously; cf. Rom. 3.28; 4.5ff). In either sense, however, the threat of eschatological judgement functions as a distinct warning for the moral life to be taken with the utmost seriousness by the Christian.

By distinguishing two different aspects of Paul's use of the eschatological sanction, therefore, we begin to see how the seemingly contradictory concepts of justification by faith and judgement by works could conceivably be integrated in his thinking. Though moral living in itself is never viewed as a means of attaining justification, it nonetheless appears to be a necessary concomitant of the faith that does, and thus serves to confirm and in some sense secure the believer's standing in God's grace; as such, it is one of the conditions of remaining within that grace. Immoral living, accordingly, is generally regarded as a mark of one who stands outside of grace; it is incompatible with a true confession of faith and, on the whole, renders it meaningless. On this basis, Paul can apply the harshest form of the judgement sanction against it – the threat of ultimate condemnation and exclusion from the kingdom. Thus, though 'works' may condemn, it is always and only faith that saves. Those passages which speak most explicitly of judgement according to merit for believers, on the other hand, are most easily understood as references not to the declaration of salvation or condemnation, but to reward or the loss of it for Christians in the new age. On this interpretation, the element of merit in Paul's ethics need not be viewed as incompatible with the doctrine of justification by faith. Admittedly, however, much hangs on our understanding of the aspect of judgement in focus in the key text 2 Cor. 5.9f; and here it is impossible to be absolutely certain. With a different interpretation, therefore, those less inclined to see an integrated, coherent structure as inherently more reasonable could perhaps equally plausibly argue that at this point Paul maintains two incompatible beliefs (old and new) in irreconcilable tension.[73]

Paul's use of the judgement sanction is not limited to the eschatological sense, of course; he also speaks of the threat of judgement upon believers' lives here and now, in this world[74] – even to the point of death (e.g. 1 Cor.

5.1–5; 11.30ff; here it is physical death that is meant, not spiritual death).[75] In this case judgement is viewed as disciplinary, and not as endangering the Christian's salvation. There are many other references to judgement that could be interpreted in a non-eschatological sense;[76] but because the temporal aspect (whether present or future) is so often left unstated, in most cases it is simply impossible to be certain. On other occasions, it is the threat of *human* judgement to which Paul appeals – though this may carry the weight of divine disfavour or punishment with it (Rom. 13.1–7;[77] 1 Cor. 4.18–21; 5.1–5, 9–13; 2 Cor. 10.2, 5f, 10f; 12.20; 13.2f, 10; 2 Thess. 3.6, 14[78]). But in no instance in Paul's writings does human judgement have the authority to decree ultimate condemnation or exclude one from God's grace, as in Mt. 18.17f – that is the prerogative of God alone.

To what extent does the Parousia function as a sanction (or as a factor more generally) in Paul's parenesis? Evidence may be found throughout the whole of the Pauline corpus suggesting that the apostle lives with the conviction that the End is near, and that life must be lived in its anticipation.[79] But whereas that belief inevitably shapes the spirit of his ethics, rarely does it seem to affect their content. At several points Paul encourages his readers to live in a way that will prove that they are ready for its coming (cf. Rom. 13.11–14; Phil. 4.5;[80] 1 Thess. 5.2–8); and though the full implications are not spelled out, it is clear that these passages carry the implicit threat of eschatological judgement (in some sense), and are intended to incite the Christian community to serious moral living in preparation for it.[81] Apart from these more general references, however, there is only one point at which the expectation of an imminent Parousia seems to shape the specific substance of Paul's parenesis – 1 Cor. 7.26–31, where Paul argues for the celibate life on the grounds of the impending End. But even here his stance is not determined by the expectation of the Parousia alone (note e.g. the desirability of maintaining an undivided loyalty and devotion to Christ alone (7.32–5) and the practical problems inherent in married life (7.28, 32*a*) – though the latter may be with special reference to the End); and this raises the question of whether the anticipation of the Eschaton is really the primary factor shaping Paul's thought at this point or not.[82] In any event, this is the only clear example of the expectation of an imminent End being a determinative factor in the particular content of Paul's parenesis.[83] In view of his frequent reference to the Parousia, it is rather surprising (and perhaps significant) that he makes no greater use of it in his ethics.

Generally speaking, Paul never views the End as so imminent as to negate the need for serious moral living or ethical instruction; indeed, from the prominence he gives to practical ethical matters, one does not get the impression of any sense of *absolute* imminence at all. The Parousia is near and life must be lived in its anticipation, but Paul's ethics are not determined by any sense of its utter immediacy.[84] (J.T. Sanders' statement, that Pauline parenesis is so bound up with a sense of the impending End that it becomes nonsense once that sense of imminence is lost,[85] apparently fails to appreciate this point.) Indeed, at one point (if one can accept the evidence of 2 Thessalonians) Paul takes pains to stress that the duties of life in this world must *not* be neglected as one awaits the Parousia (2 Thess. 3.7–10). Houlden concludes that Paul's attitude wavers: 'He veers from making provision for the realities of life in this world to abandoning the present world-order as no longer worth consideration ... and then back again.'[86] On balance, however, apart from the issue of celibacy in 1 Cor. 7, Paul rarely fails to take seriously the matter of living in this world, and to make provision for it.

### 2.3 Reward and Encouragement

So far, we have focused primarily on references to judgement; and we have observed that the fact of grace does not in Paul's thinking deny the value of the judgement sanction for ethics. But what of the concept of reward? Here again the centrality of grace in his theology, set as it is in sharp contrast to the principle of *μισθός* (Rom. 4.4f; cf. verses 1–25), would seem to leave little room for any such notion. Yet Paul does motivate by the promise of reward (cf. 2 Cor. 9.6; 11.9), and at one point insists that even Scripture itself endorses the principle (1 Cor. 9.9ff; cf. verses 13f). Even one's ultimate salvation, clearly viewed as a 'free gift' (*χάρισμα*) and not in terms of 'wages' (*ὀψώνια*: Rom. 6.23), may from a slightly different perspective be regarded as a 'reward' to be received (*ἀνταπόδοσις*: Col. 3.23f) and a 'prize' to be won (*βραβεῖον*: 1 Cor. 9.24ff; cf. Phil. 3.8). The latter terminology comes into view especially when Paul wants to stress the importance of assuming moral responsibilities seriously (cf. Rom. 6.16, 22; Gal. 6.8f). As noted above, even though salvation is a gift of grace and cannot be earned, responsible moral living is a condition for remaining 'in'; in this sense God's eschatological grace may be viewed as a reward or prize for the one who strives for it. Of course Paul also speaks of rewards in the new age for those who belong to Christ, but in quite a different sense (1 Cor. 3.8, 14; cf. 4.5; 2 Cor. 5.10). Thus, in general, even though the concept of grace is fundamental to Paul's outlook, he can still appeal to some form of eschatological reward (often without specifying its precise sense) to rouse his readers to faithful living and diligent service (cf. 1 Cor. 15.58; Phil. 3.20 – 4.1). And it would seem that this hope for reward is one of the forces driving his own life (cf. 1 Cor. 9.24ff; Phil. 3.8–15), enabling him to endure in the midst of immense difficulties: 'So we do not lose heart ... For this slight momentary affliction is preparing for us (*κατεργάζεται ἡμῖν*) an eternal weight of glory beyond all comparison' (2 Cor. 4.16f; cf. verses 7–18; Rom. 8.18f; 1 Cor. 15.19, 29ff).

For Paul, then, the Eschaton functions as a sanction in both the positive and the negative senses, i.e. as both promise and threat. The positive sense is accentuated when he wants to encourage the faithful in their suffering and opposition (Rom. 8.17ff; cf. 2 Cor. 4.16f above; 2 Thess. 1.5–10) or to comfort the bereaved in their distress (1 Thess. 4.13–18); the negative sense, when he feels the community to be in need of strong warning, from either a theological or a moral point of view.[87] His use of the eschatological sanction, then, is determined by his focus, and adjusted according to the need at hand.

One very significant point remains: Paul's recognition of the importance of affirmation and encouragement in the motivation of ethics – and in this he is an undisputed master. In the immediate context of warning his readers of the solemn consequences of living outside the 'obedience of faith', Paul frequently makes a point of reaffirming his confidence in them as those who are standing firm in God's grace – as if to say: 'But I'm sure *you* have not fallen into such things'[88] (cf. Rom. 6.17f; 8.9ff; 1 Cor. 6.11 (cf. verses 9ff); Phil. 3.20ff; Col. 3.7 (cf. verses 3f, 12; 2.4ff); 1 Thess. 5.4f, 8ff; 2 Thess. 2.13f – all of which occur in the context of warnings). Here the threat of judgement still functions indirectly as a stimulus to steadfastness in faith and moral living, but in every case it is cushioned with a word of affirmation and encouragement – and it is this which Paul consistently emphasizes. On the whole, he apparently wants his readers to feel that he is confident of their standing with God.

This may be observed also in his consistent tendency to express confidence in the theological and ethical standing of his readers at the very outset of his letters (Rom. 1.8; 1 Cor. 1.4ff; 2 Cor. 1.7, 24; Phil. 1.3ff; Col. 1.3ff; 1 Thess. 1.2–10; 2 Thess. 1.3ff; Phm. 4ff). Significantly, only in Galatians is this affirmation missing; here theological issues predominate, and the tone is rather one of distress and anxiety.[89] This is not to say that Paul never entertains doubts about the life and standing of the young Christians in the other churches (cf. 1 Cor. 3.1ff; 5.1ff; 2 Cor. 11.3; 12. 20ff; Col. 2.8, 16ff, 20ff; 1 Thess. 3.5; 2 Thess. 3.11); indeed, the very real presence of such doubts only makes his expressions of confidence that much more remarkable. From this point of view, the introductory affirmations in Paul's letters cannot always be considered accurate representations of his assessment of the actual situation; but they certainly tell us something about his understanding of the importance of affirmation and encouragement as factors in motivation – and this is confirmed by the frequency with which one encounters such statements throughout his letters.[90] In some cases (especially 2 Corinthians: cf. 7.4, 16; 8.7; 9.2f) his expressions of confidence appear quite exaggerated, and conflict so sharply with the actual picture of church life that one begins to doubt the sincerity of his words, and to suspect that at least some of his acclamations are little more than mere psychological devices – sheer flattery intended to evoke the desired response.[91] In any case here we see the way Paul prefers to motivate theological and moral response by positive rather than negative means, by affirmation and encouragement rather than threat – at least when the occasion allows it.

In general, it is not the recompense sanction at all (whether positive or negative) that functions as the primary motivational force in Paul's ethics (cf. Phil. 2.1ff), but rather the fact of God's grace in Christ and the believer's relationship to that. This, to him, is what lies at the heart of the Christian life, and therefore ultimately provides a more adequate basis for ethical living than either the threat of judgement or the promise of reward.

## 3. *Comparison of Matthew and Paul*

As a result of their common Jewish heritage, the ethics of both Matthew and Paul presuppose the fundamental principles of personal accountability to God and divine recompense for one's behaviour in life. Superimposed upon this traditional belief system is a new message of grace centred on Jesus; but in neither case does it eliminate the demand for moral living as a condition for remaining within God's favour. To fail to take the moral life seriously is, in the thinking of both, to invite God's judgement and wrath. The threat of eschatological judgement therefore remains a very real one, even for those who name the name of Jesus; and both writers make use of it accordingly as a sanction for ethics. Indeed, the two would agree that ultimately it is the most powerful sanction to which appeal may be made.[92]

Because one's eschatological destiny is thus ultimately related to the quality of one's ethical life, both writers can also appeal to the Eschaton in a more positive sense – i.e. as a prize to be won, a goal to be striven for;

and it is primarily in this future eschatological sense that both conceive of 'reward'. Neither understands the new message of grace in Jesus to be incompatible with such a perspective.

Further, both appear to think of eschatological judgement as functioning on two different levels (though in Paul's writing especially it is difficult to distinguish the two consistently), one relating to ultimate destiny, the other to rewards (Paul) or rank (Matthew) in the new age (1 Cor. 3.14f; Mt. 5.19; 18.4; 25.21, 23; cf. 24.47) – the latter of which is based on the criterion of merit. In spite of these fundamental similarities of perspective, however, the place of judgement in the overall structure of their ethics differs markedly.[93]

In Matthew's Gospel, the concept of recompense, especially eschatological recompense, heavily colours Jesus' teachings, and seems to dominate the author's outlook. The promise of eschatological reward and (even more) the threat of its loss – with the full weight of divine judgement that implies – undergird the whole of the Sermon on the Mount, and function as the primary sanctions for ethics throughout the Gospel. The picture of divine retribution is powerfully and vividly drawn, and Matthew's appeal to it is direct, explicit, and very free: there is a warning of punishment for virtually any and all behaviour (no matter how seemingly inconsequential[94]) that fails to measure up to Jesus' stringent demands for a life of deeper righteousness. The resulting picture is one in which the threat of judgement is prominent.

Paul's use of the judgement sanction, however, is much more tempered. In its strongest form, it is reserved for the kinds of behaviour which are viewed as simply incompatible with life in Christ, and which therefore characterize those who are outside the realm of God's grace; but even then it is generally cushioned with a word of encouragement – as if Paul wants to reassure his readers that he is convinced *they* are not guilty of such things. In a more moderate form, the warning of judgement underlies much of what he writes; but on the whole it remains more in the background, often hinted at but seldom made fully explicit. Paul can certainly resort to the threat of judgement when the occasion demands it, but he generally prefers to ground his injunctions in more positive sanctions. The threat of judgement therefore plays a less crucial role in Paul's ethics than in Matthew's.

Underlying these two different perspectives lie several possible factors, one of which would seem to be a difference of opinion regarding the motivation of ethical behaviour itself. The strong element of threat in Matthew's Gospel suggests that (quite in line with his legal outlook) the author believes *negative* sanctions to be the most effective way to evoke the radical obedience demanded by Jesus. The central place of affirmation and encouragement in Paul's parenesis, on the other hand, would seem to reflect his conviction that *positive* sanctions provide a more adequate basis for truly Christian living. The two writers appear to be operating with different 'psychologies', and these in turn may reflect somewhat different understandings of human nature itself. In any case, Paul seems to have more confidence than Matthew in the inherent motivation of Christians to respond ethically without having to be either threatened or enticed.

Another factor very probably shaping the ethical stances of the two writers is the *Sitze im Leben* in which they write. The sharpness of Matthew's polemic against the Pharisees and scribes, for example, may well reflect the antagonism being felt by his community from the Jewish religious leaders. Even more important, the emphasis on judgement in Jesus' ethical teachings, directed as they generally are to the disciples, would seem to suggest that the evangelist is disturbed by certain lax elements within the Christian community itself. Apparently aware of his mixed audience, Matthew seems to feel that it is more important to devote his energies to warning the negligent than to comforting the faithful; hence the stress on judgement rather than grace. The fact that he focuses more exclusively than Paul on strictly eschatological judgement does not necessarily imply that the latter's concept of judgement is more broadly based; it may simply reflect the degree of Matthew's anxiety over the moral life of his community, or at least of certain disturbing elements within it.

Paul is also aware of certain moral and theological problems in the churches to whom he writes, and it is significant that his warnings of judgement (both explicit and implicit) tend to be concentrated in the passages that deal most directly with those problems (cf. 1 Cor. 3–6, 10–11; 2 Cor. 10, 12–13; Gal. 1–5; Col. 3; 1 Thess. 4; 2 Thess. 3). It is not surprising, then, that the threat of judgement is sharpest and most explicit in his correspondence with the church at Corinth, where the moral problems are most acute and Paul's authority is most questioned; it also underlies his expressions of concern over the wavering theological position of the Galatians, but less explicitly so. On the whole, however (apart from Galatians), Paul does not seem to view the Christian community as being in quite such a mixed and precarious state as Matthew does, and the more moderate tone of his writing reflects this. The two writers' use of the judgement sanction, then, is conditioned in part by their perception of the needs of the particular communities to whom they write.

This may be seen in their references to the Eschaton more generally. Both writers live in the expectation of the End, and their ethical outlooks appear to be influenced in somewhat similar ways by that expectation. [95]

But neither sees the Parousia so imminent as to obviate the need for moral concern in this world – as is evident from the priority both give to ethical instruction; and apart from the issue of celibacy in 1 Cor. 7, neither seems to attribute the specific substance of their ethics primarily to a sense of eschatological imminence. Both, however, appeal to the Parousia to incite faithful moral living and an attitude of alert preparedness generally, especially in view of the suddenness of its expected arrival and the event of judgement associated with it. But more to the point, for both writers the Eschaton functions as a sanction in both a positive and a negative sense: when laxity of moral behaviour is the concern, it serves as a sharp warning of future judgement and loss of reward; but when the focus shifts to the needs of the faithful and suffering, then it becomes a promise of eschatological blessing. The fact that Matthew emphasizes the negative aspects, while Paul focuses more on the positive,[96] may reflect basic differences in their fundamental orientation as well as the differing needs of the communities themselves.

This in turn suggests that the two writers' use of the judgement sanction is probably also a function of their broader theological outlooks, and therefore may reflect something of their different understandings of Jesus himself – and at this point it becomes difficult to distinguish redaction from tradition in the evangelist's thought especially. The importance of eschatological recompense in Matthew's writing fits in well with his overall legal orientation; and the frequency with which he appeals to it probably reflects his conviction that 'the gate is narrow and the way is hard, that leads to life, and those who find it are few' (7.14). Behind this rather threatening picture would seem to lie a strong view of Jesus as a teacher of strict ethical righteousness, who demands absolute obedience to the will of God, and who takes on the frightening countenance of Judge for all those who fail to measure up to his exacting standards (cf. Mt. 25.24, 26f). For Matthew, ethical righteousness is of the utmost importance from an eschatological point of view, and it is this that the sanction of judgement is intended to enforce.

For Paul, however, grace has largely superseded recompense as the primary principle by which the believing community lives, and his preference for more positive sanctions reflects this; his view of the Christian life is thus less characterized by fear and threat than that of Matthew. Paul also sees Christ in the role of Judge (2 Cor. 5.10); but for him Jesus is above all the expression of God's grace, and it is this that is central to his entire ethical perspective. In Paul's view, the primary criterion of judgement is not whether one's behaviour measures up to the exacting standards of Jesus' demand for 'deeper righteousness', but whether one is (generally speaking) securely 'in Christ', and therefore safe within the circle of God's grace; i.e. to him it is ultimately a *theological* and not simply an ethical matter.

It is a difference of focus: Matthew is more directly concerned with the question of ethical righteousness, Paul with the underlying theology; i.e. for Paul, questions of ethics relate more directly to theological considerations. Elements of grace as well as judgement are found in both; but while Matthew focuses more on the threat of judgement, Paul emphasizes rather the promise of grace. In one sense, therefore, Matthew's ethics reflect a more teleological orientation than those of Paul. On the whole, the concept of recompense is much more dominant in the evangelist's writing than in the apostle's; Paul shows little of Matthew's thoroughgoing 'tit for tat' mentality with its emphasis on reciprocity in judgement.[97] We may say, therefore, that Paul's ethics are less dependent on incentives in general (whether positive or negative).

Finally, when full account has been taken of the writer's differing perspectives and audiences, there remains yet another factor that must not be overlooked: the different genre of their writings. For Matthew (whatever his redactional approach) is writing a Gospel, and is inevitably concerned to a greater degree with the actual history of the pre-Easter Jesus – and more dependent therefore on the tradition of Jesus' life and teachings that has come down to him. Paul, on the other hand, writing letters, is much less tied to the tradition. Though opinions vary widely as to just how much control is exerted by the underlying tradition (it is impossible to distinguish sharply between tradition and redaction in the Gospel), we must at least recognize it as a factor, and be careful therefore not to assume that the different outlooks expressed in the two writers can be adequately accounted for in terms of the differences of their individual perspectives alone.

There are at least four possible factors, then, underlying the different uses made of the judgement sanction by the two writers: (1) their individual attitudes toward the motivation of ethics itself; (2) the particular situations, problems and needs of the communities to whom they write – or at least their perceptions of them; (3) their overall theological perspectives – which in turn are shaped by their different backgrounds, experiences of life and perspectives on Jesus; and (4) the different genre of their writings. And in view of the interrelationship of these elements, it is virtually impossible to assess (to any degree of certainty) the relative importance of the factors individually.

3

# RELATIONSHIP TO CHRIST AND THE ROLE OF GRACE

In this chapter we shall investigate the ways in which the ethical outlooks of the two writers are shaped by their understanding of the Christian's relationship to Christ (and to the salvation event more generally) and the extent to which this relationship functions as a factor in the motivation of ethics. Special attention will be focused on the role of grace.

## 1. *Matthew*

In the Gospel, this relationship is portrayed primarily in the interaction between Jesus and the twelve disciples. Matthew sees in their relationship to Jesus the relationship of his own community to the *κύριος*, so that, generally speaking, words spoken by Jesus to the Twelve are to be understood as spoken to his own community as well.[1] (There are limits to this principle, however.[2]) The Twelve are presented not so much as models to be imitated, as simply typical or representative disciples; *Jesus* is the model, not the disciples.[3]

### 1.1 Matthew's View of Jesus

Before examining the disciples' role more closely, we look first at Matthew's portrait of Jesus. Above all, it is Jesus' authority (*ἐξουσία*) that the evangelist emphasizes,[4] and this is seen in both his words and his deeds. Many of the details are taken over directly from Mark: for example, Jesus pronounces forgiveness with authority (9.2*, 6*), heals with authority (9.6f*), exorcises demons with authority (8.32*; cf. 10.1*, 8),[5] and even controls nature with his authority (8.26f*; cf. 21.19*); he also teaches with authority (7.29*) – about the kingdom of God (4.17*; 13.11ff*, 33ff*; 19.23ff*), God's forgiveness (6.14f*; 12.31f*), eternal life (19.16ff*), the resurrection (22.30ff*), and other future events (24.2ff*; cf. 16.21*; 17.22ff*; 20.18f*). As the authoritative expounder of Scripture and interpreter of the law (19.3ff*; 22.29*, 34ff*; 23.16ff*; cf. 12.8*), Jesus enters into vigorous debate with the traditional religious leaders and denounces them (15.1ff*; 23.1ff*), and even takes it upon himself to exercise authority in the temple (21.12ff*). 'Heaven and earth will pass away', he declares, 'but my words will not pass away' (24.35*). All this is taken over from Mark.

But Matthew further accentuates the Marcan picture with his own references to Jesus' authority. For example, he alters Mark's conclusion to the story of Jesus' healing of the paralytic to emphasize that the crowd's amazement centres not on the healing itself but on Jesus' *ἐξουσία* (9.8). And while the giving of the keys of the kingdom focuses primarily on the authority of the Church, it also says something about that of Jesus; for it is ultimately from his authority that the Church's power to 'bind' and 'loose' derives, and it is by his authority that such ecclesiastical decisions are given heavenly ratification (16.19). Indeed, it is implicitly because of his authority that the Church can be confident that the *πύλαι ᾅδου* shall not prevail against it (16.18). Further, the small redactional addition *λόγῳ* to the summary account of Jesus' exorcism in 8.16 may suggest that Matthew is especially concerned with the authority of Jesus' 'word';[6] this impression is strengthened by his inclusion of the narrative about the healing of the centurion's servant, which centres precisely on this point (8.8f; cf. verse 13).

It is not surprising, then, to find in the didactic and parenetic materials some of the strongest assertions of the authority of Jesus.[7] This is most noticeable in the antitheses, where the traditional understanding of the law is opposed six distinct times by Jesus' authoritative *ἐγὼ δὲ λέγω ὑμῖν* ... Here, as Houlden points out, Jesus' word 'invites no discussion, uses no logically grounded persuasion. It simply commands obedience.'[8] Matthew's emphasis on the *ἐξουσία* of Jesus' teachings may be seen especially in the key statement he removes from its Marcan context and places at the very end of the Sermon on the Mount, where it nicely sums up his attitude to the entire Sermon: 'he taught them as one who had authority (*ἐξουσία*), and not as their scribes' (7.29*).

The centrality of this concept may be observed also in the concluding words of Jesus in the Gospel: 'All authority (*ἐξουσία*) in heaven and on earth has been given to me' (28.18) – an excellent summary of Matthew's portrait of Jesus.[9] Here we have attributed to Jesus the very authority that Jesus himself implicitly attributes to God in 11.25 (but cf. 11.27). Blair correctly concludes: 'Matthew's portrait of Jesus centers in his representation of Jesus' authority ... [28.18] simply catches up the thrust of the entire story.'[10] The fact that this concluding declaration forms the basis for the mission commission that immediately follows, addressed as it is to disciples and expressed in terms of making disciples, suggests that the acknowledgement of Jesus' ἐξουσία lies at the heart of Matthew's understanding of what it means to be a μαθητής (28.19f).

The evangelist's emphasis on Jesus' authority may also be seen in the heightened use he makes of various Christological titles;[11] for him, Jesus bears Messianic authority. Of all the titles, it is the designation 'Lord' (κύριος), with its overtones of power and authority demanding submission and obedience, that brings Matthew's ethical perspective most sharply into focus. The evangelist is especially concerned to stress that Jesus is κύριος: whereas Mark employs the term (or some variant of it) eighteen times, Matthew does so eighty times. But even more significant, whereas in Mark Jesus is generally addressed as διδάσκαλε (or ῥαββί) by friend and foe alike, in Matthew those who are true disciples consistently address him as κύριε;[12] διδάσκαλε and ῥαββί are used only by those who fail to recognize his real authority (including Judas Iscariot).[13] Thus, in numerous passages Matthew either replaces the Marcan διδάσκαλε with κύριε, or inserts κύριε as the appropriate vocative if there was none before.[14] Though some take this to be nothing more than a mere term of polite address ('sir'),[15] the reference to κύριε κύριε in 7.21f would suggest that at least in this context the term means something more. Further, it seems unlikely that Matthew would so consistently alter the respectful Marcan διδάσκαλε to the less honorific κύριε if all he intends by it is a polite 'sir' – especially in view of the importance he attaches to Jesus' role as a διδάσκαλος (cf. 23.8f). I conclude, then, that Matthew's use of the term κύριε most likely reflects his view that the appropriate relationship between the disciple and Christ is above all one in which Jesus is acknowledged as κύριος.[16]

### 1.2 Matthew's View of Discipleship

Now let us look at the picture Matthew draws of those who follow Jesus. Clearly, it is their role as μαθηταί that he wishes to emphasize:[17] note, for example, his redactional insertion of the term in 10.1, 42; 11.1; 20.17; 26.20 (cf. 28.16), and the way he shapes the Marcan miracle stories to bring out various aspects of discipleship[18] – a tendency most commonly observed in the stilling-of-the-storm episode (8.23–7).[19] But it is his formulation of the post-Resurrection mission commission in terms of 'discipling' (μαθητεύσατε πάντα τὰ ἔθνη: 28.19) that most clearly illustrates this.[20] It would seem, then, that one of the evangelist's prime concerns in writing the Gospel is to spell out what it means to be a μαθητής of Jesus.[21]

What exactly does Matthew understand by discipleship? Certainly there is a scholastic element involved (both learning and teaching), judging from the final commission (28.19f); for here the injunction to 'make disciples of all nations' is largely explicated by the following clause, 'teaching them to observe (τηρεῖν) all that I have commanded you'[22] – a passage that might be taken as reflecting a Jewish–Christian view of Jesus as a *ῥαββί* teaching his understanding of the law to his *μαθηταί*.[23] But clearly, for Matthew, the relationship involves much more than this, for Jesus is more than simply a teacher and the disciple is more than simply a learner;[24] Jesus is *ὁ κύριος*, and the disciple is above all one who submits in obedience to him. Though both learning and teaching are involved, it is this element of obedience which is most central to Matthew's understanding of discipleship and which he is most concerned to emphasize; and it is this that lies at the heart of the demand for 'deeper righteousness' in the Sermon. Just as Jesus is characterized by authority, so the disciple is characterized by submission; the *κύριος–δοῦλος* motif is much more prominent in Matthew than in Mark (cf. 8.5–13; 10.24f; 18.23–35; 20.25–8*; 21.34–6*; 22.1–10; 24.45–51; 25.14–30).[25] Of the three synoptics, it is unquestionably Matthew that gives us the strongest impression of discipleship as a life of submission and obedience.[26]

Implicit in the teachings of Jesus, for example, is the assumption that discipleship means radical submission to the will of God – a concept taken over from Mark (cf. Mt. 12.50*; 26.39*) but further emphasized by Matthew (6.10; 7.21; 26.42; cf. 21.31). The importance of the concept in the Gospel may be seen in the reference to it early in the Lord's Prayer (6.10, the chief Matthean element absent in Luke's version),[27] and more especially in 7.21–3, which emphasizes that true discipleship is marked not by mere verbal confession of Jesus as Lord but by obedient doing of the heavenly Father's will. Though explicit references to it are few, the theme underlies much of the Sermon on the Mount,[28] and is certainly implicit in Jesus' demand for radical obedience to the deepest intent of the law (5.21–48). It is a key Matthean motif, and G. Barth only slightly overstates it when he concludes that, for Matthew, 'doing the will of God is the entire essence and meaning of being a disciple'.[29]

However, discipleship also implies submission and obedience to Jesus himself as *κύριος*. In taking Jesus' 'yoke' upon oneself (11.29), one submits to his authority and acknowledges his demand for radical allegiance to himself.[30] Here again Matthew takes over Mark's picture (Mt. 10.17ff*; 13.21f*; 16.24ff*; 19.27ff*; 24.9ff*; cf. 26.35*) and further emphasizes it by his own references to the demand for unconditional commitment and single-minded loyalty (especially in 10.37–9; cf. 6.22f, 24, 33; 19.12). The disciple is thus pictured as one who is called to sacrifice everything in order to follow Jesus[31] with absolute singleness of inner intention.

More than the other synoptic writers, Matthew emphasizes that submission to Jesus' authority calls for obedience to his teachings.[32] This is the main point of the short pericope 7.24–7, which, given its position, may be taken as a reference to Jesus' teachings in the Sermon especially. The point is again made in the final mission commission (28.19f), which was cited above; here, however, 'all that I have commanded you' obviously includes the teachings of Jesus in the whole of the Gospel.[33] While it may not be strictly accurate to say (as Strecker does[34]) that in Matthew's Gospel *κηρύσσειν* and *διδάσκειν* become virtually one, and the kerygma essentially reduces to *διδαχή* (such a view ignores the element of kerygma implicit, for example, in the reference to baptizing: 28.19*b*), nevertheless this passage impresses upon us the extent to which Matthew views discipleship in terms of obeying the teachings of Jesus. For him, the Christian life is a life of obedience to Jesus' commands.

To what extent does discipleship entail the imitation of Christ, in the evangelist's thinking? Explicit references to the motif are very few.[35] The clearest example is found in 20.25–8*, where the call for an attitude of humble service is predicated on Jesus' own example. Though this passage is largely taken over from Mark, the alteration of Mark's *καὶ γάρ* to *ὥσπερ* (20.28) does perhaps bring out the *imitatio Christi* more explicitly.[36] In 10.24f, we have what appears to be a distinctly Matthean reference to imitation; but closer examination reveals that, though elements of this concept may be implicit (note the double *ὡς*), the passage functions more as a prediction of persecution than a call to imitation – i.e. disciples share the fate of their Lord.

Though relatively little explicit reference is made to the imitation of Jesus, the motif is implicit throughout.[37] The character of true disciples as portrayed in the Sermon on the Mount, for example, is in a number of respects akin to that of Matthew's Jesus himself; the attitudes and behaviour demanded of them are in many ways but a reflection of his own. The qualities of meekness and humility, for instance – so central in the disciple's life (5.3–5, 21–48; cf. 18.3f*; 19.14*; 20.25–7*; 23.8–12) – are also prominent in the evangelist's depiction of Jesus himself (11.29; 21. 5);[38] and the call for imitation of these is clearly implicit in 11.29.[39] The overall impression we get of Jesus in the Gospel, at least from one point of view, is that of a humble, compassionate, suffering servant, totally submissive and obedient to God's will, even to the point of death; and this is precisely the kind of life to which disciples are called.[40] G. Barth concludes:

'The imitation demanded of the disciples is suffering imitation.'[41] Here we see that Matthew portrays Jesus not only as the master διδάσκαλος and κύριος, but also as the ideal μαθητής, the great model of righteousness and commitment to doing the will of God.[42] Jesus himself thus exemplifies the life of deeper righteousness to which disciples are called (5.20), and it is implicitly by following him that the disciple attains this quality of life.[43] In Matthew's Gospel, then, discipleship implies both obedience to Jesus' teachings and imitation of his life and character; *both* take on normative value, for it is in his own life, above all, that his teachings are lived out.[44] As Lindars notes, such a viewpoint fits quite well into the common rabbinic notion of mimesis: 'The master lives out the ethic which he teaches, and the disciple learns as much by imitation as by listening.'[45] If 4.18–22 is in any sense a paradigmatic expression of Matthew's view of the disciple as one who is called to 'follow' Jesus, then we may assume that ἀκολουθεῖν calls for both obedience and imitation.[46] The dual emphasis is expressed well in 11.29: 'Take my yoke upon you, and learn (μάθετε) from me' – a text that sums up much of Matthew's understanding of discipleship.

I must hasten to add, however, that the *imitatio Christi* is not to be understood in any wooden, literalistic sense; it is no mere mimicry of external behaviour that Matthew has in mind, but a thoroughgoing assimilation of Jesus' inner attitude and character – a point stressed throughout the Sermon on the Mount. What is demanded is not merely formal but committed imitation and obedience.[47] There are, of course, limits to the principle of imitation; for as κύριος, Jesus bears an authority that the disciple does not, and this authority may give him the prerogative to manifest certain kinds of attitudes and behaviour that the disciple may not. (Compare his denunciation of the scribes and Pharisees in 23.17, 33 with the character demanded of the disciple in 5.22, 39, 44 – though here, as we shall see later,[48] the question of inconsistency arises.) How the disciple is seen to relate to Jesus, therefore, depends on the focus: when it is Jesus' response to the authority of God that is in view, the disciple is called to *imitate* him;[49] but when attention shifts to Jesus' own authority, then the disciple is called to *obey* him. In either case, the elements of submission and obedience are central.

In passing, it is perhaps worth mentioning the one appeal to the *imitatio Dei*. In 5.44f, disciples are called to an uncalculating love for their enemies, so that (ὅπως) they may be 'sons' of their Father who is in heaven. The immediate context (5.45*b*) makes it clear that in this case being a 'son' refers not to securing one's relationship with God, but to being *like* God;[50] and this interpretation is confirmed by the statement shortly thereafter: 'You, therefore, must be perfect (τέλειοι), as your heavenly

Father is perfect (τέλειος)' (5.48). Though interpretations of τέλειος vary somewhat, in light of the larger context in which it occurs (5.20–48) and the parallel injunction in Lev. 19.2 from which it may well be derived, the term is probably best taken as a demand for absolute goodness and freedom from wrongdoing, in line with the 'deeper righteousness' to which the disciple is called in 5.20[51] – and such an interpretation fits Matthew's other reference to τέλειος also (19.21). But these are the only explicit references to the imitation of God in the entire Gospel.[52] (Jesus' name Emmanuel (1.23) cannot be taken as evidence of a strict identification in Matthew's thinking of the *imitatio Christi* with the *imitatio Dei*, in view of the uncertain sense in which the name is to be understood.) Implicitly, of course, the fact that God is τέλειος underlies the whole emphasis of the Gospel on ethical righteousness, just as the basic conviction of God's mercy and forgiveness underlies the demand for mercy and forgiveness on the part of the disciple (cf. 5.7; 9.13; 12.7; 18.33; 23.23; 25.31). But while the nature of God functions implicitly as a factor shaping the evangelist's ethics, almost never does it function explicitly as a sanction *motivating* his ethics. In any case, his portrayal of the nature of God (especially as Judge) is in certain respects distinctly antithetical to the character required of the disciple (cf. 5.3–5, 38–42; 7.1f). On the whole, in Matthew (as in the other synoptics) the disciple's ethical behaviour is grounded not so much in the imitation of God, as in the fact that he stands confronted with the demand of God.[53]

### 1.3 The Role of Grace

The question arises, what is the relation of the 'indicative' to this strong emphasis on the 'imperative'?[54] To what extent, if any, does the concept of grace enter into Matthew's understanding of the disciple's relationship to Jesus, and what part does it play in his ethics?

Scattered throughout the Gospel are hints of an underlying concept of grace that are frequently overlooked by those who set Matthew in stark contrast to Paul. There is, for example, the recurring theme of God's mercy and forgiveness (6.12–14; 9.2, 5f*; 12.31f*; 18.23–7, 32f; 21.31), which is reflected in the demand for human mercy and forgiveness (6.12–15; 9.13; 12.7; 18.21f, 28–35); such a theme lies behind the king's free invitation to the wedding feast – extended even to the most unworthy – in the parable of the great supper, for instance (22.1–14).

There are also references to the soteriological significance of Jesus, which is declared by the angel even before his birth (1.21); and Matthew's important redactional addition (εἰς ἄφεσιν ἁμαρτιῶν) to Mark's words about Jesus' 'blood of the covenant, which is poured out for many' (26. 28), indisputably confirms his awareness of it. Though the point is not emphasized, Matthew clearly portrays Jesus' death as of fundamental significance for the new covenant relationship in which the disciple stands, and as the ground of forgiveness.[55] It is likely that such central kerygmatic elements are also presupposed in the reference to baptizing 'in the name of the Father and of the Son and of the Holy Spirit' in the final mission commission (28.19*b*),[56] though the commission itself gives us no hints as to what this implies in the evangelist's thinking.

The fact that Jesus proclaims *τὰ μυστήρια* of the kingdom of heaven (13.11) suggests that Matthew views Jesus' teaching itself as an expression of grace: it is the key to understanding the secrets of the kingdom – indeed, it provides the key to the kingdom itself. For within the context of the still valid law, it is Jesus' teaching that gives the true interpretation of Torah, defines both the degree and quality of *δικαιοσύνη* demanded, and thereby enables one to know and to do the will of God.[57] Thus, demanding though it be, it is Jesus' teaching that makes it possible in the end for one to attain the kingdom. Grace is implicit also in the fact that, apparently in contrast to the legalistic burden of Pharisaic Judaism, Jesus' yoke is described as 'easy' (*χρηστός*) and his burden as 'light' (*ἐλαφρόν*: 11.30).[58]

In addition, there are hints that Matthew sees grace as active even in an individual's commitment to discipleship. Just as the Twelve were chosen by Jesus to follow him (cf. 4.18–22), so true disciples everywhere may be described as *ἐκλεκτοί* (22.14; 24.22*, 24*, 31*); they are the 'good seed' sown in the world by the Son of Man, the 'sons of the kingdom' (13.38). Implicitly, they are also the ones with a 'wedding garment' (22.11f), and those who are 'known' by Jesus (7.23) – though the precise significance of the latter two references remains undefined, and the extent to which grace is implicit is therefore less certain.[59] There are also the strange Johannine-like references in 11.27 and 16.17 (cf. 11.25), which attribute even the disciple's knowledge of the Father and the Son to a personal revelation; similarly, disciples are those to whom 'it has been given to know' the mysteries of the kingdom (13.11).[60] In the context of his statement about the difficulties of rich men entering the kingdom, Jesus' assertion, 'With men this is impossible, but with God all things are possible' (19.26*, largely taken over from Mark), even seems to suggest that repentance itself may be viewed as ultimately effected by God; but the overall emphasis is certainly elsewhere.[61]

Other statements imply that God's grace may be experienced in the ordinary day-to-day life of the disciple. Jesus is ever among his disciples, to aid and bless them in their life of discipleship (18.20; 28.20);[62] indeed, God himself is in some sense with them in Jesus' presence (cf. 1.23). The disciple can always turn to the Lord for help in times of need (18.19f; note Jesus' response to the Matthean *κύριε, σῶσον* in 8.25; 14.30; to *ἐλέησον* in 9.27; 15.22; 17.15; 20.30, 31; and to similar requests in 8.2*, 6ff; 9.2, 18, 21, 32; 12.22; 14.35f*; 15.30).[63] Further, of all the synoptic writers it is Matthew that draws the most winsome picture of God as a kind and caring heavenly Father, concerned to meet the everyday needs of his children (6.6–13, 25–34; 7.7–11; 10.20, 29ff; 18.10–14, 19f); indeed, it is to him that disciples are implicitly invited to look for *all* their needs (cf. 24.20*; 26.36–44*).[64] By implication, then – even though Matthew nowhere draws this conclusion explicitly – the help of God may be invoked even for the attitude of heart required in order to fulfil Jesus' demands for a life of deeper righteousness and 'perfection' (5.20, 48; cf. 26.41* and the moral overtones of 6.10, 13: 'Thy will be done ... deliver us from evil'[65]); in other words, for *all that is required in order to attain the kingdom of heaven*.[66] The presence of passages on prayer in the midst of such a strong ethical section as the Sermon on the Mount (6.9–13; 7.7–11) supports this conclusion – as does the fact that God has the power to change even the most obstinate of hearts (19.26*).

It is clear, then, that there is an underlying structure of grace presupposed throughout the Gospel: in the traditional Jewish assumption of God's mercy and forgiveness; in the soteriological significance of Jesus' life and death; in the teachings of Jesus that make a life of righteousness possible; in the 'chosenness' of the individual disciple; and in the experience of Jesus' continual presence and God's fatherly care and aid for all the needs of life – presumably including that of meeting Jesus' own stringent demands for *δικαιοσύνη*. In effect, grace is implicit in the *whole story* of Jesus told by the evangelist. But the significant point is that Matthew does not exploit this assumed structure of grace, and does not build his ethics explicitly upon it[67] (rarely is ethical behaviour motivated by considerations of grace); for the most part, it remains in the background, simply taken for granted – the largely unspoken context in which the Gospel is set.[68]

In Matthew's case, then, one cannot say that the imperative is simply built upon or derived from the indicative;[69] nor, however, can one say that the indicative is simply dependent on the imperative. The writer's concern rather is to stress that the fulfilment of the imperative is a prerequisite for the ultimate, full and final expression of the indicative – a point that is made with regard to forgiveness, for example (6.12–15;

18.23–35; cf. 5.20; 7.13f, 21ff).[70] Beyond this, Matthew gives us few hints of how the two concepts are related in his thinking. One thing is clear, however: his primary focus is on the imperative, not the indicative. Though he takes over Mark's concept of election (24.22*, 24*, 31*), nowhere does he leave the impression that one can presume upon it as a guarantee of eschatological security: 'For many are called, but [in the end] few are chosen' (22.14).[71] It is only by a life of obedience and righteousness that the disciple will in the end be found among the elect – this is the point that Matthew is concerned to stress. Thus, though elements of both grace and demand are found in the evangelist's portrayal of the disciple's relationship to Jesus, it is the sense of demand that predominates and characterizes Matthean ethics.[72]

## 2. *Paul*

For Paul, it is the believer's relationship to Christ and the fact of God's grace behind it that provide not only the basis for the Christian's standing with God, but also the fundamental grounding for ethics; here we touch the heart of what motivates ethics in the Pauline epistles. Paul's parenesis, then, may be viewed as an attempt to spell out the implications of this relationship for the believer's life.

### 2.1 Relationship to Christ

This relationship is described essentially in two different ways. First, the believer is one who confesses Jesus Christ as *κύριος* (Rom. 10.9; cf. Phil. 2.9ff). It is no mere confession of a formula that Paul has in view here, but rather genuine submission and obedience to the one who has all power and authority (1 Cor. 15.24ff; Phil. 3.21; Col. 1.15ff; 2.10, 15),[73] and who is the head of his body, the Church (Col. 1.18; 2.9f, 19; cf. Eph. 5.23). That the Christian is one who lives not for himself but for the Lord, is a basic assumption of all Pauline ethics; indeed, Paul can even say that it was to this end that Christ died and rose again (Rom. 14.7–9; 2 Cor. 5.14f).[74] The underlying supposition, that the believer no longer belongs to himself but to another, is made explicit in 1 Cor. 6.19f (cf. 7.23; Rom. 7.4).[75] Christians are to live, then, as those 'under new management', and everything they do is to be done 'in the name of the Lord Jesus' (Col. 3.17; cf. 2 Cor. 8.5). Even celibacy is encouraged on the grounds that it frees one to apply oneself in single-minded devotion to *τὰ τοῦ κυρίου*, and to pleasing him (1 Cor. 7.32ff; cf. 2 Cor. 11.3; Col. 1.10); after all, even one's body belongs to the Lord (1 Cor. 6.12ff). Similarly, Christian slaves are exhorted to labour heartily and with unfeigned respect, *ὡς τῷ κυρίῳ καὶ οὐκ ἀνθρώποις*, knowing that it is a heavenly master that they really serve (Col. 3.22f; here Paul elevates even the most menial of tasks to an act of worship[76]). Indeed, every Christian is a *δοῦλος* of Christ (1 Cor. 7.22), and is to live as one who serves him faithfully (1 Cor. 4.2, 17; 7.25; Col. 1.2, 7; 4.7, 9). Thus, Tannehill is correct in stating that the concept of slavery forms a key part of the theological basis of Paul's ethics.[77] This is not to suggest, however, that Paul thinks of the Christian as being under the tyrannical rule of a harsh and merciless master; sovereign, yes – but not tyrannical. Nor is it to suggest that he lives under the delusion that all believers measure up to this demanding standard, as his parenesis itself attests; he himself admits of those accompanying him at one point that, apart from Timothy, no one is genuinely concerned for *τὰ Ἰησοῦ Χριστοῦ* – only for *τὰ ἑαυτῶν* (Phil. 2.20f). Nevertheless, it is true that, as Furnish sums it up, 'The total claim which Christ's lordship lays upon the believer is a basic and pervasive element of Pauline thought and is implied in almost every paragraph he writes'[78] – though even this is rooted in the awareness of God's grace (2 Cor. 5.14f; cf. 1 Cor. 6.19f).

Paul's own life serves as a model of submission to the Lord. He lays great stress, for example, on the fact that he is a servant or slave of Christ (*δοῦλος*: Rom. 1.1; Gal. 1.10; Phil. 1.1; *διάκονος*: 2 Cor. 11.23; cf. 1 Cor. 3.5; 2 Cor. 3.6; 6.4; Col. 1.23, 25; *ὑπηρέτης*: 1 Cor. 4.1; *λειτουργός*: Rom. 15.16; *οἰκέτης*: Rom. 14.4; cf. *οἰκονόμος*: 1 Cor. 4.1f),[79] and that there is a certain accountability associated with that (1 Cor. 3.8ff; 4.1ff; cf. 9.16f; 2 Cor. 1.21f; 2.17; 5.18ff; Gal. 1.10; Col. 1.25; cf. 4.17; 1 Thess. 2.4ff).[80] As such, he is prepared not only to suffer, but willingly to sacrifice everything – even his life – in Christ's service (Rom. 8.36f; 1 Cor. 15.31; 2 Cor. 1.5; 4.5, 8–11; 6.4–10; Gal. 6.17; Phil. 1.13, 20; 3.7ff; Col. 1.24; 1 Thess. 2.2ff). For him, 'to live is Christ', and his deepest desire is to honour Christ in all he does (Phil. 1.20f; cf. 2 Cor. 4.15; 5.13; 8.19; Gal. 2.20; Col. 3.4). Without question, there are implications here for Christian ethics; for Paul's self-portrait depicts one who is claimed by the Lord in *all* areas of life. The resulting sense of obligation, however, is never portrayed as an onerous burden, in view of the overwhelming sense of God's grace behind it.

Submission to the authority of Christ as Lord is linked in Paul's mind with submission to the will of God, the assumed need for which underlies the whole of his ethics (cf. Rom. 2.18; 12.2; Phil. 2.13; Col. 1.9; 4.12; 1 Thess. 4.3).[81] Thus, it is difficult to argue against Nieder's statement that Paul's ethics centre on obedience to the will of God[82] – though such a statement totally fails to capture the truly distinctive element. This may help to explain how he can simultaneously speak of response to the gospel in terms of *πίστις*, on the one hand, and *ὑποτάσσειν* (Rom. 10.3), *ὑποτάγη* (2 Cor. 9.13), *ὑπακούειν* (Rom. 6.17; 10.16; 2 Thess. 1.8), and *ὑπακοή* (Rom. 1.5; 6.16f; 15.18; 16.19, 26; cf. 2 Cor. 10.5f) on the other – the latter of which results in the paradoxical phrase 'obedience of faith' (*ὑπακοὴ πίστεως*: Rom. 1.5; 16.26).[83] We cannot argue from this, however (as Bultmann and Furnish do), that Paul thinks of *πίστις* primarily in terms of obedience[84] – for such a view represents a distorted understanding of his use of the term *πίστις* generally; but we can begin to appreciate just how important the elements of submission and obedience are in Paul's thinking.[85] Further, submission to the will of God is not so much a matter of obedience to specific injunctions and particular lines of conduct, as it is a radical surrender and commitment of one's whole life to God himself; i.e. it is obedience not in a legal but in a personal sense. The obligation to obey is only heightened by the believer's awareness of his *υἱοθεσία* (Rom. 8.15; Gal. 4.6f); but the obedience called for is that of a responsive son to a loving Father[86] – it is obedience rooted in grace.

Paul also speaks of the believer's relationship to Christ in 'participationist' language, or in terms of an intimate union.[87] Thus, he describes Christians as 'the body of Christ' (1 Cor. 12.13, 27; cf. Rom. 12.5);[88] 'members (*μέλη*) of Christ' (1 Cor. 6.15); 'united to the Lord' (1 Cor. 6.17); those who in the sacrament experience *κοινωνία* of the body and blood of the Lord (1 Cor. 10.16–18; 11.29) – all because they are baptized into Christ (Gal. 3.27; cf. 1 Cor. 12.13). Such an intimate relationship with the Lord clearly has implications for the believer's religious and moral life.[89] It demands, for example, a worthy appreciation of the sacrament (1 Cor. 11.27ff) and abstention from idol worship (1 Cor. 10.21f); it also requires total abstinence from sexual immorality (1 Cor. 6.15ff).[90] The underlying supposition, as E.P. Sanders points out, is that the Christian's union with Christ is considered to be wholly exclusive of certain other relationships.[91] Paul's favourite phrase for describing this relationship is *ἐν Χριστῷ*, or *ἐν κυρίῳ*[92] – a phrase that he uses to provide support for quite a wide range of statements and injunctions.[93] For Paul, all of life is to be lived *ἐν κυρίῳ* (Col. 2.6f), and the implication is that this is to shape the whole of one's outlook and ethical behaviour. Frequently, however, the phrase is used in such a general sense that it appears to mean little more than simply 'Christian' or 'as a Christian';[94] and at these points one must beware of drawing ethical implications from any supposed references strictly to the believer's union with Christ. Nevertheless, it is clear that in Paul's thinking generally, such a union does impose definite ethical obligations; for moral living is the only suitable response to an intimate relationship with Christ, and the only fitting expression of gratitude for the grace that has brought it about. In E.P. Sanders' view, participation in Christ or union with him *'is the theme, above all, to which Paul appeals both in parenesis and polemic'*.[95]

Paul also appeals to the fact that, by entering into union with Christ, believers have broken with sin and their old way of life; and for this he uses a variety of metaphors. In contrast to those who practise evil, Christians have been 'washed' and 'sanctified' (1 Cor. 6.9ff). They have experienced spiritual 'circumcision' by 'putting off the body of flesh' (Col. 2.11). Above all, they have 'died' with Christ (2 Cor. 5.14ff; cf. Gal. 2.19) – a metaphor suggested perhaps by the rite of baptism itself,[96] and developed especially in Rom. 6.3–11 (cf. Col. 2.12), where Paul applies it particularly to the question of sin. And because believers have 'died' to sin (Rom. 6.2, 6f), they are to regard themselves as 'dead' to its power and control (Rom. 6.6f, 11, 14; cf. Col. 2.20).[97] In slightly more vivid terms, Paul describes them as those who have 'crucified' their *σάρξ* with its passions and desires (Gal. 5.24; cf. 2.19; 6.14), and instructs them therefore to 'put to death' their evil inclinations (Rom. 8.13; Col. 3.5ff;[98] here we encounter the indicative–imperative paradox so frequently observed in his writings[99]). In response to the anticipated charge that justification by faith alone constitutes an invitation to licence (Rom. 6.1, 15), Paul thus argues that to be baptized into Christ is to share in his death to sin (Rom. 6.2–11), and calls upon believers to effect in their lives the full implications of that.[100] The recurrence of this theme in Paul's writings suggests something of its importance in his thought. Houlden concludes that it is in this experience of Christ's death by the believer that the moral impulse finds its deepest source for Paul.[101]

The emphasis is not entirely on the negative side, however; for just as believers have 'put off the old nature', so they have 'put on the new' (Col. 3.9f)[102] – and are to clothe themselves accordingly with all the virtues of the new life (Col. 3.12ff). Having 'put on' Christ in a theological sense (Gal. 3.27), they are to 'put on' Christ in an ethical sense (Rom. 13.14). Just as in baptism they 'die' to their old way of life, so they 'rise again' to live a wholly new one; and Paul appeals to *both* aspects of the conversion experience to motivate ethical behaviour. Though it is only in Colossians that we find explicit references to a present resurrection life (Col. 2.12f; 3.1), the concept is clearly presupposed in Rom. 6 as well (6.4f, 11, 13).[103] We see, then, how Paul's appeal to the believer's baptism functions as a moral stimulus both negatively and positively.

To what extent does the *imitatio Christi* enter into Paul's ethics? The relative infrequency of explicit appeals to the specific details of Jesus' life would certainly suggest that the motif plays no central role, contrary to the assertions of Tinsley and Stewart.[104] Nor however is it totally absent, as Michaelis would have us believe;[105] for there are certain elements (though not many) in Paul's ethical teaching that are clearly grounded in the example of Christ. Among these may be included the call for humble and obedient service (Phil. 2.5ff),[106] selfless consideration of others (Rom. 15.1–3), sacrificial generosity (2 Cor. 8.9),[107] a forgiving spirit (Col. 3.13), and acceptance and welcome of others (Rom. 15.7). Though Paul nowhere grounds the appeal for *ἀγάπη* itself explicitly in the example of Christ, the thought is clearly implicit in the above passages; the priority he gives to it may suggest something of the importance of the concept in his understanding of Christ himself.[108] As for the reference to *τὴν ὑπομονὴν τοῦ Χριστοῦ* in 2 Thess. 3.5, whether this functions as an example for imitation is unclear; the genitive is ambiguous.[109] In addition, at least once Paul calls for the adoption of Christ's attitude and behaviour in a more general sense: 'put on the Lord Jesus Christ' (Rom. 13.14; cf. verses 12f). But there are very few references to specific details of Jesus' *earthly* conduct (it apparently does not occur to Paul, for example, to appeal to Jesus as an example of celibacy or freedom from legalism); what is in focus rather is the love and grace expressed in his incarnation and death as a whole. It is 'his self-effacing love and ... the giving of himself in suffering and death' that is primarily in view when Paul thinks of imitating Christ (Phil. 3.10; cf. 1 Cor. 11.1; 2 Cor. 4.10[110]); for herein lies the real significance of Christ's life and the ultimate expression of his love, in his thinking.[111]

Underlying the apostle's appeal to the *imitatio Christi*, therefore, is a strong awareness of God's grace in Christ – and with it the conviction that such grace calls for ethical response. Thus, what appears on the surface to be an appeal for imitation may on a deeper level be yet another call for ethical response to what Christ has done: 'because Christ has ..., so you should ...'[112] At this point, response to Christ's kindness takes on the nature of imitation of his life and character, and the two concepts merge. In some cases the *imitatio Christi* may be present implicitly but in a peripheral manner – as, for example, in the analogy Paul makes between the believer's attitude to sin and Christ's death and Resurrection in Rom. 6.3–11. That at least some element of mimesis is implied (of Christ's attitude to sin in particular) may certainly be argued;[113] but this is not at all the central element in the passage.[114] For the most part, the references to the death, burial and Resurrection of Christ serve merely as the grounds for a simple comparison with what happens to the believer in baptism; i.e. they play a largely illustrative role, and little more.

Ultimately, of course, Paul does think of the believer as becoming like Christ (Rom. 8.29; cf. 2 Cor. 3.18) – and because Christ is the *εἰκὼν τοῦ θεοῦ* (2 Cor. 4.4; Col. 1.15–20; cf. Phil. 2.6), presumably like God himself. (The latter, however, is mentioned explicitly only in Col. 3.10, and is not at all emphasized by Paul.[115]) But the important point is that Paul thinks of this process as the result not of conscious imitation, but of the work of the Spirit in the heart; i.e. it is ultimately a gift of God's grace, not the achievement of human effort.[116] This fits in well, of course, with his view of *δικαιοσύνη* generally. From this point of view, the fact that the example of Christ plays such a minimal role in Pauline ethics is quite understandable.

### 2.2 The Role of Grace

We begin to see, then, the extent to which Paul grounds the believer's response to Christ in an awareness of God's grace; whichever aspect of the relationship is in focus, grace lies at its core. That the concept plays a major role in Paul's thinking goes without question. Virtually all of his letters, for example, both open and close with some invocation of the grace of God in Christ; and there are references to *χάρις* and *χαρίζεσθαι* throughout. At the very heart of Paul's theology lies the conviction that one's standing with God itself is a gift of grace (Rom. 3.21ff; 1 Cor. 1.4; Col. 1.6; 2 Thess. 2.16).[117] The apostle is entirely conscious of his own dependence on God's grace, not only for his standing with God (Phil. 3.3–11) but also for his whole ministry: it is God who sustains him in his weakness (2 Cor. 12.7–9), who delivers him out of crises (2 Cor. 1.9), and who gives him power and inspiration (2 Cor. 4.7; Col. 1.29; 1 Thess. 2.2); indeed it is God who is actually at work in and through him, effecting the results of his ministry (1 Cor. 3.5ff; 2 Cor. 1.12; 2.14; 3.5f; 4.7) – Paul is but a servant, a mere 'labourer' in God's 'garden'. Everything that Paul is and has, including his ministry (2 Cor. 4.1), is attributable to the grace of God (1 Cor. 15.10; cf. 7.25; Gal. 2.9). So it is with his churches as well: it is God who initiates the 'good work' in them (Phil. 1.6), who sustains and prospers it (1 Thess. 3.12), and who preserves them to the end (Phil. 1.6; 1 Thess. 5.23). God is the one who gives them both the desire and the ability to do what he wants (Phil. 2.13; cf. 2 Thess. 1.11f; 2.16); he is the one who sanctifies them (1 Thess. 3.13; 5.23f) and fills their hearts with love for one another (2 Cor. 8.16; 1 Thess. 3.12; 2 Thess. 3.5). All growth within the Christian community is the result of grace, and all gifts within the community stem from grace; indeed, the ministry of Christians to one another is simply the exercise of *χαρίσματα* (1 Cor. 12.4ff). Accordingly, Paul is quick to attribute whatever good he sees in the churches to its ultimate source (cf. 2 Cor. 8.1ff; 9.11ff). References to *εὐχαριστία* and *εὐχαριστεῖν* abound; because everything good is ultimately a gift of grace, thanksgiving assumes a role of fundamental importance in the believer's life.[118] In Paul's thinking, then, the whole of the Christian life is both an acknowledgement of dependence on God's grace and an expression of response to it. (One implication of all this for Paul's ethics is that there is absolutely no room left for boasting of one's own prowess or achievements: 1 Cor. 1.29–31; 4.7; 2 Cor. 10.17; cf. Rom. 15.17f; it is a categorical rejection of self-exaltation and pride.) The point is well summed up in 1 Cor. 8.6, where Paul speaks of God as the one *ἐξ οὗ τὰ πάντα* – and adds, *καὶ ἡμεῖς εἰς αὐτόν*. If the ambiguous latter phrase may be interpreted as in the RSV, 'and for whom we exist',[119] then here we have an excellent example of the close link in Paul's mind between the Christian's sense of obligation and his awareness of total dependence on God's grace – with the former deriving from the latter.

The sense of grace is heightened by Paul's consistent use of terminology that describes believers as those who are especially chosen by God: e.g. *κλητοί* (Rom. 1.6, 7; 8.28; 1 Cor. 1.2, 24; cf. *κλῆσις*: 1 Cor. 1.26; 7.20; Phil. 3.14; 2 Thess. 1.11; cf. Rom. 11.29), *ἐκλεκτοί* (Rom. 8.33; Col. 3.12), and *ἐκλογή* (Rom. 9.11; 11.7; 1 Thess. 1.4); with regard to God's action in choosing them, he uses *ἐκάλεσεν* (Rom. 8.30; 9.24f),[120] *εἵλατο* (2 Thess. 2.13), *ἐξελέξατο* (1 Cor. 1.27f), *προέγνω* (Rom. 8.29; cf. 11.2), *προώρισεν* (Rom. 8.29f), and *ἔθετο* (1 Thess. 5.9). Hence believers are likened to 'vessels of mercy' which God in his sovereign grace has created to receive his glory (Rom. 9.23). In view of their special calling and election, Paul speaks of them as *υἱοὶ/τέκνα θεοῦ* (Rom. 8.15f; 9.25f; cf. Gal. 3.26; Phil. 2.15), *ἀγαπητοὶ θεοῦ* (Rom. 1.7; 1 Thess. 1.4; cf. 2 Thess. 2.13; Col. 3.12), and *τέκνα ἐπαγγελίας* (Gal. 4.28); the concept of a new covenant is implicit in a number of passages (2 Cor. 3.6ff; Gal. 4.24; Rom. 11.27).[121] The greatness of the grace involved is brought most sharply into relief when the new status of Christians is set over against their previous status (Gal. 4.3–7) or that of the *λοιποί* as *ἀπολλύμενοι* (1 Thess. 5.6; 2 Thess. 2.13f). The point that Paul wishes to emphasize is that the believer's new standing with God is entirely the result of God's grace and initiative (Rom. 11.5; Gal. 1.6; cf. 4.9: 'now that you have come to know God, or rather to be known by God').

The resulting impression is that Christians enjoy a certain security in their relationship with God.[122] They can know that God is indeed 'for' them, and that nothing in itself has the power to break that relationship and take them away from his love (Rom. 8.31ff). Provided they remain within the embrace of that love, they can rest in the knowledge that their Lord will support them in the Judgement (Rom. 14.4), and that God has the power to keep them from falling away until then (1 Thess. 5.23f).

The Christian's knowledge of God's special calling and grace constitutes in itself a call for moral response (Col. 3.12ff).[123] Because believers are called to be *ἅγιοι* (Rom. 1.7; 1 Cor. 1.2), it is essential that *ἁγιασμός* should be effected in their lives; indeed, that is part of God's purpose in the whole saving event (Col. 1.22; 1 Thess. 4.7f). For Paul, one's theological status can never be divorced from its ethical implications (cf. the references to 'leaven' in 1 Cor. 5.6f). Thus, at several points he calls upon his readers to live in a way that is 'worthy' (*ἀξίως*) of those who have been so favoured by God's grace: 'as befits the saints' (Rom. 16.2); 'worthy of God, who calls you' (1 Thess. 2.12f); 'worthy of his call' (2 Thess. 1.11)[124] – though the very fact that the latter appeal is expressed in the form of a prayer (cf. also Col. 1.10) suggests that even this is ultimately attributable to God's grace. At some points this desire that Christians should live in a manner worthy of their calling takes on very specific form – as, for example, with regard to sexual relationships: they are not to behave 'like heathen who do not know God' (1 Thess. 4.5). In general, they are to live in a way that is entirely worthy both of their relationship to the Lord and of their divine calling (cf. Col. 1.10; Phil. 1.27), and to avoid any action that could be interpreted as unbecoming of either (cf. 1 Cor. 11.4).

At the heart of what motivates Paul's ethics, then, lies this strong awareness of God's grace.[125] Whether the appeal is to one's relationship to Christ (in any of its various forms) or to one's special calling from God, grace is always implicit. And beneath it all lies the conviction that the supreme expression of grace is Christ himself, with the focus especially on his death (which functions as the basis of everything else). Christ's death is a point of central importance, therefore, not only for Paul's theology, but also for his ethics (Rom. 6.2ff, 6f; 7.4; 8.1ff; 1 Cor. 8.11; 2 Cor. 5.14f; 8.8f; Gal. 2.20; Phil. 2.1–8; Col. 2.11ff).[126]

In general, it is this view of the Christian life as a response to grace that lies at the heart of the commonly observed link between Pauline theology and ethics.[127] The close relationship between the two is evidenced especially by the frequency with which we find parenetic passages set in the context of theological assertions, often linked by the parenetic 'therefore' (*οὖν*, *ὥστε*, etc.: Rom. 6.12; 12.1; 13.12; Gal. 5.1; Col. 3.1, 5, 12; 1 Thess. 5.6; 2 Thess. 2.15).[128] The most prominent example of this is Rom. 12.1ff, where Paul's appeal for total commitment and its ethical outworking is predicated on 'the mercies of God' as expressed in the preceding eleven chapters[129] (cf. also Phil. 2.12; Col. 3.5, 12). To a large extent, then, the sense of obligation underlying the ethics of Paul derives from a keen awareness of God's grace and the implicit claims it makes upon the believer's life; it is the obligation not of law but of grace.[130] At their core, Pauline ethics are an expression of gratitude.[131]

### 3. *Comparison of Matthew and Paul*

The ethics of both writers are fundamentally grounded in their understanding of the Christian's relationship to Christ, and may be viewed as attempts to spell out the implications of this relationship for the Christian's life. The precise nature of the relationship, however, is understood somewhat differently by the two, and as a result their ethics take on different hues. In part, this is due to underlying differences in their views of Christ himself (who nonetheless remains central for both), and also to more basic differences in their theological perspectives.[132]

The two are most alike in their common emphasis on the authority of Christ as *κύριος*,[133] and on the demand for submission and obedience to him – as may be seen, for example, in the *κύριος–δοῦλος* motif, which is prominent in the writings of both. Both also stress that the demand for submission and obedience takes the form of a radical claim for total commitment, a claim that takes priority over all self-interest and calls the Christian to self-sacrifice – even to the point of forgoing marriage in certain cases (Mt. 19.10ff; 1 Cor. 7.1, 7f, 32ff)[134] and being prepared to die (Mt. 10.17ff*, 37ff; 24.9ff*; Rom. 14.7ff; Phil. 1.20f; 3.7–10) – though Paul portrays this in a more positive light than Matthew. On the whole, the concepts of authority and submission play a more dominant role in Matthew's writing than in Paul's; whereas Matthew concentrates primarily on the *ἐξουσία* of Jesus, Paul emphasizes the *χάρις* as well. For Matthew, Jesus' authority as Christ and Lord is apparently sufficient in itself to command ethical response; but for Paul, even obedience to Jesus' authority is rooted in God's grace. Further, for Matthew Jesus' authority is expressed especially in his teachings and commands, and the life of discipleship focuses on obeying *them* (Mt. 7.24–7; 28.18–20) – a view that fits in well with his overall legal orientation and understanding of Jesus as interpreter of Torah; but for Paul, submission to the authority of Jesus is a matter of doing everything *ὡς τῷ κυρίῳ* – a more abstract concept, and one reflecting a stronger personal than legal orientation. Similarly, obedience to the will of God (which Matthew especially stresses) is linked much more closely to the specifics of Jesus' teaching in the evangelist's writing (7.21ff) than in the apostle's. Accordingly, 'learning' and 'observance' play a much greater role in the life of the Matthean disciple than they do in that of the Pauline believer. Both writers, then, think of the Christian life in terms of obedience to authority – though neither wishes to portray this as burdensome (Mt. 11.28–30; 2 Cor. 5.14f; Phil. 1.20f; 3.7ff); but Paul's conception of it is grounded to a much greater extent in the awareness of God's grace.

Neither makes any great appeal to the *imitatio Christi* (and even less to the *imitatio Dei*); yet both take it for granted that the Christian's attitude and behaviour are in certain ways to be modelled after those of Christ himself – and that not in any wooden, literalistic sense. Many of the traits of Christ set out as exemplary are surprisingly similar for the two writers: meekness and humility; self-giving, suffering service; and obedience to the divine will – characteristics especially noteworthy in view of the contrasting emphasis of both writers on Jesus' authority. But generally speaking, whereas Matthew portrays these characteristics in specific events of Jesus' life, Paul associates them rather with the larger event of his incarnation and death as a whole, which for him is of far more importance. And if we take into account their overall theological perspectives, it becomes clear that the significance of the two pictures is somewhat different: for Matthew's disciples, Jesus functions as a model primarily of *δικαιοσύνη*; for Paul's believers, he is a model of *ἀγάπη*. Paul goes much further than Matthew, of course, in providing an intermediate model for the believer – namely, himself; in certain very limited respects Matthew's Twelve function as examples also (e.g. in the way they leave everything to follow Jesus), but not in the same thoroughgoing sense. Paul also goes much further than Matthew in attributing the Christian's ultimate conformation to Christ to an act of grace in the heart. But neither writer makes any extensive appeal to the example of Christ to motivate ethical behaviour; the *imitatio Christi* remains more implicit than explicit in the ethics of both.

While Matthew portrays the Christian's relationship to Christ primarily in terms of obedience and discipleship, Paul depicts it also in terms of participation and union – and of this there is no real equivalent in Matthew at all (though to a certain extent he does speak of Jesus as identifying with his disciples, especially in the treatment they receive from others: Mt. 10.40; 18.5ff; 25.40, 45[135]). The conviction that in baptism the believer is united with Christ in death and resurrection, and thereby enters into a wholly new way of life and an intimate relationship that is exclusive of certain other relationships, is quite important in Pauline ethics; but it is (understandably) almost wholly absent in those of Matthew.

While Matthew focuses on Jesus' authority, Paul stresses the implications of his death. Matthew, writing a Gospel, makes virtually no reference to Jesus' death in his parenesis; but Paul gives it a role of central importance in his. For Paul, it is an event of cosmic significance, for *both* theology *and* ethics – the primary expression of grace from which all else flows; in it the reconciling love of God is expressed and the powers of law, sin and death are vanquished,[136] thereby making ethical living possible at last. For Paul, Christ's death provides a strong impulse for moral living, and the whole of the Christian life is viewed as a response to it. Matthew, however, makes no attempt to relate the two.

The writings of both men reflect a concept of grace, and certain basic elements are held in common – e.g. the traditional Jewish assumption of God's mercy and forgiveness. In addition, it is clear that both writers attach soteriological significance to Jesus' death; but it is Paul who develops the point into a central one, and draws out its implications for ethics – Matthew neither emphasizes nor exploits it. Both also maintain a doctrine of election;[137] but again, it is Paul who gives it greater prominence and makes it into a basis for ethical living – while Matthew discourages any attempt to presume upon it, and stresses rather that though many are κλητοί, few in the end will find themselves ἐκλεκτοί.[138] Thus, whereas Paul instructs Christians to live in a way that is 'worthy' of those who are ἐκλεκτοί, Matthew enjoins them to live in a way that would ensure at the end that they are indeed *among* the ἐκλεκτοί; Paul's writing therefore expresses a greater degree of eschatological security than Matthew's.

Both writers also think of grace as something that may be experienced in everyday life. In part, this derives from their common conviction of the continuing presence of Jesus with his people and their belief in a 'father–son' relation between God and the Christian, which results in a strong doctrine of prayer for both. The particular significance they derive from these considerations, however, differs: for Matthew, the fact that God is 'Father' means that disciples can be confident their needs will be taken care of – and Jesus' presence confirms this (i.e. it functions primarily as assurance of aid and support); but Paul focuses on the fact that as 'son', the believer is now 'free' (Rom. 8.15; Gal. 4.5ff; 5.1ff) – and for him, Jesus' presence (as experienced especially in the power of the Spirit) confirms *this* (i.e. it functions as the power that makes ethical living possible). Here again it is Paul who draws out the ethical implications.

There is one point, however, at which Matthew's conception of God's grace clearly exceeds that of Paul; and that is in his understanding of Jesus' *teachings* as an expression of grace. For Paul, the point is of no real significance; but from Matthew's legal perspective, it is of crucial importance.[139] Nonetheless, on the whole it is undoubtedly Paul who has the more comprehensive view of God's grace, and who gives it the more central role in ethics. For him, the whole of the Christian life is an expression of both dependence on grace and response to it. Whereas Matthew assumes an underlying conception of grace but leaves it largely in the background, Paul chooses to make it dominant and to build his ethics squarely upon it.[140]

Just as we must beware, therefore, of drawing too sharp a distinction between the two writers, so we must beware of failing to draw a distinction at all (i.e. of falling into the common error of reading Matthew through the eyes of Paul).[141] In the end, it is essentially a difference of focus and emphasis. Aspects of both grace and demand are present in the writings of both; but whereas Matthew largely assumes the former and stresses the latter, Paul focuses rather on the former, and builds the latter upon it.[142] Matthew seeks to arouse a sense of ethical obligation based primarily on the concepts of authority and demand (of God, of Jesus, of the law); Paul seeks to root it rather (ultimately) in an awareness of grace, so that it springs from a sense of debt and gratitude.[143] In other words, while Paul grounds the imperative firmly in the indicative, Matthew stresses that the fulfilment of the imperative is a prerequisite for the ultimate experiencing of the indicative.[144]

Finally, the differing emphases of the two writers may be illustrated by comparing the motivational considerations to which they appeal in dealing with the problem of sexual immorality (*πορνεία*, *μοιχεία*: Matthew focuses primarily on the latter, Paul deals more broadly with the former). In Matthew, the fundamental appeal is to the strict prohibition of *μοιχεία* in the Mosaic law (Mt. 5.27; 19.18; cf. the description of both *μοιχεία* and *πορνεία* in terms of 'defilement': 15.18ff), which is characteristically sharpened with the authoritative demand of Jesus (who extends the concept to include even the lustful look) and reinforced with the threat of *γέεννα* (Mt. 5.28ff). The entire construct is founded on Jesus' demand for 'deeper righteousness' (5.20) within the framework of the still-valid law; i.e. it is an appeal grounded throughout in the concept of obedience to authority. The Mosaic prohibition of *μοιχεία* is also fundamental to Paul's thinking (Rom. 2.22f; 13.9), as is the basic wrongness of *πορνεία* in general (1 Cor. 7.2; 2 Cor. 12.21); and when it is called for, he too can appeal to the judgement sanction against it (1 Cor. 5.3ff; Col. 3.5f; 1 Thess. 4.6ff), and even declare that those who engage in such behaviour will not enter the kingdom of God (1 Cor. 6.9ff; Gal. 5.19–21). But on the whole, he prefers to ground his appeal in the more positive factor of God's grace, by which believers are now established in an entirely new relationship with God and a wholly new way of life (1 Cor. 6.9ff, esp. verse 11; Col. 3.1ff). Such a calling demands purity of life and behaviour appropriate to those who know God, and this in itself rules out *πορνεία* (1 Cor. 5.1–9, esp. verse 7; 1 Thess. 4.3ff, esp. verses 5, 7). Further, as those who have 'died' with Christ to their old way of life, believers are to 'put to death' such passionate drives (Col. 3.3ff, esp. verse 5); indeed, they are to consider them as 'crucified' in their lives (Gal. 5.24; cf. Rom. 6.6f). Paul also appeals to the believer's intimate union with Christ (1 Cor. 6.12–17), and to the fact that one's body now serves as a 'temple' for the Spirit (1 Cor. 6.19; cf. 1 Thess. 4.8) – which means that to engage in illicit sexual activity is to sin against the sacred dwelling of God himself (1 Cor. 6.18). Besides, as those who now belong to the Lord who has redeemed them, believers are to regard their bodies as no longer their own anyway (1 Cor. 6.13, 19f; Gal. 5.24); these too must bring glory to God (1 Cor. 6.20). Here we see the various ways in which Paul seeks to internalize an awareness of what God has so graciously done in Christ and in the believer's life, and to draw out ethical implications from it.

# 4

# LOVE

We turn now to examine (somewhat more briefly) the concept and role of love in the ethics of the two writers,[1] and the ways in which this reflects their broader theological perspectives.

## 1. *Matthew*

### 1.1 Ἀγάπη

On the whole, Matthew emphasizes love more than Mark[2] – a fact only partially accounted for by the greater amount of didactic material in the longer Gospel. Looking first at those passages in which the terms *ἀγαπᾶν* and *ἀγάπη* occur, I shall briefly summarize the relevant points. (The extensive work already done on these passages precludes any need to labour the fine details.)

#### *5.43–48*[3]

The injunction to love one's enemies and pray for one's persecutors, given apparently in opposition to a popular conception of love as extending only to the borders of the community of the faithful,[4] is grounded in the fundamental nature of the heavenly Father, who 'makes his sun rise on the evil and on the good, and sends rain on the just and on the unjust' (5.45); and it culminates in the command to be 'perfect' as the heavenly Father himself is perfect (*τέλειος*: 5.48). Being the last of the antitheses, the injunction serves as a final example of the 'deeper righteousness' demanded of the disciples in order to enter the kingdom (5.20; cf. *περισσόν*: 5.47).[5] Taken together with the preceding antithesis, this command instructs the Matthean community to adopt a posture of determined non-retaliation and doing of good to those at whose hands they suffer.

*19.16–22*[6]

To the Decalogue commandments cited by Jesus in response to the question of the rich young man about eternal life, Matthew significantly adds to the Marcan account the final commandment, 'and you shall love your neighbour as yourself' (19.19*b*; cf. Lev. 19.18)[7] – a redactional insertion which, though properly not associated with the Decalogue at all, not only makes the list more comprehensive, but also (by virtue of its position in part) suggests that in the evangelist's view the love commandment serves as the epitome of the moral demands of the law, and of the Decalogue in particular[8] (a point already implicit in his formulation of the golden rule, 7.12[9]). Thus, in Matthew the ensuing command to 'go, sell what you possess and give to the poor ... and come follow me' (19.21*) – significantly prefaced by the evangelist with the conditional clause, *εἰ θέλεις τέλειος εἶναι* – only reinforces and accentuates the love commandment already expressed by spelling out some of its implications. Here the addition of the love commandment prepares for the climax of the story as a whole.[10]

*22.34–40*[11]

In Matthew's version of the pericope centring on the two great commandments, the legal orientation has already been observed.[12] Here *ἀγάπη* is clearly viewed as 'the great commandment in the law' (22.36). Omitting the Marcan scribe's thoughtful reflection on Jesus' response, Matthew concludes with the crucial dictum: 'On these two commandments depend (*κρέμαται*)[13] all the law and the prophets' (22.40). The law is maintained, but the dual love commandment is viewed as the most important of the law's demands and the key to its meaning – i.e. as the primary hermeneutical principle for interpreting and applying the law[14] (a principle exemplified especially in Jesus' activity on the sabbath[15]); it is a compassion-focused view of the law. Even though Matthew speaks of the second commandment as being 'like' (*ὁμοία*) the first, the explicit emphasis on the first as *ἡ μεγάλη καὶ πρώτη* (22.38) precludes the possibility of their being considered of equal importance in his thinking.[16] Matthew, like Mark, seems to view the second within the context and framework of the all-embracing first;[17] but the pairing of the two suggests that one cannot fulfil the first apart from the second (cf. 7.12; 19.19*b*). The fact that Matthew converts a Marcan *Schulgespräch* into one of a series of *Streitgespräche* (22.35),[18] and – in contrast to both Mark and Luke – intimates no agreement between Jesus and his questioner on the point at issue (namely, the correct interpretation of the law),[19] may be indicative of a basic difference of opinion between the Matthean community and the Jewish religious authorities on this point.

*24.12*

In the apocalyptic discourse, Matthew alone of the synoptic writers refers to the loss of ἀγάπη[20] to be experienced in the coming days of suffering and persecution, due to the increase in ἀνομία. One cannot logically deduce from this, however (as Furnish does), that 'lawlessness' may therefore be defined merely as 'departing from the way and the deeds of love'.[21] But one can conclude, in view of the fact that ἀνομία is probably to be understood in a broader moral sense, that ἀγάπη is here viewed as a significant part of Matthew's concept of δικαιοσύνη.[22] The immediately following context makes it clear that remaining obedient to the love commandment is an essential part of that 'endurance to the end' by which one is ultimately saved.

### 1.2 Ἔλεος

But any discussion of the concept of love in Matthew's writing cannot be limited merely to ἀγάπη terminology;[23] for when the evangelist stresses the need for compassion, it is often the term ἔλεος (or a cognate) that is used. This term, perhaps more than any other, describes the kind of concern for others that Matthew most wishes to encourage.[24]

Jesus himself is portrayed as the exemplar *par excellence* of this compassion. This is seen, for example, in the number of times Matthew applies to him the verb σπλαγχνίζεσθαι (9.36*; 14.14*; 15.32*; 20.34; cf. 18.27; note also the number of instances in which he responds to the cry, ἐλέησον: 9.27*; 15.22; 17.15; 20.30f*) and in the compassionate nature of the 'mighty acts' of chapters 8–9, performed by one who 'took our infirmities and bore our diseases' (8.17). At several points the evangelist's summary of Jesus' activity includes an explicit reference to his healing care not found in Mark (4.23f; 9.35; 14.14; 15.30f; 21.14); and similarly, when the Twelve are sent on their mission, Matthew adds that their commission is not only to proclaim that 'the kingdom of heaven is at hand', but also to 'heal the sick, raise the dead, cleanse lepers, cast out demons' (10.8) – though this may be intended to emphasize Jesus' power and authority as much as his compassion.

The importance of ἔλεος in Matthew's understanding of Jesus' ethical teaching may be seen not only in the inclusion of 5.7 in the beatitudes, but also in the crucial role it plays in the confrontation between Jesus and the Pharisees. As we have seen, twice the evangelist adds to Mark's account of Jesus' defence of his actions the citation of Hos. 6.6, 'I desire mercy (ἔλεος), and not sacrifice' (9.13; 12.7; cf. verse 11);[25] and, in a key statement that confirms the centrality of the concept in Matthew's interpretation of the law, the Pharisees are rebuked for neglecting *τὰ βαρύτερα τοῦ νόμου* (23.23) – defined as 'justice and mercy (ἔλεος) and faith'. It is this emphasis on the expression of mercy in the interpretation of the law, this compassionate administration of the law, that provides the sharpest point of contrast between Jesus' teachings and the attitudes and practices of Pharisaic Judaism in this Gospel (cf. 23.4, 23). Yet another indication of the importance of ἔλεος is the evangelist's emphasis on the related theme of forgiveness, which, though scarcely noticeable in Mark, is quite prominent in Matthew (6.14f; 18.21f, 23–35; cf. 5.9, 21–4). The compassion motif is emphasized once again at the very close of Jesus' teaching ministry, in the parable of the sheep and the goats (25.31–46);[26] though the terms *ἀγάπη* and ἔλεος nowhere appear explicitly, it is clear that the criterion upon which the judgement is based is the expression of compassion to those in need (in this case, Jesus' 'brethren'[27]). In this pericope at least, the *δίκαιοι* – whoever they are[28] – are defined by their acts of compassion.

### 1.3 The Nature and Role of Love

It is clear that Matthew's concept of love is shaped by more general theological perspectives. At a number of points, for example, it reflects an inward-focused emphasis on self-denial: love demands the subduing of self-assertive desires for retaliation, and a willingness to suffer from, pray for and do good to one's enemies (5.43ff; cf. 5.10–12);[29] it calls for the distribution of one's wealth to the poor (19.21), in a way that is free from desires for self-gratification (6.1–4); and it requires a steeled determination to persist in the doing of good, even in times of great adversity (24.12f). In some cases, self-denial calls for the giving-up of more normal forms of love: e.g. Matthew's insertion of 10.37ff makes it clear that filial love must never be allowed to conflict with the call to discipleship (cf. 4.22*; 8.18–22; 10.21f*, 34ff; 12.46–50*); indeed, those who are able to forsake marriage for the sake of the kingdom are explicitly encouraged to do so (19.12). Matthew's emphasis on self-denial builds, of course, on a similar theme taken over from Mark (16.24f*; 19.27ff*; 20.17ff*, 20ff*; cf. 10.17–22; 24.9f*), and on the Marcan picture of Jesus as the model for such a life-style (16.13 – 17.13*; 26.36–56*; 27.32–54*; cf. 10.24f). Thus, Furnish is at least partially correct in observing that in Matthew as well as Mark, it is not so much love or compassion *per se* that is held up as the ideal, as humble service and cross-bearing modelled after Jesus' own example;[30] but even this does not touch the real heart of the matter.

Significantly, in three of the four *ἀγάπη/ἀγαπᾶν* passages above (5.43ff; 19.16ff; 22.34ff), love is expressed in the form of a commandment and viewed within the framework of the law.[31] (Two *ἔλεος* references are also in the form of citations from Scripture: 9.13; 12.7.) Here the expression of love is part (indeed, the central part) of the moral obligation imposed on the disciple by the demands of the law; i.e. it is a 'must'. The fact that Jesus likewise commands it, and makes it a criterion for gaining entrance to the kingdom, only accentuates the sense of obligation associated with it. As those who live under the authority of the law and the word of Jesus, then, disciples recognize the love commandment as binding upon them.

Twice the expression of love is closely linked to the term *τέλειος* (5.48; 19.21), a term which occurs nowhere else in the synoptics but which appears to be of some importance in Matthew's picture of the Christian life. In both cases, however, the kind of love demanded calls for strong self-denial; and upon closer examination, it becomes evident that it is this self-denial – or more properly, the attitude of submission and obedience underlying such self-denial – that characterizes one who is *τέλειος*, not simply the quality of *ἀγάπη* itself. Thus, though the *τέλειος* reference in 5.48 nicely caps the immediately preceding demand for love of one's enemies (5.43ff), it more properly functions as a summary of the kind of life characterized by the antitheses as a whole, a culminating expression of the demand for deeper righteousness (5.20)[32] – just as the *τέλειος* reference in 19.21 reaches its climax not merely in the demand for sacrificial acts of charity, but in Jesus' words, 'come, follow me'.[33]

It is important to realize, then, that contrary to popular belief and what is frequently deduced from the evangelist's placing of the golden rule at 7.12,[34] the concept of *Nächstenliebe* in itself is not Matthew's most basic concern, nor does it accurately represent the essence of the Sermon on the Mount.[35] Admittedly, certain of the antitheses do seem to reflect the importance of love (5.21ff, 31ff, 38ff, 43ff); but, as a whole, even they cannot be adequately summarized as an expression of this principle alone, as is so often claimed[36] (cf. 5.27ff, 33ff).

If there is any one term that may be said to summarize the essence of the Sermon, it is not love but *δικαιοσύνη* (5.6, 10, 20; 6.1, 33; cf. 3.15; 21.32),[37] of which love is but one aspect (albeit a very important one).[38] The Sermon is not a discourse on love but a description of the attitude and behaviour that characterize a life of deeper righteousness. Those who claim that love represents the totality or essence of this deeper righteousness,[39] or the whole of the law itself,[40] fail to realize that δικαιοσύνη in Matthew's Gospel centres on the broader and more fundamental themes of submission and radical obedience to the will of God (as expressed in the law and the teachings of Jesus), and that it is these themes that lie at the real heart of the Sermon, not love.[41] This is why the virtues of humility and self-abnegation play such an important part in the beatitudes, the antitheses, and the acts of piety (cf. 11.28ff; 18.4).[42] In every case the antitheses are better understood as examples of radical submission and obedience to God's will than as simple expressions of love for others, as they appear to be on the surface.[43] Whether the issue is name-calling (5.21f), broken relationships (5.23ff), lust (5.27ff), divorce (5.31f; cf. 19.9), injustice (5.38ff), or the needy (5.42), a careful reading of the text reveals that in each case the motivating consideration is not so much an altruistic concern for the welfare of others as the demand for radical compliance with the will of God – reinforced by the threat of consequences for noncompliance (cf. 7.13f); the fundamental focus is on one's relationship to *God*, not others. Even the injunction to love one's enemies and pray for one's persecutors (5.43ff) reflects this perspective; for as Moffatt observes, Matthew's primary concern is not with the needs of the persecutors, but with the attitude of those persecuted.[44] The immediately following passage on almsgiving (6.1–4) manifests precisely the same orientation: it is not the needs of the recipients that are emphasized – or even the importance of caring for such needs – but the attitude of the giver as he stands before God; and the same could be said for other passages as well (e.g. 7.1ff).

In the Sermon on the Mount, then, the expression of love appears to be motivated at least as much by a sense of living under the demand of God as by any sense of altruism or affection. (Cf. what is said about forgiveness and not offending one's 'brothers' in 18.6–10, 21–35.) From this perspective, it is not surprising that Matthew's formulation of the golden rule and the two great commandments roots love in law (7.12; 22.34–40; cf. 19.19*b*); here the expression of charity and compassion is both shaped by and interpreted within the framework of the law and the more basic demand for δικαιοσύνη. For Matthew, therefore, the second great commandment is properly understood only when viewed within the context of the more fundamental demand of the first (22.37–9), with love for God expressed primarily in terms of obedience (cf. 4.1–11).

This may help us to understand what lies behind the apparent inconsistency in the Gospel between Jesus' teaching on loving one's enemies (5.43ff) and the attitude expressed toward the Pharisees, who are castigated as a 'brood of vipers' (3.7), '[children] of hell' (23.15), and 'blind fools' (23.17) – the latter seemingly quite in contradiction with the spirit of 5.22.[45] It may be that, having rejected and condemned Jesus, they are viewed as *ipso facto* having made themselves the enemies of God[46] – in which case the commandment to love God might possibly be interpreted as precluding the possibility of loving God's enemies. Or it may be that the evangelist regards the whole question of the interpretation and practice of the law to be of such supreme importance that severe rebuke of the Pharisees and their 'leaven' (16.11f) is felt to be a more appropriate expression of love for God than any more moderate approach. In either case, the sharpness of his words could conceivably be rationalized in terms of the absolute priority to be given to 'the great and first commandment'. Windisch suggests, alternatively, that Matthew may view Jesus' Messianic authority to be such that it simply places him outside the normal strictures governing others, i.e. that he has a right to pronounce judgement upon the enemies of God in a way that others do not;[47] but this fails to take adequate account of the extent to which Matthew himself sharpens the invective, and therefore implicitly endorses it. In any case, however, while such explanations may help us to understand how the evangelist might rationalize the sense of contradiction, they do little to eliminate the contradiction itself. For when all is said and done, there remains a basic inconsistency in Matthew's presentation between 5.43ff and the attitude shown in the Gospel to the Pharisees; at this point Matthew's Jesus himself could perhaps be viewed as guilty of the charge he levels at those who 'preach, but do not practise' (23.3). And to the extent such invective betrays the attitude of Matthew himself, he fails to measure up to his own convictions of Jesus' ideals.[48]

In summary, then, we may say that Matthew views love within the framework of the law. Of all the ethical commandments in the law, the love commandment is the most important, and epitomizes the rest; as such it functions as the major criterion for interpreting and applying the law. But within the context of the law, the expression of love must be understood essentially as an obligation, a matter of obedience; and it must be interpreted in the light of the more basic demand for righteousness (5.20). In this Gospel, then, love is a manifestation of the self-renouncing behaviour that characterizes the life of the disciple who desires to be truly good and to do what is 'right';[49] i.e. it is concerned as much with fulfilling the demands of God as with meeting the needs of others. Hence it relates closely to loving God, and is not seen as simple altruism.

## 2. *Paul*

### 2.1 The Centrality of Ἀγάπη

The centrality of love (especially ἀγάπη) in Paul's writings has been well established, and is documented in virtually every major work on Pauline theology and ethics.[50] To summarize briefly, ἀγάπη, for Paul, is the greatest of the Christian 'virtues', the most important ethical trait of the Christian life. Of greater value than the more popularly desired χαρίσματα such as tongues, prophecy, knowledge, and faith (1 Cor. 8.1; 12.31 – 13.2; 13.8, 13),[51] it is the moral quality with which believers are to clothe themselves above all else (Col. 3.12, 14; cf. 1 Thess. 5.8), and is listed first in Paul's 'fruit of the Spirit' (Gal. 5.22). Viewed as both summing up and 'fulfilling' the ethical demands of the law (Rom. 13.8–10; Gal. 5.14; cf. 5.23*b*; Lev. 19.18), love is the one unending debt that believers owe to others (Rom. 13.8) – it is the new 'law of Christ' (Gal. 6.2); and as such, it has direct bearing on one's welfare in the Judgement (Phil. 1.9f; 1 Thess. 3.12f; cf. 4.6–10). Paul's whole understanding of ethical righteousness now seems to be dominated by the concept of love.[52]

### 2.2 The Nature of Love

The frequency with which the terms πίστις and ἀγάπη occur in conjunction would suggest that together they represent the epitome of Paul's theological and ethical concerns (cf. Col. 1.28 – 2.5).[53] The fact that the initial thanksgiving sections of four of his letters begin with a reference to the faith and love of those to whom he writes (Col. 1.4; 1 Thess. 1.3; cf. 3.6; 2 Thess. 1.3; Phm. 4f)[54] attests their importance in his thinking. The pattern is so uniform, in fact, that the absence of such a reference in the other letters is noteworthy; indeed, its omission in the letters to the Corinthians and the Galatians probably reflects his problems with these churches.[55] It is not insignificant, then, that Paul's final summary exhortation in 1 Corinthians mentions these two elements specifically (16.13f), and that in contrast to Galatian concern over the question of the law he emphasizes that what really counts is πίστις δι' ἀγάπης ἐνεργουμένη (5.6)[56] – a statement that perhaps comes closer than any other to summarizing his view of the Christian life.[57]

The frequent conjunction of these two terms suggests that there is a definite relation in Paul's mind between love and δικαιοσύνη, as the above reference to 'faith working through love' implies. As the essence of the moral dimension of the law (Rom. 13.8–10; Gal. 5.14), love epitomizes the ethical outworking of the δικαιοσύνη which comes through faith.[58]

Love does not function independently of faith, but as a necessary concomitant of it – its ethical correlate.[59] Just as faith spells the 'end' of the law (τέλος νόμου) in a theological sense (Rom. 10.4), so love becomes the 'fulfilling' of the law (πλήρωμα νόμου) in an ethical sense (Rom. 13.10); the two function together as a statement of that which essentially replaces the law in Paul's thinking (Gal. 5.6). Here we observe the *theological* dimension of love.

Love is possible only because faith in Christ introduces the believer into a wholly new way of life, governed at its core no longer by his own corrupt desires but by the Spirit of God. And here we encounter the *eschatological* dimension of love in Paul's ethics: as the ἀρραβών of the new aeon (2 Cor. 1.22; 5.5; cf. 1 Cor. 10.11), the Spirit effects the power of the new age in the believer's life here and now, making a form of eschatological existence actually possible in the present.[60] Thus, freed from the enslaving powers of sin and the law, the believer is enabled to produce true 'fruit' for God (Rom. 7.4; cf. Col. 1.6), the καρπὸς δικαιοσύνης (Phil. 1.9ff)[61] – which for Paul is always 'the fruit of the Spirit'; and the first and most important element of this is love (Gal. 5.22;[62] cf. Rom. 15.30; Phil. 2.1f; Col. 1.8).[63] For the apostle, then, love is never merely a self-generated social virtue, but the result of a transformed life filled with the Spirit, which pours God's own love into the human heart (Rom. 5.5; cf. Gal. 4.6f). The absence of love therefore implicitly calls into question the presence of the Spirit in one's life, and hence one's whole relationship to God (cf. Rom. 8.1–14). The fact that his injunctions to love are frequently voiced in the form of a prayer (Phil. 1.9ff; 1 Thess. 3.12; cf. Col. 1.8ff; 2 Thess. 3.5) is simply in keeping with his basic conviction that ἀγάπη (and indeed everything good) derives ultimately from God himself (cf. 2 Cor. 8.16; 1 Thess. 4.9).

There is also a strong *Christological* dimension to the Pauline view of love. It derives fundamentally neither from Jesus' teachings nor from the nature of his earthly life and ministry,[64] but from a theology of the cross that views Christ's death as the supreme expression of God's own love (Rom. 5.8; 8.31–9; cf. 2 Thess. 2.16).[65] Christian love, then, is but the appropriate ethical response to a theology grounded at its core in the awareness of divine love in Christ.[66] (Note the focus of the *imitatio Christi* in Rom. 15.2f, 7; 1 Cor. 11.1; 2 Cor. 8.8f; cf. Gal. 2.20; Phil. 2.5–8; Col. 3.12–14.) It is significant in this regard that Paul nowhere emphasizes a reciprocal love for God (a concept he mentions only infrequently[67]) or Christ; the focus throughout is on God's love (or Christ's) 'for us', and the response is portrayed primarily in terms of loving others.[68] Because both theology and ethics are so fundamentally rooted in the conviction of God's love in Christ, it is of crucial importance to Paul that believers should have the clearest awareness and deepest possible appreciation of it (cf. 2 Thess. 3.5[69]); indeed, the strong sense of Christ's own love is a prime driving force in Paul's own life and ministry (2 Cor. 5.14f;[70] cf. Gal. 2.20).

There is also a major *ecclesiological* dimension to love in Paul's writings; for when a person is baptized into Christ, he is baptized into 'one body' (1 Cor. 12.12ff), and thus brought into a fellowship of *ἀγάπη* (Col. 3.12–14) or *φιλαδελφία* (Rom. 12.10; 1 Thess. 4.9).[71] Though it cannot be maintained that the expression of love in his letters has only the Christian community in view (Rom. 12.14, 17–21; Gal. 6.10; 1 Thess. 3.12; 5.15), the Christian community is certainly the primary focus (cf. Rom. 12.13; Col. 1.4; 1 Thess. 5.15; 2 Thess. 1.3; Phm. 4f).[72] Because Paul's predominant concern is always the welfare of the Body of Christ, the expression of love within the community is a matter of supreme importance; it is that which knits the members of the Body together in 'perfect harmony' (Col. 2.2, 19; 3.14). His repeated emphasis on love and unity[73] reflects the importance of this matter to him – as does his repeated caution against anything disruptive.[74] As 'members one of another' (Rom. 12.5), Christians are to care for one another (1 Cor. 12.25f; cf. Phm. 7) and to be concerned with building one another up (1 Cor. 8.1; 14.3–5, 12, 17, 26; Rom. 14.19; 15.2; Phil. 2.1–4; 1 Thess. 5.11). The fact that Paul's classic chapter on love (1 Cor. 13) occurs in the midst of his discussion of the use of gifts for the edification of the Church (1 Cor. 12, 14), is itself a significant indication of the ecclesiological orientation of love in his thinking.[75] For Paul, it is always the community and not simply the individual believer that is important.[76]

That the Christian is to live not for himself but for others, is a theme emphasized by the apostle at several points (Rom. 15.1f; 1 Cor. 10.23f, 31f; Phil. 2.4ff) and spelled out in detail in his description of love in 1 Cor. 13.4–7.[77] Jesus (Rom. 15.2f; 2 Cor. 8.8f; Gal. 2.20; Phil. 2.5ff), Timothy (Phil. 2.19ff), and especially Paul himself (Rom. 9.3; 1 Cor. 9.19ff; 10.33; cf. 11.1; 2 Cor. 1.6; 4.5; 13.9; Phil. 1.23ff; 2.17; Col. 1.24ff; 1 Thess. 2.9ff; and implicitly throughout his writings) are all set forth as models for such a way of life. Paul's concept of love, then, includes a strong element of self-abnegation motivated by concern for what is genuinely best for others (Rom. 14.13, 15, 20f; 1 Cor. 8.9–13; 10.23–33; Gal. 5.13);[78] at this point it is shaped by his understanding of the love of Christ in which it is grounded (cf. Rom. 14.15; 1 Cor. 8.11). This is what Furnish has in mind when he writes: 'For Paul love's character is determined by theological [Christological], not humanitarian considerations.'[79] The nature and role of love in Paul's ethical thinking, therefore, is shaped by a complex of theological, Christological, eschatological and ecclesiological factors.[80]

There is one further point to note, which is rarely mentioned: love in Paul's thought is not simply a matter of service or doing good, or of showing mercy to those in need (cf. 1 Cor. 13.3: 'If I give away all I have ... but have not love...'); it must also include a sense of genuine care and compassion, and brotherly affection. Love is not just a matter of *doing*, it is also a matter of *being*.[81] The importance of this aspect is seen both in his frequent urging of his readers to communicate their affection to one another (for example, with a 'holy kiss';[82] cf. Rom. 12.10; 16.16; 1 Cor. 16.20; 2 Cor. 2.8; 13.12; 1 Thess. 4.9f; 5.26) and in the repeated affirmation of his own affection for them (1 Cor. 16.24; 2 Cor. 2.4; 6.11ff; 7.3; 11.11; 12.15; Phil. 1.7f; 4.1; 1 Thess. 2.8; 3.12; Phm. 9). His frequent use of the terms *ἀγαπητός/ἀγαπητοί* and (to a lesser degree) *ἀδελφοί* expresses the same thing[83] – as do his 'parent'/'father'/'nurse'–'children' terminology (2 Cor. 6.13; 12.14f; 1 Thess. 2.7, 11).[84] and certain references to his fervent desire to see them (e.g. 1 Thess. 2.17f; 3.1, 10; cf. Phil. 2.19, 24, 25). Galatians stands apart as the one letter in which his expression of affection remains somewhat cool (there is no *ἀγαπητός/ἀγαπητοί* terminology, no expression of joy or thanksgiving, and no final greetings);[85] but this simply reflects the seriousness with which he takes the Galatians' theological deviancy. (He still addresses them as *ἀδελφοί* and *τέκνα*, and the genuineness of his concern for their return to the gospel is implicit throughout; cf. 4.16–20.) Parts of 2 Corinthians, on the other hand, are permeated by an almost desperate attempt to convince his readers of the sincerity of his care and affection for them, in an effort to regain their confidence (e.g. 2 Cor. 2.4; 6.11–13; 7.3; 11.11; 12.15; cf. also 1.6, 24; 4.5, 15; 5.13; 7.6ff; 8.16; 10.8; 11.2f, 8f, 28; 12.14f, 19; 13.7, 9f); hence the repeated mention of his confidence and pride in them, and of the joy they bring to him (1.14; 7.4, 14, 16; 8.7, 22, 24; 9.3; cf. Phil. 4.1; 1 Thess. 2.19f; 3.9). Here, perhaps as much as anywhere in Paul's writings, we sense the keenness of his desire that the churches know his care and affection for them; certainly he seems to have derived no little comfort and encouragement from the knowledge of their love for him (2 Cor. 7.6f; 8.7; cf. Gal. 4.14f; Phil. 4.10; 1 Thess. 3.6ff).[86] The extent to which this particular emphasis reflects Paul's own psychological needs for acceptance and recognition is difficult to assess (cf. however Gal. 1.10; 1 Thess. 2.4–6); but the expression of his care is certainly linked in many places (explicitly or implicitly) to genuine theological concerns (cf. 2 Cor. 13.5).[87] In general, then, when Paul speaks of love, he is thinking not only of practical acts of charity (as in 2 Cor. 8.8, 24; 1 Thess. 1.3; cf. Gal. 5.6) but also of the heartfelt expression of care and affection (cf. 1 Cor. 4.21) – both of which are of crucial importance to him.

### 2.3 The Limits of Love

It remains only to comment on the question of Paul's consistency in carrying through the implications of his own teachings. Furnish, for example, has raised the question with regard to the attitude expressed in 2 Thess. 1.5ff, in which he sees 'a certain vindictive aspect not typical of the apostle';[88] but the attitude expressed here is little different from that found in 1 Thess. 2.16 (cf. Rom. 1.18–3.20) – and both passages must be understood in light of the Jewish opposition being encountered by the Thessalonian Christians. Here Paul's overriding concern is for the spiritual welfare of the young church in their conflict with the unbelieving community. With regard to heaping 'burning coals' on the head of one's enemy (Rom. 12.20), though the precise meaning of the idiom remains obscure,[89] the immediately following context (12.21) certainly suggests that it need not be interpreted as contradicting the spirit of the previous injunction to bless (and not curse) one's persecutors (Rom. 12.14; cf. verses 18–20; 1 Cor. 4.12f; 1 Thess. 5.15). Whether the same can be said of the harsh words spoken against those who are upsetting the Galatians, however (Gal. 1.8f;[90] cf. 5.12; Phil. 3.2), is much more doubtful. When the gospel of God's grace is at stake, theological considerations obviously take precedence in Paul's thinking over the love commandment (at least with regard to the troublemakers); here his primary concern is to defend the truth of the gospel for the sake of the *Church* (cf. Gal. 2.5). (The fact that the love commandment comes immediately on the heels of such a statement as Gal. 5.12 shows that the expression of love is envisaged primarily within the context of the Christian community.) But one could go further and ask whether the general tone of the Galatian letter as a whole[91] – and of 2 Cor. 10–13 as well – does not in itself violate some of the principles he lays down elsewhere (e.g. Rom. 12.10, 18; 1 Cor. 16.14; Gal. 5.22f; Col. 3.12–14). The apostle himself acknowledges that some of his letters had the reputation of being 'weighty and strong' (*βαρεῖαι καὶ ἰσχυραί*: 2 Cor. 10.10), and there is no question but that his sharpness at points reflects very poorly on what he says about the importance of gracious speech in Col. 4.6. However, to acknowledge this is but to recognize that for him, certain basic theological and moral considerations are of such supreme importance that they simply cannot be compromised, and may therefore require tough action and attitudes – especially when they touch the Christian community (cf. Rom. 16.17f; 1 Cor. 5.1ff, 9–13; 1 Thess. 5.14; 2 Thess. 3.6, 10ff); and, in practice, these considerations simply overrule some of the principles he lays down elsewhere regarding the expression of love. In other words, love is not gentleness at any price. Indeed, Paul insists that it is precisely out of genuine concern for the Church that such harsh words and confrontive actions arise (1 Cor. 4.14; 2 Cor. 2.4; 7.8ff; 12.19; 13.9f; Gal. 2.11, 14f; cf. 1 Cor. 5.6; 6.9f; 2 Cor. 5.11; Gal. 5.2–4; Col. 2.4, 8, 16, 20ff). Stretching the point somewhat, in fact, he attempts to rationalize even his 'boasting' (2 Cor. 10–11) – by which he is obviously somewhat embarrassed (11.1, 16–18, 30; 12.1, 6, 11; cf. 1 Cor. 4.7; 13.4; Phil. 2.3) – on this basis (2 Cor. 12.19)! There are clear theological and moral limits, then, both to the validity of some of his statements about love and to his own carrying them out. There are times when love does *not* endure all things (1 Cor. 13.7), and when love *does* insist on its own way (1 Cor. 13.5), even rather harshly – especially when that way is identified with God's way (1 Cor. 14.37f; 2 Thess. 3.14; cf. 2 Cor. 13.3; Gal. 1.1); and when the doctrine of grace is at stake, love is *not* greater than πίστις (1 Cor. 13.13). In Paul's own life, then, it is clear that the expression of love is conditioned by certain theological and moral considerations of even greater importance than love itself, and that love is understood primarily in terms of what is best for the *Christian* community.

### 3. *Comparison of Matthew and Paul*

When it comes to specific moral qualities, both writers emphasize the importance of love especially. Both, for example, have come to a re-interpretation of the law in terms of love (though from different perspectives), and thus to a new understanding of the love commandment itself as the essence of the law. Both also link the concept of love (at least superficially[92]) with the notion of perfection or completeness (Mt. 5.43–8; 19.19–21; Col. 3.14), in a way that suggests it is viewed in some sense as the epitome of the ethical life. It is not surprising, therefore, that both portray it as a criterion for God's judgement (Mt. 25.31–46; cf. 19.16–21; Phil. 1.9ff; 1 Thess. 3.12f), with the expression of love or non-love to Christ's people interpreted as the expression of love or non-love to Christ himself (though Paul restricts himself to the negative side of this: 1 Cor. 8.12).[93]

Both writers also ground their conceptions of love in certain Christological and theological factors. Matthew, for instance, regards love as a prime element in Jesus' own teaching, and it is very possible that Paul does also (cf. the 'law of Christ': Gal. 6.2). Both certainly root their emphasis on love in the example of Jesus' own life, though the particular points on which they focus differ: while Matthew concentrates on Jesus' compassion in healing and his role as suffering servant in a hostile world (perhaps reflecting the evangelist's own *Sitz im Leben*), Paul stresses the love implicit in his incarnation and death from a soteriological point of view. Both, however, point to Jesus as *the* example of suffering, self-giving love. Both writers also root their emphasis on love in the character of God;[94] but again, the particular aspects to which they link it differ. Matthew's injunction to love one's enemies is based on the long-suffering beneficence of the One 'who makes his sun rise on the evil and on the good', and who calls disciples to be τέλειοι as he himself is τέλειος; and in his Gospel, the demand for interpersonal forgiveness is tied to the fact of God's forgiveness, with the ultimate expression of the latter conditional upon the former. Nowhere, however, does he seem to draw ethical implications from the fact of God's gracious, fatherly care for his children,[95] even though he emphasizes the point in other contexts. Paul, on the other hand, firmly grounds his emphasis on love in the fact of God's grace, revealed above all in Christ's death. For him, love (and indeed the whole of the Christian life) is an expression of gratitude for God's grace in Christ. Of the two writers, therefore, it is clearly Paul who has the stronger view of Christ himself as an expression of God's love,[96] and who draws out the ethical implications more explicitly.

The different concepts of love reflect more basic differences in their overall theological perspectives. For Matthew, love is a commandment of the law, a commandment to be obeyed – indeed, the most important of all the moral commandments, the very essence of the law's ethical demands. As such it is also an important hermeneutical principle to employ when confronted with problems in applying the law. The emphasis on love in Jesus' teaching, therefore, is significant precisely because it reveals the centrality of love in the true interpretation of the law, and makes possible a real fulfilment of the law on a deeper level. At the same time, however, it intensifies the rigour of the law's demands. For Matthew, then, love is perceived within the framework of the law; the second commandment finds its meaning within the context of the obedience demanded by the first.

The essential orientation of Paul's ethics, however, is not legal but eschatological;[97] he portrays love not primarily in terms of law, but as the characteristic expression of new life in Christ brought about by the eschatological power of the Spirit. True, he does speak of love as the 'law of Christ', and the moral demands of the law, though summarized in the love commandment, do appear to retain their validity implicitly at the core of his thinking.[98] But unlike Matthew, Paul does not emphasize this aspect, and grounds his appeal instead in more positive factors. Both writers find in Jesus a new basis for a love-oriented ethic; but whereas Matthew appears to find it in Jesus' teaching, which for him gives new meaning to life as viewed from the traditional perspective of law, Paul finds it largely in the grace manifest in Jesus' death, which he sees as making possible a whole new way of life through the power of the Spirit. While the evangelist fits Jesus' emphasis on love into the framework of the past, the apostle integrates it into a wholly new construct linked to the power of the future.

Because the theological perspectives from which the two writers view love differ, the underlying attitudes toward it (and motivations) differ accordingly. Viewed by Matthew within the framework of law and the authority of Jesus, the expression of love is understood fundamentally as a matter of obedience and not as simple altruism; it is part of the deeper righteousness *demanded* of those who would enter the kingdom, of those who would be *τέλειοι*. And because it is subsumed under the more basic category of *δικαιοσύνη*, it reflects the sublimation of self-will and radical submission to God's will that characterize *δικαιοσύνη* in the evangelist's writing – a gentle but determined meekness of spirit that does not seek its own rights, but suffers long and patiently in the persistent doing of good that gains God's approval.[99] In the First Gospel, then, the focus is not so much on love *per se*, as on love as an expression of the attitude and behaviour appropriate to being good and doing good.

The frequent conjunction of faith and love and the role of love in relation to the law suggest that Paul also thinks of love in relation to *δικαιοσύνη*; he too conceives of it in terms of obedience, suffering and self-denial.[100] But while the concepts of obedience and duty lie in the background of his thought, his primary stress is a much more positive one – on love as the natural outflow of eschatological existence in the Spirit, linked to the joy and freedom of the justified state. Thus, while Matthew's view of love reflects a strong element of self-subjugation and (at least in part) an introspective concern for doing what is 'right', Paul stresses the importance of an outgoing love in its own right,[101] and emphasizes that it must be genuine in its expression – a demonstration of sincere care and unfeigned affection for others. His overall orientation is more outward in its focus, and somewhat less centred on the question of 'oughtness' in general – at least with regard to the law (the sense of obligation arises primarily from one's relationship to God in Christ); unlike Matthew, he prefers to motivate love by affective rather than prescriptive means. While both writers, then, are concerned with the attitudes behind charity, their conceptions of what constitutes the proper attitude (at least in its essence) would seem to differ: for Matthew, it is a spirit of radical submission and obedience to the demands of God; for Paul, it is a matter of authentic concern and care for others.[102]

The two writers also focus on somewhat different forms of the expression of love. While Matthew concentrates on acts of *ἔλεος* directed to those in need generally, Paul emphasizes the expression of *ἀγάπη* to the members of the Christian community in particular. Though Paul's ethical concern is not restricted exclusively to the Church (as in John), his is a more Church-oriented view of love than Matthew's;[103] and as H. Montefiore points out, such a difference in the object of love is almost the same as a difference in meaning of the word itself.[104] Paul's more ecclesiologically-oriented perspective is reflected in the prominence he gives to both the edificatory and the affective aspects of love. Keenly aware of the importance of maintaining harmonious relationships both with and within the churches, he knows it is not enough merely to engage in practical deeds of charity (though that too is a necessity); love must be expressed with a sense of genuine care, warmth and affection if it is to be truly *perceived* as love. Not only must love be communicated, it must be felt; not only is it important to love, it is important to *know* that one is loved. The obvious danger of superficiality in such an expression is mitigated by the apostle's emphasis on loving sincerely.[105]

Finally, there also appears to be a distinction between the two writers with regard to their understanding of the source of love. Paul, for his part, is quite explicit: love derives not from oneself, but from the eschatological power of the Spirit within; it is a natural outflow of the divine love poured into the believer's heart. Matthew, on the other hand, makes no mention of any special 'power' behind love, and his Gospel seems simply to presuppose its possibility; here love is basically an obligation to be fulfilled, a commandment to be obeyed – like any other aspect of the law[106] (though, as we shall see in the next chapter, even for this God's help is implicitly available).

Both writers, it would seem, fail to carry through the implications of their own teaching with complete consistency, especially when it comes to dealing with their opponents. At this point, their zeal to uphold the truth of God as they know it, and to denounce what to them is clearly heresy, apparently takes precedence over everything else – including love. Both writers seem to feel that their opponents, by making themselves the antagonists of God's truth in Christ, have *ipso facto* excluded themselves from any claim to receiving the love of God's people – and this in spite of what both say about behaving in a generally loving way to one's enemies.

To be fair, however, it must be acknowledged that neither, strictly speaking, states that one must feel either affection for one's enemies or genuine, heartfelt concern for their welfare (though that would seem to be implied in Mt. 5.44f);[107] what is in focus rather is a response of meekness and non-retaliation, and the returning of good for evil – which is quite a different thing. But in any case, even this does not seem to be the attitude expressed by Matthew and Paul when actually confronting their opponents. It may be concluded, then, that neither lives fully up to his own ideals. Viewed from a different perspective, however, this simply says that neither regards love as the sole norm of ethics or the ultimate value in life, and that, for both, certain crucial theological factors take precedence even over the love commandment – at least in practice, if not in theory; i.e. the expression of love is theologically conditioned. But whether either would recognize this as a point of inconsistency is perhaps another question.

# 5

# INNER FORCES

We come at last to consider briefly what the two writers have to say about the inner sources of ethical motivation and behaviour, and the relationship between these inner dynamics and the writers' overall theologico-ethical perspectives.

## 1. *Matthew*

We note first the absence in Matthew of any developed doctrine of the Spirit as a moral force in the life of the disciple. Though he has twice as many references to the Spirit as Mark (Mt.: 12 Mk.: 6),[1] the majority relate to Christology (1.18, 20; 4.1*; 12.18, 28, 31*, 32) and reflect the Old Testament view of the Spirit as a special endowment of power upon a chosen individual for a divinely appointed mission[2] – in this case, usually upon Jesus as the anointed Messiah. Only three texts suggest a link between the Spirit and the disciple's life; two of them occur in the context of statements about 'baptism' (3.11*; 28.19 – both of which are problematic[3]) and the third (10.19f*) reflects exceptional circumstances that exclude it from being considered as normative for daily life. In any case, none of them makes any specific reference to ethics generally. This absence of any explicit link between ethics and the Spirit and the fact that Matthew deals with ethical matters almost wholly apart from reference to the Spirit may imply that the two remain largely unintegrated in his thinking.

Apart from these rather ambiguous texts relating to the Spirit, the closest that the evangelist comes to the concept of a divine presence in the life of the Christian is in what he says of the ongoing presence of Jesus in the life of the community (18.20; 28.20; cf. 1.23). But this is portrayed more as a presence 'with' the community (*μεθ' ἡμῶν, ἐν μέσῳ αὐτῶν, μεθ' ὑμῶν*) than one 'within' the individual,[4] and more as a promise of general aid (in the form of deliverance, authoritative support and encouragement) than a source of personal moral strength and ethical stimulus.[5] The concept of Jesus' continuing presence with the community is as little explicitly integrated with the evangelist's ethics as his view of the Spirit.[6]

### 1.1 The Nature of the Heart

When Matthew speaks of the inner source of moral attitudes and actions, he speaks not of the Spirit, but of the heart; herein, for him, lie the roots of both good and evil. The nature of a person's behaviour is therefore a measure of what lies in his heart (12.35). The state of one's inner being (or inner 'eye': 6.22f[7]) is, then, a matter of crucial importance, for from it flow the issues of life – and indeed, all of ethics; this is what fundamentally determines a person's outlook and behaviour. The metaphor most commonly used to illustrate this point is that of the tree and its fruit (3.8, 10; 7.16–20; 12.33–5). Though the precise function of the metaphor differs somewhat from reference to reference, in each case it is tied to a strong warning of judgement (3.10; 7.19; 12.31f, 36) directed against those whose lives fail to exhibit truly good 'fruit';[8] implicitly, therefore, it functions also as an ethical stimulus for true disciples to demonstrate by their own 'fruits' the real nature of their own hearts.

As we might expect, it is the Pharisees and scribes who serve as the primary foil for Matthew's emphasis on the heart and inner attitudes. The strong charges of hypocrisy against them centre precisely on this point (15.7f; 22.18; 23.13, 15, 23, 25, 27, 28, 29; cf. 6.2, 5, 16); in their legalistic and egocentric preoccupation with externals, they neglect the more important matters of inner righteousness, integrity and compassion (cf. 23.3f, 23f) – and in neglecting these, they show that the very core of their lives is corrupt. Further, in failing to realize that defilement is fundamentally a matter not of what goes into the mouth but of what comes out of the heart (i.e. a matter not of outward acts but of inward disposition: 15.11, 17–20[9]), they reveal their basic misunderstanding of the demands of the law itself (cf. 7.12; 9.13; 12.7; 23.23).

It is perhaps significant that in the passage dealing with the question of defilement Matthew focuses more specifically than Mark on what comes 'out of the mouth' (cf. Mt. 15.11, 18 with Mk. 7.15, 20),[10] and takes pains to emphasize that it 'proceeds from the heart' (15.18). Precisely the same point is made earlier, again in a passage directed against the Pharisees (12.34f); in this case the Pharisees' words themselves are evidence of the perversity of their hearts, and therefore a valid criterion for their ultimate judgement and condemnation (12.36f). (The seemingly contradictory statement in 23.3 concerns a quite different point – namely, their failure to practise what they preach.)

### 1.2 Inner Goodness

In contrast to Pharisaic concern for what is *outwardly* correct, the Sermon on the Mount stresses the importance of being *inwardly* correct. Characterized by humility, submission and radical obedience to the deepest intent of the law, the correct attitude is defined in the beatitudes (5.1–12) and illustrated especially in the antitheses and the acts of piety (5.21 – 6.18); indeed it underlies the whole of chapters 5–7. The entire Sermon, then, may be viewed as an attempt to spell out the disposition required of the disciple, and the kind of behaviour that truly reflects it; i.e. on the deepest level Matthew is concerned more with inner attitudes than with behaviour *per se*.[11] The kind of *δικαιοσύνη* demanded of a would-be disciple of Jesus is of a deeper level than that practised by the scribes and Pharisees (5.20) because it requires that one should be *δίκαιος* (and, indeed, *τέλειος*) inwardly as well as outwardly, i.e. in both attitude and behaviour. This is why Green speaks of the sixth beatitude ('Blessed are the pure in heart': 5.8) as 'the key beatitude, and crucial to Mt's understanding of the Christian ethic'.[12]

Fundamental to Matthew's conception of human existence, it would seem, is the traditional Jewish dichotomy between good and evil. This may be inferred in part from the relative frequency with which good–evil terminology occurs in his writing (compared, for example, with that of Mark[13]). People are therefore divided according to whether they are good (i.e. righteous) or evil (5.45; 13.41, 43) – and the terminology applies to behaviour and disposition equally (what is true of one will be true of the other: 7.16–19; 12.33–5). The Pharisees and scribes are portrayed as those who think evil (9.4; 22.18), speak evil (9.34*; 12.24, 34f; cf. 5.11), and do evil (cf. 12.34; 21.35–9; 23.13, 34f), because they essentially *are* evil (12.33–5; 23.25–8). Indeed, the whole present generation is said to be evil (12.39, 45; 16.4; cf. 17.17), as are some even of those among the *μαθηταί* (7.22f; 18.32; 24.48ff; 25.26, 30; cf. 22.11–14). The true 'sons of the kingdom', on the other hand, are likened to good soil (13.8*, 23*), good seed (13.24, 27, 37f) and good servants (25.21, 23), and are called to a life of good works (5.16).[14] It is not surprising, then, that Matthew speaks of the Judgement as a time when the 'good' are sorted out from the 'bad', the righteous from the evil (13.24–30, 36–43, 47–50; 25.14–30; cf. verses 31–46).

Thus, what lies at the heart of ethical behaviour in this Gospel is 'an essential inner goodness'[15] – or to use Matthew's favourite term for it, *δικαιοσύνη* (5.20; cf. 3.15; 5.6, 10; 6.1, 33; 21.32).[16] The meaning of this term in Matthew's usage has been discussed at length;[17] suffice it to say that Strecker, Hill and Przybylski have all clearly demonstrated that the word is consistently used by the evangelist in an ethical, and not a forensic–eschatological sense[18] – and this correlates well with his use of the related terms *δίκαιος/δίκαιοι* (9.13; 10.41; 13.17, 49; cf. verses 41, 43; 23.28f, 35; 25.37, 46; 27.19).[19] What is important to realize, however, is that the term *δικαιοσύνη* does not refer simply to correct behaviour or conduct, as is so often stated or implied[20] – i.e. it is not simply something that one 'does' (though this is often the central focus); it includes also the element of inward goodness, so essential to everything else. *Δικαιοσύνη* to Matthew, then, embraces both being and doing; it refers both to a mode of behaviour and to the fundamental inner disposition from which that behaviour derives. It is, as Osborn states it, 'an all-inclusive term for goodness and obedience'.[21]

The crucial question, then, is how the disciple attains to this life of *δικαιοσύνη*. In general, the assumption seems to be that it is basically a matter of submission and obedience: submission to the will of God and radical obedience to the law and Jesus' teachings (5.20–48; cf. 19.21). The question of the possibility of such an existence is not even raised; the potential for obedience is (apparently) simply presupposed – provided, of course, that one is a follower of Jesus' teachings (which define the nature of true righteousness). The underlying assumption appears to be a traditional Jewish one: if God commands something to be done, it must be within the power of humans to do it (cf. Ecclus. 15.15). In this Gospel, then, *δικαιοσύνη* would seem to be a way of life that is simply commanded (cf. 23.26), one to be sought with all diligence (5.6; 6.33[22]); and Christians are to assume full responsibility for its implementation in their lives.

Yet even though the full weight of responsibility is placed squarely on the shoulders of the disciple himself (cf. 11.29f), he is not left alone; for Jesus is always with him (18.20; 28.20; cf. 1.23), ever ready to lend a helping hand. And, as we have seen, the invitation to look to God for all one's needs (6.6–13; 7.7–11; 18.19) presumably applies even to the need for inward goodness and an obedient heart.[23] Thus, even though Matthew's emphasis on demand and obedience results in a Gospel almost totally devoid of explicit reference to God's aid in the moral–ethical realm, there are statements throughout that by extension clearly imply that such help is available for those who truly 'hunger and thirst' for *δικαιοσύνη*. Behind the focus on demand and obedience, then, lie implicit elements of grace that, though rarely emphasized or drawn out, must not be overlooked.

## 2. *Paul*

Paul's experience of Jesus has resulted in[24] an understanding of *δικαιοσύνη* that, in both its forensic and ethical aspects,[25] is rooted at its core in the concept of grace; no matter how we define it, Paul is convinced that the *καρπὸς δικαιοσύνης*[26] comes only through Jesus Christ (Phil. 1.11; cf. Rom. 7.4, 24f; 1 Cor. 1.30). In the ethical realm, it is the Spirit of God in particular that makes moral living possible; for human beings, according to the apostle, simply do not have the capacity for it in themselves (Rom. 3; 7).[27] True goodness, therefore, cannot be attained merely by a determined effort to be good or to obey the law, but only by living in Christ 'according to the Spirit' (Rom. 7.4–6; 8.4ff, 13f; Gal. 5.16–25).[28] Apart from this, even should one find within himself the desire to do what is right, he will only be frustrated by his continual inability actually to do it; for a human by nature is *σάρκινος*, not *πνευματικός*, and is therefore a slave to sin (Rom. 7.14–25).[29] Here the fundamental moral problem is not one of knowing what is right, but of finding the power to do it.

### 2.1 The Role of the Spirit of God

For Paul, therefore, the proclamation of God's grace in Jesus Christ can never be separated from the ethicizing action of the Spirit that must accompany it, if it is to be truly efficacious in the believer's life (cf. Rom. 15.16).[30] The close conjunction of the two in Paul's soteriology may be seen especially in 1 Cor. 6.11 ('you were washed, ... sanctified, ... justified in the name of the Lord Jesus Christ and in the Spirit of our God')[31] and in 2 Thess. 2.13 ('saved, through sanctification by the Spirit and belief in the truth';[32] cf. Rom. 15.30; Gal. 5.5f, and the frequent conjunction of the terms 'faith' and 'love'[33]). Apart from the Spirit, one cannot attain the kingdom at all (1 Cor. 6.9ff; Gal. 5.19ff; cf. 6.8); indeed, apart from the Spirit one cannot have a valid relationship with Christ (Rom. 8.9). Thus, in Paul's thinking, the pronouncement of *δικαιοσύνη* forensically cannot be considered apart from the experience of *δικαιοσύνη* ethically; i.e. the power of *δικαιοσύνη* must be realized in the believer's life[34] – and this is possible only through the work of the Spirit (cf. 2 Cor. 3.8f[35]). At the heart of Pauline ethics, then, lies the concept of the Spirit as the primary driving force behind morality and ethics.[36]

There can be no question that the idea of the divine presence in the life of the believer is of central importance to Paul. Most commonly this is spoken of in terms of the indwelling Spirit (Rom. 5.5; 8.9, 11, 23; 15.16; 1 Cor. 2.12; 6.19; 2 Cor. 1.22; 5.5; Gal. 3.2, 5; 4.6; 1 Thess. 4.8), but occasionally reference is made to God himself (2 Cor. 6.16; cf. 1 Cor. 3.16f;[37] Phil. 4.9) and even to Christ as living within the believer (Rom. 8.10; 2 Cor. 13.3, 5; Gal. 2.20; Col. 1.27; cf. 2 Cor. 4.11; Gal. 4.19; Col. 1.29)[38] – for the Spirit is the very Spirit of God and the Spirit of Christ (Phil. 1.19; cf. Gal. 4.6).[39] Thus, though they never lose their individual identities, there is a considerable degree of free interchange of the terms God, Christ, Lord and Spirit in this context (cf. Rom. 8.9f; Paul can even say, 'the Lord is the Spirit': 2 Cor. 3.17f),[40] which may simply imply that Paul's focus is on the broader concept of the divine presence within. Not every reference to the divine presence, of course, concerns ethics, for the apostle applies the concept to a wide variety of issues;[41] in some cases, it functions as an ethical sanction in itself (1 Cor. 6.13*b*–20; 2 Cor. 6.14 – 7.1; 1 Thess. 4.8; cf. 1 Cor. 3.16f), especially with regard to the problem of sexual immorality. But the significant point is the extent to which the indwelling Spirit provides for Paul a whole new basis and potential for ethical living.

Such a way of life is possible, he argues, because the gift of the Spirit is linked to certain fundamental changes effected by Christ's death and Resurrection, both on a cosmic level and in the life of the individual believer, which free the Christian from the grasp of evil.[42] Released from the enslaving power of *τὰ στοιχεῖα τοῦ κόσμου* (Gal. 4.3, 8f;[43] Col. 2.8, 20; cf. Rom. 8.37ff; 1 Cor. 2.6, 8; 2 Cor. 4.4; Col. 2.15) and the law (Rom. 6.14f; 7.1–4, 6; Gal. 2.19; 5.18), believers are potentially freed from the power of sin itself (Rom. 6.6f, 14, 18, 22; 8.2; cf. 7.14–25).[44] What has transpired is a crucial transfer of believers from the domain of sin to the realm of God's grace (Rom. 6.14; cf. 3.10ff; Col. 1.13) – or in eschatological terms, from the old aeon to the new, in accordance with Paul's understanding of the purpose of Christ's coming (Gal. 1.4: 'to deliver us from the present evil age').[45] It is important to realize, however, that this cannot be viewed as an absolute transfer,[46] for Christians are obviously still susceptible to the influences of evil and the old way of life. The resulting picture of the believer seems to be that of a person living in two different worlds at the same time.[47] It is precisely at this point, however, that we see the significance of the Spirit in Paul's ethics; for it is the Spirit that, as the *ἀρραβών* of the new aeon (2 Cor. 1.22; 5.5; cf. 1 Cor. 10.11), brings its full power into the believer's life, making eschatological existence effectively possible in the present[48] – even though the power of the old aeon continues to exert its influence. But it is only to the extent that the Christian lives 'according to the Spirit' that he actually finds the power to experience such existence, and to live a life of true moral goodness (Rom. 8.4–8, 12ff; Gal. 5.16–25);

for it is only by the Spirit that one is able to 'put to death' the evil inclinations of the body (Rom. 8.13) and to produce true 'fruit' for God (Rom. 7.4–6; Gal. 5.22f; note the distinction between the 'works' of the flesh and the 'fruit' of the Spirit in the latter context). Thus, in Bultmann's words, the new status of the believer in Christ is 'not a magical guarantee against the *possibility* of sin ... but release from the *compulsion* of sin'.[49]

### 2.2 Tensions with Human Nature

The primary human factor that inhibits a life of genuine goodness is the *σάρξ*, which in Paul's view stands in perpetual and irreconcilable conflict with the divine *πνεῦμα* (Gal. 5.17).[50] The believer is never free from the resulting tension, and is therefore faced with the constant question of which authority he will allow to rule his life.[51] If he yields to the controlling power of the *σάρξ* and allows himself to live *κατὰ σάρκα*, evil will soon come to dominate his life (Gal. 5.19–21); and the consequences of this, Paul warns, are fatal (Rom. 6.16, 21, 23; 8.6f, 13), for such a course places one in direct opposition to God (Rom. 8.7f). If, on the other hand, he opens his life to the Spirit of God and chooses to live *κατὰ πνεῦμα*, he is opting for the 'fruit of the Spirit' (love,[52] joy, peace, patience, kindness, goodness, faithfulness, gentleness, self-control)[53] and a life of unlimited potential for *δικαιοσύνη* (even to the point of fulfilling the essential demand of the law: Rom. 8.4;[54] cf. 2 Cor. 3.17; Gal. 5.22f: 'against such there is no law') – and ultimately for life itself (Rom. 8.6, 10f, 13). What makes the latter option difficult, of course, is the essential negation it demands of one's own human nature (Rom. 8.13; cf. 13.14; Gal. 5.24; cf. 1 Cor. 9.26f); but, as Paul goes on to say, it is only those who allow themselves to be governed (NEB: 'moved') by the Spirit who are truly the 'sons of God' (Rom. 8.14; cf. verse 9).[55] Here, then, we seem to have two sharply delineated and mutually exclusive options. In reality, however, the situation in many of the churches is much more mixed, and Paul's actual response much less clear-cut: even within the Christian community he distinguishes between those who are *πνευματικοί* and those who are not (1 Cor. 2.13 – 3.3; Gal. 6.1),[56] and frankly even speaks of some as *σαρκικοί* (1 Cor. 3.1, 3) – and this in spite of the 'holy' status he attributes to them elsewhere (1 Cor. 1.2; 6.11).

Though Paul sees the full power of the new age as now available for ethical living, it is up to the believer whether he will draw upon it or not. As the dynamic behind ethics, the work of the Spirit is portrayed as neither automatic nor irresistible, and certainly not coercive; it is not a relentless moral force asserting its way in a person's life irrespective of his will.[57] Hence, even though Paul's ethics are fundamentally grounded in the concept of grace and thoroughly dependent on the initiating and energizing work of God himself in the human heart (cf. Phil. 1.6; 2.13; 4.13), in no way does this negate or lessen the responsibility of the individual to respond to it;[58] indeed, it is emphasized throughout that the full implementation of God's grace in the believer's life depends on his response to it. The very fact that Paul occasionally states explicitly what he prays for the churches (Col. 1.9ff; 2 Thess. 1.11ff; cf. the invocations in 1 Thess. 3.12; 5.23; 2 Thess. 2.16f; 3.5) attests this.

It is precisely this juxtaposition of divine and human elements in Paul's thinking, reflected in the dual nature of the believer's existence, that gives rise to the indicative–imperative paradox: cf. (*a*) Rom. 6.2ff, 6ff; Col. 2.12; 3.1, 3 – with Rom. 6.11; (*b*) Rom. 6.7, 14, 18, 20, 22; 8.2ff; Gal. 5.24 – with Rom. 6.12ff; 8.12f; Col. 3.5ff; (*c*) Rom. 3.21f; 1 Cor. 6.11; Col. 1.22; 2 Thess. 2.13 – with Rom. 6.13, 19, 22; 2 Cor. 7.1; 1 Thess. 4.2–7; (*d*) 2 Cor. 3.18; 4.16 – with Rom. 12.2; (*e*) Gal. 3.27 – with Rom. 13.14; (*f*) 2 Cor. 5.17; Col. 3.9f – with 1 Cor. 5.6f; Gal. 4.9; (*g*) also Gal. 5.25; Phil. 2.12f; Col. 2.20ff; 1 Thess. 4.9f. There is no need here to spell out the details.[59] It should be noted, however, that this is not simply a failure on Paul's part to reconcile his ethics with the doctrine of justification by faith,[60] but rather a reflection of the inherent complexity of his eschatological thought itself, and the tensions within it due to the realities of the human situation. The powers of the old aeon are conquered, but not destroyed – and certainly not rendered totally ineffective (in either the theological or ethical realm: 1 Cor. 7.5; cf. 2 Cor. 2.11; 4.3f; 11.14f; Gal. 4.9; 2 Thess. 2.9ff);[61] and though the believer is effectively transferred from the dominion of sin to the realm of grace (Rom. 6.14), the human *σάρξ* persists, constantly pulling in the opposite direction. On the one hand, Paul wants to see the person who is in Christ as a *καινὴ κτίσις*, for whom *τὰ ἀρχαῖα* have been superseded by *καινά* (2 Cor. 5.17; cf. Gal. 6.15); yet he is forced by the reality of the situation to acknowledge that this is not fully the case. The human element, then – in spite of the disclaimer in 2 Cor. 5.16 – constantly places a check on the eschatological element in Paul's theology. The power of the Spirit is therefore no guarantee of a sin-free existence,[62] and it is precisely this that renders the imperatives not only valid in Paul's thinking, but indeed necessary. Whereas the indicatives arise out of the new situation in which Paul sees believers to be in Christ, the imperatives reflect the fact that they still have to deal with the realities of the old; the sense of paradox derives from the fact that both obtain simultaneously. And because Paul is unable fully to reconcile the two realities, it remains a genuine paradox.[63] Still, the significant point is the extent to which he builds the imperative on the indicative, and thereby roots his ethics firmly in God's grace.

### 2.3 The Role of the Heart, Mind and Human Spirit

There is no need to reduplicate here the extensive work already done on Paul's anthropological concepts.[64] But since the focus in this chapter is on the inner dynamics of ethics, it is perhaps worth inquiring briefly into the relationship in Paul's thinking between the work of the divine *πνεῦμα* and the human *καρδία*, *νοῦς* and *πνεῦμα* – those elements which constitute a person's essential inner being, the state of which will therefore be assessed on that day when God judges the inner secrets of humans by Jesus Christ (Rom. 2.16; 1 Cor. 4.5).

It is clear that, on the individual level, Paul views the work of the Spirit as taking place primarily in the heart (Rom. 5.5; 8.27; 2 Cor. 1.22; 3.3; Gal. 4.6; cf. 2 Cor. 4.6), and that in line with Jewish prophetic—eschatological hopes, he interprets the results in terms of a transformed or 'circumcised' heart (Rom. 2.29; cf. 2 Cor. 3.3; Jere. 31.31–4).[65] Just as evil reigns in the heart, enslaving and corrupting a person's whole life (cf. Rom. 1.24; 2.5), so the renewing power of the Spirit is focused on the heart, making possible a life of true goodness. Because the state of the heart determines the quality of one's life, it is essential for Paul that the *καρδία* should come under the influence of the Spirit.

However, at the root of all evil lies not only a corrupt heart, but also a corrupt mind (Rom. 1.28ff); hence the *νοῦς*[66] also must experience the transforming power of the new age (Rom. 12.2). For Paul, the renewal of the mind (implicitly, by the Spirit) is a key both to a changed life and to a proper understanding, assessment and doing of *τὸ ἀγαθὸν καὶ εὐάρεστον καὶ τέλειον*, i.e. the will of God (Rom. 12.2; cf. 3.11).[67] Apart from the Spirit, there is no way that one can truly come to know the mind of God, for it is the divine *πνεῦμα* that reveals the thoughts of God to the human *νοῦς* (1 Cor. 1.18 – 2.16; 3.18ff). The close relationship between a Christian's understanding of the divine will and the activity of the Spirit is seen in 1 Cor. 2.6–16 especially, where Paul suggests that those who are truly spiritual[68] have the *νοῦς Χριστοῦ* (1 Cor. 2.16). This does not necessarily imply that *νοῦς Χριστοῦ* is here synonymous with *πνεῦμα Χριστοῦ*[69] (though there is a close link between the two), but rather that the Spirit has the power to effect Christ's perspective – and God's will – in the mind of the believer given over to it,[70] thus making possible a true assessment of all things (1 Cor. 2.15f). Though the immediate context is not related directly to ethics, there are certainly ethical implications inherent.[71] (Cf.

Phil. 2.5, which, at least on one interpretation, calls on the Christian community to let the νοῦς of Christ rule all their relations with one another[72] – though the focus here is on the *imitatio Christi.*) Although the implications are not fully drawn out, here Paul lays a potential basis for Christian ethics in the spiritual renewal of the human νοῦς, which allows all of life to be perceived from Christ's point of view.[73] (Νοῦς itself, however, is never viewed as an energizing force for ethics in the same sense that the divine πνεῦμα is.[74]) Truly ethical living, therefore, demands a spiritual transformation of both heart and mind.[75]

The precise relationship between the divine Spirit and the human spirit in Paul's thinking is not clear, and the fact that his use of the term τὸ πνεῦμα is notoriously ambiguous[76] only obfuscates the picture. There is certainly little support for the idea of a specifically Christian πνεῦμα, distinct both from one's personal πνεῦμα and from the πνεῦμα θεοῦ, as suggested by Stacey.[77] In general, it is clear that the believer's human πνεῦμα is not simply replaced by the divine πνεῦμα, for both retain their separate identities (cf. Rom. 1.9; 8.16; 1 Cor. 5.5; 16.18; Phil. 4.23; 1 Thess. 5.23; Phm. 25);[78] yet 1 Cor. 6.17 would seem to suggest that Paul envisages a certain joining of the two elements (ἕν πνεῦμα; cf. 6.15ff). It may be that he conceives the human πνεῦμα as taken over (absorbed? possessed? dominated?) by the divine πνεῦμα,[79] and thus transformed (cf. Rom. 7.6: ἐν καινότητι πνεύματος) in a manner similar to that of the καρδία and νοῦς; but we cannot be absolutely sure. In any case, the human spirit also has a role to play in moral living, and it too must be 'sanctified', just as the heart and mind (1 Cor. 7.34; cf. 2 Cor. 7.1). There are many references to τὸ πνεῦμα that relate (directly or indirectly) to ethical living (Rom. 2.29; 7.6; 8.2ff, 13; 12.11; 15.30; 1 Cor. 5.3ff; 6.17; Gal. 5.16ff, 22f, 25; Phil. 2.1; Col. 1.8; 2 Thess. 2.13); but again the problem is knowing whether Paul has in mind a renewed human πνεῦμα or the indwelling divine πνεῦμα, and on this point differing commentary opinion may be found for almost every text.

As those elements which constitute the essential inner being of a person, then, the human καρδία, νοῦς and πνεῦμα all play basic and interrelated roles in ethical living.[80] (Although Paul sees it possible for the human πνεῦμα to act independently of the νοῦς in ecstatic worship (1 Cor. 14.14ff) – and yet paradoxically remain under the control of the individual's will (14.32)[81] – there is no indication that the πνεῦμα is ever viewed as acting independently of the νοῦς in ethical matters.) And each must implicitly experience some form of renewal by the Spirit if the 'new person' (Col. 3.10) is to be fully manifest in the believer's life (cf. 2 Cor. 4.16: 'our inner nature is being renewed every day'). But overall, when

Paul thinks of the inner dynamics of ethics, his primary focus is not on a transformed heart, mind, or human spirit, but on the Spirit of God itself as the ultimate agent of change, able to effect the will of God in the believer's life (Rom. 8.26–9; 1 Cor. 2.10–16; 2 Cor. 3.18); this for him is the fundamental source of moral living.

In Paul's view, therefore, the Spirit's role in the believer's life is a comprehensive one: it renews and transforms his inner being (Rom. 2.29; 5.5; 12.2); it enables him to see life from God's perspective (1 Cor. 2.10–16; cf. 2 Cor. 5.16: 'from now on ... we regard no one from a human point of view'; Col. 1.9), and to acknowledge the lordship of Christ (1 Cor. 12.3); by it (presumably) God gives him both the desire and the ability to do what pleases him (Phil. 2.12f); it enables him to conquer sin (Rom. 8.2ff), and to express a life of love and true goodness (Gal. 5.22f; cf. Col. 1.11); it even intercedes on his behalf that he may truly do the will of God, and works to transform him into the likeness of Christ (Rom. 8.26ff; 2 Cor. 3.18). So we see that the Spirit provides a truly comprehensive basis for ethical living – but not a coercive one; for its outworking always depends on the extent to which the believer opens himself to its influence (Rom. 8.13f) and chooses to live *κατὰ πνεῦμα*.

### 2.4 The Question of Specific Guidance

Finally, to what extent (if any) does the Spirit provide guidance for the individual's moral conduct in specific ethical situations? Part of the Spirit's role, as we have seen, is to give understanding of the thoughts of God and the mind of Christ (1 Cor. 2.6–16), and Paul clearly acknowledges that the full knowledge of 'his will' comes only with a certain spiritual wisdom and understanding (Col. 1.9); but there is no evidence that he thinks of this in terms of individual guidance for specific ethical decisions in general. The lone reference that suggests such a possibility (1 Cor. 7.40: *κατὰ τὴν ἐμὴν γνώμην, δοκῶ δὲ κἀγὼ πνεῦμα θεοῦ ἔχειν*) is equivocal in its sense: it may simply imply that, in contrast to the Corinthians' claim that their opinions are backed by the authority of the Spirit, Paul wants to assert that such claims are always 'dangerously exposed to contradiction' and carry no real weight at all, as Barrett suggests;[82] or it may refer to Paul's own spiritual authority as an apostle (cf. 1 Cor. 14.37). Most likely it is an understatement; but if not, *δοκῶ* takes away its forcefulness in any case. Further, in what is probably the most extended and concrete hortatory section in Paul's writing (Rom. 12.1 – 15.13), there are only three isolated references to the work of the Spirit (12.11; 14.17; 15.13); and not one of them refers to the Spirit as the means by which one discerns the precise will of God in specific situations.[83] It may be that such knowledge is possible within the larger context of the Christian fellowship as a whole, through the *χαρίσματα* of wisdom, knowledge, prophecy, discernment, teaching, tongues, interpretation, etc. – all of which apparently function in one way or another to reveal God's will to the members of the community; but if so, there is no explicit mention of it. Generally speaking, Paul seems to regard such gifts as intended primarily for the broader edification of the community as a whole (1 Cor. 14.1ff, 12), rather than as means by which an individual obtains guidance for particular ethical problems; but the possibility of the latter cannot be ruled out.

A number of scholars see in Paul's view of the Spirit a suggestion of more specific guidance.[84] Cullmann, for example, with regard to the concept of *δοκιμάζειν* (cf. Rom. 12.2), asserts: 'the working of the Holy Spirit shows itself chiefly in ... the *capacity of forming the correct Christian ethical judgment at each given moment* ... Certainty of moral judgment in the concrete case is in the last analysis the one great fruit that the Holy Spirit ... produces in the individual man.'[85] Schubert's claim that the believer is enabled by the Spirit 'to know the will of God in every concrete situation' [86] is similar – and both are overstatements. J.D.G. Dunn speaks of 'a spontaneous awareness of what is God's will in the concrete situation and the ethical dilemma', but sees this as the result not so much of the direct impulse of the Spirit at the moment, as of the transformation of the Christian's inner motivations and moral consciousness – a view that certainly comes closer to being truly Pauline; but at the same time he speaks of 'a more inspirational (charismatic) perception, sense or feeling for what is right and appropriate in the given situation'.[87] None of these views, however, does justice to the large number of Pauline imperatives, and the need the apostle obviously feels to provide specific ethical instruction on a wide variety of topics (see 1 Corinthians especially).

Rom. 12.2 seems to be a more accurate reflection of Paul's thinking on this point. Here discernment of the will of God is portrayed not in terms of direct, revelatory impulses of the Spirit in specific situations, but as the outcome of a renewed and transformed *νοῦς*. The Spirit thus functions not so much as a source of specific ethical guidance, as a power that shapes one's understanding and orientation on a deeper level, thereby enabling the believer to see life from a different viewpoint (cf. 1 Cor. 2.16).[88] It does not automatically guarantee the proper response at any given moment, but it shapes the whole perspective from which one views the problem. To the extent a believer's life is ordered *κατὰ πνεῦμα*, therefore, he will be able to respond to particular ethical decisions not out of self-interest but in genuine ἀγάπη, and thus truly do the will of God. In no way, however, does this preclude in Paul's thinking the need for specific moral instruction (cf. Rom. 15.14f; 1 Thess. 4.9f); nor does it necessarily imply that the believer will have all the wisdom he requires in every ethical situation to make the very best choice (cf. 1 Cor. 8.2; 13.9). So with a degree of caution, I conclude that it is unlikely that Paul conceives of the Spirit as a source of the 'spontaneous' knowledge of right and wrong.[89]

Here again, then, we see that Paul's ethics, though rooted in God's grace, in no way negate the individual's responsibility; at the same time, the individual's response cannot be considered apart from the event of God's grace that makes it possible.[90] The two are inextricably linked (cf. Phil. 2.12f): it is an ethic of both grace and demand.

### 3. *Comparison of Matthew and Paul*

Both writers clearly recognize the necessity of dealing with ethical issues on a level deeper than the merely external; i.e. neither is a behaviourist. Both see human actions, whether good or bad, as determined by the quality of one's inner life and attitudes; and both therefore emphasize the importance of being inwardly 'right'. But their conceptions of how this comes about – their understanding of the inner dynamics – would seem to differ considerably.

In Matthew's Gospel, it is the state of one's heart that matters; whether one engages in good or bad behaviour all depends on the nature of one's inner being. At the core of all ethical behaviour, in his thinking, lies an essential inner goodness, without which there can be no truly good living; δικαιοσύνη must be conceived radically, in inward as well as outward terms, if one is to do the will of God from the heart. Paul's focus, however, is on the Spirit that transforms the heart (and the mind as well); for him the divine πνεῦμα is the real dynamic behind morality and ethics. Both writers speak of virtuous living in terms of 'fruit'; but whereas for Matthew it is the fruit of inner goodness (i.e. of a good heart), for Paul it is the fruit of the Spirit. Though both speak of the continuing presence of Christ in the community, Matthew's writing reflects no well-developed doctrine of the divine presence within the individual believer, as Paul's does;[91] nor does it explore the ethical implications of the concept. For Paul, however, the Spirit provides a whole new basis and potential for ethical living (and indeed for the entire Christian life), on a truly comprehensive scale.

Paul certainly appears more concerned than Matthew with the question of how one finds the power to live a life of moral goodness. Matthew, for his part, does not even raise the question, but in good Jewish fashion seems simply to presuppose its possibility – at least for those who genuinely want to obey Jesus' teachings. Paul, however, is convinced that humans in themselves lack the capability to do it,[92] and argues that such a life is possible only through the transforming power of the Spirit; for him, therefore, everything depends on the extent to which believers open their lives to spiritual renewal and choose to live not *κατὰ σάρκα* but *κατὰ πνεῦμα*. Matthew makes no mention at all of an inner transformation by the Spirit as a prerequisite for ethical living.[93]

Both are clearly aware of the need for divine aid, but it is Paul that emphasizes the fact and draws out its ethical implications. Neither, however, is a thoroughgoing determinist; i.e. neither views ethical living as simply 'spontaneous' or automatic[94] (as is evident from their parenesis). The same is true with regard to the question of knowing God's will in specific moral situations: neither implies the Christian is free from making ethical decisions – though Paul suggests that such decisions are made with a mind renewed and transformed by the Spirit (which has the power to effect Christ's own understanding and viewpoint in the believer), while Matthew would see them informed by Jesus' love-centred interpretation of the law. Elements of both grace and demand are present, therefore, in the writing of both; the difference lies in their emphasis. While Matthew stresses the demand for ethical goodness, Paul focuses on the grace that makes it actually possible. Of the two, there can be no doubt that it is Paul who has the stronger and more comprehensive view of the Christian life as one energized at its core by the working of God.

In general, Matthew has a much simpler approach than Paul: in his Gospel, it all boils down to an attitude of submission and obedience – submission to the will of God and obedience to the law and the teachings of Jesus; but it must be radical submission and obedience, and he emphasizes this to a much greater degree than Paul. Paul, interpreting the gift of the Spirit from an eschatological perspective, is much more interested in the whole range of theologico-ethical dynamics (both on a cosmic scale and in the life of the individual believer) that make eschatological existence (and therefore a life of true goodness) now effectively possible. As a result, his is a more complex formulation. Presenting a more radical view of sin, it offers a more radical answer to the problem of sin – and the possibility of genuine liberation from it. However, the very complexity of Paul's view in itself reflects something of the difficulty he encounters in attempting to integrate the various elements into a coherent whole (note the indicative–imperative paradox especially); the reality of the human situation constantly reasserts itself, placing a check on all claims to eschatological existence. As a result, Paul is caught in somewhat of a dilemma – and this is reflected in his dualistic view of the believer as a person living in two different worlds simultaneously, torn between the opposing pulls of two different authorities (*πνεῦμα/σάρξ*)[95] and therefore capable of manifesting two quite different natures. At this point, the simplicity of Matthew's Gospel has a certain attractiveness about it. And yet we must acknowledge that the more complex formulation of Paul, with all its duality and tensions, is not an inaccurate depiction of the struggles and ambivalence that characterize the actual life experience of many Christians.

## CONCLUSION

### *Brief Summary*

In this study I have tried to analyse the basic factors underlying the ethics of Matthew and Paul, to show how these relate to one another and to their theological views more generally, and to compare their perspectives. Focusing on motivational considerations has proved to be a useful way of getting at the underlying structure of their ethical thought. We have found that though there is a fundamental difference of perspective between the two, the contrast is not as simple as it appears at first sight; and I have accordingly attempted to give it more careful expression than it commonly receives,[1] with attention being given to implicit as well as explicit elements.

Generally speaking, the various aspects of the two writers' ethics fit together into coherent wholes, and are clearly integrated with their total theological perspectives. Matthew's emphases on the related themes of obedience, righteousness and judgement reflect a moral system based on law as the fundamental premiss of life – though the primary focus has now shifted to the teachings of Jesus as Lord; the essential orientation in any case is one of submission to authority. The structure of Paul's ethics is much more complex; but the core of it is clearly rooted in the central theological conviction of God's grace in Christ, which dominates Paul's whole view of life. Eschatological existence in the Spirit is for him both a result of and response to that grace.

The two viewpoints may not be contrasted, however, in terms of a simple dichotomy of law and grace; for as we have seen, the actual situation is much more complex, with elements of both law and grace being found in each of the writers. Thus, Matthew also has a doctrine of grace – but not in the thoroughgoing Pauline sense; for it is neither as explicitly emphasized nor as fully developed as that of Paul, and its precise relationship to ethics is much less clearly worked out. But Matthew's primary concern is obviously elsewhere. So it is a difference of focus and emphasis as much as of basic perspective; and it is this basic difference of focus that, more than any other single factor, gives each his distinctive quality.

As a result, their writings reflect somewhat different views of the essential nature of the Christian life. Matthew portrays the life of discipleship as one of submission and radical obedience to the will of God (as expressed in the law and interpreted by the life and teachings of Jesus); it is a very demanding life, governed by the dictates of authority – though the load is lightened by Jesus' presence, and still regarded as easier than the burden of Pharisaic legalism. Paul also depicts the Christian life in terms of submission to Jesus as Lord, but his general emphasis is not so much on the demand for obedience, as on living in committed and grateful response to God's grace in Christ – and on the whole new possibility this opens up for truly ethical living by the power of the Spirit. The total impression is a much more positive one.

Both are concerned to effect a radical form of ethical righteousness on a level deeper than the merely external; but their conceptions of how this comes about appear to differ markedly. For Matthew it would seem to be essentially a matter of obedience: the proper inner disposition – an attitude of self-abnegation, absolute commitment to the will of God and compassion and kindness to others – is in his Gospel the result, above all, of submission and obedience to the law of God and the authority of Jesus. For Paul, however, it is a matter of the liberating work of the Spirit within the heart, the power of the new age that frees believers from the enslaving dominance of sin and effects true goodness in their lives, thereby making a form of eschatological existence effectively possible in the present. In his view, radical righteousness is the result not of determined effort, but of being filled with the Spirit and choosing to live not *κατὰ σάρκα* but *κατὰ πνεῦμα*; for him, it is the Spirit that is the primary driving force behind morality and ethics. Compared with Matthew, he appears to have a much stronger conception of grace as a presence and power active within the Christian's life. Both writers are convinced that ethical living on the very highest plane is indeed possible for Christians (Mt. 5.48; Rom. 8.2ff); but whereas Matthew portrays it as the result of heightened obedience to the ultimate demands of the law, Paul insists that it is the result rather of being freed from the law to live by the Spirit. Matthew would bind Christians more tightly to the law, Paul would free them from it.

Thus, while Matthew emphasizes the imperative, Paul focuses rather on the indicative from which the imperative derives. Both see a close relationship between theology and ethics, but Paul obviously feels a greater need to work out the details of how the one provides a basis for the other. (In part, he is pressed to do so by the position he adopts with regard to the law.) The result, in any case, is that while Matthew focuses directly on ethics (i.e. on what one must do), Paul's primary interest lies in the theological dynamics behind ethics (i.e. in what God has done). The one stresses human responsibility, the other God's grace; but it is not an absolute dichotomy.

### *Factors Underlying Their Differences*

But suppose now that we press the matter one stage further, and inquire into the factors that may underlie these differences of perspective and emphasis. Here we must recognize that there is no one single parameter (or simple *Sitz im Leben* statement) that by itself will ever be able to explain all the differences, for many different factors are involved.[2]

There is a *social* factor, for instance: the different outlooks of the two writers would seem to reflect the fact that they live and work among two quite different communities, which themselves have undoubtedly had some shaping influence on their perspectives. Thus, as has been noted throughout, Matthew's viewpoint reflects the more traditional outlook of a predominantly Jewish–Christian community (albeit one that has broken with the synagogue and stands in favour of the gentile mission[3]) – and no argument to the contrary has yet disproved this thesis;[4] while Paul's more radical reformulation, representing as it does a much sharper break with the traditional Jewish viewpoint, fits his sense of being called to the pagan communities of the Hellenistic world,[5] and reflects the need to work out an entirely new basis for ethics accordingly. (Precisely how much his thought is influenced by early Hellenistic–Christian understanding and formulations is difficult to ascertain.)

There is also a *polemical* factor, related to the *Sitz im Leben*: the different emphases of the two writers undoubtedly reflect the different problems that engage their attention. A number of the key Matthean motifs, for example, may be explained by the hypothesis that the evangelist is concerned with two basic problems: that of Pharisaic–Jewish opposition to his community from the outside, and that of the threat of moral laxity on the inside. This would account for his emphasis not only on the validity of the law, but also on the demand for radical obedience and a deeper level of δικαιοσύνη, reinforced by the threat of judgement – rather than on the assurance of grace and eschatological security. Paul's emphasis on an ethic of freedom grounded in grace, on the other hand, is in certain cases clearly attributable (at least in part) to his polemic against the Judaizers – as are some of his more extreme statements about the law. The detail in which he works out the ethical implications of Christ's death and the believer's status in Christ may in turn reflect the charge of antinomianism against him, or at least the threat of it in the Christian communities to whom he writes[6] – perhaps as a result of the extremes to which his own teachings are being carried. In general, the differing emphases in their writings reflect the differing situations and needs of the communities to whom they write – or at least their perceptions of them.

There is also a *motivational* factor: the differing emphases of the two writers would seem to express different understandings of how ethical behaviour is most effectively inspired. Matthew's focus on the imperative, for example, may well reflect his conviction that ethics are essentially a matter of obedience; the fact that they are typically reinforced (implicitly if not explicitly, within the framework of the law) by the promise of reward or the threat of judgement (both in an eschatological sense) further suggests that, in his view, a strong, external incentive is often needed to make people do what is right. The evangelist's heavy reliance on the latter especially would incline me to believe that he sees the threat of judgement as the most effective means to this end, particularly if the problem is one of moral laxity. Paul, however, distinctly shies away from motivating ethics by the mere use of compensatory sanctions. In his thinking, reliance on external compulsion and the use of incentives is an inadequate basis for the motivation of ethical behaviour; what is needed instead is an enlarged awareness of God's grace in Christ, especially as it touches the individual believer's life. For Paul, authentic goodness arises out of the heart as a free response to God's grace, not out of a sense of mere duty or external compulsion. Laying down the law has its place when the situation demands it, but demand and threat in themselves cannot effect the quality of goodness ultimately desired. In general, Paul has a much greater appreciation than Matthew of the value of motivating ethics by positive means.

Related to the above is a *psychological* factor: it would seem that the two writers have somewhat different conceptions of human nature. Matthew's consistent emphasis on the demand for obedience seems to reflect (for lack of any explicit assertion to the contrary) the traditional Jewish assumption that, if God commands something to be done, it must be within the power of humans to do it. Paul, however, specifically denies this assumption, and insists rather that it is only by the transforming power of the Spirit that one is enabled to do the will of God. For him, all true righteousness (whether conceived in theological or in moral terms) must be viewed as a gift of grace; anything less will ultimately prove inadequate. Clearly, Paul has a more pessimistic view of the potential (if not the tendency) of human nature itself. But just as his understanding of human weakness and sin is more radical than Matthew's, so is his view of God's grace.

There is also a *Christological* factor, related to their different understandings of the role of Jesus with regard to ethics – or at least their different emphases in this regard. Matthew's primary focus is on Jesus as a teacher, who both authoritatively explicates the demands of the law and commands radical obedience to its ultimate intent. Paul's focus, however, is on Jesus' incarnation and death, which he sees as the supreme expression of God's grace to which believers respond, and that which ultimately makes ethical living possible by bringing in the transforming power of the new age. Both see Jesus as in some sense a model to imitate, but again from quite different perspectives: while Matthew portrays him as a model of *δικαιοσύνη*, Paul points to the example of his self-giving love and service. The fact that the two writers focus on such different aspects of Jesus' life probably reflects not only their different experiences and understandings of him, but also their somewhat different perceptions of what God was doing in him.

But *literary genre* is also a factor; for when all is said and done, we must remember that Matthew, unlike Paul, is writing a Gospel, and therefore works with certain constraints that Paul does not – imposed both by the peculiar nature of the genre and by the tradition of Jesus' life and teachings itself, as it has come down to him. I have made the simple assumption that, by and large, Matthew subscribes to what he writes (irrespective of its derivation) – and the analysis has given me no cause to doubt the validity of that assumption; but this does not imply that the evangelist is any less dependent on the underlying tradition, or that the Gospel necessarily represents the totality of his thinking. This difference in genre, then, and the limits it imposes on Matthew in particular, provides perhaps the single greatest difficulty for any attempt to compare the two writers' thought comprehensively.

Finally, there is the *interpretative* factor: both writers are involved in a process of reinterpretation or reformulation, and certain of their ethical statements reflect tensions inherent in that process and inconsistencies resulting from the lack of total integration of new and old belief systems. Evidence of such phenomena in Matthew's work suggests that the evangelist is attempting to resolve a number of conflicting traditions or viewpoints. For example, he apparently wants to maintain the overall Marcan picture of Jesus, yet feels bound to adjust it to a more Jewish–Christian perspective at the points of sharpest conflict. He wants to insist that the Mosaic law must be upheld in every detail, yet knows that Jesus' life and teaching represent a radical reinterpretation (and in some cases an effective disregarding) of it. Possibly a converted scribe himself, he apparently feels compelled to recognize the authority of the scribal system in matters of legal interpretation generally, yet finds himself called by Jesus to a critical evaluation of the lives and teachings of the scribes themselves. Such tensions would seem to reflect the fact that Matthew belongs simultaneously to two different communities and traditions (Jewish and Christian), the relation between which is only very imperfectly worked out in his thinking; the line between them is not at all sharply delineated, as it is in Paul. Matthew and his community seem to be still struggling to find their way; they are a community in transition.[7] As a serious attempt to portray the significance of Jesus and his ethical teaching from the viewpoint of a Christian standing within the traditional framework of Judaism, then, Matthew's Gospel is an excellent example of the way the Jewish–Christian community tried to integrate the 'new' with the 'old' (in spite of the basic incompatibility of the two implied in 9.16f*).

Paul's much more thoroughgoing reformulation expresses, it would seem, both the creative brilliance of his intellect and the profundity of his thought;[8] yet neither is it without its points of conflict. Believers are considered redeemed from the 'curse' of the law, yet its moral standards remain implicitly valid as a measure for their lives. The freeing power of the new age has come, yet Christians still feel the effects of the old. The many Pauline statements reflecting the indicative–imperative paradox especially, expressing as they do the conflict between the realized and non-realized aspects of the new age, show the tensions between the 'new' and the 'old' in Paul's reformulation. But by any measure, it must be acknowledged that his work represents a truly creative attempt to spell out the significance of God's grace in Christ and its ethical implications in the context of the wider mission of the Church as a whole.

Here, then, are two different views of Jesus and his significance for the Christian life, two examples of how the early Christian community perceived Jesus to provide a new basis for ethical living. From the perspective of the common Jewish background of the two writers, one may be labelled 'conservative', the other 'radical'. As we have seen, their differences of outlook and emphasis cannot be adequately explained in terms of any single parameter, but must be understood as the result of many different factors, of which it is not always possible to determine which particular one is determinative for any given emphasis or viewpoint. In any case, one thing is clear: it is the figure of Jesus that is central for both writers. It is he who has reshaped their whole understanding of life and called them to a critical evaluation of their past; and it is he that provides the key to truly ethical living. The question remains open which of the two builds upon a more accurate understanding of human nature, and which provides a more adequate basis for ethical living. Both, with some justice, can make such a claim;[9] but we cannot enter into that issue here. With regard to the question of their relevance for Christian ethics today, suffice it to say that, in my judgement, both are of value and both are needed;[10] the emphases of the two are complementary, and the Christian community needs to hear at various times both the word of grace and the word of demand. And in the gracious (but paradoxical!) providence of God, both have become part of Christian Scripture, and speak the word of God to those who have ears to hear.

## NOTES

### Introduction

1 Cf. Gardner, p. 99.
2 In this study, the term 'Matthew' (Mt.) designates both the Gospel and its writer, yet presupposes nothing about the actual identity of the latter.
3 See Furnish, *Theology*, pp. 92ff. Herein lies the weakness of Merk's study.
4 So also Ropes, pp. 37, 92f; Farrer, pp. 85f; Goulder, 'Q', pp. 218–34; cf. Drury, *Tradition*, pp. 40f, 82ff, 120ff; 'Midrash', p. 292; Goodspeed, pp. 107f; Butler, pp. 1ff *et passim*. Gardner, p. 104, writes: 'The doctrine that we should make all we can of our extant documents before we make hypotheses about lost earlier ones has always been honoured in theory'; cf. Butler, p. 1; Green, 'Georg Strecker', p. 362.
5 On the possibility of a more direct relation between Mt. and Lk., see Drury, 'Midrash', p. 292; *Tradition*, pp. 120ff; Ropes, p. 93; Goulder, 'Q', pp. 218–34; *Calendar*, p. vii. For a different approach, see Léon-Dufour, pp. 9ff.
6 Cf. Schweizer, *Good News*, p. 14: 'Matthew must not be pictured as a modern scholar, copying Mark precisely and consciously considering every modification. Obviously he is freely recounting the narratives before him ... His rendition of Mark should not be pictured too mechanically.'
7 *Bergpredigt*, p. 101.
8 Cf. Piper, pp. 140f; Bornkamm, 'Authority', p. 44: 'In no instance does he include a saying or group of sayings just because source and tradition provided it. We observe no thoughtless mechanism in his reproduction of traditional material.'
9 *Ethics*, pp. 4f, 54. Houlden emphasizes that a Gospel must be viewed *first* as a witness to the thought of the writer himself.
10 Cf. Smith, p. xii; Stendahl, 'Matthew', p. 769.
11 Cf. Stendahl, 'Matthew', p. 769.
12 See Pesch, *Matthäus*, p. 75.
13 Cf. H.D. Betz, 'Matt 11.28–30', p. 23: 'we must presuppose that in the final redactions of the gospels we are dealing with theologically consistent thought'.
14 Catchpole, pp. 94–6, sees lapses of logic in Matthew's writing.
15 On these, see Moule, 'Commentaries', p. 141; Goulder, *Midrash*, p. 21.
16 So also Dibelius, *Paul*, pp. 7ff; Kümmel, *Introduction, ad loc.*; Campenhausen, *Ecclesiastical Authority*, p. 30.

17 See E.P. Sanders, *Paul*, p. 431; Conzelmann, *Theology*, p. 155.
18 Cf. Campenhausen, *Ecclesiastical Authority*, p. 30; E.P. Sanders' opposing view, *Paul*, pp. 431f, is only valid on the assumption of their non-authenticity.
19 See Hurd's useful discussion in 'Chronology'.
20 So also Kümmel, *Introduction, ad loc.*
21 See Kümmel, *Theology*, p. 139; Jewett, *Terms*, pp. 1ff; Drane, *Paul*, pp. 3 *et passim*; Hurd, *I Corinthians*, pp. 5f; 'Chronology', p. 247; Wire, pp. 6, 10; Stendahl, *Paul*, p. 5; Beker, 'Contingency', pp. 141ff; *Paul*, pp. 23ff; cf. W.D. Davies, 'Paul and Israel', p. 19; Chadwick, pp. 273f.
22 See Stendahl, *Paul*, p. 5; Hurd, *I Corinthians*, p. 5; Beker, 'Contingency', pp. 147f. Thus R.M. Grant, *Historical Introduction*, p. 175, cautions against treating Rom. as normative.
23 For documentation, see esp. E.P. Sanders, *Paul*, p. 432, n. 9, and Hurd, *I Corinthians*, p. 10, n. 2; p. 11, n. 1; cf. Beker, 'Contingency', p. 142; *pace* Perrin, *New Testament*, p. 94. Though not entirely conclusive in itself, it is significant that Paul's letters were written within a relatively narrow time-span at a fairly mature stage in his Christian life.
24 Cf. Merk, p. 246; see further ch. 1, nn. 194, 206; ch. 2, n. 79; ch. 3, n. 103 below.
25 On Gal., see Drane, 'Diversity', pp. 3f, 9ff, and Kümmel, *Introduction*, pp. 301–4; on the problem of Pauline chronology in general, see Hurd, 'Chronology', and Jewett, *Chronology*; cf. Ogg.
26 See E.P. Sanders, *Paul*, pp. 433, 518ff; cf. Kümmel, *Theology*, p. 139.
27 See esp. E.P. Sanders, *Paul*, pp. 434–47; cf. the viewpoints of Kümmel, *Theology*, pp. 141f; Furnish, *Theology*, pp. 114, 141ff, 214; Bultmann, *Theology*, vol. I, p. 191; Käsemann, 'Righteousness', pp. 168ff; Bornkamm, *Paul*, pp. 115ff; Stendahl, *Paul*, pp. 1ff, 7ff.
28 Cf. Gager, pp. 326f.
29 See Merk, pp. 233ff; Wilder's distinction between 'essential' and 'formal' sanctions (*Eschatology and Ethics*, p. 133) is a useful one, but inaccurately applied.
30 C.A.A. Scott (1930; 2nd ed. 1934); Preisker (1933; 3rd ed. 1968); Marshall (1946); Dewar (1949); Lillie (1961); Schnackenburg (1962; ET 1965); Flew (1963); Spicq (1965); Wendland (1970); Schelkle (1970); Houlden (1973); J.T. Sanders (1975).
31 An outstanding example of an earlier analysis that accurately characterized the SM (as *Gehorsamsethik*), and attempted to contrast it with Paul's outlook, is Windisch, *Bergpredigt* (1928; 2nd ed. 1937).
32 See esp. G. Barth, 'Law'; Blair; Strecker, *Weg*; Sand, *Gesetz*; Przybylski.
33 Major works include Kilpatrick; Stendahl, *School*; Hummel; W.D. Davies, *Setting*; Trilling, *Das Wahre Israel*; Pesch, *Matthäus*; Hare; W.G. Thompson; Schweizer, *Gemeinde*; Goulder, *Midrash*; Cope.
34 Ernesti (1868, 3rd ed. 1880); Juncker (1904, 1919); Alexander (1910); Benz (1912); Sommerlath (1923, 2nd ed. 1927); Enslin (1930); Cleland (1954); Furnish (1968); Corriveau (1970); Murphy-O'Connor (1974). For an excellent historical survey of various interpretations of Paul's ethic, see Furnish, *Theology*, pp. 242–79.
35 Zillessen; Dobschütz, 'Motives'; Andrews, 'Motive'; A.A. Thompson; Nieder; Campenhausen, *Begründung*; Grumm; Romaniuk; Merk.

36 Beker, *Paul*, and another important book on Paul, Hooker and Wilson (eds.), *Paul and Paulinism* (see under Wilckens, 'Law'), appeared too late to be incorporated into my study.

37 See Furnish, 'Jesus-Paul Debate'.

38 For brief comparative remarks on the issue, see Bacon; Kilpatrick; Käsemann, 'Sentences'; G. Barth, 'Law'; Stendahl, 'Matthew'; Grundmann, *Matthäus*; Conzelmann, *Theology*; Wendland; Albright–Mann; H. Günther; Ziesler; Osborn; Meier; Dunn, *Unity*; Lehmann-Habeck; H.D. Betz, 'Makarismen'; cf. discussion of relevant passages in recent commentaries. For more extended treatment, see Smith; Joest; Hunter, *Design*; W.D. Davies, 'Matthew, 5, 17–18'; Strecker, *Weg*; 'Makarismen'; Hummel; Stuhlmacher, *Gerechtigkeit*; Bornkamm, 'Risen Lord'; M.P. Brown; Sand, *Gesetz*; Green, *Matthew*; Luz, 'Erfüllung'; B.L. Martin; D. Marguerat; Przybylski.

39 Windisch, *Bergpredigt*, contrasts the *Gehorsamsethik* of the SM with the grace-oriented thought of Paul; McArthur compares their differing viewpoints on the necessity of an inner transformation by the Spirit for ethical living; Hill, *Greek Words*, analyses the difference in the two writers' concepts of δικαιοσύνη; Campenhausen, *Formation*, provides a concise study of their different understandings of the law; Wendland, though slight with regard to Mt., provides a comprehensive analysis of Paul's ethics; Houlden, *Ethics*, attempts to identify the major elements of both writers' ethics, and briefly to describe their overall perspectives; and Furnish, *Love*, critically examines their understanding of love and its relation to the law. See also J.T. Sanders, *Ethics*, who provides a useful analysis of the different nuances of love in the two writers, but focuses primarily on their use of 'holy law'; and E.P. Sanders, *Paul*, who provides a comprehensive comparison of Paul's viewpoint with that of traditional Judaism. See further the comparative studies of H.D. Betz on discipleship and imitation (*Nachfolge*), and Schweizer on the hidden nature of true piety ('Der Jude im Verborgene'). The articles by Dodd ('Matthew and Paul'), Via and Argyle ('M and the Pauline Epistles') pertain less to ethics.

40 W.D. Davies' extensive discussion of the question of law and grace in the two writers (*Setting*) concludes that their perspectives are similar: both see Christ as a lawgiver (a 'new Moses') and the Christian life as a way based on that law, and both portray the imperative as originating in the indicative; see ch. 3, nn. 135, 140, 141 below. Feuillet's comparison, 'Mt V. 17–20', is similar. Goulder (*Midrash, Calendar*) argues that Mt. is heavily influenced by Pauline theology, and sees the evidence for a direct literary link as nothing less than 'massive'. (Many of the parallels cited, however, simply reflect the common Jewish background of the two writers.) See also Sand, 'Gesetzlosigkeit', whose contrast of the writers' understanding of 'lawlessness' appears somewhat forced.

41 Cf. E.D. Hirsch: 'It is of the utmost importance to determine the horizon which defines the author's intention as a whole, for it is only with reference to this horizon, or sense of the whole, that the interpreter may distinguish those implications which are typical and proper components of the meaning from those which are not' (cited by Kee, pp. 1ff); Minear: 'The term remains an empty cipher until we grasp the constellation of ideas within which this idea belonged ... [One] must reconstruct the perspective as a

whole to understand the bearing of any single command' (*Commands*, pp. 22, 27); A. Farrer: 'The pattern of the whole comes first. Every sentence of a book is formulated by the mind which writes the whole' (cited by Neill, p. 263).

**1. Law**

1 See pp. 128, 130f below.

2 Mt. has eight references to *νόμος*, Mk. none at all; the term generally refers to the written Torah (see Gutbrod, p. 1059; Meier, p. 135, n. 24; Banks, *Jesus*, p. 89; Sand, *Gesetz*, p. 207).

3 See Harrington, p. 387, for recent attempts to deal with this complexity.

4 Cf. the following statistics (see also ch. 2, n. 2 below), taken from G. Barth, 'Law', pp. 58f :

| | | | |
|---|---|---|---|
| *δικαιοσύνη* | (Mt: 7 | Mk: 0 | Lk: 1) |
| *κελεύω* | (Mt: 7 | Mk: 0 | Lk: 1) |
| *τηρέω* | (Mt: 6 | Mk: 1 | Lk: 0) |
| *ἀνομία* | (Mt: 4 | Mk: 0 | Lk: 0) |
| *ὑποκριτής* | (Mt: 13 | Mk: 1 | Lk: 3) |
| *φρόνιμος* | (Mt: 7 | Mk: 0 | Lk: 3) |
| *ποιεῖν τὸ θέλημα τοῦ πατρός* | (Mt: 6 | Mk: 1 | Lk: 5) |

5 See e.g. Blair, pp. 117ff; Trilling, *Das Wahre Israel*, pp. 167–86; Hübner, *Gesetz in der synoptischen Tradition*, pp. 15–40; Zumstein, pp. 107–29; and esp. Meier's exhaustive study, pp. 46–124.

6 Cf. Suggs, p. 117. For summaries of different opinions, see G. Barth, 'Law', pp. 67–9; Blair, pp. 117–22; Meier, pp. 73–82; Banks, *Jesus*, pp. 208–13; Hamerton-Kelly, pp. 24f, n. 18; and esp. Ljungmann's study on 5.17ff.

7 So Zahn, Schniewind, Schlatter (as cited by G. Barth, 'Law', p. 68, n. 1); also Esser, 'Law', p. 443; cf. Suggs, p. 117. Contrast Meier, p. 80.

8 So Bächer, Fiebig, Schrenk, Branscomb, Schlatter, Jocz and Percy (as cited by Banks, *Jesus*, p. 208); cf. Jeremias, *Theology*, p. 83.

9 So McNeile, p. 58; Carlston, 'Things', p. 79; Fenton, p. 84; Green, *Matthew*, pp. 36, 65; Campenhausen, *Formation*, pp. 15f; Micklem, p. 43; cf. Hill, *Matthew*, p. 117; see additional references in Banks, *Jesus*, p. 208, n. 1, and G. Barth, 'Law', p. 67, n. 7. Hummel, pp. 49f, 75, interprets it as explication of the original intent of the will of God (cf. 19.8: ἀπ' ἀρχῆς). Several (e.g. Schweizer, *Good News*, p. 202; Hübner, *Gesetz in der synoptischen Tradition*, p. 196; Strecker, *Weg*, pp. 146f; cf. Goulder, *Midrash*, p. 20) interpret *πληρῶσαι* in terms of the love command; but cf. Meier's critique, p. 164.

10 See esp. Meier, pp. 73–82; Banks, 'Matthew 5:17–20', pp. 229ff. This may be understood in either a *heilsgeschichtlich* or ethical sense (see Hamerton-Kelly, pp. 24f, n. 18). Apart from Ljungmann, most who adopt this interpretation opt for the ethical sense: W.D. Davies, *Setting*, pp. 100ff; Perrin, *New Testament*, pp. 174f; cf. Banks, *Jesus*, p. 242; Schweizer, 'Matth. 5, 17–20', p. 400; *Good News*, p. 107.

11 See Carlston, 'Things', p. 80, n. 6; Meier, p. 122 *et passim*. Trilling, *Das*

*Wahre Israel*, p. 175, however, argues that Mt. 'genau zwischen πληροῦν und τελεῖν unterscheidet'.

12 For detailed discussion of Mt.'s phrase 'the law and the prophets', see Meier, pp. 70 ff; Berger, pp. 209–31; Trilling, *Das Wahre Israel*, pp. 172ff; and esp. Sand's detailed study, *Gesetz*; cf. also Gutbrod, p. 1059; Suggs, pp. 118f. Sand argues that for Mt., it is the prophets who supply the decisive key to the proper understanding of the Torah (p. 208; cf. pp. 183–221; Grundmann, *Matthäus*, p. 144); but see Carlston, 'Things', p. 79, n. 4.

13 To make this the prime criterion for exegesis, however, is to adopt a linguistically faulty methodology that takes insufficient account of both the immediate context and idiomatic usage, and ignores the limited size of the data sample.

14 Cf. Banks, 'Matthew 5:17–20', p. 229; see n. 92 below for references to the fulfilment of prophecy.

15 See Eissfeldt, pp. 209ff; cf. Esser, 'Law', p. 443; Bonnard, *Matthieu*, p. 61.

16 So Grundmann, *Matthäus*, p. 145; Blair, pp. 123f; Bonnard, *Matthieu*, p. 61; Trilling, *Das Wahre Israel*, pp. 174–9, 202ff; Dunn, *Unity*, p. 246; McConnell, p. 28; cf. Allen, pp. 45f; Micklem, p. 43; Hill, *Matthew*, p. 117; Feuillet, 'Mt V. 17–20', p. 124; Schweizer, *Good News*, pp. 107f; Gaechter, p. 164; G. Barth, 'Law', pp. 69f. Goulder, *Midrash*, pp. 261f, suggests that Mt.'s ambiguous use of the term in the dual sense of 'deepen' and 'abrogate' serves as a smoke-screen to ease the tension between Mk.'s more liberal tradition and his own thought; but this is unlikely.

17 For detailed discussion, see esp. Meier, pp. 41–124; cf. Grundmann, *Matthäus*, pp. 142ff; Suggs, pp. 116f; Trilling, *Das Wahre Israel*, pp. 167–86; G. Barth, 'Law', pp. 64ff; Hamerton-Kelly, pp. 24ff; Banks, 'Matthew 5:17–20', pp. 226ff; W.D. Davies, 'Matthew, 5, 17–18', pp. 431ff; Carlston, 'Things', p. 79, n. 6; p. 91, n. 1. On 5.18–19 as Jewish–Christian tradition taken over by Mt. that does not, at least in its original strict sense, represent Mt.'s own viewpoint, see Trilling, *Das Wahre Israel*, p. 179; Hübner, *Gesetz in der synoptischen Tradition*, p. 39; Smith, p. 96; Schweizer, 'Matth. 5, 17–20', pp. 400ff; Green, *Matthew*, pp. 80f; Hill, *Matthew*, pp. 117f; Hummel, p. 67 – all of whom suggest that 5.18–19 must be interpreted in the light of the framework (5.17, 20 ± verse 18*c*) within which Matthew has set it; cf. Carlston, 'Things', pp. 79–83; G. Barth, 'Law', p. 70, n. 3; Käsemann, 'Beginnings', p. 85; Suggs, pp. 119f; Wilder, *Eschatology and Ethics*, p. 130, cf. n. 30. Contrast Allen, pp. 45f; Bonnard, *Matthieu*, p. 62; Goulder, *Midrash*, p. 284.

18 However, this does not necessitate assuming with Goulder, *Midrash*, pp. 283f, that 5.17–20 derives entirely from the pen of Mt. and reflects no underlying tradition.

19 So Suggs, p. 119; Bonnard, *Matthieu*, p. 62; Dunn, *Unity*, p. 246; cf. Käsemann, 'Beginnings', p. 85, who sees the meaning of the passage as essentially 'unambiguous'. 5.17–19 is sufficient in itself to deny Cave's assertion, p. 98, that the SM entails 'an abandonment of the legal conception of religion' (cf., ironically, Sandmel, *Jewish Understanding*, p. 167: 'Matthew has little regard or respect for the Jewish law').

20 So McKenzie, 'Matthew', p. 71; Meier, pp. 56f, 61ff; Hamerton-Kelly, pp. 21, 30f; Trilling, *Matthew*, vol. I, pp. 79f; Goppelt, *Christologie*, p. 34; cf. Green, *Matthew*, pp. 80f; W.D. Davies, *Setting*, p. 334; also Schlatter, Zahn, and Roux, as cited by Bonnard, *Matthieu*, p. 62. For various interpretations of 5.18*c*, see Hill, *Matthew*, p. 118. Most take it as a Matthean addition to the tradition.

21 Cf. W.D. Davies, *Setting*, p. 158.

22 So Bonnard, *Matthieu*, p. 62, who cites Schniewind also; cf. Sand, *Gesetz*, p. 38; Carlston, 'Things', p. 78, n. 5; Hasler, *Amen*, pp. 56f.

23 Kümmel, 'Jüdische Traditionsgedanke', p. 127.

24 So Hamerton-Kelly, p. 31; Schweizer, 'Observance', p. 215; *Good News*, pp. 108f; Carlston, 'Things', pp. 78, n. 2, 79, 82f – who is typical of those who see a reference to the Mosaic laws only in the original meaning of the *logion*; cf. Green, *Matthew*, p. 81. Contrast Fenton, p. 85; Hill, *Matthew*, p. 118; Hummel, p. 67.

25 Goulder, *Midrash*, pp. 15–17, suggests that, as a Christian scribe doing midrashic exegesis of Mk., Mt. is embarrassed by Mk.'s radical position. Cf. Bacon, pp. 348–56; Hummel, pp. 36ff, esp. 53f; Banks, *Jesus*, pp. 153ff.

26 On these passages, see G. Barth, 'Law', pp. 79, 81–3; Sand, *Gesetz*, pp. 59–63; Hübner, *Gesetz in der synoptischen Tradition*, pp. 124ff, 136ff.

27 See e.g. W.D. Davies, *Setting*, p. 100; Hull, pp. 137f.

28 Asterisks denote material taken over from Mk. without significant alteration.

29 Bornkamm, 'End-Expectation', p. 31, n. 2.

30 Cf. Suggs, pp. 106f; McNeile, p. 166.

31 So G. Barth, 'Law', p. 81; Sand, *Gesetz*, p. 60; Kilpatrick, p. 116. But cf. Carlston, 'Things', p. 87, who argues that no rabbinic allowances were made for hunger.

32 So Hill, 'Hosea VI. 6', p. 114; McNeile, p. 168; Lohmeyer, *Matthäus*, pp. 183f.

33 Cf. Schlatter, p. 398.

34 See W.D. Davies, *Setting*, p. 103; Stendahl, 'Matthew', p. 784; Wilder, *Eschatology and Ethics*, p. 131; but cf. Cohn-Sherbok, pp. 36ff. Levine, pp. 481f, finds in 12.5 a reference not to the sacrificial duties of the priest, but to 'the widely contested and rigorously defended Pharisaic practice of reaping the first sheaves (i.e., '*omer*) offering' on the second day of Passover, even though it be a sabbath (cf. Daube, p. 67; *Mish*. Men. 10.3, 9). Here, suggests Levine, p. 480, is an example of Mt.'s excellent knowledge of the law.

35 Cf. G. Barth, 'Law', p. 81; Schweizer, 'Observance', pp. 214f; Green, *Matthew*, p. 123: 'It would seem that for Mt Jesus' attitude to the law of sabbath is not one of abrogation but of liberal casuistry.'

36 '... and the action is justified on ethical-cum-legal rather than deeply theological principles' (Houlden, *Ethics*, p. 50); see ch. 1, n. 39 below.

37 So G. Barth, 'Law', p. 83; Houlden, *Ethics*, p. 50.

38 Both W.D. Davies, *Setting*, p. 104, and Hill, *Matthew*, p. 213, see Jesus' argument in 12.11 based on oral tradition (cf. *Mish.* Yoma 8.6; Shab. 18.3); contrast Banks, *Jesus*, p. 126; see S.-B., vol. I, pp. 629–30.

39 Houlden, *Ethics*, p. 49, noting Mt.'s purely legal treatment of issues that

in Mk. are raised on a theological level, maintains that Mt. frequently turns 'episodes which in Mark have a theological point into stories where the reasoning and the message are ethical'.

40 Cf. Kilpatrick, p. 116; G. Barth, 'Law', pp. 81, 91f.

41 Cf. Hübner, *Gesetz in der synoptischen Tradition*, p. 139: '*Der Sabbat ist kein Sabbat, wenn er nicht auch dem Menschen dient*.'

42 To make Mt.'s view more stringent than even that of the strictest form of contemporary Judaism (S.-B., vol. I, pp. 952f; Carlston, 'Things', p. 86) does not accord well with his more liberal emphasis elsewhere on allowance for the expression of mercy (12.7, 11f). Cf. Banks, *Jesus*, p. 102; Schlatter, p. 706; G. Barth, 'Law', pp. 91f.

43 On this passage see G. Barth, 'Law', pp. 86–9; Hübner, *Gesetz in der synoptischen Tradition*, pp. 176ff; Berger, pp. 497–505.

44 In Mt., the question 'Why do your disciples transgress ...?' is immediately countered by Jesus' response, 'And why do you transgress ...?' Houlden, *Ethics*, p. 51, however, finds deeper significance in the fronting of the Corban reference, which he sees as limiting the applicability of the ensuing Isaiah quotation to the specific abuse of Corban, not to the observance of the tradition in general, as in Mk.

45 G. Barth, 'Law', p. 80; contrast Banks, *Jesus*, p. 143.

46 But cf. 24.15*, where a similar Marcan parenthesis is retained.

47 So Dunn, *Unity*, pp. 247f; cf. Schweizer, *Good News*, pp. 325f.

48 Cf. Green, *Matthew*, p. 143.

49 Cf. Dunn, *Unity*, p. 248. This brings into question Berger's assertion, p. 243, that 'einen kultischen und rituellen Teil des "Gesetzes" gibt es für Mt nicht' (cf. pp. 582f).

50 So Green, *Matthew*, pp. 36, 143f; cf. Hill, *Matthew*, pp. 250ff; Filson, pp. 176f; Micklem, pp. 155ff (but cf. p. 219); Davies, *Setting*, p. 104; Fenton, p. 252; Hübner, *Gesetz in der synoptischen Tradition*, p. 181; Bacon, p. 354; Dunn, *Unity*, pp. 63, 247ff; cf. p. 360. Blair, pp. 112ff, speaks of Jesus' opposition to 'the bulk at least, of Pharisaic tradition'.

51 Cf. Sand, *Gesetz*, pp. 69f, 211; Bonnard, *Matthieu*, pp. 227f; G. Barth, 'Law', pp. 86–9.

52 Cf. Hummel, p. 47; see pp. 13f below.

53 *Ethics*, p. 51; see n. 44 above; cf. Hummel, pp. 46ff, 55f.

54 Fitzmyer, however, questions this (p. 205, n. 30).

55 See Houlden, *Ethics*, pp. 48, 78; W.D. Davies, *Setting*, p. 104; Blair, p. 116. Houlden sees this as a 'shift from theology to Church law'; but even in Mk. the pericope centres on a question of law: εἰ ἔξεστιν ... (10.2).

56 Most recently, by Moloney, pp. 44f, who with Stock, pp. 25–8, Fitzmyer, pp. 207–11, and Meier, pp. 147ff, 150, n. 61, follows Baltensweiler and Bonsirven in understanding it as a reference to the consanguinity restrictions of Lev. 18.6–18, cited for the benefit of new gentile converts to the Jewish–Christian community (see Fitzmyer, p. 210, n. 52, and Moloney, p. 56, n. 14, for bibliography); but cf. Banks, *Jesus*, p. 155.

57 Cf. Dunn, *Unity*, p. 247: 'Thereby he transforms a general question and sets it within the rabbinic debate between the schools of Hillel and Shammai; the Matthean formulation in fact presupposes the then current practice of divorce and asks Jesus for a verdict on the then dominant Hillelite

position ... Jesus is thus shown as ... favouring the stricter viewpoint of the Shammaites.' For the different views of Hillel and Shammai, see S.-B., vol. I, pp. 312–20. Branscomb, p. 55, affirms the ascendancy of the Hillelites in the post A.D. 70 era, but not before.

58 See esp. Meier, pp. 143ff; Sand, *Gesetz*, pp. 72–5, 211.

59 Cf. Houlden, *Ethics*, p. 78: 'The former then appears as the basic law, which is modified or glossed, first by Moses' rule and now by the greater law of Jesus.'

60 *Setting*, pp. 105f.

61 See p. 19 below.

62 See pp. 95f below.

63 On the authenticity of the reading *νομικός*, see Metzger, *Textual Commentary*, p. 59.

64 Cf. G. Barth, 'Law', p. 64.

65 Matthew's supposed redaction of the Q version of 11.13 (cf. Lk. 16.16) is viewed by some as an attempt to soften the implication that the era of law is now finished (G. Barth, 'Law', pp. 63f, 159f; Hill, *Matthew*, p. 66).

66 Banks, *Jesus*, p. 138.

67 See Westerholm, pp. 126f; Haenchen, pp. 30f, observes that here scribal authority bears the same authority as that of Torah itself; cf. Hübner, *Gesetz in der synoptischen Tradition,* p. 207.

68 *Pace* Banks, *Jesus*, pp. 179f, who wrongly sees this denied by the gnats and camel saying that follows (23.24). On the extension of tithing to herbs in scribal tradition, see Green, *Matthew*, pp. 191f; McNeile, p. 335; Micklem, p. 223; Allen, p. 247.

69 So Banks, *Jesus*, p. 238; Jeremias, *Theology*, pp. 208–11; McKenzie, 'Matthew', p. 65; Carlston, 'Things', p. 77, n. 2; p. 82, n. 4; cf. Smith, p. 95; Filson, p. 29; see also n. 50 above.

70 So Hare, pp. 142f; Blair, pp. 113f; McConnell, p. 84; Strecker, *Weg*, pp. 16, 139; Trilling, *Das Wahre Israel*, pp. 203f; Branscomb, p. 225; Green, *Matthew*, pp. 188f; cf. Haenchen, pp. 31, 39f; Schweizer, *Good News*, pp. 437f. Grundmann, *Matthäus*, p. 484, sees them as bits of early Jewish–Christian tradition retained by Mt. for tactical reasons, to show that it is not the Christian community that is responsible for the break with the synagogue. Carlston, 'Things', p. 85, n. 2, cites some who attribute it to Mt.'s desire for reconciliation with Judaism (cf. Hummel, pp. 31f; Lohmeyer, *Matthäus*, p. 335); but the strong anti-Pharisaic diatribe throughout rather gives the impression that Mt. views the Jewish leadership as beyond repentance.

71 So Banks, *Jesus*, p. 238; Johnson, 'Matthew', p. 529; Stendahl, 'Matthew', p. 792; Suggs, pp. 106f; Hill, *Matthew*, p. 310; Sand, *Gesetz*, p. 88; Jeremias, *Theology*, p. 210; Filson, p. 29; Trilling, *Matthew*, vol. II, p. 170; Lohmeyer, *Matthäus*, pp. 334f; cf. Carlston, 'Things', pp. 84f.

72 So LaVerdiere–Thompson, p. 578, n. 28; Munck, p. 255, insists: 'Either the text [23.2f] cannot be right, or we have not yet understood its real meaning.'

73 Clearly 23.2f, 23 must be interpreted in the light of 15.1–20; 16.11f; 23.4, 16–22; see pp. 20f below; cf. Allen, p. 244; McNeile, p. 335; Green, *Matthew*, pp. 188f.

74 Cf. G. Barth, 'Law', pp. 86ff, esp. p. 89 : 'Thus Matthew does not reject the Rabbinic tradition in principle and as a whole.' Cf. also Bornkamm, 'End-Expectation', p. 31; Campenhausen, *Formation*, pp. 14, 16; Suggs, pp. 106f; Merkel, pp. 198f; W.D. Davies, *Setting*, p. 106; Hummel, pp. 47, 75; Goulder, *Midrash*, pp. 14f; Bonnard, *Matthieu*, pp. 227, 334, 340; Micklem, p. 219; Kilpatrick, p. 108.

75 Cf. Hasler, *Amen*, p. 81.

76 Cf. W.D. Davies, *Setting*, p. 106; Micklem, p. 219; Bonnard, *Matthieu*, p. 227; Perrin, *New Testament*, p. 188.

77 See pp. 21ff below; W.D. Davies, *Setting*, p. 290, n. 3, defends Mt.: 'is not the ambiguity ... what we should expect if he was presenting the Christian Dispensation to Judaism and so within the framework of it?'

78 E.g. 'Pharisees', 'elders'; cf. Mt. 9.11, 34; 12.24; 17.14; 21.23; 22.34, 35, 41; 26.3, 47; 27.1. Not all negative references are eliminated, however: cf. 5.20; 7.29; 9.3; 12.38; 15.1; 16.21; 21.15; 23.2, 13, 15, 23, 25, 27, 29; 26.57; 27.41.

79 Suggs, pp. 120–7, finds three references also to the 'commissioning' of Christian scribes (5.11–16; 16.17–19; 28.16–20); but the analysis lacks cogency.

80 So T.H. Robinson, p. 124; McKenzie, 'Matthew', p. 88.

81 See esp. Cope's monograph; cf. Goulder's evidence, *Midrash*, pp. 5–27, esp. 21ff. So, originally, Dobschütz, 'Matthäus', pp. 338–48, followed by Bacon, pp. 81, 131f; Clark, p. 15; M.P. Brown, p. 39; Rigaux, p. 55; Kilpatrick, pp. 106f; Blair, pp. 114, 157f; Minear, 'Disciples', pp. 40f. Pesch, *Matthäus*, pp. 59ff, 67ff, 76, sees Mt. as both a *Schriftsteller* and *Seelsorger*. Goulder, *Midrash*, pp. 5, 9–13, 131, views him as a provincial *sôphēr,* teacher-cum-lay-reader, rather than a sophisticated member of a Jerusalem *beth-hamidrash*. Contrast Moule, 'St. Matthew's Gospel', pp. 98f, and Strecker, *Weg*, pp. 15–35, 39.

82 So Trilling, *Matthew*, vol. II, p. 31; Fenton, p. 230; Zumstein, pp. 156–63; cf. Grundmann, *Matthäus*, p. 357. Contrast Bonnard, *Matthieu*, p. 342; Walker, pp. 24–9; and Sand, *Gesetz*, p. 83, who see no conclusive evidence for such a view; but cf. Bornkamm, 'End-Expectation', pp. 50f, n. 5.

83 *Pace* Filson, p. 165; Micklem, p. 146; Allen, pp. 154f; cf. p. 250, and Minear, 'Disciples', p. 32.

84 Cf. Bonnard, *Matthieu*, p. 210.

85 *Setting*, p. 106; cf. Smith, p. xiii; *pace* Green, *Matthew*, pp. 138, 193, who insists that Christian scribes do not deal with Torah (cf. also Fenton, p. 231).

86 On the confused use of this and related terms, see Kraft, pp. 81–92; Riegel, pp. 410–15; cf. Klijn, pp. 419–31.

87 Cf. Johnson, 'Matthew', p. 529. Minear, 'Disciples', p. 32, suggests the question of whether Israel will follow the Pharisees and their scribes, or Jesus and his, is of prime importance to the author.

88 23.34 may indicate that *προφήτης*, *σοφός* and *γραμματεύς* are more acceptable terms; cf. Dunn, *Unity*, pp. 117f.

89 Cf. Hare, p. 143.

90 So Schweizer, *Gemeinde*, pp. 148f; 'Observance', pp. 228f; *Good News*, pp. 343, 371; cf. Smith, pp. xiii f; Hummel, pp. 61f; Plummer, *Matthew*,

p. 231; McNeile, p. 243; Bornkamm, 'Authority', p. 48; W.D. Davies, *Setting*, pp. 396f; cf. p. 106. Dunn, *Unity*, p. 360, sees in these two references evidence that Jesus' teaching has replaced oral tradition; but this ignores 23.2f, 23.

91 Cf. Green, *Matthew*, p. 153; Schweizer, *Good News*, p. 371; Jeremias, 'κλείς', pp. 751ff; Micklem, pp. 167, 183; also Dodd, 'Matthew and Paul', p. 59; Bornkamm, 'Authority', p. 40.

92 1.22f; 2.5f*, 15, 17f, 23; 3.3*; 4.14–16; 8.17; 11.10*; 12.18–21; 13.35; 21.4f; 26.31*; cf. 11.3ff; 26.54, 56*. For bibliographical references on Mt.'s use of the OT, see Meier, p. 3, n. 6.

93 Hummel's statement, however, that Mt. never makes a declaration against either the commands of the Torah or the customs of the Pharisees without producing evidence from Scripture for it (p. 56), is exaggerated.

94 21.16*, 42*; 22.23–33*, 34–40*, 41–6*.

95 *Pace* Meier, pp. 162–70, who builds too much on the obscure reference 11.13.

96 See Zumstein, pp. 171ff.

97 *Pace* G. Barth, 'Law', pp. 74f; Sand, 'Gesetzlosigkeit', pp. 112–25; so, correctly, Carlston, 'Things', p. 85. Hill, 'False Prophets', pp. 338, 340, concludes: 'The nomistic significance of the word has been greatly exaggerated.'

98 So, e.g. with regard to 7.23: Bauer, pp. 71f; W.D. Davies, *Setting*, pp. 202–5; Hill, 'False Prophets', pp. 340f; cf. Gutbrod, p. 1086; Carlston, 'Things', p. 81, n. 2.

99 So J.P. Martin, pp. 45f; Carlston, 'Interpreting', p. 5; G. Barth, 'Law', p. 66; cf. Hill, *Matthew*, p. 117. Sand, *Gesetz*, p. 207, sees the Gospel written within the context of a community in tension over the question of law; but cf. Stendahl, *School*, pp. xi f. McConnell, p. 8, attributes Mt.'s legal concern in part to his Jewish missionary interests; but the issue is clearly more fundamental than this.

100 So Moule, 'St. Matthew's Gospel', p. 93; 'Intention', p. 168. Suggs, p. 119, and Hummel, pp. 66f, see it directed against the lax observance of the law *both* in the church and in Pharisaism; Hill, *Matthew*, pp. 67f, sees 5.17–19 directed rather against Pharisees who are 'undermining the validity of the Law and the Law's real intention by their emphasis on "tradition"'. While this is a genuine Matthean concern, it is not the point of 5.17–19. (Cf. his seemingly contradictory statement on p. 117.) Sand, *Gesetz*, pp. 101, 104, believes there is no single group in focus, but that it is all a question of the 'richtige Auslegung der Tora': 'Seine "Gegner" sind vielmehr alle diejenigen, die dem Gesetz irgendwie Gewalt antun, so dass nicht mehr der Wille Gottes sichtbar wird'; cf. p. 221.

101 'St. Matthew's Gospel', p. 93.

102 See W.D. Davies, *Setting*, p. 200; G. Barth, 'Law', pp. 74f; Dunn, *Unity*, p. 117; Hamerton-Kelly, p. 22.

103 So Hill, *Matthew*, p. 67; 'False Prophets', pp. 337–40; J.P. Martin, p. 49; cf. G. Barth, 'Law', pp. 162f; Käsemann, 'Beginnings', p. 84; Grundmann, *Matthäus*, p. 235; Dunn, *Unity*, p. 249.

104 *Pace* Schweizer, 'Observance', p. 224; Hamerton-Kelly, pp. 31f. Schweizer is on questionable ground when he asserts that Mt.'s concern over the

false prophets may be attributed to their 'main doctrine' of *ἀνομία* that results in loss of love (24.12).

105 See Hill, 'False Prophets', pp. 327ff, for various interpretations; cf. ch. 1, n. 138 below and Sand, *Gesetz*, pp. 168–77.

106 Cf. G. Barth's assertion, 'Law', p. 75, that 'in 5.17ff. and 7.15ff., Matthew has put the Sermon on the Mount in brackets, which are clearly directed against the antinomians, and thus he understands the whole Sermon on the Mount in relation to the question about the law'. The statement may be challenged on three points: (1) it identifies the 'antinomian' concern of 5.17ff with the *ἀνομία* of 7.15ff; (2) it omits the beatitudes and ignores major parts of the SM that have little to do with the law; (3) it assumes that the material bracketed by two statements exhibiting a common theme must as a whole be directed to that theme. Barth's exegesis reflects a tendency to overextend the contextual influence of a reference at several points (cf. pp. 73, 79f, 84); see ch. 4, n. 34 below.

107 So Bacon, p. 339; Brandon, pp. 233ff, 242; H.D. Betz, 'Makarismen', p.5; Smith, p. xiii; Hunter, *Design*, p. 47; cf. M.P. Brown, pp. 41f; for additional references see Sand, *Gesetz*, pp. 99ff; G. Barth, 'Law', pp. 160ff. Bacon, pp. 88, 356, sees Mt. as a neo-legalistic reaction to the Pauline Mk.; but cf. Kee's argument, p. 6, against describing Mk. as 'Pauline'. ἐλάχιστος (Mt. 5.19) is viewed as a subtle reference to Paul himself (cf. 1 Cor. 15.9) by T.W. Manson, *Sayings*, p. 154, and by Holtzmann and Loisy (as cited by Feuillet, 'Mt V.17–20', p. 123); cf. H.D. Betz, 'Makarismen', p. 5; Bultmann, *Theology*, vol. I, p. 54; but this is unlikely (cf. Dunn, *Unity*, p. 250; Meier, p. 95).

108 See Goulder, *Midrash*, p. 155; note however that Paul himself makes only one reference to his work in Syria (Gal. 1.21).

109 Those who find little or no evidence of anti-Paulinism in Mt. include Bauman, p. 549; G. Barth, 'Law', p. 162; Hummel, p. 65; W.D. Davies, *Setting*, pp. 320–36.

110 Cf. Campenhausen, *Formation*, p. 11; Strecker, *Weg*, p. 137, n. 4; thus Carlston, 'Things', p. 85, speaks of antinomianism in Matthew as 'a rather ill-defined error or system of errors'.

111 *Paul*, p. 420; note however Neusner's critical review.

112 *Paul*, p. 426.

113 Cf. Hasler, *Amen*, pp. 78f: 'Das Tun des Gesetzes nach der messianischen Interpretation aber ist die Voraussetzung für die Aufnahme ins Himmelreich.'

114 See pp. 95, 98 below, and Banks, *Jesus*, pp. 159–64, for further discussion of the text. This does not, however, necessitate Banks' view of the initial endorsement of the law (19.17f) as a mere first step, the ultimate goal of which is to 'surpass its demands and, in the end, leave it quite out of sight' (p. 177; cf. pp. 162f; Meier, pp. 87f). Cf. McKenzie, 'Natural Law', pp. 9f, who sees it not as an affirmation of the law at all, but as a statement of its insufficiency. It could equally well be understood as an assertion that true fulfilment of the law is possible only with a radical commitment to follow Jesus. See ch. 4, n. 33 below.

115 The reference to tax-collectors and harlots in 21.31f is no argument to the contrary: their *μετάνοια* is presupposed.

116 Carlston, 'Things', pp. 79f.

117 The contrast of 'least' and 'great' suggests the term does not imply exclusion from the kingdom (cf. 11.1); *pace* Bonnard, *Matthieu*, p. 62, and Schweizer, *Good News*, p. 105; correctly, Meier, pp. 92–5, 100; Filson, p. 84; Allen, p. 46; cf. Green, *Matthew*, p. 81.

118 Cf. Carlston's argument against Hummel in 'Things', p. 81, n. 2: 'It is pure assumption that Matthew would assert flatly "Ohne Tora gibt es überhaupt keine Gerechtigkeit ..." '; but see Campenhausen, *Formation*, pp. 13f. Note also that Mt. never raises the circumcision issue; but see pp. 44f below.

119 Cf. Sand, *Gesetz*, p. 207; Houlden, *Ethics*, p. 48; Clark, p. 209; J.T. Sanders, *Ethics*, pp. 44f; Carlston, 'Things', p. 77, n. 1; *pace* Gaechter, p. 162, who states that Mt.'s Jesus proclaims a Messianic era without law. The omission of any reference to law (pp. 416f) thus argues against Donfried's analysis of 25.1–13 as a summary of Matthean theology.

120 See esp. Meier's detailed study, pp. 124–61; cf. Hübner, *Gesetz in der synoptischen Tradition*, pp. 40–112; Schmahl, pp. 284–97; Lohse, 'Ich aber ...', pp. 189–203.

121 Guelich, p. 456, and Sand, *Gesetz*, p. 53, argue that nos. 3, 5, 6 (the 'redactional' antitheses) annul the law; but McArthur, pp. 44f; Hamerton-Kelly, p. 22; Jeremias, *Theology*, pp. 251f; Meier, pp. 135–61; and Dunn, *Unity*, pp. 97f, point rather to nos. 3, 4, 5. Hummel, p. 72, and Hübner, *Gesetz in der synoptischen Tradition*, p. 207, argue that only no. 5 totally abrogates the law. Cf. Carlston, 'Things', pp. 80f, n. 6; Hamerton-Kelly, p. 22, n. 11; Suggs, p. 113; McConnell, p. 96.

122 See G. Barth, 'Law', p. 94; Suggs, p. 113; Meier, pp. 140–61.

123 W.D. Davies, *Setting*, p. 102; he adds: 'To interpret on the side of stringency is not to annul the Law, but to change it in accordance with its own intention.' Cf. also Daube, p. 60; Tasker, *Matthew*, pp. 66f. Sand, however (*Gesetz*, p. 53), rejects this thesis, as does Meier, pp. 125ff.

124 The insertion of 5.17–19 at this point may be intended to prevent misunderstanding of the antitheses that follow; cf. Meier, p. 66; Hill, *Matthew*, p. 117.

125 Houlden, *Ethics*, pp. 48f, thus speaks of Mt. 'transforming the Law by adding to its rigour (v, 20–48)'. Cf. Sand, *Gesetz*, p. 109: 'das Tun ist nicht mehr nur ein Tun des Gesetzes, des Buchstabens also, sondern ist Tun des Willens Gottes ...' (also pp. 120, 216).

126 So G. Barth, 'Law', p. 73; see p. 98 below.

127 See Dunn, *Unity*, p. 249; Bauman, p. 562.

128 Cf. Banks, *Jesus*, pp. 182–203, 225; S.-B., vol. I, pp. 353ff; Meier, pp. 137ff. See ch. 4, n. 4 below, however, for parallels in the Qumran literature.

129 See pp. 13f above. Neither however is there evidence for Hamerton-Kelly's thesis, p. 23, that in 5.21–48 Mt. *opposes* Christian Sadducees who deny Jesus' halakic authority.

130 Cf. Filson, p. 29; Hummel, pp. 74f. W.D. Davies, *Setting*, pp. 103ff, argues that even though Mk.'s position remains somewhat ambiguous, Mt. makes it 'perfectly clear that not the validity of the Law as such is in dispute but its interpretation in the tradition'.

131 Mt.'s somewhat free alternation of the terms Pharisee, scribe, Sadducee, elder, and chief priest (9.34; 12.24, 38; 16.1, 6; 22.41; 23.2; 26.3; 27.12,

20, 41; but see p. 14 and n. 78 above) suggests that he treats them as a single group representing the opposition of the Jewish religious leaders (see Sand, *Gesetz*, pp. 76–84, 94; Hare, p. 81; Meier, pp. 111f; cf. Banks, *Jesus*, p. 174, n. 3). The Pharisees, however, remain the primary centre of focus.

132 Note Mt.'s tendency to turn Mk.'s *Schulgespräche* into *Streitgespräche*; Sand, *Gesetz*, p. 41; Bornkamm, 'Doppelgebot', p. 92.

133 See esp. Beilner, pp. 9–88, 174–238; Zumstein, pp. 47–68. Hummel, p. 55, sees Jesus as the exegete before whom the rabbis are cast (against their will) as students (9.13; 12.3, 5, 7; 19.4). On ch. 23, cf. Mk. 12.37*b*-40 and see Sand, *Gesetz*, pp. 84–95; Hare, pp. 80–96.

134 But 16.11f does not imply a straight rejection of oral tradition, as is claimed by Blair, p. 113; see pp. 13f above. Mt.'s lumping together of such clearly diverse teachings as those of the Pharisees and Sadducees suggests to Houlden the possibility of διδαχή meaning something rather more general here, such as 'influence' (in correspondence; cf. Filson, p. 183: 'teaching and influence') – which would avoid a straight conflict with 23.2f. Meier, p. 19, sees 16.12 as clear evidence that Mt. is quite ignorant of Sadducean doctrine.

135 Carlston's statement, 'Things', p. 76 (see n. 1), that in many passages the Pharisees represent Judaism as a whole (blind and reprobate), while partially true (15.14), overlooks the fact that the focus is often specifically on the Pharisees.

136 Mt.'s order of 'does' and 'teaches' in 5.19 is perhaps a significant expression of his priorities, in contrast to those of the Pharisees.

137 For criticism of Mt. on this point, see C.G. Montefiore, *Synoptic Gospels*, vol. II, pp. 296f; cf. Banks, *Jesus*, pp. 58ff. Himmelfarb, p. 62, concludes that the Pharisees are 'straw men'; cf. Bacon, pp. 342f.

138 Cf. Hill, 'Hosea VI.6', p. 113; 'False Prophets', pp. 344–8; Hill suggests it is the Pharisees who are the 'false prophets'. For further discussion of the tensions between Mt.'s community and Pharisaic Judaism, see esp. the studies of Hummel and Hare; the latter suggests the debate centres on the larger question of the exegetical authority of Jesus and his Church *vis-à-vis* that of the rabbis (p. 143); cf. also Kilpatrick, p. 106; Green, *Matthew*, pp. 30f. W.D. Davies, *Setting*, pp. 286–315, hypothesizes that the Gospel may be an attempt to meet the internal demands of the community for a Christian counterpart to the mishnaic developments of Jamnia; so also LaVerdiere–Thompson, pp. 572ff, who however overstate the scholarly endorsement of this position.

139 See esp. Beilner, pp. 89–122.

140 *Setting*, pp. 291f.

141 For Mt.'s emphasis on inward as opposed to purely outward concerns, cf. 5.1–11, 21–48; 6.1–8, 16–18; 15.1–20*; 23.2–28; Bacon, p. 343; see ch. 4, n. 5 below.

142 See p. 26 and n. 187 below.

143 P. 95.

144 Cf. G. Barth, 'Law', p. 88.

145 See p. 97 below. Cf. G. Barth, 'Law', p. 81; Furnish, *Love*, p. 74; Hummel p. 52; Bornkamm, 'Doppelgebot', p. 86; Carlston, 'Things', p. 82, n. 3.

But for evidence of rabbinic regard for love as a principle of interpretation, see S.-B., vol. I, pp. 353ff, 459f, 907f.

146 See pp. 11f above.

147 Cf. G. Barth, 'Law', p. 79; Windisch, *Bergpredigt*, p. 47; Blair, p. 123; Sand, *Gesetz*, pp. 207f: 'Das Verhalten gegenüber dem Mitmenschen hat mehr Gewicht als die Sorge um kultische Reinheit und religiöse Korrektheit.'

148 See ch. 4, n. 14 below.

149 Cf. Berger's correct qualification of the sense of 22.40, p. 230: 'Nicht gemeint ist in diesem Satz, dass, wer diese beiden Gebote erfüllt, damit auch alle anderen erfüllt habe oder dass man die anderen nur in dieser Grundgesinnung erfüllen brauche'; also McConnell, p. 13.

150 Cf. Hill, 'Hosea VI.6', p. 115: 'Matthew has evidence that the Torah can set one law over another, even to the extent of allowing, in the case of conflict, one to be broken for the sake of the other'; cf. p. 116. G. Barth, 'Law', p. 89, concludes that, even though Mt. is reluctant to move outside the rabbinic system of oral tradition as a whole, 'With this critical attitude as the deciding factor the whole idea of the Rabbinical tradition is, of course, broken through'; cf. pp. 85, 103f; Blair, p. 113. Carlston, 'Things', p. 87, adds: 'The man who insists on the priority of love over law in connexion with sabbath observance ... is on fundamentally different ground from that occupied by the rabbis' (though, strictly speaking, it is not correct to speak of the priority of love *over* law for Mt.; see pp. 98ff below). Cf. G.F. Moore, vol. II, p. 93; S.-B., vol. I, pp. 900–5.

151 Cf. Strecker's references to Q and *Sondergut, Weg*, p. 12; he thus speaks of two lines of tradition: that which portrays Jesus within the OT tradition, and that which shows him critical of it (p. 146).

152 Those who identify the rigorist position with the strict Jewish–Christian tradition and the more liberal viewpoint with Mt. himself, include Schweizer, 'Matth. 5, 17–20', pp. 400ff; Green, *Matthew*, pp. 80f; Hill, *Matthew*, pp. 117f; Hummel, pp. 66f; Carlston, 'Things', pp. 81, 90f; Strecker, *Weg*, pp. 16ff; Käsemann, 'Beginnings', p. 85; Smith, p. 96; Hamerton-Kelly, pp. 31f; see further ch. 1, nn. 17, 70 above. G. Barth, 'Law', pp. 64ff, 70f, identifies Mt. with the more rigorous position; Goulder, *Midrash*, pp. 15ff, concurs, but identifies the more liberal position with Mk. (cf. pp. 261f); many of the contradictory elements, however, occur in the non-Marcan materials.

153 So Trilling, *Das Wahre Israel*, pp. 214–16, and Abel, pp. 142ff, who see the work of both a Jewish–Christian and a gentile redactor; but cf. Rohde, pp. 80, 87; W.D. Davies, *Setting*, pp. 326ff.

154 See e.g. ch. 1, n. 71 above for those who attribute little significance to 23.2f, 23 in view of the overriding concern of the context with other factors.

155 Cf. G. Barth, 'Law', pp. 94f; Hummel, pp. 66ff; Carlston, 'Things', pp. 80f; Dunn, *Unity*, pp. 249f; see further below.

156 So Bornkamm, 'End-Expectation', p. 25; cf. Goulder, *Midrash*, p. 20; C.G. Montefiore, *Synoptic Gospels*, vol. II, p. 298; M.P. Brown, p. 42. Meier, however, pp. 43f, 124, denies that Mt.'s is 'a confused position that has not been carefully thought out'; 'on the whole, Mt has done

a masterful job of welding together disparate Jewish–Christian material to create a unit that speaks his own mind'.

157 Cf. G. Barth, 'Law', pp. 94f.

158 See esp. Tagawa, pp. 158–62. Cf. Campenhausen, *Formation*, p. 17: 'Matthew stands on the borderline between two eras. He is the last witness to a Christian faith which sought ... to be sincerely loyal to the old law. But this was an untenable position.' The conclusion however does not follow; see Dunn, *Unity*, pp. 250f; cf. pp. 239ff.

159 P. 114; cf. pp. 107, 114, 127. But see Banks' criticism in *Jesus*, p. 259, n. 2; also ch. 1, n. 183 below. Note that Mt. nowhere uses the term *νόμος* to refer to Jesus himself (Sand, *Gesetz*, pp. 33ff). Suggs' argument that Mt. portrays Jesus as Wisdom-incarnate in 11.19, 25–30; 23.34–6 (pp. 31–127) is based on the assumption of an underlying Q document with a Wisdom emphasis (pp. 5–29).

160 See pp. 24f below.

161 So Bacon, pp. 168, 342; Branscomb, p. 97; Perrin, *New Testament*, p. 174; Freyne, p. 156; Sandmel, *Jewish Understanding*, p. 145; Schnackenburg, p. 203; T.W. Manson, *Ethics*, p. 52; Windisch, *Bergpredigt*, p. 45; cf. pp. 10, 61; Wilder, 'Sermon', p. 160; Kilpatrick, p. 108; Dodd, *Gospel*, pp. 64ff; Vidler, p. 88; Smith, p. xii; so also Wellhausen, J. Weiss, Schniewind, and C.G. Montefiore (cited by G. Barth, 'Law', p. 153, n. 1); cf. J. T. Sanders, *Ethics*, p. 41.

162 See Banks, *Jesus*, pp. 230ff; cf. W.D. Davies, *Setting*, pp. 14ff, 107.

163 See Banks, *Jesus*, pp. 72–80, who criticizes W.D. Davies' methodology on this point (p. 80); cf. Davies, *Setting*, pp. 156ff, 184; G. Barth, 'Law', pp. 149, 153–7; Filson, p. 29. Contrast Bruce, 'Paul and the Law', p. 263, who builds perhaps too confidently on Baeck's assertion that in Jewish belief the Messianic age was to supersede the law; cf. E.P. Sanders, *Paul*, p. 496.

164 Cf. W.D. Davies, *Torah in Messianic Age*, pp. 84ff; Blair, pp. 125ff, 130f; Moule, *Christology*, p. 150.

165 Cf. Vermes, pp. 130–40; W.D. Davies, *Setting*, pp. 109–90.

166 Cf. 2.16–18, 19f; 4.1f; 5.1; see W.D. Davies, *Setting*, pp. 25–93; Blair, pp. 133ff; Dunn, *Unity*, p. 248; Sand, *Gesetz*, pp. 101f. Davies identifies the greatest point of similarity: 'Matthew has draped his Lord in the mantle of a teacher of righteousness like Moses' (p. 102; cf. p. 118). The parallels, however, liken Jesus as much to Israel as to Moses (cf. p. 61).

167 See Trilling, *Das Wahre Israel*, p. 186; McConnell, p. 94; cf. Sand, *Gesetz*, pp. 102, 104; W.D. Davies, *Setting*, pp. 83, 86, 92f, 107f, who notes the absence of the term at key points where we might otherwise have expected it.

168 *Setting*, p. 99.

169 See Hummel, p. 75; Bornkamm, 'End-Expectation', p. 35, n. 2; Stendahl, 'Matthew', p. 776; Guelich, p. 457; Carlston, 'Things', p. 83; cf. Hill, *Matthew*, p. 69; T.W. Manson, *Teaching*, p. 301.

170 E.g. Hasler, *Amen*, p. 82: 'Die Antithesen stellen uns mitten in die schriftgelehrte Arbeit des Evangelisten zur Formulierung einer für Katechese oder Paränese gültigen messianischen Halacha'; cf. Hummel, p. 64, who asserts that parallel to and distinguished from Pharisaic Judaism,

Mt.'s church has its own full set of Christian halakoth (cf. pp. 57ff; Bornkamm, 'Authority', p. 48; Sandmel, *Jewish Understanding*, pp. 145, 160), and that the Gospel is basically an attempt to defend and legitimate the halakic practices of the community against Pharisaic opposition (pp. 53ff).

171 Cf. Westerholm, p. 21: 'halakhah is casuistic law. The categorical imperatives and prohibitions of apodictic law, addressed directly to the hearer and intended to guide his future behaviour, do not belong to the sphere of halakhah. Halakhah posits, objectively and in detail, a concrete case and states the legal consequences.' Carlston, 'Things', p. 82, n. 3: 'In what sense would the rabbis have recognized as "halachoth" what Matthew actually does with this (to them) reduction and subordination of the Law?' (cf. pp. 86, 88). Meier, p. 159, n. 81, observes that Jesus' opinion is always decisive and final (7.29*; 22.17*), not couched in terms of exegetical subtlety and the weighing of opinions, but proclaimed as authoritative pronouncement (cf. pp. 109f). Daube, p. 58: 'The setting in life of the Rabbinic form is dialectic exposition of the Law; that of the Matthean is proclamation of the true Law.' Cf. Suggs, p. 115; W.D. Davies, *Setting*, pp. 422ff; Sandmel, *First Century*, p. 94; Manns, pp. 3–22; Blair, pp. 135ff; McConnell, pp. 91, 95; Campenhausen, *Formation*, pp. 14f; Dibelius, *Jesus*, pp. 96ff; Hunter, *Design*, pp. 27, 116f; Sand, *Gesetz*, pp. 213f; Dodd, *Gospel*, pp. 60f, 76f; Houlden, *Ethics*, p. 112; Stendahl, *School*, p. xiii; Barton, pp. 60ff. However, this does not warrant Schweizer's conclusion, 'Matth. 5, 17–20', p. 406, that for Mt. *all* casuistry and legalism is basically unsatisfying.

172 *Sayings*, p. 37.

173 See Kilpatrick, p. 108; Himmelfarb, p. 59; Hummel, pp. 57f – who finds evidence of Christian halakoth in 5.32, 33–7; 6.1–18; 15.20; 18. 15–17, 18, 21f; 19.9; 23.8–10, 16–22, 26; cf. Manns, pp. 17–22; Carlston, 'Things', p. 86; G. Barth, 'Law', pp. 71, 141.

174 McArthur, p. 159; cf. W.D. Davies, *Setting*, pp. 387ff, 400f:

> 'Not catechism but casuistry lies behind all this: in this casuistry a Christian gemaric element is noticeable: words of Jesus from some sources become the occasion for the insertion of related material by way of enlargement or comment, and in the material peculiar to Matthew the rabbinization of the Church is seen at work ... In the process [the Church] took what was radical, modified it, and made it regulatory.'

Davies thus speaks of Mt. as 'the Gospel of Christian Rabbinism' (*Paul and Rabbinic Judaism*, p. 149), and suggests it is only Mt.'s proximity to Judaism that prevents him from explicitly calling Jesus' teaching 'new law' (*Setting*, p. 414). Käsemann, 'Beginnings', pp. 84, 93, also sees the community 'well on the way to a Christian rabbinate'; cf. Houlden, *Ethics*, p. 15. Conzelmann, *Theology*, p. 148, is more cautious, but sees it as an easy step from Mt.'s Gospel to a new legalism.

175 Cf. Fenton, p. 95; see pp. 98f below.

176 Cf. Houlden, *Ethics*, p. 14; see pp. 49f below.

177 Cf. Meier, p. 169: 'It is in this sense, and only in this sense, that it would be legitimate to use in reference to Mt the ambiguous phrase, "new Law".'

178 Blair, p. 139, and W.D. Davies, *Setting*, p. 107, thus speak of Jesus as a

new 'Torah-giver' – taking 'Torah' in its more basic sense of 'teaching' or 'instruction'; cf. Blair, p. 129, n. 26; McConnell, p. 91; Vidler, pp. 153ff.

179 Cf. W.D. Davies, *Setting*, p. 107; Hasler, *Amen*, pp. 78f; Hummel, pp. 55f; Green, *Matthew*, p. 168; Tasker, *Matthew*, p. 67; Schweizer, *Good News*, p. 541.

180 *Ethics*, p. 42.

181 See p. 74 below.

182 See p. 15 above; Banks, *Jesus*, p. 251; cf. Hare, pp. 5, 135f, 143; Stonehouse, p. 210; McConnell, pp. 90, 96.

183 P. 108; cf. p. 117; Hummel, pp. 49f; Meier, pp. 87–9. But note Bornkamm's qualification: 'This does not mean that Jesus is put *in the place* of the law' ('End-Expectation', p. 35, n. 2); cf. 'Authority', pp. 41, 45; Suggs, pp. 114f. Thus W.D. Davies' reference to the 'substitution of Christ for the Torah' (*Paul and Rabbinic Judaism*, p. 150) is not entirely accurate; nor is Banks' statement about Jesus' teachings 'surpassing' or 'transcending' the law (*Jesus*, pp. 203, 250; cf. Spicq, *Agape*, vol. I, p. 55; Meier, pp. 87f); cf. Hare, pp. 5, 135f, 143; Wilder, *Eschatology and Ethics*, p. 130; Bauman, pp. 546, 565. Nor is it strictly correct to say that Jesus has power 'over' the law.

184 G. Barth, 'Law', pp. 135f, falls into this error: 'In the preaching of the law ... the kingly rule of Jesus Christ comes to men ... From this it follows that the preaching of the law occasions the presence of the Risen One in the congregation ... the presence of Christ ... comes to a man with the proclamation of the word, which indeed is the proclamation of the law'; cf. Hummel, p. 62. It is Christ that is central to Mt.'s proclamation, not the law.

185 W.D. Davies, *Setting*, p. 422, comments: 'there was a marked difference between a life dedicated to study at the feet of a rabbi, in which the aim was an increasing knowledge of the Law which would eventually "qualify" a student himself to become a rabbi, and the life of the Christian disciple (often, to judge from "the Twelve", not markedly studious by nature!) called to personal loyalty to Jesus in his way'. Cf. Filson, p. 31; Carlston, 'Things', pp. 83ff; Meier, pp. 87ff; Freyne, pp. 152ff.

186 See p. 79 and ch. 3, n. 58 below.

187 See G. Barth, 'Law', pp. 158f; Lagrange, p. 229; Gutbrod, p. 1060; Maher, p. 97.

188 Houlden, in correspondence; so also H.D. Betz, 'Matt 11.28–30', p. 24; for other explanations, see Plummer, *Matthew*, p. 170; Bultmann, *Jesus*, p. 83; Suggs, p. 108.

189 W.D. Davies, *Setting*, p. xvi, thus epitomizes 11.28–30 as 'the quintessence of the Matthaean interpretation of Christianity as Gospel and Law'. On 'yoke' as an image of submission to authority, see Maher, pp. 98ff; Micklem, p. 118; Plummer, *Matthew*, p. 171. Suggs, p. 106, interprets this as the traditional yoke of Torah, offered by Jesus as Wisdom-incarnate; but Green, *Matthew*, p. 122, probably correctly takes it as a reference simply to discipleship.

190 Cf. J. Knox, *Ethic*, pp. 41f. Houlden, *Ethics*, p. 48, concludes that Mt.'s Jesus is 'the authoritative teacher of ... strenuous moral lessons'.

191 Of the 191 occurrences of the term *νόμος* in the NT, 119 occur in Paul's

letters, esp. Rom. (72) and Gal. (32; Esser, 'Law', p. 442). Paul's use of the term varies: generally it refers to the whole system of Mosaic regulations superimposed with Pharisaic halakoth, but occasionally it refers specifically to the ethical laws (Rom. 13.8–10; Gal. 5.14) or even to a single statute (Rom. 7.2f; Sanday–Headlam, p. 173; Dodd, *Romans*, p. 101); at other times he uses it in the more general sense of 'Scripture' (Gal. 4.21), 'divine law' (Rom. 2.14*c*; Caird, *Principalities*, p. 49, speaks of 'natural law'), 'legal system' (Gal. 3.21), or simply 'principle' (Rom. 3.27; 7.21, 23, 25; 8.2); see Dodd, *Bible and Greeks*, pp. 34–7; Burton, pp. 447–60; Gutbrod, pp. 1069ff; W.D. Davies, 'Law', p. 99; J.A. Sanders, 'Torah and Paul', pp. 13( Cranfield, 'Paul and the Law', p. 44; Bruce, 'Paul and the Law', p. 259. The meaning of *ὁ νόμος τοῦ Χριστοῦ* (Gal. 6.2; cf. 1 Cor. 9.21) is disputed (see p. 40 below; cf. Gutbrod, p. 1071; Bultmann, *Theology*, vol. I, pp. 328, 344). *Ἀνομία* is generally used in the non-legal sense of 'sinfulness', 'wickedness' (2 Thess. 2.3, 7f; Gutbrod, pp. 1085f). Paul nowhere employs the plural *οἱ νόμοι* (Gutbrod, p. 1070).

192 Apart from the question of whether *νόμος* is to be taken here as a reference to the law of Moses or to law as a general principle (so Sanday–Headlam, p. 284), the precise meaning of the term *τέλος* in Rom. 10.4 is hotly contested: it can mean either 'termination', 'cessation' (so Bammel, pp. 120ff; Schoeps, *Paul*, pp. 171ff; but see p. 171, n. 5), or 'goal', 'fulfilment' (so Cranfield, 'Paul and the Law', pp. 48ff; G.E. Howard, p. 337; Flückiger, pp. 153ff). Both interpretations are attested in Paul's writings and compatible with his thought (Moule, 'Obligation', pp. 402ff; cf. Joest, p. 138; Esser, 'Law', p. 445; Vidler, p. 80; Gogarten, pp. 238ff; Bruce, 'Paul and the Law', p. 264), though the general consensus is that the former fits the immediate context of Rom. 10.4 better. Cf. Gutbrod's qualification, however, p. 1075: 'Only for him who in faith appropriates the righteousness of God in Christ is the Law abolished.' Moule, 'Obligation', p. 392, proposes the following solution: 'Paul saw Christ as the *fulfilment* of law, when law means God's revelation of himself and of his character and purpose, but as the *condemnation* and *termination* of any attempt to use law to justify oneself.'

193 For a good brief review of recent work, see J.A. Sanders, 'Torah and Paul', who concludes, p. 132: 'Paul's attitude toward the Law has been one of the most puzzling and seemingly insoluble in biblical study' – though his own proposed solution (distinguishing between the *muthos* and *ethos* aspects of Torah) fails to account for many specific texts, and is criticized by W.D. Davies, *Land*, p. 24, n. 19, for its overemphasis of the *muthos* aspect in Paul's thinking.

194 See Hübner, *Gesetz bei Paulus*, pp. 16–81 (Gal.: the end of the Mosaic law; Rom.: the end of the fleshly misuse of the law); cf. Drane, *Paul*, pp. 132f; Buck–Taylor, p. 255, who suggest that in Rom. Paul 'takes pains to soften the harsher statements of Galatians about the law'; W.D. Davies, 'Paul and Israel', p. 19: 'in Romans he abandoned the unqualified dismissal of the Law expressed in Galatians'; cf. Drane, 'Diversity', p. 3; Wilckens, 'Law', pp. 17ff. See ch. 1, n. 246 below.

195 See Kümmel, *Introduction*, pp. 303f.

196 Pp. 58, 60.

197 Attempts to establish a single, consistent meaning of the term δικαιοσύνη in Paul's writings are of doubtful value, in view of the clear differences of meaning demanded by the widely varying contexts in which the term occurs. See esp. Hill, *Greek Words*, pp. 139–62, and the extended discussion of E.P. Sanders, *Paul*, pp. 491–5 *et passim*, who criticizes the sharp distinction made by Ziesler between the nominal and verbal nuances of the term (δικαιοσύνη, δίκαιος: ethical terms; δικαιόω: forensic term; Ziesler, pp. 162, 168ff, 212; cf. also Watson's critique and E.P. Sanders, 'Patterns', pp. 477f). Sanders also criticizes the views of Bultmann (δικαιοσύνη primarily an eschatological/forensic term; *Theology*, vol. I, pp. 271ff; cf. Furnish, *Theology*, pp. 146f), and Bornkamm and Conzelmann (δικαιοσύνη: something achieved in the present as a precondition to life), as well as the recent attempts of Käsemann and Stuhlmacher to derive a single, uniform meaning of righteousness from the supposed technical term δικαιοσύνη θεοῦ (see Brauch, pp. 523–42; cf. Schrenk, pp. 202ff, esp. n. 48). The whole approach reflected in recent German attempts to interpret the term in a uniform, consistent sense fails to do justice to the fundamental principle of contextual interpretation. E.P. Sanders concludes: 'He does not use the righteousness terminology with *any one* meaning' (*Paul*, p. 495) – though he himself sees it primarily as a 'transfer term'. See ch. 5, n. 25 below.

198 For differing views, see C.A.A. Scott, *Christianity*, pp. 16ff, 38ff; Furnish, 'Jesus–Paul Debate', p. 358; J. Knox, *Ethic*, pp. 103f; Caird, *Principalities*, pp. 52f; Bruce, 'Paul and the Law', pp. 260ff; *Paul*, pp. 188ff; W.L. Knox, *Jerusalem*, pp. 98ff; J.A. Sanders, 'Torah and Christ', p. 375; Keck, 'Justification', pp. 200f, 207; Sandmel, *Jewish Understanding*, pp. 68f; Schoeps, *Paul*, pp. 171ff; W.D. Davies, 'Matthew, 5, 17–18', pp. 446f; 'Paul and Israel', pp. 4f; Stendahl, *Paul*, pp. 1ff, 7ff; Bornkamm, *Paul*, p. 23; White, p. 204; Gutbrod, pp. 1071, 1077f; and esp. E.P. Sanders, *Paul*, pp. 474ff.

199 Moule, 'Obligation', pp. 391ff, suggests that, strictly speaking, it is not 'law' but 'legalism' that Paul sets in antithesis to grace. For criticism of Paul's portrayal of Judaism on this point, see G.F. Moore, vol. III, pp. 150f; Schoeps, *Paul*, pp. 213–18; E.P. Sanders, *Paul*, pp. 2–7, 549–52. The bulk of Sanders' book is devoted to showing that the motifs of covenant and grace play a much more central role in Judaism than is commonly thought or portrayed by Paul. Cf. 'Patterns', p. 472: 'His argument with Judaism, at least on this point, is a classic case of two ships passing in the night, firing their guns away from each other.' See further below.

200 So Furnish, *Theology*, p. 158; Cranfield, 'Paul and the Law', pp. 55, 62ff; cf. Moule, 'Obligation', p. 393; Ladd, *Theology*, pp. 497ff.

201 Cf. G.F. Moore, vol. III, p. 151.

202 Here I follow E.P. Sanders' conviction (*Paul*, pp. 442ff, 474ff), that in Paul's mind, the analysis of the problem does not precede, but follows the solution – in spite of the opposite direction of the argument in Romans: 'Paul's logic seems to run like this: in Christ God has acted to save the world; ... it must follow that the law could not ...' (p. 475; cf. 'Fulfilling the Law', pp. 103ff); see ch. 5, n. 24 below.

203 Moule, 'Obligation', p. 401, suggests that here Paul penetrates to the very

heart of the ethical dilemma; cf. W.D. Davies, *Setting*, p. 150. See p. 33 below on Gal. 1.13; Phil. 3.4–6.

204 Cf. Cranfield, 'Paul and the Law', pp. 45ff; Bushell, pp. 114f.

205 Cf. Acts 7.53; Heb. 2.2; S.-B., vol. III, pp. 554ff; Sandmel, *Jewish Understanding*, p. 68. Caird, *Principalities*, pp. 40f, sees this statement directed against those rabbis who asserted that the Torah lay on the knees of God before the creation of the world. Drane, *Paul*, pp. 33f, suggests that here Paul throws into question the divine origin of Torah; but this ignores Rom. 7.12. At this point Drane's insistence on treating Galatians independently of Romans must be viewed as methodologically inadequate.

206 See Houlden, *Patterns*, p. 30; J. Knox, *Ethic*, pp. 78f. Caird, *Principalities*, pp. 41f, sees the law taking on the functions of Satan in Paul's writings: accuser (Rom. 2.12; 3.19), executioner (Rom. 7.9ff; 8.2; 1 Cor. 15.56; 2 Cor. 3.6f), and tempter (Rom. 7.7f); he concludes that, for Paul, 'when the law is isolated and exalted into an independent system of religion, it becomes demonic' (p. 41); it becomes 'a destructive power' (p. 43). But this assessment is somewhat extreme.

207 Herein lies the essential 'weakness' of the law (cf. Gal. 4.9: τὰ ἀσθενῆ καὶ πτωχὰ στοιχεῖα; see ch. 5, n. 43 below).

208 See Philipose, p. 445, however, for a different interpretation.

209 Cf. Campenhausen, *Formation*, p. 35, n. 57: 'That the παιδαγωγός of Gal. 3:24 was no kindly and beneficent "tutor", must by now be universally agreed'; Lightfoot, *Galatians*, pp. 148f; Stendahl, *Paul*, pp. 17f; Smith, p. ix.

210 See Lohse, 'Gesetz', on 3.31; cf. Campenhausen, *Formation*, p. 33; Gutbrod, p. 1076; Gulin, p. 120; Cranfield, *Romans*, vol. I, p. 224; Leenhardt, p. 112; Bruce, *Romans*, p. 109; T.W. Manson, 'Romans', p. 943; J. Knox, 'Romans', p. 438; Black, p. 71.

211 Cf. Kilpatrick, p. 108.

212 See Houlden, *Ethics*, p. 32: 'For Paul, law is a theological before it is a moral category.'

213 Paul's attitude to Jewish Christians however is less clear: cf. Stendahl, *Paul*, p. 2: 'In none of his writings does he give us information about what he thought to be proper in these matters for Jewish Christians'; Young, p. 330: 'nowhere in his epistles did Paul suggest that Jewish converts should cease to be Jews'; so also Gutbrod, p. 1066; Flückiger, p. 156; W.D. Davies, *Paul and Rabbinic Judaism*, p. 321; Drane, *Paul*, pp. 51f.

214 Cf. Ladd, *Theology*, p. 510; Houlden, *Ethics*, p. 33.

215 But see Hollenbach, pp. 254–61, for a different exegesis.

216 See esp. Gunther, pp. 95ff. The latter passage is only peripherally concerned with food regulations, however. Drane's view, *Paul*, pp. 67ff, that Gal. 2.11ff and 1 Cor. 8–10 represent identical situations but quite different responses by Paul, wrongly assumes a Jewish setting for 1 Cor. 8–10.

217 Contrast Acts 15.28f; nowhere does Paul explicitly cite the 'Jerusalem decree' against gentile Christians eating meat sold by pagan butchers. For various explanations, see Hurd, *I Corinthians*, pp. 253–70.

218 The reference is to complete vegetarians, not necessarily Jewish Christians (cf. Barrett, *Romans*, pp. 256f).

219 At this point, suggests W.D. Davies, 'Matthew, 5, 17–18', p. 443: 'To be ἔννομος Χριστοῦ could demand submission to the Law of Moses.'
220 Perhaps an original word of Paul to the Corinthians that they have misconstrued; cf. Drane, *Paul*, pp. 67f.
221 Ebeling, p. 272, finds significance in the fact that Paul does not say the law itself is dead, but rather that Christians have died to it.
222 See Bultmann, 'Theology', vol. I, pp. 340f.
223 See ch. 5, n. 43 below.
224 Cf. E.F. Scott, *Spirit*, p. 164; Schubert, pp. 384f; W.L. Knox, *Jerusalem*, p. 100; thus, at a number of points Paul contrasts life in the Spirit with life under the law (e.g. Rom. 7.6; Gal. 3.3f).
225 Note the singular; contrast the plural in Rom. 2.26; Schrenk, p. 221.
226 E.P. Sanders, *Paul*, pp. 508ff, noting this 'rich and well-developed conceptualization of man's plight', suggests that the really original contribution of Paul lies in his anthropology, not his theology: 'In comparison with his analysis of the human plight, Paul's statements directly about God are only a collection of standard opinions' (p. 510).
227 Cf. E.P. Sanders, *Paul*, p. 443, n. 4; p. 479, n. 23; he speaks of Kümmel as striking the decisive 'death blow' to the strictly autobiographical interpretation of Rom. 7.
228 So most commentators; acknowledged by Dunn, *Jesus*, p. 313; cf. Käsemann, *Römer*, pp. 191ff; Conzelmann, *Theology*, p. 230; Bornkamm, *Ende*, p. 67; *Paul*, pp. 125–7; Bultmann, *Theology*, vol. I, p. 247; Kümmel, *Theology*, p. 177; Kuss, vol. I, p. 482.
229 See e.g. Dunn, *Jesus*, pp. 313ff.
230 In Rom. the conflict is between the individual's νοῦς and the σάρξ, in Gal. between the divine πνεῦμα and the σάρξ. The latter is clearly the conflict of a Christian, the former not necessarily so at all. Cf. Bornkamm, *Ende*, p. 68.
231 See e.g. Dunn, *Jesus*, p. 314; J. Knox, *Ethic*, pp. 116f, n. 24; but cf. Bornkamm, *Paul*, p. 125; Ladd, *Theology*, p. 500.
232 See e.g. Dunn, *Jesus*, pp. 314f, 316. If, as is likely, 7.25*a* is an intrusive exclamation anticipating ch. 8, 7.25*b* would still serve as a perfectly adequate summary of the chapter without necessitating an interpretation of the passage in terms of Christian experience; nor is it necessary to emend the order of the text, as Neill suggests (pp. 79f).
233 Cf. Käsemann, 'Spirit', p. 146. Stendahl, *Paul*, pp. 81f, 88–91, notes that Paul never speaks of himself (in his Christian life) as a 'sinner'; rather, he is confident that his conscience is clear (Rom. 9.1; 1 Cor. 4.4; 2 Cor. 1.12).
234 Cf. Stendahl, *Paul*, p. 94; Conzelmann, *Theology*, p. 285; Bornkamm, *Ende*, pp. 53ff.
235 *Pace* Gutbrod, p. 1072; Bruce, 'Paul and the Law', p. 266; J. Knox, *Ethic*, p. 99; Banks, *Jesus*, p. 109.
236 This argues against E.P. Sanders' statement that Paul's acceptance of the Jewish moral standards is 'not ... by virtue of their being commandments' (*Paul*, p. 513).
237 So Gulin, p. 121; Grosheide, p. 169; cf. Orr–Walther, p. 216; but note Barrett, *First Corinthians*, p. 169. See ch. 4, n. 56 below.

238 Cf. Campenhausen, *Formation*, p. 29.

239 See Ladd, *Theology*, pp. 504, 510, 517; Houlden, *Ethics*, pp. 15, 33; Wendland, p. 57; but cf. J. Knox, *Ethic*, p. 101. Gutbrod, p. 1069, speaks of the Decalogue as the 'gist of the law' in Paul's thought.

240 So Moule, 'Obligation', pp. 392, 397; Ladd, *Theology*, pp. 509f; Conzelmann, *Theology*, p. 225; Kümmel, *Theology*, p. 184; Campenhausen, *Ecclesiastical Authority*, p. 48; *Formation*, pp. 29ff; Furnish, *Love*, pp. 95f; E.P. Sanders, 'Fulfilling the Law', pp. 124f (see n. 1); Bultmann, *Theology*, vol. I, pp. 260ff; cf. Thomas, p. 91; Ebeling, p. 271; Cranfield, 'Paul and the Law', p. 66; *pace* Schoeps, *Paul*, pp. 171ff, who claims that Paul flatly denies the validity of the law in every way, disclaiming not only its saving character, 'but in spite of Rom. 7:12 even its revelational character' (p. 183; cf. pp. 192f, 198f).

241 See further pp. 101ff below; cf. Hübner, 'Ganze und eine', p. 256; J.T. Sanders, *Ethics*, p. 60. Bultmann, *Theology*, vol. I, p. 341, sees evidence here that 'freedom from the Law ... actualizes itself in the freedom to differentiate between the valid and the non-valid ... within the Law' (cf. Rom. 12.2; Phil. 1.10); Hübner, *Gesetz bei Paulus*, p. 42, makes a distinction between the quantitative and qualitative fulfilment of the law in Paul's thinking; cf. 'Identitätsverlust', pp. 182–5.

242 'Sentences', pp. 66ff; cf. Wilckens, *Römer*, p. 127.

243 *Ethics*, pp. 48ff.

244 1 Cor. 11.23 and 1 Thess. 4.15 relate more to kerygma (cf. 1 Cor. 15.3).

245 Cf. Goulder, *Midrash*, p. 144; Gulin, p. 127; Kümmel, *Theology*, p. 227, terms them the 'ultimate norm'.

246 The fact that the majority of these occur in 1 Cor. is taken by Drane as evidence of a clear shift away from the rigorist position adopted in Gal. to a more legal ethic: 'the whole tone of I Corinthians is intensely legalistic' ('Diversity', p. 8; cf. *Paul*, pp. 69, 76; Hurd, *I Corinthians*, pp. 258, 294). He thus speaks of Paul's 'ways in Christ' (1 Cor. 4.17) as 'moral principles comparable with the *Halacha* of the Jewish rabbis' (*Paul*, pp. 63ff; cf. pp. 160f, n. 5; W.L. Knox, *Jerusalem*, p. 318, n. 3). Drane, *Paul*, pp. 109ff, views 2 Cor. and especially Rom. as later attempts to resolve the opposing tendencies, in which Christians are viewed as free from the law but still under specific moral directions. His overall thesis may be criticized on three grounds: (1) it greatly exaggerates the 'legal' element in 1 Cor. (see p. 38 below) – and ignores it in Gal.; (2) it fails to take adequate account of the quite different problems addressed by Paul in the two letters; (3) it thus fails to distinguish adequately between ethical and non-ethical senses and functions of law. Cf. Hurd's equally questionable reconstruction of the Corinthian correspondence (summarized *I Corinthians*, pp. 289ff), which he views too narrowly in terms of issues arising out of the Apostolic decree.

247 Cf. Campenhausen, *Ecclesiastical Authority*, pp. 44f.

248 *Paul*, p. 211.

249 *Ethics*, p. 66.

250 J. Knox, *Ethic*, pp. 102f, seems to concur.

251 *Ethics*, p. 30; cf. p. 29: 'when he looks towards the End, Paul forbids vices

on the grounds that they are against God's law and can be expected to produce an adverse verdict in the Judgement'.

252 *Ibid*. p. 34.

253 *Paul and Rabbinic Judaism*, pp. 16, 70 (see n. 2 for a similar statement by W.L. Knox); the refs. however are to Acts. Cf. 'Torah and Dogma', p. 103.

254 Pp. 201f. Ellison's position, like Davies', is based more on the Lucan portrait of Paul in Acts than on the writings of Paul himself; cf. Drane, *Paul*, pp. 51f.

255 *Setting*, p. 343, n. 4.

256 Cf. *Setting*, pp. 353ff: 'Almost certainly it is a comprehensive expression for the totality of the ethical teaching of Jesus that had come down to Paul as authoritative'; *Paul and Rabbinic Judaism*, pp. 142ff; Dodd, *Gospel*, pp. 47, 64ff; Dunn, *Unity*, pp. 68f; Kümmel, *Theology*, p. 227.

257 *Setting*, pp. 363f; *Paul and Rabbinic Judaism*, pp. 144, 148f.

258 *Paul and Rabbinic Judaism*, p. 226; cf. Dodd, *Gospel*, pp. 68ff; Ladd, *Theology*, p. 502.

259 *Setting*, pp. 348f.

260 *Paul and Rabbinic Judaism*, p. 323; *Setting*, pp. 363f.

261 *Setting*, p. 353; cf. *Paul and Rabbinic Judaism*, p. 142.

262 *Paul and Rabbinic Judaism*, p. 145; but cf. Ladd, *Theology*, p. 512.

263 'Sentences', p. 73.

264 Of the examples cited by Käsemann, at least three (Rom. 2.12; 1 Cor. 16.22; Gal. 1.9) occur in the context of theological rather than ethical statements; and a further two (1 Cor. 14.38; 2 Cor. 9.6) contain no unequivocal reference to 'the divine law of *jus talionis*' – leaving relatively few authentic examples. Cf. Barrett, *First Corinthians*, p. 334; *Second Corinthians*, pp. 235f; see ch. 2, n. 97 below.

265 See Roetzel, pp. 148–54, who notes confusion regarding the meaning of the term itself.

266 Cf. Bornkamm, *Paul*, p. 183.

267 But cf. Hunter's references to the 'tacit' use of Jesus' sayings in Paul's parenesis (*Paul*, pp. 45–51); also W.D. Davies, 'Teaching', pp. 325ff, and Dungan, *passim*, who notes a number of similarities between Mt. and Paul especially. Many of these apparent 'allusions', however, cannot with certainty be identified as deriving uniquely from Jesus.

268 Bornkamm, *Paul*, p. 182; Cranfield, 'Paul and the Law', pp. 65f; cf. Ladd, *Theology*, p. 514; Bruce, 'Paul and the Law', p. 278; Ahern, 'Spirit', p. 227.

269 See p. 59 below. Chadwick, p. 266, suggests that in some cases the assertion of authority may indicate that Paul is on the defensive.

270 Cf. Campenhausen, *Ecclesiastical Authority*, pp. 50ff.

271 See p. 36 above.

272 See p. 36 above.

273 Cf. Enslin, p. 87; J. Knox, *Ethic*, p. 61. Current NT scholarship has swung back to an appreciation of the importance of Paul's Jewish background; cf. E.P. Sanders, *Paul*, p. 7.

274 Cf. Barrett, 'Idols', p. 147.

275 See Acts 21.17–26; cf. Bruce, 'Paul and the Law', p. 264; Bornkamm, 'Stance', pp. 194–207; Chadwick, pp. 273ff. Hurd's limitation of the

passage to the issue of eating idol meat (*I Corinthians*, pp. 128–31) is too narrow for the context of ch. 9.

276 See Drane's critique, *Paul*, pp. 55–8; cf. E.P. Sanders, *Paul*, pp. 511ff.

277 Cf. Ladd, *Theology*, p. 514; *pace* Lampe, p. 82. For Davies' opinion, see *Paul and Rabbinic Judaism*, pp. 136ff (note his rebuttal of criticism on this point, p. 146, n. 1); 'Teaching', pp. 325ff, esp. 327ff, n. 44. Cf. Drane, *Paul*, pp. 134f.

278 So Esser, 'Law', p. 446; Ladd, *Theology*, pp. 509, 514; Goulder, *Midrash*, p. 158; Bultmann, *Theology*, vol. I, pp. 262, 344; Vidler, p. 79; Bruce, 'Paul and the Law', pp. 266, 277; *Paul*, p. 201; Furnish, *Theology*, pp. 59–65, 228, 235; cf. Merk, pp. 76f; Schnackenburg, p. 202.

279 As W.D. Davies himself points out, *Setting*, p. 343, n. 4, even the virtues lists are too generalized to constitute a new law; see Ladd, *Theology*, p. 514; J. Knox, *Ethic*, pp. 98f. Cf. Bornkamm, *Paul*, p. 182:

> 'The elements which elsewhere form indispensable concomitants of law and the bases of a community founded on it – a fixed law, an authoritative court that makes the law or interprets it in mandatory fashion, authorities which possibly enforce it and punish offenses against it – these either play no part at all or at best have a subordinate and indefinite role.'

Dodd, *Gospel*, p. 73; Vidler, p. 79; Bruce, 'Paul and the Law', p. 266.

280 Cf. Ladd, *Theology*, p. 514; Campenhausen, *Ecclesiastical Authority*, p. 49.

281 *Ethic*, p. 97.

282 *Ibid*. pp. 75f: 'It is not an accident that the only places in the New Testament where the antinomian question is explicitly raised are in Paul's letters.' No matter how much he denies it, claims Knox, 'Paul's doctrine of justification has in itself the seeds of antinomianism, and Paul's critics ... were not merely being perverse in saying so.' Cf. Smith, p. xi; W.L. Knox, *Jerusalem*, p. 310.

283 *Ethic*, pp. 89, 110.

284 Pp. 33ff.

285 Cf. the responses of Moule, 'Obligation', p. 397; E.P. Sanders, *Paul*, pp. 500f.

286 Cf. Campenhausen, *Formation*, pp. 25ff; *Begründung*, p. 41; Käsemann, 'Spirit', pp. 155ff; Meier, p. 169.

287 Cf. J. Knox, *Ethic*, p. 101; Campenhausen, *Begründung*, pp. 37ff; E.P. Sanders, *Paul*, p. 456; Gulin, p. 119: 'This reserve in regard to citing the Old Testament is all the more significant as an external norm of the law would have facilitated considerably his difficult task of ethical instruction among the heathen.' Nieder, pp. 107f, somewhat overstates the case; cf. Drane, *Paul*, p. 69.

288 Cf. Gutbrod, p. 1077: 'the proof from the Law is not adduced as the decisive argument, but as confirmation of what is already known to be right on other grounds'; also Merk, pp. 234, 244f; Bornkamm, *Paul*, p. 184; Campenhausen, *Formation*, pp. 30f (see n. 40); Esser, 'Law', p. 446. But cf. Rom. 13.8–10.

289 Cf. Steensgaard, pp. 110–18, on Phm. and 2 Cor. 8–9.

290 Cf. Houlden, *Ethics*, p. 26; Bornkamm, *Paul*, pp. 204f, 208f; Merk, p. 232: '... er will den verstehenden Gehorsam seiner Gemeinden, nicht den "blinden"'; Campenhausen, *Ecclesiastical Authority*, p. 52: 'The hortative and not the imperative is really the mood of the verbs in Pauline parenesis.' Cf. Paul's desire for 'reasoned' worship in 1 Cor. 14.1–19, esp. verses 14f. Pierce, p. 76, suggests that the real reason in these instances is the intractable response of the Corinthian church to any imposition of external authority; also Hurd, *I Corinthians*, pp. 258, 294.

291 Cf. Bornkamm, *Paul*, p. 184; Campenhausen, *Ecclesiastical Authority*, pp. 46f, 52.

292 Both appear to be converts from Pharisaic Judaism.

293 Cf. Moule, 'Obligation', pp. 404f.

294 Cf. Houlden, *Ethics*, p. 17.

295 Cf. Hummel, pp. 69f; Kilpatrick, p. 129.

296 See p. 128 below.

297 Houlden, *Ethics*, p. 106, suggests that, of all the NT writers, it is only Mt. and, probably, James who see the whole law as still binding on Christians.

298 Cf. Houlden, *Ethics*, pp. 48f: 'Here [in Mt.] we find none of the subtle combining of continuity with discontinuity, acceptance with rejection, which makes Paul so paradoxical and profound in his understanding of the role of Law ... Rather, the Law is accepted in principle and largely in content.'

299 So H.D. Betz, 'Makarismen', p. 19; *pace* W.D. Davies, *Setting*, p. 366; Hunter, *Design*, p. 16.

300 W.D. Davies, 'Torah and Dogma', p. 96; cf. Windisch, *Meaning*, pp. 79ff.

301 For Paul's teaching on sabbath observance, see Gal. 4.10; Col. 2.16ff; cf. Rom. 14.5ff.

302 The parallels Goulder observes between Mt. 6 and Rom. 14 (*Calendar*, p. 229) are largely superficial; the senses are quite different.

303 *Midrash*, p. 170.

304 See pp. 113ff below.

305 Cf. M.P. Brown, p. 43; Kilpatrick, p. 130; Hummel, p. 70.

306 Cf. Moule, 'Obligation', p. 405. W.D. Davies, *Setting*, p. 413, claims that though neither manifests the intricate, detailed casuistic exegesis of the rabbis, both nonetheless reveal an 'incipient casuistry': 'What we find in Matthew, and to a lesser degree in Paul, is that the revelatory and radical demands are used in what we may loosely call a regulatory, rabbinic manner, that is, they come to constitute a base, or given ground, from which halakoth are deduced or to which they are attached'; cf. *Torah in Messianic Age*, p. 92. The seeds of second-century neo-legalism are to be found in both, claims Davies; but he overemphasizes this aspect for both writers.

307 See pp. 106f below; cf. Jüngel, *Paulus und Jesus*, p. 272.

308 Thus J.T. Sanders, *Ethics*, p. 42, suggests the similarities of Mt. 22.40 and Rom. 13.9 are more apparent than real: 'for what Paul means is that the Torah may be dispensed with in view of the all-inclusive command to love, whereas Matthew views the command to love as "principle of interpretation," on the basis of which one may reinterpret the Torah'; cf. Houlden, *Ethics*, p. 107: 'The other evangelists and Paul are clearer

in giving pride of place to the command to love ... by it the Law is not merely newly interpreted but rivalled and supplanted.' But see pp. 107f and ch. 4, n. 98 below.

309 Cf. Green, *Matthew*, pp. 36f.

310 J.T. Sanders' distinction between the two, however (*Ethics*, p. 48), is a dubious one: in his view, Matthew uses 'tenets of holy law' to stimulate righteousness in view of the coming kingdom, while Paul uses them in a more isolated, arbitrary and absolute sense.

311 W.D. Davies, *Setting*, pp. 365f, sees in this a common understanding of the 'law of Christ': 'The upshot of all this is that Paul, who is usually set in antithesis to Matthew, would probably not have found the Matthaean emphasis on the "law of Christ" either strange or uncongenial. He too knew of the same law, although the circumstances of his ministry demanded from him greater concentration on other aspects of the Gospel.' See, however, Goulder, *Midrash*, p. 170, and pp. 37f above.

312 Bornkamm, 'End-Expectation', pp. 24f, speaks of an 'unrecognized' inconsistency; but cf. Suggs' critique, pp. 113f, and Carlston, 'Things', pp. 81, 90f.

313 Hummel, e.g. pp. 65f, sees Mt.'s polemic directed against Pharisees and antinomians, and Paul's against legalists and libertines; he overlooks the similarities of the issues, however. Cf. Kilpatrick, p. 108.

314 Cf. Goulder, *Midrash*, p. 170: 'whenever there is a point of decision ... Paul always opts for a radical, Matthew for the conservative position.'

## 2. Reward and Punishment

1 For clarity's sake, in this chapter the term 'eschatological' is used only in its futurist sense.

2 Cf. Houlden, *Ethics*, p. 52; G. Barth, 'Law', pp. 58f, includes the following statistics:

| | | | |
|---|---|---|---|
| *κρίσις* | (Mt: 12 | Mk: 0 | Lk: 4) |
| *ἡμέρα κρίσεως* | (Mt: 4 | Mk: 0 | Lk: 0) |
| *μισθός* | (Mt: 10 | Mk: 1 | Lk: 3) |
| *εἰς τὸ σκότος τὸ ἐξώτερον* | (Mt: 3 | Mk: 0 | Lk: 0) |
| *ἐκεῖ ἔσται ὁ κλαυθμὸς καὶ ὁ βρυγμὸς τῶν ὀδόντων* | (Mt: 6 | Mk: 0 | Lk: 1) |
| [cf. also *γέεννα* | (Mt: 7 | Mk: 3 | Lk: 1)] |

He adds, p. 153: 'the emphasising of the judgment of God is a consequence of the attitude to the law'.

3 Note the emphasis on judgement in the immediate contexts: 5.21–30; 18.6–10.

4 See Meier, p. 40 (cf. ch. 2, n. 15 below); Bacon, p. 428.

5 Kinniburgh, pp. 414ff, suggests that Mt. makes Jesus a preacher of judgement like John the Baptist.

6 On 5.25f as a reference to eschatological judgement, see Allen, p. 50; Stendahl, 'Matthew', p. 776.

7 For the distinction between *γέεννα* and *ᾅδης*, see Jeremias, '*ᾅδης*', p. 148; Bietenhard, 'Hell', p. 208; cf. J.A. Baird, pp. 218–24; Wilder, *Eschatology and Ethics*, p. 99.

8 Though similar in imagery to many non-eschatological parables in Jewish literature, 7.24–7 almost certainly functions as an eschatological sanction in view of the overall tenor of the Sermon; see Windisch, *Bergpredigt*, p. 10; Wilder, *Eschatology and Ethics*, p. 105; Green, *Matthew*, p. 97; Bonnard, *Matthieu*, pp. 107ff; T.H. Robinson, p. 66; *pace* Tasker, *Matthew*, pp. 84f.

9 Cf. Windisch, *Bergpredigt*, pp. 19f: 'Die Bergrede als Ganzes ist eine Predigt, die die eschatologische Gerichts- und Heilserwartung zum Fundament, zum entscheidenden Richtpunkt für Leben und Tun, für die Haltung gegenüber den Menschen im diesseitigen Leben wie für die Haltung gegenüber Gott macht ...'

10 In Mk., only in 9.43–9.

11 Elsewhere only in Lk. 13.28; cf. Houlden, *Ethics*, p. 52.

12 Bornkamm, 'End-Expectation', p. 22, speaks of a 'more richly developed' Parousia in Mt. than in Mk., and sees this as an example of Mt.'s tendency to sharpen the futurist element in Jesus' eschatology. Houlden, *Ethics*, p. 53, attributes Mt.'s emphasis on the future Eschaton partly to 'his love of structure and scheme: ... the picture must be full and detailed, right to the End'. The primary factor, however, is his conviction of the importance of judgement as a sanction for ethics; here eschatology serves a pragmatic end.

13 Cf. the general tenor of ch. 24 as a whole. The fact that many eschatological statements are expressed in the second person rather than the third may also be indicative; J.A. Baird, pp. 144f.

14 Cf. Bornkamm, 'End-Expectation', p. 23; 'Verzögerung', pp. 116f; Meier, pp. 39f. Houlden, *Ethics*, p. 20, suggests that 'the fact that the teaching of Jesus occupies so much of the book is itself evidence that the Church is to reckon on a period of life in the conditions of the present age before the Lord returns at its end'; cf. pp. 47, 49; Dodd, *Apostolic Preaching*, p. 121. Lillie, p. 144, detects no sense of imminent expectation in the SM, and concludes that the Sermon is more suited to the life of a settled community than to one living under an emergency ethic; also Wilder, *Eschatology and Ethics*, pp. 140f. J.T. Sanders, on the other hand (*Ethics*, pp. 45–9), sees Mt.'s ethics so bound up with a sense of imminent expectation that they may only be considered as *Interimsethik*. In any case, it is clear that even with the ethical emphasis, the Parousia is expected in the not-too-distant future.

15 Cf. Braumann–Brown, p. 894. Meier, pp. 39f, however, sees the focus rather on the *stringency* of judgement.

16 J.T. Sanders, *Ethics*, p. 40, suggests that though Mt. falls far short of Lk. in building a consistent theology out of the delay, he makes more of an attempt to deal with its practical implications for living in the present.

17 See ch. 5, n. 19 below.

18 So Allen, p. 42; Stendahl, 'Matthew', p. 775; T.H. Robinson, pp. 27f; Filson, p. 77; Wellhausen, p. 13; McNeile, p. 50; Fenton, pp. 79f; see also Hill, *Matthew*, pp. 109f; Bonnard, *Matthieu*, p. 55; cf. Wilder, *Eschatology and Ethics*, pp. 106, 108f, who sees many of the promises as having a double referent.

19 Cf. Houlden, *Ethics*, p. 53; Allen, p. 213; Bonnard, *Matthieu*, p. 289; Smith, p. 167; Fenton, p. 317; Hill, *Matthew*, p. 284; Plummer, *Matthew*,

pp. 270f; McNeile, p. 282; Bornkamm, 'End-Expectation', pp. 29f; Micklem, p. 192.

20 Some are indefinite (6.1, 4, 6, 18 – but note the future reference in verses 19–21; 7.1f, 7–11). Similarly, not all of Mt.'s references to the kingdom of heaven are unambiguously future in sense (cf. 11.2; 12.28; 13.24ff, 31f, 33, 41, 47ff; 16.19; 20.1ff; 21.31, 43); *pace* Bornkamm, 'End-Expectation', pp. 34, 44.

21 Cf. Sand, *Gesetz*, p. 115.

22 Cf. Houlden, *Ethics*, pp. 52f: 'He consistently binds commands and exhortations to promises for the future assize, sometimes giving to sayings which could in themselves easily be read as maxims for present conduct a clear reference to reward or punishment on the Last Day'; see 10.39–42; 16.24–7; 19.27–30.

23 See p. 56 and ch. 2, n. 40 below. Mt.'s use of the term *δίκαιοι* in the context of judgement is significant in itself (cf. 13.43; 25.31ff, 37; Bornkamm, 'End-Expectation', p. 43).

24 Cf. Moule, 'As we forgive', p. 74: 'forgiveness, though not conditional on merit, is, nevertheless conditional – conditional on response to the gift, conditional on the capacity to receive it'.

25 The specific sense of the genitives is debated, but the phrases are probably best understood as referring to the reward that prophets and righteous men will receive; so Allen, p. 112; Smith, pp. 124f; Fenton, p. 167; Filson, p. 134; Micklem, p. 108. Plummer, *Matthew*, p. 158, denies that the reward is offered as a motive for action: 'the motive in each case is love and reverence ... The reward is a support to this motive.' But a 'support' to a motive surely functions as a motive in itself, even though it be secondary.

26 A similar point may underlie 16.19 and 18.18.

27 Thus, W. Schneider's view, p. 366, 'The human principle of "tit for tat" has no place in the divine judge's dealings with men', is different from Mt.'s understanding; cf. Sand, *Gesetz*, p. 117, who argues against Käsemann's description of this as 'eschatologischen Jus talionis'.

28 Hill, *Matthew*, pp. 159, 180, argues that *ὡς* and *κατά* are to be taken as causative, not comparative, but offers no supporting evidence (see also Micklem, pp. 92, 160; Bonnard, *Matthieu*, pp. 116, 138); cf. Bauer, p. 898; Lagrange, p. 310; Lohmeyer, *Matthäus*, p. 256; Grundmann, *Matthäus*, p. 254; S.-B., vol. I, p. 478.

29 Sand, *Gesetz*, p. 115, however, correctly observes that one cannot characterize the relation of the Christian to Christ in the Gospel as simply *Lohnverhältnis*; see ch. 3 below. Wilder, *Eschatology and Ethics*, seeks to demonstrate that the eschatological sanction, though most prominent, is really merely a 'formal' and 'stylistic' one (pp. 87ff), and not the most basic one – which he identifies as the nature of God underlying the eschatological sanction (pp. 116ff), and which in turn is ultimately subordinated to an appeal to human reason and moral discernment (the 'final' sanction: pp. 116ff, 125; cf. p. 103). It is this ultimate appeal to reason and the 'God-conscious moral nature of man' that most clearly distinguishes the ethics of the Gospel from the law-based ethics of Judaism, according to Wilder (pp. 125, 132). Such an overdrawn contrast, however, overlooks the strong Jewish background

and outlook of Mt., and reflects the fundamental biases that distort Wilder's analysis of the text.

30 Note that it is Mt. alone who makes explicit the self-acknowledged guilt of the Jews before Pilate (27.24f).

31 On the significance of 22.7 for a post A.D. 70 dating of the Gospel, see Fenton, p. 348; Bonnard, *Matthieu*, p. 320; Smith, p. 174; Micklem, p. 210; Allen, p. 234; Stendahl, 'Matthew', p. 791; Hill, *Matthew*, p. 302; cf. Green, *Matthew*, p. 181. Contrast J.A.T. Robinson, *Redating*, pp. 19–21.

32 See ch. 1, n. 131 above.

33 Cf. Kinniburgh, pp. 415f. Hare, pp. 164–6, and Green, *Matthew*, pp. 35f, point out a difference here between Mt. and Paul: whereas Paul does not view the rejection of the Jews as final, Mt. does; the difference is attributed to the fact that Mt. is written at a later time.

34 See Meier, pp. 9ff, for an excellent discussion.

35 See ch. 1, n. 105 above.

36 So Bornkamm, 'End-Expectation', p. 19; Green, *Matthew*, pp. 134, 136f; Smith, pp. 139–41; Filson, pp. 164f; T.H. Robinson, p. 124; Hill, *Matthew*, pp. 237, 239; cf. Bonnard, *Matthieu*, pp. 204, 208; for alternative explanations, see Fenton, p. 220; Stendahl, 'Matthew', pp. 785f; Plummer, *Matthew*, p. 193; McNeile, pp. 202f, 204.

37 Cf. Wilder, *Eschatology and Ethics*, p. 104; Hill, *Matthew*, pp. 302f; Stendahl, 'Matthew', p. 791; Filson, pp. 233f; Bonnard, *Matthieu*, p. 320; Fenton, p. 350.

38 'End-Expectation', p. 19; in Bornkamm's view, the Matthean text that best characterizes this church is 22.14: 'Many are called but few are chosen'; cf. J.A. Baird, p. 139. Thus, the 'elect' in 24.22*, 24*, 31* are not to be strictly identified with the present community of disciples as a whole. In view of this, Houlden's description of the Matthean community as one 'living in expectation of the End and assured of its role on that day' (*Ethics*, p. 53), while true in the first respect is inaccurate in the second.

39 See ch. 4, n. 28 below.

40 The identity of *ἑνὶ τούτων τῶν ἀδελφῶν μου τῶν ἐλαχίστων* (25.40) is debated. Green, *Matthew*, p. 207, sets forth convincingly the argument for the above interpretation; see also LaVerdiere–Thompson, p. 581, n. 35. Note esp. the Matthean references to *οἱ μικροί* (see ch. 3, n. 66; ch. 4, n. 29 below) and the post-Resurrection designation of the disciples as 'brothers' of Christ (28.10; cf. 6.9; 12.49f). The description of them as hungry and thirsty, strangers, naked, sick, and imprisoned, would seem to anticipate times of persecution; cf. Stendahl, *Paul*, pp. 62f.

41 See pp. 78ff below.

42 See Roetzel, pp. 142–62, on 1 Cor. 16.22.

43 Dodd, *Romans*, pp. 20ff, was perhaps the first to suggest that Paul's use of *ὀργή* implies an impersonal, almost mechanistic force that, set in progress, executes the natural consequences of sin – rather than a personal attribute of God expressing anger against an individual; cf. Macgregor, pp. 102–5, who cites Cave: 'they are almost personified powers, which, owing to God their origin, act on in partial independence of God, and are hostile to men as He is not'; Caird, *Principalities*, p. 40; Roetzel, pp.

79ff. Whiteley, *Theology*, pp. 61–72, concludes that Paul uses the term in an effectus and not an affectus sense. But as Stählin has argued, 'ὀργή', pp. 423ff, the emotive aspect of ὀργή in Paul's writing cannot be dismissed as simply as this.

44 Cf. Bruce, *Romans*, p. 195; Murray, *Romans*, vol. II, pp. 33ff; Barrett, *Romans*, p. 189; Nygren, *Romans*, pp. 370f; contrast Leenhardt, p. 258, note.

45 See Roetzel, pp. 170ff. E.P. Sanders, *Paul*, p. 503, apparently fails to appreciate the multi-dimensional character of Paul's argumentation when he asserts with regard to this passage: 'It is not the transgressions *qua* transgressions which exclude one (as a punishment for them).'

46 A difficult passage to interpret; those who see the threat of judgement as eschatological in some sense include J.T. Sanders, *Ethics*, pp. 47f; Robertson–Plummer, p. 67; Barrett, *First Corinthians*, pp. 90ff.

47 'Corruption' (*φθορά*) here is to be understood in the eschatological sense; note the contrast with 'eternal life'.

48 The majority of commentators take this as a reference not to the threat of judgement, but to living in awe and humility before others; but see Houlden, *Letters*, p. 87; Jones, p. 37; Müller, p. 91.

49 *ἀπρόσκοποι* can mean either 'blameless' (R.P. Martin, *Philippians*, p. 69; Lightfoot, *Philippians*, p. 85; Plummer, *Philippians*, p. 16; Beasley-Murray, p. 986) or 'not causing others to stumble' (Beare, *Philippians*, p. 55; Jones, p. 9; Caird, *Letters*, pp. 108f).

50 Nieder's statement, however, pp. 109f, 137, that aside from Rom. 13.2 all of Paul's threats of judgement stand at the end of *Lasterkataloge*, is inaccurate.

51 Note that here Paul's use of *ἄδικοι* is ethical and not forensic in sense. Gager's observation, p. 334, that the eschatological sanction is only one of many acting here, is correct; but it is the following and not the preceding context that makes this most clear (the link with verses 2–8 is tenuous).

52 The textual variant that adds 'upon the sons of disobedience' is indicative of later scribal attempts to bring the text into line with Pauline theology as delineated elsewhere.

53 Cf. E.P. Sanders, 'Fulfilling the Law', p. 124; Donfried, 'Justification', p. 102 *et passim*. Mattern, pp. 133, 136, fails to take adequate account of the fact that these are addressed to the Christian community (cf. Nieder's assertion that Paul's threats of judgement are never aimed directly at Christians, p. 138). Note that when confronted with an actual problem of immorality, Paul makes greater allowance for God's graciousness than when he discourses more generally on the subject (cf. 1 Cor. 5.5).

54 In Rom. 3.6 and 14.10, the judgement is said to be 'God's'; but cf. Rom. 2.16: 'God judges the secrets of men by Christ Jesus' (cf. 1 Cor. 15.24–8). See Barrett, *Second Corinthians*, p. 160.

55 Keck, 'Justification', pp. 208f.

56 Cf. W.D. Davies, *Setting*, pp. 347ff; E.P. Sanders, *Paul*, pp. 515ff; Houlden, *Ethics*, p. 16.

57 Rom. 2.6–16 especially seems to stand in tension with the principle of justification by faith alone, for here Paul appears to speak of judgement by works in the most thoroughgoing sense; even 'righteousness' is defined

in terms of works (cf. E.P. Sanders, *Paul*, p. 516; Barrett's interpretation of 2.7 as a reference to 'those who with patient endurance look beyond their own well-doing to the glory, honour, and incorruption God alone can give' (*Romans*, p. 46) is unconvincing, and fails to appreciate the overall sense of 2.6–10; cf. Cranfield's criticism, *Romans*, vol. I, pp. 147ff). But this passage must be interpreted in light of the larger section Rom. 1–3, which – based on traditional Jewish views of ultimate recompense – seeks to demonstrate that *everyone* is guilty of sin and therefore deserving of God's judgement, i.e. that *no one* will be justified on the basis of doing 'good'. The focus, then, is on the negative side (cf. Best, *Romans*, p. 25; Murray, *Romans*, vol. I, p. 63; Bruce, *Romans*, pp. 88ff; Nygren, *Romans*, p. 130; Leenhardt, pp. 78f; Mattern, p. 68; Synofzik, p. 81; T.W. Manson, 'Romans', p. 942; Cranfield, *Romans*, vol. I, p. 152). The principle of recompense here cited functions not as a statement of the basis on which one finds acceptance with God, but as a statement of the grounds on which the entire world stands condemned and therefore in need of grace – and an entirely different principle by which to find his favour. Cf. E.P. Sanders, *Paul*, p. 516: 'Once we see that here the righteousness terminology refers to the question of *punishment*, and not to whether or not one is *saved* ... the difficulty vanishes'; Nygren, *Romans*, pp. 127ff, 130; Synofzik, pp. 85, 90; and esp. Cranfield's discussion, *Romans*, vol. I, pp. 151ff. (Cranfield's argument against this position is weak; for him, 2.6–16 is to be interpreted rather in the light of the fact that faith opens up the possibility of truly moral living; *ibid.* pp. 147, 152; so also Black, pp. 55f; Mattern, p. 179; cf. Murray, *Romans*, vol. I, pp. 62ff.) See further the two excursuses of Wilckens, *Römer*, pp. 127–46.

58 Cf. *Paul*, p. 517: 'the distinction between being *judged on the basis of deeds* ..., on the one hand, and being *saved by God's gracious election*, on the other, was the general view in Rabbinic literature. It is a very straightforward distinction, and it should occasion no surprise when it meets us in Paul.'

59 Cf. *Patterns*, p. 64: 'The future judgment was, in a sense, anticipated, its verdict assured: but II Cor. 5.10 shows that the old picture remained alongside'; also *Ethics*, p. 30.

60 *Paul*, pp. 515–18; cf. McComiskey, p. 370. Sanders fails, however, to show precisely *how* the two doctrines fit together.

61 Recent major works on this topic include those of Roetzel, Mattern, and Synofzik; see also the extensive bibliographical references in Donfried, 'Justification', pp. 90ff, n. 3; Roetzel, ch. 1. Roetzel unfortunately omits serious discussion of several crucial passages (e.g. 2 Cor. 5.10; Gal. 5.19ff) and fails to get to the heart of the problem. Mattern analyses the different aspects of judgement in a much more satisfying way, but Donfried's criticism of her Lutheran conclusion ('Justification', pp. 105ff) is entirely valid. Donfried does an excellent job of showing the close link between justification and obedience, but restricts the interpretation of 1 Cor. 3.1–15 too narrowly to apostolic workers, fails to deal adequately with the whole matter of rewards, wrongly understands 1 Cor. 11.27ff, and has to distort the meaning of 1 Cor. 5.1–5 to maintain his (too) neat analysis. Synofzik's concern with the tradition history behind the Pauline

formulations results in a study that sheds little light on the real problem; but see his useful evaluation of previous works, pp. 9ff, 151ff.

62 See pp. 66f below.

63 See p. 115 below.

64 E.P. Sanders, *Paul*, p. 517, sees moral living as the condition of remaining 'in'; cf. Donfried, 'Justification', pp. 93, 96f.

65 See esp. Roetzel, pp. 163ff; Mattern, pp. 168–79.

66 So Stumpff, pp. 889f; Mattern, pp. 176ff; Thrall, *Corinthians*, p. 32; Robertson–Plummer, pp. 64f; Morris, *First Corinthians*, pp. 68f; Héring, *First Corinthians*, pp. 23f; Grosheide, p. 87; Barrett, *First Corinthians*, pp. 88ff; *pace* Orr–Walther, pp. 173f. On the meaning of ζημιόω, see Stumpff, pp. 889f.

67 Cf. Col. 2.18; Barrett, *First Corinthians*, p. 218; Goudge, *First Corinthians*, p. 79; Grosheide, p. 216; Moffatt, *First Corinthians*, pp. 128f; *pace* Morris, *First Corinthians*, p. 140.

68 Cf. Conzelmann, *1 Corinthians*, p. 162; Caird, *Letters*, p. 140.

69 *Ibid*. p. 145; Beare, *Philippians*, p. 135. On the meaning of εἴ πως, see Caird, *Letters*, p. 140; R.P. Martin, *Philippians*, pp. 135f; Jones, pp. 54f; Bonnard, *Philippiens*, p. 67; Vincent, p. 106.

70 Cf. Beasley-Murray, pp. 987f; Donfried, 'Justification', p. 100.

71 See Mattern, pp. 179–86; on ὁ ἔπαινος, cf. Rom. 2.29; Barrett, *First Corinthians*, p. 104; Bruce, *Corinthians*, p. 48.

72 So Héring, *Second Corinthians*, p. 39; Mattern, pp. 151–7; cf. pp. 158–62, 178; Bruce, *Corinthians*, p. 206; Hughes, pp. 181ff; Menzies, p. 37; Plummer, *Second Corinthians*, pp. 155, 160; cf. Murray, *Romans*, vol. II, p. 184; Strachan, p. 104. Barrett, *Second Corinthians*, pp. 160f, fails to distinguish the two and provides a somewhat inadequate exposition – as does Synofzik, pp. 74–7.

73 See ch. 2, n. 59 above.

74 This is totally apart from the natural consequences of perversion (Rom. 1.27).

75 *Pace* Donfried, 'Justification', p. 107; note the distinction between κρίνω and κατακρίνω. On these passages, see Roetzel, pp. 115–25, 137–42; cf. ch. 2, n. 53 above.

76 See pp. 58f above.

77 See ch. 2, n. 86 below.

78 See Roetzel, pp. 132f, on 2 Thess. 3.1–16.

79 E.P. Sanders, *Paul*, pp. 447ff, asserts that nothing is 'more certain, or more consistently expressed'. Cf. Nineham, *Use*, pp. 141f; Kallas, p. 367; Rom. 13.11f; 1 Cor. 1.7f; 5.5; 7.29, 31; 10.11; 15.23, 51ff; 2 Cor. 1.14; Phil. 1.6, 10; 2.16; 3.11, 20f; 4.5; Col. 3.4; 1 Thess. 1.9f; 3.13; 4.13 – 5.11, 23; 2 Thess. 2.1–8. There is still no conclusive evidence for any clear development in the major elements of Paul's eschatological thought: cf. Ellis, 'II Corinthians V. 1–10', pp. 212, 224; A. L. Moore, *Parousia*, pp. 108ff; Merk, p. 246, esp. n. 50; W. Baird, p. 327; E.P. Sanders, *Paul*, p. 432. (For résumés of attempts to trace such a development, see C. Brown, pp. 922–7; Hurd, *I Corinthians*, pp. 8f, nn. 2, 3; cf. E.P. Sanders, *Paul*, pp. 432f, n. 9; see p. 4 and Intro, n. 23 above.) It is quite possible that there is a subtle shift of focus in the later writings, however, correlated

with Paul's growing recognition of the likelihood of his own death before the Parousia: see esp. Harris, pp. 32–57. Sanders accepts Moule's thesis of a basic consistency behind varying formulations; cf. *Paul*, p. 448: 'the fact that Paul does not always describe "the end" in precisely the same terms does not mean that he held no unified conception of it'; p. 433, n. 9: 'It seems safest to take such changes as developments in *presentation* and *argument*.'

80 ὁ κύριος ἐγγύς (4.5*b*) is equivocal in its sense; those who take it in a temporal sense include Plummer, *Philippians*, p. 93; Beasley-Murray, p. 988; Lightfoot, *Philippians*, p. 158; R.P. Martin, *Philippians*, p. 155, who also cites Gnilka and Dibelius; Bonnard, *Philippiens*, p. 75; Beare, *Philippians*, p. 146; Caird, *Letters*, pp. 150f; Vincent, pp. 133f; Houlden, *Letters*, p. 110; Bornkamm, *Paul*, pp. 205f.

81 Synofzik, pp. 107f, apparently fails to recognize the link between Paul's *Gerichts- und Vergeltungsaussagen* and his appeal to the *Naherwartung*.

82 Cf. A.L. Moore, *Parousia*, pp. 114ff; Houlden, *Ethics*, pp. 28f; Wendland, p. 77. Opinions vary as to the importance of the eschatological factor: Schoeps, *Paul*, p. 102, sees it as absolutely central (cf. also Merk, p. 233; Nineham, *Use*, p. 159). Wilder, 'Kerygma', pp. 524ff, sees the real crisis to be not the Parousia, but some grave danger posed to the church by the world around it – albeit as viewed from an eschatological perspective; 1 Cor. 7 is thus not interim ethics but 'emergency ethics' for a young and struggling church in a hostile culture. Gager, p. 333, views the crisis in Parousial terms, but sees Paul's preference for celibacy shaped more by popular philosophy than the Parousia: 'the end-time language is introduced as an additional support'. Both Doughty, pp. 70ff, and Bornkamm, *Paul*, pp. 206ff, suggest that the eschatological factor is used to highlight the relationship of the believer to Christ in the present: 'The sole leitmotiv and criterion in Paul's counsel is the believer's relationship to the coming Lord' (*ibid*., p. 208). Most commentators, however, see the eschatological sanction as the primary one in the chapter.

83 Whiteley's suggestion, *Theology*, p. 215, that a sense of imminent expectation may lie behind Paul's failure to mention procreation as an end of marriage – 'which for a Jew was a really astonishing omission' – fails to take into account the fact that (1) procreation was almost certainly assumed to be part of normal marriage, and therefore would have called for no special mention; (2) the supporting non-eschatological factors (1 Cor. 7.28, 32–5) would explain such an omission equally well.

84 Thus e.g. with regard to Rom. 13.11–14, Dodd, 'Mind', II, p. 111, hears more the voice of 'an earnest preacher' than the 'herald of an imminent catastrophe'; cf. *Romans*, pp. 209ff. Similarly, Harris, p. 51, perceives no sense of personal urgency, but only that of the 'perpetual "imminence"' of the Parousia; cf. Leenhardt, p. 339; Black, p. 163; Murray, *Romans*, vol. II, pp. 167ff. Merk, pp. 242f, suggests that what is most important to Paul is not so much the *Naherwartung* itself as the certainty of God's future action; thus the motives of eschatological reward and punishment are not in essence tied directly to the *Naherwartung* itself. Contrast J.T. Sanders, *Ethics*, pp. 61f.

85 *Ethics*, pp. 56f.

86 *Ethics*, p. 32; cf. Bornkamm, *Paul*, pp. 205–10. Houlden adduces the contrasting attitudes to government expressed in 1 Cor. 6.1ff and Rom. 13.1ff as evidence of this wavering tendency (pp. 11f; also Dodd, 'Mind', II, pp. 113ff); but 1 Cor. 6.1ff expresses not so much a negative attitude to government as the importance of dealing with Christian problems strictly within the church itself – for which the reference to the End serves merely as a supportive sanction. At another point, Houlden seems to suggest that even the Rom. 13 passage, with its emphasis on acquiescence to the 'powers that be', may be evidence of Paul's view of the near End (p. 81; contrast Kallas, pp. 367f, who takes exactly the opposite view and therefore sees the passage as an interpolation) – as may be also the acceptance of slavery evidenced in 1 Cor. 7.20ff; Col. 3.22 – 4.1; and Phm. (p. 21; also Thomas, p. 96; cf. Wilder, 'Kerygma', p. 535). The latter two phenomena, however, are probably better explained as examples of simple, non-critical acceptance of normal socio-cultural institutions (cf. Klausner, pp. 565ff, 575ff), reinforced – as Houlden points out – by the status of the Christian community as a small minority lacking any political power or influence.

87 *Pace* Nieder, pp. 137f, who consistently interprets the eschatological sanction in Paul's parenesis in a positive sense – 'a matter of joy to the Christian'. Nieder's undervaluation of negative motivation may be due in part to his conviction that Paul presupposes a deep drive on the part of every Christian to do consistently what is right (p. 138).

88 Cf. Houlden, *Ethics*, p. 30. Nieder thus suggests that Paul's use of the judgement sanction often carries a sidewise glance at the fate of the *λοιποί* (1 Thess. 5.3, 5), the ἀπολλύμενοι (2 Thess. 2.12), the ἄδικοι (1 Cor. 6.9), etc.; but see ch. 2, n. 53 above.

89 Cf. Faw, p. 25; see Gal. 1.6; 3.3f; 4.11; 5.2–4.

90 Apart from those appearing in epistolary introductions (cited above), see Rom. 6.17f; 15.14; 16.19; 1 Cor. 6.11; 11.2; 2 Cor. 1.24; 7.4, 7, 11, 14ff; 8.7, 24; 9.2, 4; Phil. 2.12; 3.20 – 4.1; 4.15f; Col. 1.21f; 2.5, 10; 3.3f, 7, 9f, 12; 1 Thess. 2.13f, 19f; 3.6ff; 4.1, 9f; 5.1, 4ff, 8ff, 24; 2 Thess. 2.13; 3.4; Phm. 7, 21; cf. Campenhausen, *Ecclesiastical Authority*, pp. 49f.

91 But cf. 1 Thess. 2.5!

92 Cf. Plummer, *Second Corinthians*, p. 157: 'men are not much influenced by the prospect of losing possible blessings; the dread of possible pains is more influential' (attributed to Chrysostom; cf. G.F. Moore, vol. II, pp. 89f); Plummer's addition, 'But *present* gains and losses are the most influential of all', represents a point of view that Mt. at least would dispute.

93 Cf. J.T. Sanders, *Ethics*, pp. 48ff.

94 Cf. Mt. 5.22f, 28ff.

95 J.T. Sanders, *Ethics*, p. 49, suggests that Mt.'s position with regard to a new law represents the normal development still awaited in the Pauline writings – the obvious 'next step' following the recognition of a delay in the Parousia; but the analysis fails to do justice to either the evangelist's legal or his eschatological perspectives.

96 Note the relative occurrences of ἐλπίζω (Mt: 1 Paul: 15) and ἐλπίς (Mt: 0 Paul: 29); cf. Hoffmann, p. 241.

97 The clearest examples in Paul are 2 Cor. 9.6; Gal. 6.7f – both of which appear to be traditional proverbs.

## 3. Relationship to Christ and the Role of Grace

1 Cf. Freyne, pp. 184, 197. Luz thus speaks of the *Transparenz* of Matthew's portrait of the disciples: 'Kennzeichnend für den matthäischen Jüngerbegriff ist also die Tendenz, gerade – was Matthäus betont – das Vergangene für die Gegenwart transparent zu machen' ('Jünger', p. 160 *et passim*; cf. Sheridan, p. 242). Jesus' words to the Twelve are not to be taken as applying only to the leaders of the Christian community; cf. G. Barth, 'Law', pp. 96ff; Luz, 'Jünger', p. 159; Freyne, pp. 185ff, 189.

2 See 10.5ff; 19.28. Luz' attempt to find *Transparenz* in 10.5ff ('Jünger', pp. 143f) is unconvincing.

3 *Pace* Strecker, *Weg*, pp. 193f; Sheridan, p. 255; Houlden, *Ethics*, pp. 47f. It is rather only in very limited respects that the disciples function as models – e.g. in the immediate and total response of the four fishermen to Jesus' call. Mt. does shade out certain negative aspects of the disciples' behaviour in Mk., esp. their non-comprehension. (See 13.19, 23, 51; 14.33; 17.23; cf. 16.12 and 17.13 – which latter, however, may be little more than explanatory devices; note that 15.16* retains the reference to ἀσύνετοι. Though many of the omissions may be accounted for by a propensity to abbreviate the Marcan narrative, Sheridan, pp. 238ff, suggests that understanding is essential if discipleship centres on obedience to Jesus' teachings, and mission involves their propagation; see G. Barth, 'Law', pp. 105–12, 118; Zumstein, pp. 203ff; Kretzer, pp. 97ff, 113ff; Houlden, *Ethics*, p. 48; Luz, 'Jünger', pp. 147ff; Sheridan, pp. 244ff; cf. Kee, pp. 152f, and Best, 'Disciples', pp. 379ff, on the role of disciples in Mk. Note also the close relation between understanding and obedience in Psa. 119.27, 32, 34, 73, 125, 144, 169; cf. verses 99f, 103f; Conzelmann, 'συνίημι', pp. 890ff. For Mt. it is not the disciples but the unrepentant Jews who fail to understand.) But in other cases he brings their failings even more sharply into focus (esp. ὀλιγοπιστία: cf. G. Barth, 'Law', pp. 119f; 'Glaube', pp. 282ff; Strecker, *Weg*, pp. 233ff).

4 On ἐξουσία in Mt., see esp. Hübner, *Gesetz in der synoptischen Tradition*, pp. 196–207.

5 On Mt.'s omission of Mk. 1.23–8, with its otherwise significant reference to Jesus' authority in exorcism, see pp. 9f and ch. 1, n. 27 above.

6 Held, p. 171; cf. Hull, p. 135, who suggests that the author's concern is rather to set Jesus' authority over against mere (magical) methods or techniques.

7 Hull, pp. 132f, 135, 137, 141, 144, suggests that Jesus' miracle-working authority is subordinated in Mt.'s thought to his moral authority, and therefore a witness to it (8.23–7; 14.22–34; 17.14–21); cf. Campenhausen, *Ecclesiastical Authority*, pp. 6f; Hübner, *Gesetz in der synoptischen Tradition*, p. 200: 'Für ... Matthäus besteht die Autorität Jesu in der Macht seiner Predigt.' But such a distinction is too sharp; see Vermes, p. 123; Dunn, *Unity*, p. 50.

8 *Ethics*, p. 14: 'the content of what is commanded is secondary in importance

to the mere fact that it is commanded'. Here, Houlden suggests, submission to authoritative commands is more important than logical consistency of behaviour.

9 Michel, 'Matthäusevangeliums', sees in 28.18–20 a summary of the entire Gospel; cf. Hubbard, p. 98, and esp. Zumstein, pp. 86–106.

10 P. 46.

11

| | |
|---|---|
| *Χριστός* | (Mt: 17 Mk: 7) |
| *κύριος/κύριε* | (Mt: 80 Mk: 18) |
| *υἱὸς θεοῦ* | (Mt: 9 Mk: 4) |
| *υἱὸς ἀνθρώπου* | (Mt: 31 Mk: 14) |
| *Ἐμμανουήλ* | (Mt: 1 Mk: 0) |
| *υἱὸς Δαβίδ* | (Mt: 10 Mk: 3) |

*βασιλεὺς τῶν Ἰουδαίων*, *διδάσκαλος*, and *προφήτης* are used of him as well.

12 W.D. Davies, *Setting*, pp. 96f; cf. Foerster, '*κύριος*', p. 1093. It is not only true disciples who so address him, however (7.22; 8.21; 25.11, 24, 44). In Mk., only the Syrophoenician woman calls him *κύριε* (7.28).

13 See 8.19; 12.38; 19.16; 22.16, 24, 36; 26.5, 49; Bornkamm, 'End-Expectation', p. 41.

14 8.2, 6, 8, 21, 25; 9.28; 17.4, 15; 20.31, 33; 26.22; for additional uses of the term see 7.21f; 14.28, 30; 15.22, 25, 27; 16.22; 18.21; 25.11, 37, 44. Lk. generally prefers to substitute *ἐπιστάτα*, though he often parallels Mt.'s use of *κύριε* in non-Marcan materials.

15 So Moule, *Christology*, pp. 35f, 149, who argues that *κύριε* cannot be taken as evidence of Mt.'s Christology.

16 Cf. Freyne, pp. 163f; Sheridan, p. 246; Bornkamm, 'End-Expectation', p. 42.

17 Cf. H.D. Betz, *Nachfolge*, pp. 33ff; Freyne, pp. 151f. Luz, 'Jünger', p. 166, finds no evidence for the presence of the term *μαθητής* in 'Q', and thus attributes special significance to Mt.'s highlighting of it.

18 On the redactional insertions, see Freyne, p. 168; H.D. Betz, *Nachfolge*, p. 10; on the miracle stories, Held, pp. 181–92, 200–6; Hull, p. 132.

19 See Bornkamm, 'End-Expectation', pp. 54–7; Hull, p. 135. It is not accurate, however, to see in Mt.'s redaction of this pericope a radical revision of the *essence* of Mk.'s miracle story, and thus to describe it as 'a call to imitation and discipleship' or 'a kerygmatic paradigm of the danger and glory of discipleship' (Bornkamm, 'Storm', p. 57). In the larger context of chs. 8–9, it remains basically a miracle story that reveals Jesus' authority – albeit with overtones for discipleship that are not present in Mk. Cf. Bornkamm's own caution against eisegesis, p. 57.

20 Cf. Trilling, *Das Wahre Israel*, pp. 49f. Sheridan, p. 241, concludes, 'For Matthew the twelve are essentially disciples and their function is essentially to pass on the teaching of Jesus and, in doing so, to make other disciples' (cf. p. 254; Luz, 'Jünger', pp. 162ff; cf. pp. 150ff). Freyne, pp. 159, 162, thus speaks of Mt.'s ethic as a 'discipleship ethic'; cf. J.P. Martin, p. 51.

21 However, the Gospel as a whole cannot be accurately characterized as a 'manual of discipleship' (*pace* Sheridan, p. 241); for as J.P. Martin observes, p. 42, what Mt. writes is not a Didache, but a Gospel – albeit one with particular emphasis on discipleship; cf. Franzmann, p. v.

22 Note Mt.'s use of μαθητευθεὶς in 13.52, and the apparent emphasis on σύνεσις (see ch. 3, n. 3 above); cf. Minear, 'Disciples', p. 32; J.P. Martin, p. 51. Perrin, however, *New Testament*, p. 175, focuses too exclusively on this aspect.

23 Note Mt.'s redactional emphasis on Jesus' teaching in 4.23; 9.35; cf. Bultmann, *Jesus*, pp. 57ff; Thysman, pp. 144f; Lindars, 'Pharisees', pp. 51ff.

24 The verb μανθάνω itself occurs only three times in Mt. (9.13; 11.29; 24.32); cf. Rengstorf, 'μανθάνω', pp. 406f, 444–55; T.W. Manson, *Teaching*, pp. 239f; Hengel, *Nachfolge*, pp. 46ff, 55ff. Thus Houlden's description of disciples as 'pupils, after the rabbinic manner' (*Ethics*, p. 47) is somewhat inaccurate.

25 The term δοῦλος occurs thirty times in Mt., five times in Mk. (Morgenthaler, p. 90).

26 Cf. Rengstorf, 'μανθάνω', p. 406; Spivey–Smith, pp. 119, 146. On Joseph as a model of obedience, see Spicq, 'Joseph', pp. 206–14.

27 Cf. Sand, *Gesetz*, pp. 38f.

28 Cf. Lehmann-Habeck, pp. 47–53, who however defines it too narrowly in terms of *Nächstenliebe*; see pp. 98f below.

29 'Law', p. 102, n. 1; see Sand, *Gesetz*, pp. 106–24; Trilling, *Das Wahre Israel*, pp. 187–211.

30 See ch. 1, n. 189 above.

31 Meier, pp. 87f, sees this as the ultimate demand of Mt.'s Jesus; cf. p. 110, n. 166.

32 '... worin das Wesen der Jüngerschaft besteht'; Luz, 'Jünger', p. 163; cf. Houlden, *Ethics*, p. 52.

33 Cf. Freyne, p. 153. H.D. Betz, 'Matt 11.28–30', p. 24, in an attempt to find corresponding elements in 11.27–9 and 28.18–20, suggests it means 'nothing else than learning ... what it means to say: πραΰς εἰμι καὶ ταπεινὸς τῇ καρδίᾳ'; but this is too limited.

34 *Weg*, pp. 40, 127f, 175.

35 Mt. nowhere uses the term μιμέομαι or its derivatives.

36 Cf. Strecker, *Weg*, pp. 183f.

37 G. Barth, 'Law', pp. 102–5, suggests it functions implicitly as a principle for interpreting the law.

38 Cf. Bornkamm, 'End-Expectation', p. 37. G. Barth, 'Law', pp. 103ff (esp. p. 104, n. 1), 125–31, sees Mt.'s entire Christology dominated by the theme of Jesus' lowliness and meekness. Cf. J.P. Martin, p. 51; H.D. Betz, 'Matt 11.28–30', p. 24.

39 μάθετε here clearly implies more than simply learning Jesus' teachings (*pace* Thysman, p. 151); cf. H.D. Betz, 'Matt 11.28–30', p. 23: '"learning" means that the disciple himself takes over such πραΰτης and ταπεινότης'.

40 Cf. Bornkamm, 'End-Expectation', p. 30: 'Readiness to suffer (10.17ff.; 16.24ff.), poverty (19.23ff.; 6.19ff.), lowliness (18.1ff.), love (25.31ff. and often), renunciation of worldly honour (23.7ff.) and service (20.20ff.), these are the marks of discipleship'; G. Barth, 'Law', p. 105.

41 'Law', p. 101; cf. 5.11; 10.25, 38; 16.24f*; 19.29; 20.22f.

42 Note Mt.'s redactional emphasis on Jesus' δικαιοσύνη in 3.15; 27.19; cf. Strecker, *Weg*, pp. 177ff. On doing the will of God, see 4.4, 10, and Mt.'s

redactional insertion in 26.42 (cf. 26.39*); cf. G. Barth, 'Law', pp. 125ff; Strecker, *Weg*, pp. 183f; Freyne, pp. 158, 165ff; Sand, *Gesetz*, pp. 121ff. Mt.'s emphasis on Jesus' commitment to the fulfilment of Scripture, even at his own expense, highlights this point.

43 Cf. W.D. Davies, *Setting*, p. 96: 'just as his words reveal the essence of the Law of God, so does his life, so that to obey the Law of God comes to mean, for Matthew, to follow Christ' (19.16–20); G. Barth, 'Law', pp. 102f: 'The following of Christ and radical fulfilment of the law are one and the same'; H.D. Betz, *Nachfolge*, p. 34; Maher, p. 103; Tinsley, *Imitation of God*, pp. 136f.

44 Cf. Tinsley, *ibid*. p. 115. Tinsley's emphasis on the *imitatio Christi*, however, is motivated in part by his concern to establish it as a limiting principle on the early Church's creativity – 'an influence which controlled the preaching, teaching and liturgy of the early Church, and prevented them from being the instruments of elaboration and fabrication to the extent that used to be supposed' (p. 176).

45 'Imitation', p. 401; cf. Larsson, pp. 38ff.

46 Attempts such as those of Thysman, pp. 143–56; Osborn, p. 23; Schulz, *Nachfolge*, p. 269; and H.D. Betz, *Nachfolge*, p. 186, to draw a sharp line between the *Nachfolge Christi* of the twelve disciples and the *Nachahmung Christi* emphasized by the later Church, simply do not fit Mt., for whom the ἀκολουθεῖν of the Twelve is descriptive of discipleship for his own day and contains implicit elements of mimesis in it. So the neat distinction between an earlier 'religious' category of ἀκολουθεῖν and a later 'ethical' category of μιμεῖσθαι simply does not stand up; see 20.24–8; cf. Thysman, pp. 148f, 155; Schweizer, *Lordship*, p. 77.

47 See Thysman, p. 172; cf. Tinsley, *Imitation of God*, pp. 177ff; Bultmann, *Jesus*, pp. 73ff: 'Radical obedience exists only when a man inwardly assents to what is required of him ... when he is not *doing something obediently*, but *is* essentially obedient'; see ch. 5, n. 21 below. This raises questions about Houlden's statement, *Ethics*, p. 49, that the relationship between the Christian and Jesus in Mt.'s Gospel may be described in the 'more external language' of obedience and discipleship.

48 See pp. 99f below.

49 Cf. Lindars, 'Imitation', p. 402: 'the concept of the imitation of Christ only comes in ... as the means of reproducing that response in his followers'.

50 *Pace* Schnackenburg, pp. 162f.

51 So Windisch, *Bergpredigt*, pp. 60f; Furnish, *Love*, p. 54; cf. Lohse, 'Ich aber ...', p. 202; Sand, *Gesetz*, pp. 54ff; G. Barth, 'Law', pp. 97, 99; Hasler, 'Herzstück', p. 91; Lindars, 'Imitation', p. 402; R.M. Grant, *Historical Introduction*, p. 333; Freyne, pp. 160f, n. 2. Some however link it more closely to the immediate context of 5.43, with its emphasis on love: so Thysman, p. 170; Yoder, pp. 119f; but see p. 98 below. Bruppacher's thesis that the Aramaic term behind τέλειοι has been wrongly pointed and actually relates to the verb *vergelten* (p. 145), fits the context well, but involves too much speculation to carry any real weight.

52 Przybylski, p. 90, adds 6.33; but τὴν δικαιοσύνην αὐτοῦ could mean 'the righteousness he demands'.

53 Cf. Lindars' valid critique of Tinsley's and Cupitt's analyses, 'Imitation', pp. 394f, 402.

54 For bibliographical references on the relationship of law and grace in the Gospel, see esp. Banks' note, *Jesus*, p. 254; cf. pp. 15f; Himmelfarb, p. 63; G. Barth, 'Law', pp. 112, 147; Gutbrod, p. 1064; Esser, 'Law', p. 443; McArthur, pp. 69ff; McConnell, p. 90; Gulin, p. 22.

55 Cf. Hoskyns–Davey, p. 98.

56 See Conzelmann, *Theology*, p. 148; Trilling, *Das Wahre Israel*, pp. 32ff.

57 Cf. Schweizer, *Good News*, p. 538: 'he gives to all who follow him the possibility of fulfilling God's will in word and deed'.

58 See C.G. Montefiore, *Rabbinic Literature*, p. 240; Banks, *Jesus*, p. 254; Hunter, *Design*, pp. 16f.

59 The focus of both references is strictly on the negative side – i.e. on the one *without* a wedding garment, and on those who are *not* known by Jesus; see esp. Jeremias, *Parables*, pp. 187ff, on the former.

60 G. Barth, 'Law', p. 110, suggests that *συνιέναι* is portrayed as a gift by Mt., but correctly notes exceptions to this (13.15; 15.10; 16.9; 17.12).

61 Windisch, *Meaning*, p. 78, sees it as an isolated instance, and therefore not representative; cf. Kee, p. 154, on the Marcan version.

62 Cf. Nineham, *Use*, p. 146. Luz, 'Jünger', p. 161, wrongly focuses on this as the centre of Mt.'s concept of salvation: 'Negativ heisst das: Nicht das Kerygma von Tod und Auferstehung Jesu ist das Heil. Positiv ist das Heil die fortdauernde Präsenz Jesu in der Gemeinde.' Via's focus is likewise distorted, p. 283, when he identifies the presence of Christ with the 'power of prayer'.

63 Held, p. 265, points out that nearly all the healing miracles in Mt. are expressed as Jesus' response to a request for aid.

64 In the Lord's prayer we see a certain duality in the disciple's response to God: he both bows in submission to his rule and will (6.9f), and looks to his fatherly care for the meeting of personal needs (6.11ff). The same duality is seen in 10.28ff: God is to be feared as the one who can destroy both soul and body in hell, and yet the disciple is instructed to 'fear not'. Cf. Dodd, *Gospel*, p. 59: 'The immediacy of His care is balanced by the immediacy of His demands upon us.'

65 See Evans, *Lord's Prayer*, p. 68.

66 Cf. the eschatological interpretation of 'bread for the morrow' by Jeremias, *Prayers*, pp. 100ff, and Evans, *Lord's Prayer*, pp. 52–5. Houlden, *Ethics*, p. 51, writes: 'His scheme is no mere code presented for man to obey independently and in his own strength (xviii, 20)'; cf. p. 15; see also Hunter, *Design*, pp. 115f, 121, who overstates the case, however. G. Barth, 'Law', pp. 121, 124ff, sees intimations of this also in the designation of the disciples as *οἱ μικροί*; but in context the term is more likely a reference to their vulnerability than to their moral weakness, see ch. 4, n. 29 below.

67 Attempts to anchor Mt.'s ethics in a framework of grace on the basis of the structure of the SM itself and the context in which it occurs in Mt.'s overall construct, fail to be convincing. W.D. Davies, for example, views the SM as embedded in the framework of Jesus' ministry of compassion and founded on the proclamation of God's grace in the beatitudes: 'Jesus first appeared, not making a demand, but offering succour, his first concern,

not the exaction of obedience, but the proclamation of blessing (iv.23ff.; v.3–11). For Matthew, therefore, the Sermon is set within a framework of healing and pity'; *Setting*, p. 96; cf. pp. 365f, 435; 'Ethics', p. 168; so also Hill, *Matthew*, p. 69; Friedlander, p. 18; T.W. Manson, *Ethics*, p. 51: 'First the congratulations, the status, the promise; and only after that the charge, the responsibilities, the tasks.' Manns, pp. 17f, similarly feels the beatitudes 'soulignent la gratuité de l'élection'. But this misunderstands the parenetic nature of the beatitudes, and reads too much into the structure.

68 Thus Jeremias, *Sermon on the Mount*, pp. 24–33, speaks of the concept of grace in the Sermon as 'unexpressed', 'not specifically stated', 'ostensibly missing'.

69 See Strecker, *Weg*, pp. 149–58. Schulz' description of the Christian life in Mt. as 'a movement of trust and gratitude, towards God's antecedent grace' (cf. Moule, 'Schulz', p. 364) would seem to be an example of reading Mt. through the eyes of Paul.

70 Cf. Strecker, *Weg*, p. 149; Piper, p. 173. However, this is not to suggest that Mt.'s community knows no sense of present forgiveness: cf. 9.2ff*; 18.23–35; 26.28. Nor does it imply that forgiveness is not viewed essentially as a gift (*pace* Strecker, *Weg*, pp. 157f).

71 H.D. Betz, *Nachfolge*, pp. 35f, suggests that there is no indication that disciples know themselves to be among the 'elect' and 'chosen'; they only know themselves to be among the 'called'. Cf. the surprised responses of the 'righteous' in 25.37ff and the man without the wedding garment in 22.11–14. For discussion of the analogy of the safety of the disciples in the stilling of the storm to their security in the church, see Bornkamm, 'Storm', pp. 54–7; Luz, 'Jünger', p. 153; cf. 16.18; the analogy breaks down, however, on the mixed nature of the church in Mt. (cf. 13.24–30, 36–43, 47–50).

72 Thus Windisch's description of the SM as *Gehorsamsethik* (*Bergpredigt*, p. 51) is essentially correct.

73 Moule, *Phenomenon*, p. 26, sees Χριστός used primarily in the context of kerygmatic indicatives, and κύριος reserved generally for ethical imperatives (cf. 1 Cor. 4.15; Phil. 4.2; note the fusion of the two in Col. 2.6); Kramer, pp. 169ff, 179, 182, sees in this a break with the pre-Pauline tradition, which uses κύριος more in the context of worship. But cf. Foerster, 'κύριος', p. 1091.

74 E.P. Sanders, *Paul*, p. 466, suggests that Paul sees the significance of Christ's death 'more in terms of a *change of lordship* ... than in terms of the expiation of past transgression'. See ch. 5, n. 30 below.

75 See also 1 Cor. 1.2; 3.16, 23; 6.13; 15.23; 2 Cor. 1.1; 10.7; Gal. 3.29; Phil. 3.12; cf. Col. 1.16; Nieder, p. 127.

76 See Corriveau on Paul's view of the daily life as worship.

77 P. 16.

78 *Theology*, p. 169.

79 Cf. Gal. 6.17: τὰ στίγματα τοῦ 'Ιησοῦ, the identifying marks of a slave; but see Campenhausen, *Ecclesiastical Authority*, p. 62.

80 It is significant that when Paul picks out individuals for special citation and greetings, it is most commonly their faithful commitment and service to Christ that he chooses to emphasize (Rom. 16.1f, 3f, 6, 7, 9, 12; 1 Cor.

16.10, 15f; Phil. 2.19ff, 25ff; Col. 4.7, 9, 10f, 12f; cf. 4.17; 1 Thess. 3.2; Phm. 1f, 23f).

81 Wire, p. 31, argues that Paul's view implicitly suggests that God cannot ultimately be characterized in terms of 'authority' (cf. p. 261); but Paul is certainly not aware of these implications!

82 P. 104.

83 See Furnish, *Theology*, p. 187.

84 Bultmann, *Theology*, vol. I, p. 314; Furnish, *Love*, p. 98; cf. Stewart, p. 185, n. 1.

85 Cf. Schlier, *Grundzüge*, pp. 218ff; Furnish, *Theology*, p. 226: 'For Paul, obedience is neither preliminary to the new life (as its condition) nor secondary to it (as its result and eventual fulfillment). Obedience is *constitutive* of the new life.'

86 Ahern, 'Spirit', p. 224, comments: 'No human law could ever be as exacting as this spirit of sonship.'

87 See esp. E.P. Sanders, *Paul*, pp. 453–63; cf. p. 440, n. 49. Furnish, *Theology*, p. 176, is correct: it is more accurate to speak of this in 'relational' than 'mystical' terms.

88 See Best, *Body*, and J.A.T. Robinson, *Body*, for more extended discussion of the term; cf. E.P. Sanders, *Paul*, pp. 456f.

89 See Bornkamm, *Ende*, pp. 34ff, on the ethical implications of baptism.

90 Cf. Houlden, *Ethics*, p. 29: 'Peculiarly and radically such behaviour offends against a Christian's attachment to Christ, which involves the allegiance of his whole person ... Union with Christ is described in the most exclusive terms.' Houlden goes on to argue that, logically speaking, Paul could equally well have excluded marriage on this basis.

91 Cf. *Paul*, pp. 454ff: 'The argument is that one participatory union can destroy another ... A person cannot participate in two mutually exclusive unions ... it is not simply that a *transgression* removes one from union with Christ; rather, union with Christ and union with demons are mutually exclusive.'

92 There is no significant distinction between the two in Paul's usage; cf. Foerster, '*κύριος*', p. 1091; Bietenhard, 'Lord', p. 517; *pace* Neugebauer.

93 See Best, *Body*, pp. 1–33; E.P. Sanders, *Paul*, pp. 458ff; Moule, *Christology*, pp. 54ff; W.D. Davies, *Land*, pp. 219f. Stewart, p. 194, speaks of the phrase as the 'sheet-anchor' of Paul's ethics. W.D. Davies, *Paul and Rabbinic Judaism*, p. 136, suggests it is often the mark of the apostle's 'Christianization' of those elements taken over from pagan ethics. The two phrases 'in Christ' and 'Christ in me' are not simply to be equated (*pace* Bultmann, *Theology*, vol. I, pp. 328, 335, and Grossouw, p. 95), for their functions sometimes differ: cf. Gal. 2.20; Col. 1.27; 3.11 – where the latter phrase refers not so much to a state of existence as to divine activity in an individual. Moule, *Phenomenon*, pp. 24ff, is correct: the union of Christ and the believer cannot simply be viewed as the 'mutual interpenetration of two individuals in intimate relationship'.

94 So Moule, *Christology*, p. 54; *Phenomenon*, p. 23; Bornkamm, *Paul*, pp. 154f; Grossouw, p. 93. Bultmann's analysis of 'degrees of existence' in Christ (1 Cor. 3.1: 'babes in Christ'; Rom. 16.10: 'approved in Christ';

1 Cor. 4.10: 'wise in Christ') errs precisely because it fails to recognize this broader sense of the phrase in Paul's usage.

95 *Paul*, p. 456. Sanders sees participation in Christ as central to all of Paul's thought; cf. pp. 434–41; Stewart, pp. 168ff.

96 Schweizer, 'Dying', p. 8, n. 1, sees Paul as the first to understand baptism in terms of 'dying with Christ'; cf. Larsson, pp. 19f; but see J.K. Howard, pp. 147ff.

97 Cf. Caird, *Principalities*, p. 93: 'Baptism, therefore, signifies the Christian's initial victory over the powers of evil.'

98 Ladd, *Theology*, pp. 485ff, argues that the metaphor of crucifixion here is 'not a subjective statement of something that happens in the Christian consciousness but a theological [objective] statement of one's position in Christ'. But for Paul, 'dying with Christ' includes both elements (cf. Col. 2.20 with Gal. 5.24), and he thus speaks of it in both the indicative and imperative senses.

99 See pp. 118f below.

100 Thus, what happens 'once and for all' in baptism is to be realized daily anew; in this sense the believer continually dies with Christ (cf. Tannehill, pp. 75–83, 128f; Rey, p. 629; Murray, *Principles*, pp. 211f).

101 *Ethics*, p. 26: 'baptism "into Christ" brings about the destruction of the believer's orientation to sin. It is a wholesale acceptance of Christ's cross – and a dedication to the self-giving that is consistent with it.'

102 Tannehill, pp. 24ff, argues that the 'old self' and 'sinful body' of Rom. 6.6, and the 'old nature' of Col. 3.9f, refer not to individual entities but to a collective one that was destroyed in the death of Christ – indeed to 'the physical body which Christ "wore"' (pp. 49f; cf. Col. 2.11); there is thus only one 'old man' and one 'new man', in his view.

103 So also Moule, *Christology*, p. 124; Styler, pp. 181ff; Tannehill, p. 10. Furnish's interpretation of ὡσεί in Rom. 6.13 as 'as' rather than 'as if' (*Theology*, pp. 195, 217; cf. Barrett, *Romans*, p. 128) supports this view. Those who sharply distinguish between the views of resurrection in Colossians and Romans – 1 Corinthians on the basis of tense (Col.: past tense; Rom. – 1 Cor.: future tense) fail to note that Rom. 6 clearly implies the living of a new life here and now (6.4f, 11, 13; cf. E.P. Sanders' concession, *Paul*, pp. 449f: 'even though in a certain sense the Christian already "lives" to God'), and also frequently fail to distinguish between literal and metaphorical references to resurrection. The fact that the past tense is not used in Rom. 6 may acknowledge merely that Christians commonly express less than total newness in their present living. Thus I cannot agree with Schweizer, 'Dying', p. 7, who, because he now holds Col. to be non-authentic and the Rom. 6 references to be future, concludes that Paul nowhere speaks of a present, existential resurrection life for the Christian, but only of a future resurrection (so also E.P. Sanders, *Paul*, pp. 449f). Nor can I agree with those who, holding Col. to be authentic, see a clear-cut development in Paul's thought from Rom. to Col. on this point (e.g. Dunn, *Unity*, p. 25; cf. pp. 345f) – though there may be a shift in focus and development in the *expression* of the concept. Wilson and Faw suggest that the development in Paul's later letters of the existential aspects of resurrection is linked to his own brush with death in Ephesus at about the

time 2 Cor. was written (Tannehill's objection, p. 134, n. 4, reflects a failure to distinguish between literal and metaphorical references; pp. 10f); cf. Rey, pp. 614ff.

104 Tinsley, *Imitation of God*, pp. 134ff; Stewart, p. 287; cf. Thysman, p. 164.

105 P. 672: 'The call for an *imitatio Christi* finds no support in the statements of Paul'; cf. Rengstorf, 'μανθάνω', p. 455.

106 See Furnish, *Theology*, p. 218; Yoder, pp. 124ff; contrast Stewart, pp. 158f. The related reference in 2 Cor. 10.1 must be interpreted in the light of the charge against Paul of being ταπεινός and ἀσθενής (cf. Furnish, *Theology*, p. 223, n. 41; Leivestad, pp. 161ff).

107 This example alone refutes Nieder's thesis, p. 120, that Paul's references to the example of Christ invariably occur in the context of an appeal for patience and forbearance with a weaker Christian.

108 Cf. Houlden, *Ethics*, p. 31; Betz, *Nachfolge*, p. 177; see pp. 102f below.

109 Alternatively, 'the ὑπομονή which Christ inspires'.

110 Furnish, *Theology*, p. 223, suggests that Paul's references to the imitation of himself also centre on self-giving, suffering service (1 Cor. 4.6, 16f; 11.1; Phil. 3.17; 4.9; 2 Thess. 3.7, 9; cf. 1 Cor. 4.10–13; 2 Cor. 1.5–9; 11.23–8; 12.10; Phil. 1.29f; 3.10; Col. 1.24); cf. Tinsley, *Imitation of God*, pp. 139f.

111 Ladd, *Theology*, p. 516. Cf. Furnish, *Theology*, p. 223:

> '... it is noteworthy that none of these imitation passages singles out any particular qualities of the earthly Jesus with the insistence that they be emulated. Rather, it seems always to be the humble, giving, obedient *love* of the crucified and resurrected Lord to which the final appeal is made. Paul sees the meaning of love ... revealed first of all in the grand humiliation of Christ's incarnation and death ..., not primarily in his earthly deeds of compassion and humility.'

Dodd, 'Ethics of Pauline Epistles', p. 302; H.D. Betz, *Nachfolge*, pp. 137f; Beardsley, pp. 129ff; Yoder, p. 134. Betz' assertion, that Paul's mimetic references to the qualities of Christ's incarnation suggest he is fighting against gnostics, lacks adequate support.

112 Cf. Thysman, pp. 172f. A number of the small but key particles on which the interpretation of many appeals for imitation turn (ὡς, καθώς, οὕτως, γάρ; cf. Rom. 15.3, 7; 2 Cor. 8.9; Col. 3.13) may be understood as marking either a simple comparative or a causal relationship; cf. Bauer, pp. 151f, 391, 393, 597f, 897–9. The addition of καί, however, suggests the focus is generally on the comparative aspect.

113 Cf. Tinsley, *Imitation of God*, p. 156; Larsson, pp. 46ff; H.D. Betz, *Nachfolge*, p. 175; Thysman, p. 159.

114 Tannehill, pp. 70ff; cf. Lindars, 'Imitation', pp. 401f.

115 See also 1 Cor. 11.7; Kittel, pp. 395ff. Thysman, pp. 159ff, and Rey, p. 629, overemphasize the *imitatio Dei*. Cf. Eph. 5.1.

116 Cf. Tinsley, *Imitation of God*, pp. 161f; Tannehill, p. 103; Thysman, pp. 168ff.

117 Even faith itself is a gift of grace (Phil. 1.29; cf. Rom. 8.28ff; 9.6ff); cf. Bultmann, *Theology*, vol. I, pp. 329f.

118 Cf. Schnackenburg, p. 275; Rey, p. 628; note also the central role of

ingratitude in Paul's catalogue of human sin (Rom. 1.21; Minear, *Obedience*, pp. 106ff; Tannehill, p. 124). In Rom. 14, εὐχαριστεῖν is seen as the mark of one who seeks to honour God in what he does, of one who 'lives to God' (Rom. 14.6ff). Cf. Minear's paraphrase of 14.23: 'Whatever does not proceed from gratitude is sin' (*Obedience*, p. 108).

119 So Barrett, *First Corinthians*, p. 192; Moffatt, *First Corinthians*, p. 107; Lietzmann, p. 37; cf. Héring, *First Corinthians*, p. 70.

120 Cf. the references to καλέω and καλέομαι in Rom. 9.12; 1 Cor. 1.9; 7.15, 17–24; Gal. 1.6; 5.8, 13; Col. 3.15; 1 Thess. 2.12; 4.7; 5.24; 2 Thess. 2.14.

121 See Bornkamm, *Paul*, p. 140.

122 Nieder, pp. 139f, argues that Paul's consistent use of 'past' rather than 'present' categories to describe the Christian's call is evidence of his tendency to ground his parenesis in historical references, and that it is this which provides security and certainty for the believer's life; but Paul is not concerned merely with 'historical references'.

123 See Campenhausen, *Begründung*, pp. 29ff.

124 See Foerster, 'ἄξιος', pp. 379f; Nieder, p. 126.

125 Cf. Alexander, p. 165; Bornkamm, *Paul*, pp. 201–5; Nieder, p. 139; Dunn, *Jesus*, pp. 204f.

126 Houlden, *Ethics*, p. 26, suggests that the striking thing about Paul's ethics is the way that he so often brings this central fact to bear upon the solution of moral problems; cf. Strecker, 'Strukturen', p. 126; Bornkamm, *Paul*, pp. 201, 204. Nieder, pp. 143ff, asserts it to be the Pauline *Hauptmotiv*; cf. pp. 117ff. Thomas, p. 87, thus speaks of Paul's ethic as an 'ethic of redemption'; cf. Merk, pp. 239ff.

127 Cf. Nauck, p. 135: 'Sie ist weder eine autonome, noch eine finale, sondern eine konsekutive Ethik; eine Ethik, die aus dem gnädigen Handeln Gottes die Folgerung im Vollzug der Lebensführung zieht.'

128 See *ibid*. pp. 134f.

129 If τὴν λογικὴν λατρείαν ὑμῶν (12.1) is interpreted 'your reasonable service', the link between the preceding theological statement and the ensuing ethics is brought out more clearly; cf. Corriveau, p. 178.

130 Cf. Moule, 'Obligation', p. 394; Bultmann, *Theology*, vol. I, p. 324; Käsemann, 'Righteousness', p. 175; W.D. Davies, 'Ethics', p. 168. Note Paul's use of ὀφειλέτης (Rom. 1.14; 8.12) and ὀφείλειν (Rom. 13.8; 15.1, 27; 1 Cor. 11.7, 10; 2 Cor. 12.14; 2 Thess. 1.3; 2.13; Phm. 18); cf. Hauck, pp. 563f.

131 Cf. Nauck, p. 135: 'Christliche Ethik ist Ethik der Dankbarkeit.'

132 Houlden, 'Jesus', pp. 104f, suggests that the writers' thoughts about God are ultimately determinative of all else.

133 Houlden, 'Jesus', p. 112, reminds us that Christological terms such as 'Lord' may have meant different things to the different authors by the time they were given written expression in the NT.

134 Both writers realize this can only apply to those gifted for it (Mt. 19.11f; 1 Cor. 7.7ff).

135 Via, pp. 271–86, and W.D. Davies, *Setting*, pp. 97f, see in these passages evidence that Mt., like Paul, thinks of the Church as the Body of Christ, and therefore as incorporated into the Lord in a sense akin to the Pauline

ἐν Χριστῷ; but the references cited make no explicit mention of either concept, and at the most speak of Jesus as identifying with his disciples in their weakness and need – which is quite different from the fully developed Pauline concept of participation and union.

136 See pp. 116f below.

137 G. Barth, 'Law', p. 112, suggests that both writers view the Christian's 'understanding' (of Christ and his message) as a gift of grace; but see ch. 3, n. 60 above.

138 The term κλητοί thus takes on different nuances in the two writers: for Paul, it is roughly equivalent to ἐκλεκτοί.

139 Cf. Houlden, *Patterns*, p. 66: 'what has "made all the difference" is Jesus' teaching ... rather than his death'; but see 20.28*; 26.28.

140 It is the failure to recognize this distinction that lies behind the over-emphasis of W.D. Davies on their similarities (*Setting*, pp. 365f; cf. C.A.A. Scott, *Christianity*, p. 220).

141 Emphasized by Przybylski, pp. 2f, 105ff, 123. W.D. Davies seems to fall into this error (see ch. 3, n. 135 above); cf. his assertion that Mt.'s imperatives are based on the indicative, just as Paul's (*Setting*, pp. 98f; 345f, n. 1; 433ff; so also Conzelmann, *Theology*, p. 148). He concludes that the SM 'spans the arch of Grace and Law, conjoins demands ... with the Pauline profundities' (p. 440). A.M. Hunter reflects a similar tendency: though he denies that the moral demands of the SM are intended as a 'propaedeutic to a Gospel for sinners', they are still an impossible ideal, and therefore only to be understood as preceded by the proclamation of grace. Indeed, 'the *prius* and presupposition of every saying in it is the Good News of the advent of God's New Order of grace – the Kingdom of God'. 'In every instance, the gift of God – his grace – precedes the demand.' Supporting Jeremias, he claims: 'the Sermon is not really law but Gospel ... The Sermon outlines the response of the men of the Kingdom to the experienced grace of God ... an ethic of appropriation which illustrates ... the ways in which men enter ever more fully into the experience of grace.' Hunter concludes, 'if Paul's eyes had ever fallen on Matthew's Sermon we doubt if he would have found much in it incompatible with his understanding of the Gospel' (*Design*, pp. 16, 103f; cf. W.D. Davies' similar statement, *Setting*, p. 366, and G. Barth's claim, 'Law', p. 147, that Mt.'s Jesus takes the place of sinners, and by fulfilling all righteousness brings grace and forgiveness; Feuillet, 'Mt V.17–20', pp. 131ff). Neither Davies nor Hunter equates the position of Mt. with that of Paul; but in their overemphasis on grace in the Gospel they bring the two closer together than they really are (see ch. 3, n. 140 above). With regard to Mt., Kilpatrick is essentially correct: 'The Pauline doctrine of grace is absent' (pp. 130f).

142 Cf. Marshall, p. 24: 'The ethical life at its highest might be compared to an ellipse whose two foci are the experience of the power of God and the obedience of man. Jesus largely assumes the former and stresses the latter; St. Paul largely assumes the latter and lays the stress on the former'; but Paul does not simply 'assume' the latter.

143 However, Mt. is also aware of human indebtedness: note the reference to 10,000 talents owed by the ὀφειλέτης in 18.23ff (cf. 23.16, 18; Hauck, pp. 562f), and the request for the forgiveness of ὀφειλήματα in 6.12;

but the sense of debt in these passages derives more from an awareness of sin than the awareness of grace.

144 Green, *Matthew*, p. 37, writes: 'For Paul ... God is gracious before he is demanding; for Mt ... God's graciousness is contained in his demand' (cf. Strecker's statement, *Weg*, p. 175, that in Mt. the imperative is entirely identified with the indicative); but this fails to describe the relationship precisely.

## 4. Love

1 Major NT studies of the twentieth century on this theme include the following: James Moffatt, *Love in the New Testament* (1929); Anders Nygren, *Agape and Eros* (1932, 1938, 1939; rev. ed. 1953) – a classical–philosophical approach; Viktor Warnach, *Agape: Die Liebe als Grundmotiv der neutestamentlichen Theologie* (1951); Ceslaus Spicq, *Agapè dans le Nouveau Testament* (3 vols., 1958–9), translated into English as *Agape in the New Testament* (1963–6) – a voluminous study restricted solely to ἀγάπη terminology and lacking a sufficiently critical methodology (so also Nygren, Warnach); Victor Paul Furnish, *The Love Command in the New Testament* (1973) – a careful, critical study that attempts to avoid some of the weaknesses of preceding works; and John Piper, '*Love your enemies*' (1979) – a history-of-traditions approach of more limited scope. Also very useful are two recent redaction-critical works on NT ethics more generally: J.L. Houlden, *Ethics and the New Testament* (1973), and J.T. Sanders, *Ethics in the New Testament* (1975).

2 Statistically (excluding references to love for God):

| | | |
|---|---|---|
| ἀγαπᾶν | (Mt: 7 | Mk: 3) |
| ἀγάπη | (Mt: 1 | Mk: 1) |
| φιλεῖν* | (Mt: 2 | Mk: 0) |
| ἐλεεῖν | (Mt: 1 | Mk: 0) |
| ἔλεος | (Mt: 3 | Mk: 0) |
| ἐλεήμων | (Mt: 1 | Mk: 0) |
| ἐλεημοσύνη | (Mt: 3 | Mk: 0) |

*A number of studies have demonstrated that the meanings of ἀγαπᾶν and φιλεῖν cannot always be differentiated in the NT: cf. Moffatt, *Love*, pp. 44–8; Günther–Link, p. 542; and esp. Furnish, *Love*, pp. 49f, 219–31 – whose criticism of Spicq's arbitrary distinction between the two terms is valid.

3 For more detailed discussion of this passage, see esp. Furnish, *Love*, pp. 45–54; Zumstein, pp. 309–26; Piper, *passim*.

4 Cf. 1QS 1.3f: 'Love everyone whom God elects, hate everyone he hates', cited by Günther–Link, p. 542; Stauffer, p. 43.

5 Cf. Furnish, *Love*, p. 53; Schweizer, *Good News*, p. 202; Hübner, *Gesetz in der synoptischen Tradition*, p. 196. On περισσόν, see Spivey–Smith, p. 146; it is best taken as a demand not for more 'extensive' obedience, but for more 'intensive' obedience; G. Barth, 'Law', p. 98; Freyne, p. 161, n. 2; *pace* Przybylski, pp. 85ff; cf. Banks, 'Matthew 5:17–20', p. 242; Strecker, *Weg*, pp. 141f; Bauer, p. 651.

6 See Berger, pp. 444–53; R.P. Martin, 'Matthew', p. 133, n. 1.
7 See Nygren's valid caution against reading too much into the phrase 'as yourself' (*Agape*, pp. 100f).
8 Cf. Furnish, *Love*, p. 75; Strecker, 'Strukturen', pp. 142f. R.P. Martin, 'Matthew', p. 133, n. 1, sees it as 'an epitome of the Decalogue for Gentile Christians'.
9 Cf. Windisch, *Bergpredigt*, pp. 46f; Furnish, *Love*, p. 64.
10 Cf. Furnish, *Love*, p. 75. Banks, *Jesus*, pp. 162f, and Meier, pp. 87f, distinguish too sharply between the love commandment as the essence of the law and the prophets, and Jesus' own more radical demands that follow. Jesus' demands embrace the love commandment and build upon it.
11 Several important redaction-critical studies of this pericope have been published: G. Bornkamm, 'Das Doppelgebot der Liebe' (1954); C. Burchard, 'Das doppelte Liebesgebot in der frühen christlichen Überlieferung' (1970); K. Berger, *Die Gesetzesauslegung Jesu* (1972), pp. 56–257; Furnish, *The Love Command in the New Testament* (1973), pp. 30–4; B. Gerhardsson, 'The Hermeneutic Program in Matthew 22:37–40' (1976). For characteristics of Mt.'s redaction, see Bornkamm, 'Doppelgebot', pp. 92f; Burchard, pp. 60f; Berger, pp. 202–8; Furnish, *Love*, pp. 30ff; Gerhardsson, pp. 129–50.
12 See pp. 12f above.
13 See Berger, pp. 227–32, on the meaning of the term.
14 Cf. Gerhardsson, pp. 134, 140: '... a very carefully formulated *hermeneutic program*. What we are faced with in these verses is nothing less than the Matthean Church's principles for interpretation and application of the inherited holy scriptures ... an instrument for evaluation, selection, and radical interpretation'; Furnish, *Love*, p. 34; J.T. Sanders, *Ethics*, p. 42; G. Barth, 'Law', pp. 78, 103f; Bornkamm, 'Doppelgebot', p. 93; Houlden, *Ethics*, p. 49; Sand, *Gesetz*, pp. 40–4, 188–93, 203; Hummel, p. 68; Strecker, *Weg*, p. 147; Piper, p. 152. Carlston, 'Things', p. 82, n. 2, wrongly takes 22.40 to imply that the love commandment is exalted *above* the law and the prophets. Also inaccurate are Spicq's view that love is here depicted as the motive enabling one to obey all the commandments (*Agape*, vol. I, p. 44; cf. Furnish, *Love*, p. 34, n. 29) and Schnackenburg's suggestion that all other commandments can be derived from it (p. 93).
15 See pp. 9ff above.
16 Cf. Nygren, *Agape*, p. 123; *pace* Furnish, *Love*, pp. 31, 33, and Burchard, pp. 60f.
17 Cf. Gerhardsson, pp. 140f; see p. 99 below.
18 Bornkamm, 'Doppelgebot', p. 92; cf. Berger, pp. 202f; Furnish, *Love*, pp. 31f.
19 Furnish, *ibid.* p. 32, suggests, 'the real question on the lawyer's "hidden agenda" is whether Jesus accepts all the statutes of the Torah as of equal importance. Jesus' singling out of two commandments as "great" is interpreted by Matthew (vs. 40) as a negative response, whereby Jesus is set over against Judaism' (cf. G. Barth, 'Law', pp. 77f; Spicq, *Agape*, vol. I, p. 27). This interpretation, however, is difficult to sustain in view of the common Jewish practice of defining *kelal* (see e.g. Bowker, *Jesus and the Pharisees*, pp. 32, 44; *Targums*, p. 51; cf. Aboth 1.2; S.-B., vol. I, pp. 900–8).

20 The object is unspecified; cf. Spicq, *Agape*, vol. I, p. 35; Gerhardsson, p. 147.
21 Furnish, *Love*, p. 83.
22 Cf. Bauer, p. 71. See p. 16 above.
23 A major weakness of Spicq's study; cf. Furnish, *Love*, p. 20.
24 Cf. Sand, *Gesetz*, pp. 40f, 124; Gerhardsson, p. 147. See Moffatt, *Love*, p. 85, for discussion of the proximity of ἔλεος and ἀγάπη, esp. in citations from the LXX where ἔλεος translates the Hebrew *ḥesed.*
25 See p. 21 above and Hill, 'Hosea VI.6'; cf. G. Barth, 'Law', pp. 79, 83; Hummel, p. 45: 'Es legitimiert die Freigabe des Sabbats für die Liebestat gegenüber dem Pharisäismus.'
26 See esp. Zumstein, pp. 327–50; Furnish, *Love*, pp. 79, 83; Goodspeed, pp. 95f; Stendahl, *Paul*, pp. 62f.
27 See ch. 2, n. 40 above.
28 LaVerdiere–Thompson, p. 581, suggest: 'Matthean scholars are more and more convinced that the Gentiles are being judged.' Not all are, however: cf. Furnish, *Love*, p. 80.
29 Mt.'s use of the term οἱ μικροί may reflect this (10.14f, 40ff; 18.6, 10; note the redactional insertion 10.16); cf. Bonnard, *Matthieu*, p. 159; Hill, *Matthew*, p. 196; see ch. 3, n. 66 above.
30 *Love*, p. 79; cf. Bornkamm, 'End-Expectation', p. 30.
31 See Windisch, *Bergpredigt*, pp. 59ff, on 5.43ff as a *Gebot*.
32 Cf. Piper, pp. 146–8; see p. 78 and ch. 3, n. 51 above.
33 *Pace* Minear, *Commands*, p. 104, who sees the real focus more on voluntary poverty, a further commitment beyond that of keeping the law. Houlden, *Ethics*, p. 91, also sees here possible evidence of a two-stage view of the Christian life, but acknowledges that Mt.'s use of τέλειος in 5.48 does not support this interpretation. There is little in the Gospel as a whole to suggest that Mt. thinks in terms of a two-level morality: see esp. G. Barth, 'Law', pp. 96ff; cf. p. 18 above.
34 E.g. G. Barth, 'Law', pp. 73, 79f, asserts that the golden rule represents the summary and essence of all the preceding directives in the SM, which are therefore to be understood as grounded in and subordinated to the love commandment; also McConnell, pp. 11f; W.D. Davies, 'Matthew, 5, 17–18', p. 430; Schweizer, *Good News*, p. 202 – who sees 7.12 and 5.17–20 as a 'frame' for the SM (so also Lehmann-Habeck, p. 48). But cf. Meier, p. 42, n. 4, and see ch. 1, n. 106 above.
35 Ridderbos' statement is typical of many: 'what Jesus in the Sermon on the Mount asks for is the complete, universal, radical application of the law of love' (*Matthew*, p. 30); cf. Strecker, 'Strukturen', p. 142.
36 E.g. by J.T. Sanders, *Ethics*, p. 45; cf. Schweizer, 'Matth. 5, 17–20', p. 404.
37 Cf. Günther, p. 117. Przybylski, however, argues that the essence of discipleship in Mt. is not righteousness but *doing the will of God*, and that righteousness plays no part in Mt.'s self-understanding as a disciple but serves merely as a 'point of contact' with the Jewish community (pp. 111–23). But this is a clear case of overdifferentiation that obscures the close link between the two concepts and the fact that many of the righteousness texts *are* directed to disciples.

38 Cf. Hill, 'Hosea VI.6', pp. 110, 117.

39 So Berger, p. 243; Sand, *Gesetz*, pp. 203, 205; cf. G. Barth, 'Law', pp. 79ff; Strecker, 'Strukturen', p. 143: 'Die Forderungen von *δικαιοσύνη* und *ἀγάπη* interpretieren sich gegenseitig. So ist die Gerechtigkeitsforderung das Thema der Bergpredigt (5, 20), das durch das Gebot der Feindesliebe (5, 43f) aufgenommen und durch die Goldene Regel (7, 12) abgeschlossen wird.' Cf. Furnish, *Love*, pp. 54, 75, 83, who speaks of the love commandment as 'the essential content of the "higher righteousness" which distinguishes Jesus' followers'.

40 Carlston, 'Things', p. 83, n. 1, is correct: [Mt.] does not reduce the Law to the love-commandment'; cf. Banks, *Jesus*, pp. 227f, 243f.

41 Minear, *Commands*, perhaps comes as close as anyone to identifying correctly the fundamental importance of the attitude of self-renunciation in the Gospel. While recognizing the key role of love in Mt.'s world-view, he correctly refrains from making it the centre. Perhaps the single greatest weakness of Furnish's study is his failure to explore fully the subtle but fundamental connexions in Mt.'s thought between love and these more basic concepts, which determine the real nature and function of love in the Gospel.

42 On *δικαιοσύνη* and the beatitudes, see Dupont's massive study, esp. vol. III, pp. 207–667; cf. Frankemölle, p. 65; Zumstein, pp. 284–308; Strecker, 'Makarismen', pp. 255ff; Pokorný on the core of the SM; H.D. Betz, 'Makarismen', pp. 18f. The primary function of the beatitudes in Mt. is clearly parenetic.

43 Cf. Windisch, *Bergpredigt*, pp. 46–51. Przybylski's thesis, pp. 81ff, that the antitheses represent a rabbinic-like attempt to 'build a fence' around Torah, fails to account for Mt.'s emphasis on the importance of inner attitudes.

44 *Love*, p. 108; cf. Windisch, *Bergpredigt*, p. 60. Furnish's brief argument to the contrary (*Love*, p. 52) fails to take adequate account of the themes of self-denial and tolerant submission running throughout the chapter.

45 Noted esp. by Houlden, *Ethics*, p. 118 (Friedlander, p. 264, earlier raised the question of inconsistency with regard to Mt.'s Jesus himself); note however that 5.22 refers to words spoken against Christian 'brothers', not outsiders. Furnish, *Love*, p. 78, finds a similar tension between the love commandment and passages relating to church discipline in ch. 18: 'There is no explicit word about love or forgiveness.'

46 Cf. Sand, *Gesetz*, p. 81.

47 *Bergpredigt*, p. 76.

48 Cf. Mitton, pp. 47–54. Hare, p. 170, views it from a different perspective: 'Despite his hostility toward the synagogue and its Pharisaic leadership, Matthew strives to be loyal to Jesus' insistence on loving one's enemies.'

49 In Gustafson's terms, pp. 103–17, Mt.'s is basically an 'agent-oriented ethic' rather than an 'action-oriented ethic'. Hence we must seriously question the point of view expressed by Keck, 'Sermon on the Mount', p. 321, that the SM is 'not Gesinnungsethik'; for such an understanding apparently fails to grasp the primacy and centrality of the basic underlying disposition called for, of which all the behavioural injunctions are but expressions (see p. 113 below). Mt. *is* concerned about behaviour – but

behaviour that grows out of the proper disposition; cf. Strecker, 'Makarismen', pp. 259, 264.

50 Cf. Furnish, *Love*, p. 91: 'There is no Pauline letter in which the term "love" ... does not appear and in which exhortations to love do not figure prominently.' The dominance of ἀγάπη terminology is evident from the following frequency count (with reference to love for God omitted): ἀγαπᾶν, 9; ἀγάπη, 45; ἀγαπητός, 21; φιλαδελφία, 2; φιλοξενία, 1; φιλόστοργος, 1; ἄστοργος, 1; ἔλεος, 1. Unlike Mt., Paul applies the term ἔλεος almost exclusively to God. His lone use of φιλεῖν (1 Cor. 16.22) refers to love for Christ.

51 Cf. Moffatt, *Love*, pp. 178, 204–9.

52 Furnish's tendency to categorize whole chapters of parenesis under the umbrella of love, however, overextends the concept exegetically (see *Love*, pp. 96ff, 102ff).

53 Occasionally 'hope' is added to form a triad: 1 Cor. 13.13; Gal. 5.5f; Col. 1.4f; 1 Thess. 1.3; 5.8.

54 In typical Pauline fashion, these references probably fulfil a parenetic function as well; cf. O'Brien, p. 263.

55 See *ibid*. p. 265, on the latter.

56 ἐνεργουμένη may be either middle or passive; with most commentators I assume the former, though Furnish argues for equal consideration of the latter (*Theology*, pp. 201f), and suggests the two may be viewed as complementary: '*God's* love makes faith possible and *man's* love gives it visibility and effect in the world' (*Love*, p. 94). Noting the parallelism of 1 Cor. 7.19 and Gal. 6.15 with this passage, Furnish identifies 'faith working through love' with 'keeping the commandments of God' and 'a new creation' (*Theology*, pp. 200ff; cf. *Love*, pp. 96f; Moffatt, *First Corinthians*, p. 87; Bruce, *Corinthians*, p. 71). But a simple parallelism in form does not necessarily imply an equation in content; the foci of the three phrases are distinctly different.

57 Cf. Houlden, *Ethics*, p. 31.

58 See ch. 1, n. 197 above and p. 115 below, on Paul's understanding of δικαιοσύνη.

59 Cf. Furnish, *Love*, p. 92 – who identifies the two too closely, however: 'faith is first of all obedience in love ... Love is both the context and the content of faith' (pp. 94, 96).

60 See pp. 116ff and ch. 5, n. 48 below; cf. Bultmann, *Theology*, vol. I, pp. 330, 344; Houlden, *Ethics*, pp. 27, 31f; Furnish, *Theology*, pp. 115–35; *Love*, pp. 93f; Kümmel, *Theology*, p. 227.

61 The genitive is ambiguous; Schrenk, p. 210, suggests it may be one of either apposition, origin or quality.

62 Furnish, *Love*, pp. 93, 98f (cf. *Theology*, pp. 87f), and Spicq, *Agape*, vol. II, p. 43, see love here as *the* fruit of the Spirit, of which the other virtues cited are but expressions; but not all the others fit happily under the category of love. Cf. Moffatt, *Love*, p. 170.

63 Furnish, *Love*, pp. 93, 96, identifies the Spirit and love too closely: for him, love itself is 'the power of the new age already present' – indeed, love is '*the new aeon itself, powerfully present and active in history*' (*Love*, p. 93). Cf. J.T. Sanders, *Ethics*, pp. 56ff: 'For Paul, ἀγάπη

designates the *eschaton*.' Sanders thus sees Paul as taking a step in the direction of understanding transcendence qualitatively rather than temporally, and concludes that Paul is one of the few NT writers who offer the possibility of an ethic that is not fundamentally grounded in an imminent eschatology (p. 63; cf. p. 66).

64 See however Rom. 13.9; Gal. 5.14; cf. 6.2.

65 Cf. Furnish, *Love*, p. 92; Günther–Link, pp. 544f. Schnackenburg, p. 220.

66 Cf. Furnish, *Theology*, pp. 202, 205; for a comparison with the role of love in contemporary Jewish and Hellenistic views of the relationship between God, the individual, and others, see Günther–Link, pp. 540–4.

67 Rom. 8.28; 1 Cor. 2.9; 8.3; 16.22; and if Spicq is correct in interpreting τὴν ἀγάπην τοῦ θεοῦ as an objective genitive, 2 Thess. 3.5 also. Nowhere does Paul cite Jesus' command to love God. Nygren's thesis, that Paul drops the idea because ἀγάπη 'cannot fit man's attitude to God' (*Agape*, pp. 125, 129), is based on his peculiar definition of ἀγάπη as something spontaneous.

68 Faith and obedience, more than love, represent the appropriate response to God in Paul's thinking (cf. Furnish, *Love*, pp. 94, 97; *Theology*, pp. 202f).

69 With the majority of commentators, I take τὴν ἀγάπην τοῦ θεοῦ to be a subjective genitive; see esp. Best, *Thessalonians*, p. 330.

70 I take ἡ ἀγάπη τοῦ Χριστοῦ to be a subjective genitive; so also Bauer, p. 6; Plummer, *Second Corinthians*, p. 173; J.H. Moulton, p. 211; Strachan, p. 107; Hughes, p. 192; see esp. Barrett, *Second Corinthians*, pp. 167f; *pace* Spicq, *Agape*, vol. II, p. 188.

71 Even though the term occurs only twice, J.T. Sanders suggests φιλαδελφία is 'always for Paul the primary mode of *agapē* in Christian existence' (*Ethics*, p. 59).

72 Cf. Stauffer, p. 51. Paul's primary concern with regard to the outside world is a theological and not a social one; but statements like H. Montefiore's, that 'Paul did not regard it as a Christian duty to go out of his way to love a non-Christian' (p. 162), are quite misleading.

73 Rom. 12.10, 16, 18; 14.1, 19; 15.5f; 1 Cor. 1.10; 10.16f; 2 Cor. 13.11; Gal. 3.27f; 5.22f; 6.1; Phil. 1.27; 2.1ff; 4.2; Col. 2.2, 19; 3.12ff; 1 Thess. 5.13f.

74 Rom. 12.16; 14.1–12; 16.17; 1 Cor. 3.3ff; 4.6; 11.18–22; Gal. 5.15, 19ff; Phil. 2.3f; Col. 3.8f.

75 For various interpretations of ch. 13, see J.T. Sanders, 'First Corinthians 13'; I take it to be primarily parenetic and not Christological or eschatological in nature. The view that ch. 13 represents a later insertion fails to take sufficient account of Pauline excursus, and overlooks the way the chapter functions as the basis for the following one; cf. Schneeberger, p. 152.

76 See Moffatt, *Love*, pp. 190, 204–9, for the contrasting emphasis on the individual in Hellenistic thought; cf. Furnish, *Love*, p. 98.

77 As Furnish notes, *Love*, p. 99, the passage is somewhat parallel to Gal. 5.22f.

78 Furnish's view that Paul regards love more as an act of freedom than as a restriction of freedom (*Love*, pp. 111f), does not fit well here.

79 *Theology*, p. 205, n. 154.
80 Furnish makes no mention of the ecclesiological factor in *Theology* (pp. 213–24), and gives it only slight attention in *Love* (p. 95).
81 Furnish seems to overlook this aspect; cf. *Theology*, p. 205: 'Love always assumes the form of "service".'
82 On φίλημα, see Stählin, 'φιλέω', pp. 138ff; Günther–Brown, p. 549.
83 In some cases ἀγαπητοί refers to those loved by God (Rom. 1.7; 9.25; 11.28; Col. 3.12?; 1 Thess. 1.4; 2 Thess. 2.13).
84 The primary reference, however, is to his 'begetting' of them in Christ (cf. 1 Cor. 4.15; Gal. 4.19; Furnish, *Theology*, pp. 90f).
85 See pp. 66f above.
86 These reminders function implicitly as a spur for the further expression of love – as do the references to Paul's own love (cf. 1 Thess. 3.12).
87 A positive response to Paul could be interpreted as an affirmation of their commitment to his message.
88 *Love*, p. 119; Furnish views 2 Thess. as non-Pauline.
89 See Furnish, *Love*, pp. 107f; Piper, pp. 115ff.
90 These words must be understood in the light of Gal. 3.10, however.
91 Cf. 3.1ff; 4.20; whether ἀνόητοι connotes simple ignorance or stupidity, however, is uncertain.
92 See p. 98 above.
93 See ch. 2, n. 40 above, on Mt. 25.31–46.
94 G. Barth, 'Law', p. 85, suggests rather that Mt.'s view of God 'is itself determined by the love-commandment'; but this cannot account for the whole of Mt.'s conception of God.
95 *Pace* Piper, pp. 150, 173.
96 But note Mt. 3.17; 17.5.
97 Cf. Furnish, *Theology*, pp. 114ff.
98 On this basis the contrast J.T. Sanders makes between the relation of love and law in Mt. and Paul (see ch. 1, n. 308 above) is overdrawn.
99 Cf. Dodd, 'Beatitudes', pp. 7f.
100 Cf. Rom. 12.14–21; 14.13–21; 15.1ff; 1 Cor. 8.1–13; 10.23–33; 13.4–7; 2 Cor. 5.13ff; Gal. 5.13ff; Phil. 2.3–8, 20f; 1 Thess. 2.6–9; 2 Thess. 3.7–9.
101 See Conclusion, n. 10 below.
102 Cf. Stendahl, *Paul*, p. 54.
103 However, cf. Mt. 10.42; 18.5–35; 25.31–46.
104 P. 165; cf. pp. 161ff, where Montefiore speaks of Paul's 'narrowing' of Jesus' concept of love.
105 See Moffatt, *Love*, pp. 193–6.
106 Schnackenburg, p. 104, suggests with regard to Mt. 5.43–8 that 'imitation of God will make those who love God capable of a similar attitude'; but there is little exegetical support for this.
107 It is certainly inaccurate to say, as Schnackenburg does, that 'For St. Paul too Christian love attains its utmost in love for enemies' (p. 219).

## 5. Inner Forces

1 Mt. 1.18, 20; 3.11*, 16*; 4.1*; 10.20*; 12.18, 28, 31*, 32; 22.43*; 28.19. πνεῦμα occurs with a different sense in 5.3; 12.43; 26.41*; 27.50.
2 Cf. Schweizer, 'πνεῦμα', pp. 397, 404; Hamilton, pp. 84f.
3 Mt.'s redactional addition *καὶ πυρί* and the context of eschatological judgement in which the pericope is set (3.7–10, 12) leave unclear precisely what he understands by being baptized *ἐν πνεύματι ἁγίῳ* in 3.11*; cf. Hill, *Matthew*, pp. 94f; *Greek Words*, pp. 244f; Green, *Matthew*, p. 63; Bauer, p. 730; Argyle, *Matthew*, p. 36; Allen, pp. 25f; Tasker, *Matthew*, p. 47; Plummer, *Matthew*, pp. 28f; Schweizer, *Good News*, pp. 51f. The authenticity of the trinitarian-like reference itself in 28.19 is questioned. See esp. Hill, *Greek Words*, p. 252; McNeile, pp. 436f; Green, *Matthew*, pp. 230f; but cf. Schweizer, 'πνεῦμα', p. 401; *Good News*, pp. 530f.
4 Mt. 10.40 and 25.40, 45 are no exception; the underlying principle here is one of representation, not mystical indwelling. Hull, p. 120, thus speaks of 'the external nature of the Spirit' in Mt. (12.31f). But cf. Green, *Matthew*, pp. 56, 164f, on 1.23; see p. 78 above.
5 See Hill, *Matthew*, p. 80; cf. Perrin, *New Testament*, p. 192.
6 There is no identification of Jesus' presence and the Spirit; cf. Green, *Matthew*, p. 232.
7 With Schweizer (*Good News*, p. 163) and Hill (*Matthew*, pp. 142f), I take this in the context of 6.19–24 as a reference to singleness of commitment to God, rather than to generosity and meanness. Dewar, p. 46, suggests that what is required is a 'single eye, which fills the inner man with light, an essential inner goodness'.
8 Cf. also 13.3–8*, 18–23*; 21.19*, 33–43 – all of which speak of a failure to produce 'fruit'.
9 The initial term, 'evil thoughts', suggests to Dewar that Mt. here focuses on the 'internal' thought underlying each of the 'external' offences (pp. 36f).
10 Cf. Schweizer, *Good News*, p. 325; McNeile, p. 229.
11 But see ch. 4, n. 49 above; cf. Dewar, pp. 32f, 46, 62ff.
12 *Matthew*, p. 77. Green emphasizes the singleness of intention underlying this beatitude, a theme especially prominent in 6.19–34.
13 Statistically (including only references to moral qualities or ethical behaviour):

| | | |
|---|---|---|
| κακός | (Mt: 4 | Mk: 2) |
| πονηρός | (Mt: 26 | Mk: 2) |
| καλός | (Mt: 14 | Mk: 2) |
| ἀγαθός | (Mt: 13 | Mk: 4) |

Cf. the related terms:

| | | |
|---|---|---|
| δίκαιος | (Mt: 16 | Mk: 1) |
| ἀνομία | (Mt: 4 | Mk: 0) |

14 In contrast with God, however, they remain 'evil' (7.11).
15 Dewar, p. 46; see ch. 5, n. 7 above.
16 The word occurs nowhere in Mk. and only once in Lk. (1.75).

17 See Schrenk, pp. 198f; Hill, *Greek Words*, pp. 127ff; Ziesler, pp. 130ff; Sand, *Gesetz*, pp. 197–205; Reumann, pp. 124–35; and esp. Strecker, *Weg*, pp. 149–58, and Przybylski, pp. 77–104.

18 Strecker, *Weg*, pp. 149–58; Hill, *Greek Words*, p. 129; Przybylski, pp. 77–104; so also Blair, pp. 120f; Ziesler, p. 133; cf. Schrenk, p. 198. *Pace* Bultmann, *Theology*, vol. I, p. 273; G. Barth, 'Law', pp. 123f, 139ff. Barth's criticism of Schrenk's position offers no supporting evidence (p. 124, n. 1).

19 Dewar, p. 33, observes that here there is no distinction between 'good' and 'righteous', as in the Pauline writings (cf. Mt. 19.7 and Rom. 5.7). Note that *δίκαιος* is the term Mt. applies to Joseph (1.19), whom he portrays as a model of obedience (1.19, 24; 2.14, 21, 22). Cf. Schrenk, p. 190; Ziesler, pp. 138ff. Hill's thesis that the term refers especially to Christian teachers ('ΔΙΚΑΙΟΙ', pp. 296ff) is unconvincing.

20 E.g. Banks, 'Matthew 5:17–20', p. 242; cf. Ziesler, pp. 133f, 141: '"Righteousness" is always something one *does*.' Even Ziesler's modified definition of it as 'loving activity' (p. 142) does not quite hit the mark; cf. pp. 98f above.

21 P. 18; cf. Blair, pp. 142, 137: 'The true disciple is like Jesus both inwardly and outwardly'; 'The higher righteousness and perfection, about which Matthew talks, mean simply being and acting like Jesus.'

22 See esp. Strecker, *Weg*, pp. 154f, and Przybylski, pp. 89ff, 96ff, who correctly refute the common assertion that *δικαιοσύνη* in Mt. is portrayed as a 'gift', esp. in 5.6; 6.33 (so G. Barth, 'Law', pp. 104f, 139f; Feuillet, 'Mt V.17–20', pp. 132ff; Dewar, p. 45; Schrenk, pp. 198f; Ziesler, pp. 134f; see Sand, *Gesetz*, pp. 204f for additional references) – a clear example of reading Mt. through the eyes of Paul.

23 See p. 80 above.

24 The wording of the formulation expresses my agreement with the fundamental tenet of E. P. Sanders, that the beginning point of Paul's theology lies in his soteriological convictions, not his anthropological ones: cf. *Paul*, pp. 433f, 442ff, 497, 499ff. See ch. 1, n. 202 above.

25 See ch. 1, n. 197 above. In context, at least the following references to *δικαιοσύνη* would seem to be best taken in an ethical sense: Rom. 6.13, 16, 18, 19, 20; 10.5; 14.17; 2 Cor. 6.7, 14; 9.9, 10; 11.15; Phil. 1.11; 3.6, 9 – as well as the references to *δίκαιος* in Rom. 2.13; 3.10; 5.7; 1 Thess. 2.10 (cf. Du Toit; Schrenk, pp. 190f). These texts make it clear that the term can in no way be interpreted merely as a 'legal fiction' or 'as if' (so, correctly, Bornkamm, *Paul*, p. 138); there is a 'making righteous' as well as a 'pronouncing righteous'. See further below.

26 See ch. 4, n. 61 above; cf. Paul's use of the term *καρπός* in Rom. 7.4; Gal. 5.22; Col. 1.6, 10; Schweizer, '*πνεῦμα*', p. 431.

27 On the apparent statements to the contrary in Rom. 2.6–10, 14f, 27, see ch. 2, n. 57 above. However, Paul's assertion that God's power is most effective when human potential is weakest (2 Cor. 12.9f; cf. 4.7–11; 11.30) is not spoken in an ethical context. See Schweizer, '*πνεῦμα*', p. 432, and Andrews, 'Motive', p. 212, on the contrast between Paul and the Stoics on this point. Houlden, *Ethics*, p. 34, and Schrenk, p. 210, note the absence of the standard Hellenistic notion of 'virtue' in Paul's writings.

28 The role of the Spirit in ethics is developed most fully in Rom. and Gal.; there is no clear evidence of a shift or development in Paul's thinking with regard to the concept.

29 On this passage, see pp. 32f above.

30 Cf. Schrenk, pp. 208ff; Schweizer, 'Gottesgerechtigkeit', p. 465: 'Gabe- und Machtcharakter sind also nicht zu trennen.' Linked to this in Paul's thinking is the dual nature of sin: it is both a transgression for which one is held accountable and a power that enslaves; deliverance from sin must therefore of necessity be accomplished on both levels. E.P. Sanders, *Paul*, pp. 500f, suggests that Paul's primary concern is with the latter and not the former; this, he suggests, is why the concepts of repentance and forgiveness – and transgression as guilt – are so inadequately dealt with by Paul (cf. J. Knox, *Chapters*, pp. 142ff; so also Bultmann, *Theology*, vol. I, p. 287; Bornkamm, *Paul*, p. 151; Andrews, 'Repentance', p. 125; Stendahl, *Paul*, pp. 23ff, 82, n. 5).

31 On the theological *and* ethical dimensions of the first two terms, see E.P. Sanders, *Paul*, pp. 451f.

32 Cf. Schweizer, 'πνεῦμα', p. 431: 'when πνεῦμα is the power of sanctification (R. 15:16; 1 C. 6:11; also 2 Th. 2:13), one cannot say whether Paul's emphasis is that the Spirit sets us in God's saving action and justifies us, or that He enables us to live thereby in concrete obedience. The two are one and the same.'

33 See pp. 101f above.

34 Cf. Schweizer, 'Gottesgerechtigkeit', p. 508; Käsemann, 'Righteousness', p. 175: 'The key to this whole Pauline viewpoint is that power is always seeking to realize itself in action and must indeed do so.' For discussion of Käsemann's view of the righteousness of God as active power, see Brauch, pp. 523–42.

35 Note the identification of the dispensation of δικαιοσύνη with the dispensation of the Spirit.

36 Cf. E.P. Sanders, *Paul*, p. 513; Bultmann, *Theology*, vol. I, pp. 157, 162, 337. Paul's emphasis on the key role of the Spirit in ethics is clearly linked to his theology of grace, and is not simply the result of a new-found moral power in his own life (as Cave suggests, p. 77) or a desire to play down current interest in the more phenomenal χαρίσματα (cf. Schnackenburg, p. 172; Hunter, *Paul*, p. 97; Schweizer, 'πνεῦμα', p. 432). A major weakness of Whiteley's *Theology* is the minimal attention it gives to the role of the Spirit in Paul's theology.

37 However, this passage probably refers to the church, not individuals. See esp. Moule, *Christology*, pp. 89ff, and Corriveau, pp. 36–72, on the temple metaphor in Paul.

38 Cf. Moule, *Christology*, pp. 56ff; Ladd, *Theology*, p. 488. C.A.A. Scott, *Christianity*, p. 144, and Hunter, *Paul*, pp. 90, 95, suggest that Paul was the first to link the indwelling Spirit with Christ himself.

39 The precise sense of the genitives, however, remains a matter of conjecture; Bultmann, *Theology*, vol. I, p. 153, interprets the latter as 'Christ's gift'.

40 See esp. Kümmel, *Theology*, pp. 167ff; Schweizer, 'πνεῦμα', pp. 433f; cf. E.F. Scott's more questionable analysis, *Spirit*, pp. 177ff. See E.P. Sanders, *Paul*, p. 462, and Lampe, p. 79, on Rom. 8.9f.

41 See Rom. 8.15ff, 23, 26f; 9.1; 12.11; 15.13, 19; 1 Cor. 2.4, 10ff; 7.40; 12.1–13; 14.2, 12; 2 Cor. 1.22; 5.5; Gal. 2.20; 3.5; 4.6f, 29; Phil. 1.19; 4.9; 1 Thess. 1.5f; 5.19. These references reflect the extent to which Paul's view of ministry is grounded in grace, and based on the active working of God himself (cf. also Rom. 1.11; 12.6ff; 15.16, 18f; 1 Cor. 9.11; 15.10; 2 Cor. 3.6; 10.4; 13.3f; Gal. 2.20; Col. 1.29); see pp. 86ff above.

42 Cf. Kümmel, *Theology*, p. 189: 'God's saving action in Jesus Christ cannot have decisive significance unless the power of evil also were thereby affected to the very core.' On the cosmic aspects of Christ's death, see esp. Caird, *Principalities*, pp. 80–101.

43 The context (esp. 4.5, 10, 21ff) makes it clear that *τὰ στοιχεῖα τοῦ κόσμου* (4.3) and *τὰ ἀσθενῆ καὶ πτωχὰ στοιχεῖα* (4.9) are in some way linked to the law; see esp. Caird, *Principalities*, pp. 43ff; Burton, pp. 510–18; cf. Delling, '*στοιχεῖον*', pp. 684f; Schlier, *Principalities, passim*; Drane, *Paul*, pp. 36ff; E.P. Sanders, 'Patterns', p. 468; Ridderbos, *Galatia*, pp. 153f, 161f; *Paul*, pp. 148f; Stamm, pp. 521f. The precise relationship between the two, however, is unspecified. Several see the linkage in Paul's reference to angels in 3.19: Bruce, *Paul*, pp. 421f; Reicke, pp. 261f; Duncan, pp. 134ff; cf. Neil, *Galatians*, pp. 63f; Allan, p. 70; Schlier, *Principalities*, p. 27; *Galater*, pp. 104f. It is probably best to take 4.9 as a metaphorical reference to the bondage resulting from reversion to the law, here likened to the previous bondage to pagan *στοιχεῖα*. For discussion of the former term as used in Col. 2.8, see esp. R.P. Martin, *Colossians*, pp. 10–14; Lohse, *Colossians*, pp. 96–9; Delling, '*στοιχεῖον*', pp. 685f; Bornkamm, *Ende*, pp. 139ff.

44 Cf. Kümmel, *Theology*, pp. 158, 192: 'Paul sees sin first of all as a power to which men are subject as slaves'; Bultmann, *Theology*, vol. I, p. 245; Houlden, *Ethics*, p. 32; E.P. Sanders, *Paul*, pp. 468, 499f. See Caird, *Principalities*, on 'powers' in Paul.

45 See esp. Kümmel, *Theology*, pp. 145f; Tannehill, p. 15; E.P. Sanders, *Paul*, p. 507; cf. Paul's references to 'this aeon' in Rom. 12.2; 1 Cor. 1.20; 3.18; and 'this world' in 1 Cor. 1.20; 3.19; 5.10; 7.31.

46 Cf. E.P. Sanders, *Paul*, p. 497: 'One could say, from one *sphere* to another ... as long as "sphere" is not understood to imply that the complete change has taken place.'

47 Cf. Kümmel, *Theology*, p. 149.

48 Furnish, *Theology*, pp. 129f, speaks of the Spirit as 'a power representative of the coming age'; cf. Bultmann, *Theology*, vol. I, pp. 155, 335; Kümmel, *Theology*, pp. 169, 217f; J.A.T. Robinson, *Body*, p. 73; Hamilton, p. 39.

49 *Theology*, vol. I, p. 332; it is precisely this that suggests most strongly that Rom. 7.14–25 does *not* apply to the Christian; see pp. 32f above.

50 On the meaning of *σάρξ*, see esp. Bultmann, *Theology*, vol. I, pp. 232ff; Sand, *Fleisch*. The *σάρξ–πνεῦμα* dichotomy is to be equated neither with the body–soul antithesis common in Hellenism (cf. Paul's use of *σάρξ* in Rom. 7.5; 8.3; 1 Cor. 3.3; Phil. 3.3), nor with the outward–inward contrast drawn elsewhere by Paul himself (Rom. 2.28–9; 7.22–5; 2 Cor. 4.16, 18; cf. Phil. 3.3; Col. 2.11, 23; Murphy-O'Connor, pp. 37–41). The body–soul division represents a *partim-partim* mode of analysis, while the

*σάρξ–πνεῦμα* terminology denotes concepts (authorities and powers) that apply to the whole person (cf. Kümmel, *Theology*, pp. 174ff). The *σάρξ–πνεῦμα* conflict is to a certain extent related to the outward–inward contrast, in that truly spiritual matters are consistently viewed essentially as matters of the heart, and not matters of mere external observance (Rom. 2.28f; 7.22ff; Phil.3.3; cf. Col. 2.20–3; Bultmann, *Theology*, vol. I, pp. 234f); but there are limits to the degree of overlap (Gal. 5.19–23). And whereas the *σάρξ–πνεῦμα* conflict relates strictly to the believer (cf. Ladd, *Theology*, p. 471), the *ἔξω– ἔσω* tension applies to a broader spectrum of humankind (Rom. 7.22–5; cf. 2 Cor. 4.16, 18). The meaning of the term *ὁ ἔσω ἄνθρωπος* therefore varies somewhat in different contexts: cf. Bultmann, *Theology*, vol. I, p. 203; Conzelmann, *Theology*, p. 180. The crucial point is that for Paul, *ὁ ἔσω ἄνθρωπος* is never in itself the source of moral strength (Rom. 7.15–25).

51 Cf. Bultmann, *Theology*, vol. I, pp. 331ff; Ladd, *Theology*, p. 524; Dunn, *Jesus*, pp. 308–17. It is wrong to see the 'lower nature' as 'transmuted' by the Spirit, as E.F. Scott does (*Spirit*, p. 138).

52 Schweizer's comment, '*ἀγάπη* is simply life in the Spirit which is freed from trust in the *σάρξ*' ('*πνεῦμα*', p. 431), misses the point; the prerequisite for love is not so much freedom from trust in the *σάρξ*, as freedom from preoccupation with and domination by the demands of the *σάρξ*.

53 C.A.A. Scott, *Christianity*, p. 220, sees in the nine qualities listed three levels of spiritual activity, corresponding to 'the inmost, the inner, and the outer forms of the personality'. The analysis, however, is forced.

54 See p. 32 above.

55 Cf. Dunn, *Unity*, p. 191: 'It is such experience of the Spirit that he evidently regards as *quintessentially Christian*.'

56 This does not imply that 'one may possess the Spirit in varying quantity or intensity', as Bultmann suggests (*Theology*, vol. I, pp. 158f), or that those with particular *χαρίσματα* are given a special designation; it simply means that some are living more *κατὰ πνεῦμα* than others (cf. Dunn, *Jesus*, pp. 287f).

57 *Pace* Schubert, p. 385. Cf. Richardson, p. 111; Ladd, *Theology*, pp. 494, 518f; Conzelmann, *Theology*, pp. 277, 283; Bornkamm, *Paul*, p. 201; Bultmann, *Theology*, vol. I, p. 336: 'to be "led by the Spirit" ... does not mean to be dragged along willy-nilly (cf. 1 Cor. 12:2) but directly presupposes decision in the alternative: "flesh" or "Spirit"'; Furnish, *Theology*, pp. 195, 244ff: 'For Paul, obedience means surrender to God's power but not abject capitulation to it'; 'The new is not wholly spontaneous and irresistible. It exists in a dialectical tension with the old.' Thus, to assume that Paul views morality as the inevitable, 'spontaneous' outcome of being 'in Christ', and therefore to criticize him for the illogicality of his parenesis (cf. Enslin, p. 119), is to misread Paul.

58 Cf. Beardsley, pp. 65, 76. On Ladd's overemphasis of the objective, *heilsgeschichtlich* aspects of certain texts (*Theology*, pp. 483ff; but cf. pp. 493f), see ch. 3, n. 98 above; so also Schnackenburg, pp. 173, 277.

59 See e.g. Bultmann, *Theology*, vol. I, pp. 332f; vol. II, pp. 79, 170, 176f, 180, 203ff; Bornkamm, *Paul*, pp. 201f; Furnish, *Theology*, pp. 97f, 224ff; E.P. Sanders, *Paul*, pp. 468f.

60 *Pace* Holzmann, Wernle, Windisch and Weinel (as cited by Schnackenburg, p. 271, n. 8); cf. Andrews, 'Motive', p. 206.

61 Cf. Kümmel, *Theology*, pp. 226f; Tannehill, pp. 75–8; C.A.A. Scott, *Christianity*, p. 174; Schnackenburg, pp. 271f. Dunn, *Jesus*, pp. 308ff, thus speaks of the tension between the 'already' and the 'not yet'. See Rom. 16.20; 1 Cor. 5.5; 10.20; 2 Cor. 4.3f; 12.7; 1 Thess. 2.18.

62 Cf. Tannehill, pp. 78ff; Furnish, *Theology*, p. 173, n. 110, thus criticizes Whiteley's statement (*Theology*, p. 168) that in 1 Cor. 6.11 'St. Paul clearly supposed that those who had been through the purifying waters would have ceased from the practice of sinning.'

63 Cf. Sand, *Fleisch*, p. 304.

64 See e.g. Bultmann, *Theology*, vol. I, pp. 191ff; *TDNT, ad loc.*

65 See Dunn, *Jesus*, pp. 201f, 223; *Baptism*, pp. 135, 146f, 156; cf. Sorg, p. 183; Conzelmann, *Theology*, p. 183.

66 On the overlap of the terms *καρδία* and *νοῦς*, see Bultmann, *Theology*, vol. I, pp. 220ff; Stacey, pp. 196ff; cf. Behm, '*νοῦς*', pp. 958f. In general, *νοῦς* emphasizes more the cognitive aspects. On the relationship between *νοῦς* and *ὁ ἔσω ἄνθρωπος*, see Bultmann, p. 212.

67 One cannot, however, contrast Pauline and Jewish *δοκιμάζειν* of the divine will quite as simply as Dunn does (*Jesus*, pp. 223f), with one based on a renewed *νοῦς* and the other on law. In reality, the situation is more complex, with *νόμος* playing an active role in both.

68 See Barrett, *First Corinthians*, p. 78, on the significance of 'we'; cf. Conzelmann, *1 Corinthians*, p. 69. There is little to support Ruef's suggestion, p. 21, that Paul is here quoting the Corinthians.

69 *Pace* Conzelmann, *1 Corinthians*, p. 69; also W.L. Knox, *Gentiles*, pp. 117f, who understands the passage in terms of the Hellenistic–Jewish equation of the Spirit with the divine Mind.

70 Cf. Evans, *Explorations*, p. 114.

71 Cf. Orr–Walther, pp. 116f; Lampe, p. 81.

72 So Larsson, p. 233; Schulz, *Nachfolge*, p. 274; Moule, 'Philippians 2:5–11', pp. 264ff; but see Losie, pp. 52f, on the difficulties of interpreting the text.

73 Cf. Bultmann, *Theology*, vol. I, p. 207.

74 Cf. Stacey, p. 201; *νοῦς* may will to do the right, but in itself it lacks the power to carry it out.

75 Cf. Dodd, 'Ethics of Pauline Epistles', p. 296; E.F. Scott, *Spirit*, pp. 164f; Cerfaux, p. 308 – whose concept of a 'spiritual zone' surrounding the Christian's spirit and mind (p. 310), however, is too localized.

76 See esp. Bauer, pp. 674ff; Cole, pp. 159f. Barclay, p. 14, fails to distinguish between the two, and sees the latter concept as part of the human make-up only in the Christian; but in Paul's thinking the human *πνεῦμα* is neither restricted to Christians (1 Cor. 2.11; 5.5) nor identified with its divine counterpart (see below).

77 Pp. 129ff; cf. Bultmann, *Theology*, vol. I, pp. 207f.

78 Cf. Schweizer, '*πνεῦμα*', p. 436.

79 Cf. Thornton, p. 112. This does not however support Cerfaux's statement that the two form a 'single *pneuma*' (p. 301).

80 Cf. the conjunction of *καρδίας* and *ἐν πνεύματι* in Rom. 2.29.

81 This would argue against Barclay's definition of πνεῦμα as 'the ruling part of man ... which controls the thoughts and the emotions, the mental activities and the passions' (p. 13).
82 *First Corinthians*, p. 186; cf. Furnish, *Theology*, p. 231; Lampe, p. 84.
83 Furnish, *Theology*, pp. 231f; cf. Ladd, *Theology*, p. 518; *pace* Schubert, p. 385.
84 Cullmann, p. 228; Schubert, p. 385; E.F. Scott, *Spirit*, pp. 172f; cf. Marshall, p. 270; Styler, p. 186; Whiteley, *Theology*, p. 213; C.A.A. Scott, *New Testament Ethics*, p. 83.
85 P. 228.
86 P. 385.
87 *Jesus*, p. 224.
88 Cf. Ladd, *Theology*, p. 524: 'the will of God is not a decision that arises from within in answer to each moral decision that must be made'; Furnish, *Theology*, p. 189.
89 Cf. Ladd, *Theology*, p. 518; Lampe, pp. 84f; Furnish, *Theology*, pp. 231ff.
90 Paul's ethics are thus valid only within the Christian community.
91 Cf. Green, *Matthew*, p. 35.
92 Cf. Marshall, pp. 22f: 'Jesus held *that man could lead the good life if he would* while St. Paul held *that man would lead the good life if he could*.' Sorg, pp. 182f, is typical of those who generalize the Pauline view of human 'inability' to the whole of the NT.
93 Cf. McArthur, pp. 74f:

> 'Grace and forgiveness are assumed to be needed after man has done his best, but they do not appear to be indispensable – as they are in Paul – before a man can begin to do his best. Whereas Paul affirmed the need for a transformed nature, the Sermon affirms only the need for a transformed will and presupposes that this transformation is a human possibility ... there is no hint, in Matthew, that the bad can become sound only through the activity of God's Spirit. There is only the insistence that good acts must proceed from a good will. Whether the good will is a human possibility is a question not even raised.'

Cf. E.F. Scott's slightly less accurate statement, *Spirit*, pp. 164f.
94 The strongest suggestion of compulsion in Mt.'s ethics is found in 7.17f ('every sound tree bears good fruit'). The point, however, is not that the fruit is spontaneous, but that the tree must be good at its core. Certainly Bacon's understanding of the simple spontaneity of Matthew's ethics ('the impulse of native disposition': p. 513) is inaccurate.
95 The only Matthean reference to a conflict between πνεῦμα and σάρξ is 26.41*, and here the reference is to the human rather than the divine πνεῦμα.

**Conclusion**

1 Meier, p. 169, correctly observes that most comparisons of the two have been 'too facile and superficial'; he adds: 'To try to harmonize the two would be as misleading as to try to play one off against the other.'
2 See Trilling, *Das Wahre Israel*, pp. 216–24, and Sand, *Gesetz*, pp. 220f, who lists a number of the various attempts to describe the *Sitz im Leben* of

the Gospel; cf. p. 206: '... seine theologischen Gedanken ... sind zu vielfältig, als dass man sie einem einheitlichen und alle sonstigen Fragen lösenden Hauptgedanken unterordnen könnte'; Meier, pp. 21ff.

3 Tagawa, however, p. 162, suggests that the gentile mission in the strict sense of the term is not a part of Mt.'s thinking: 'The Gentile mission in Matthew is the mission in order to introduce the Gentiles into the Israel–Christian community. For Matthew there can be no Gentile church'; cf. Goulder, *Midrash*, p. 160: 'Non-Jewish Christians are Gentiles no more, but members of God's Israel.' But contrast Stendahl, *School*, p. xiii, and Dunn, *Unity*, pp. 47f. See Meier, pp. 163, 169.

4 Cf. Hill, 'Hosea VI.6', p. 113. For a different view, see Nepper-Christensen, p. 202 *et passim*; Strecker, *Weg*, pp. 15–35, 39; Sandmel, *Jewish Understanding*, pp. 165–8; Trilling, *Das Wahre Israel*, pp. 214–16; Abel, p. 142; see Meier, pp. 14ff, for discussion. Irenaeus speaks of the Ebionites as using the Gospel of Mt. only, and repudiating Paul as an apostate from the law (Stevenson, p. 97).

5 Both Munck (pp. 24ff) and Stendahl (*Paul*, pp. 1ff, 7ff), see Paul's call to the gentiles as the central fact governing his theology and writings (cf. Gal. 1.15–17).

6 For various attempts to define more precisely Paul's opposition in the individual writings, see among others Robinson–Koester, pp. 144ff; Dunn, *Unity*, pp. 275ff; Munck, pp. 87–209; Drane, *Paul*, pp. 78–124; Gunther, *passim*; and Georgi on 2 Cor. See also Bornkamm, *Paul*, p. 185.

7 See p. 22 and ch. 1, n. 158 above; cf. Meier, pp. 22ff.

8 Cf. Stendahl, *Paul*, p. 71:

> 'Poor Paul, he was a theologian, an intellectual, and perhaps the only one in the whole first-generation church. In any case, he was the only one among the New Testament authors who had an M.Div. or its equivalent. Perhaps Matthew was something of an academician also, but Paul, the purist, is plagued by his professional antecedents. He stands out rather uniquely.'

9 Mt., e.g., provides a stronger basis for a sense of ethical obligation; but Paul's less introspective approach has greater potential for fostering genuine concern for others. See pp. 108f above.

10 On the modern-day relevance of Mt., see LaVerdiere–Thompson, pp. 567–71, 593–7.

## BIBLIOGRAPHY


Abbott, T.K. *A Critical and Exegetical Commentary on the Epistles to the Ephesians and to the Colossians* (ICC). Edinburgh: T. and T. Clark, 1897.

Abel, E.L. 'Who Wrote Matthew?' *NTS* 17 (1971), 138–52.

Ahern, B.M. 'The Christian's Union with the Body of Christ in Cor, Gal, and Rom', *CBQ* 23 (1961), 199–209.

'The Spirit and the Law', *The Way* 6 (1966), 219–29.

Albright, W.F., and Mann, C.S. *Matthew* (AB). Garden City, N.Y.: Doubleday and Co., 1971.

Alexander, A.B.D. *The Ethics of St. Paul.* Glasgow: James Maclehose and Sons, 1910.

Allan, J.A. *The Epistle of Paul the Apostle to the Galatians* (TBC). London: SCM Press, 1951.

Allen, W.C. *A Critical and Exegetical Commentary on the Gospel According to S. Matthew* (ICC). Edinburgh: T. and T. Clark, 1907.

Anderson, H. *The Gospel of Mark* (NCB). London: Oliphants, 1976.

Anderson, J.N.D. *Morality, Law and Grace.* London: Tyndale Press, 1972.

Andrews, M.E. 'Paul and Repentance', *JBL* 54 (1935), 125.

'The Problem of Motive in the Ethics of Paul', *JR* 13 (1933), 200–15.

Argyle, A.W. 'M and the Pauline Epistles', *ExT* 81 (1970), 340–2.

'"Outward" and "Inward" in Biblical Thought', *ExT* 68 (1967), 196–9.

*The Gospel According to Matthew* (CBC). Cambridge University Press, 1963.

Bacon, B.W. *Studies in Matthew.* London: Constable and Co., 1930.

Baelz, P. *Ethics and Belief.* London: Sheldon Press, 1977.

Baird, J.A. *The Justice of God in the Teaching of Jesus* (NTL). London: SCM Press, 1963.

Baird, W. 'Pauline Eschatology in Hermeneutical Perspective', *NTS* 17 (1971), 314–27.

Baltensweiler, H. 'Die Ehebruchsklauseln bei Matthäus: Zu Matth. 5, 32; 19, 9', *Theol. Zeit.* 15 (1959), 340–56.

Balz, H. 'φοβέω, κ.τ.λ.', *TDNT* 9. Grand Rapids, Mich.: Wm B. Eerdmans Pub. Co., ET 1974, pp. 189–219.

Bammel, E. 'Νόμος Χριστοῦ', in *Studia Evangelica* 3 (TU 88), ed. F.L. Cross. Berlin: Akademie-Verlag, 1964, pp. 120–8.

Banks, R. *Jesus and the Law in the Synoptic Tradition* (SNTS Monograph Series 28). Cambridge University Press, 1975.
'Matthew's Understanding of the Law: Authenticity and Interpretation in Matthew 5:17–20', *JBL* 93 (1974), 226–42.
Barclay, W. *Flesh and Spirit: An Examination of Galatians 5.19–23.* London: SCM Press, 1962.
Barrett, C.K. *The Epistle to the Romans*, rev. ed. (BNTC). London: Adam and Charles Black, 1962.
*The First Epistle to the Corinthians*, 2nd ed. (BNTC). London: Adam and Charles Black, 1971.
*The Holy Spirit and the Gospel Tradition*. London: S.P.C.K., 1947.
*The Second Epistle to the Corinthians* (BNTC). London: Adam and Charles Black, 1973.
'Things Sacrificed to Idols', *NTS* 11 (1965), 138–53.
Barth, G. 'Glaube und Zweifel in den synoptischen Evangelien', *ZThK* 72 (1975), 269–92.
'Matthew's Understanding of the Law', in *Tradition and Interpretation in Matthew* (NTL), ed. G. Bornkamm *et al.* London: SCM Press, ET 1963, pp. 58–164.
Barth, K. *The Epistle to the Philippians*. London: SCM Press, ET 1962.
*The Epistle to the Romans*. Oxford University Press, ET 1933.
Barton, G.A. 'The Meaning of the "Royal Law", Matt. 5:21–48', *JBL* 37 (1918), 54–65.
Bauder, W., and Link, H.-G. 'Goal, Near, Last, End, Complete: ἐγγύς', *NIDNTT* 2. Grand Rapids, Mich.: Zondervan Pub. House, ET 1976, pp. 52–5.
Bauer, W. *A Greek–English Lexicon of the New Testament and Other Early Christian Literature*, 2nd ed., rev. F.W. Gingrich and F.W. Danker. Chicago–London: University of Chicago Press, ET 1979.
Bauman, C. 'The Sermon on the Mount: Its History of Interpretation in Modern Times'. Elkhart, Ind.: Associated Mennonite Biblical Seminaries, no date (unpublished thesis).
Beardsley, W.A. *Human Achievement and Divine Vocation in the Message of Paul* (SBT 31). London: SCM Press, 1961.
Beare, F.W. 'The Epistle to the Colossians', *IB* 11. New York–Nashville: Abingdon Press, 1955, pp. 133–241.
*The Epistle to the Philippians*, 3rd ed. (BNTC). London: Adam and Charles Black, 1973.
Beasley-Murray, G.R. 'Philippians', *Peake's Commentary on the Bible*. London: Thomas Nelson and Sons, 1962, pp. 985–9.
Behm, J. 'καρδία, κ.τ.λ. (NT)', *TDNT* 3. Grand Rapids, Mich.: Wm B. Eerdmans Pub. Co., ET 1965, pp. 611–14.
'νοῦς', *TDNT* 4. Grand Rapids, Mich.: Wm B. Eerdmans Pub. Co., ET 1967, pp. 951–61.
Beilner, W. *Christus und die Pharisäer: Exegetische Untersuchung über Grund und Verlauf der Auseinandersetzung*. Wien: Verlag Herder, 1959.
Beker, J.C. 'Contingency and Coherence in the Letters of Paul', *Un. Sem. Qtr. Rev.* 33 (1978), 141–51.

*Paul the Apostle: The Triumph of God in Life and Thought.* Philadelphia: Fortress Press, 1980.

Benz, K. *Die Ethik des Apostels Paulus* (BS). Freiburg im Breisgau: Herdersche Verlagshandlung, 1912.

Berger, K. *Die Gesetzesauslegung Jesu: Ihr historischer Hintergrund im Judentum und im Alten Testament*, vol. I (WMANT 40). Neukirchen-Vluyn: Neukirchener Verlag, 1972.

Best, E. *One Body in Christ: A Study in the Relationship of the Church to Christ in the Epistles of the Apostle Paul.* London: S.P.C.K., 1955.

*The First and Second Epistles to the Thessalonians* (BNTC). London: Adam and Charles Black, 1972.

*The Letter of Paul to the Romans* (CBC). Cambridge University Press, 1967.

'The Role of the Disciples in Mark', *NTS* 23 (1977), 377–401.

Betz, H.D. 'Die Makarismen der Bergpredigt (Matthäus 5, 3–12). Beobachtungen zur literarischen Form und theologischen Bedeutung', *ZThK* 75 (1978), 3–19.

*Nachfolge und Nachahmung Jesu Christi im Neuen Testament* (BHT 37). Tübingen: J.C.B. Mohr (Paul Siebeck), 1967.

'The Logion of the Easy Yoke and of Rest (Matt 11.28–30)', *JBL* 86 (1967), 10–24.

Betz, O. 'Paulus als Pharisäer nach dem Gesetz. Phil. 3, 5–6 als Beitrag zur Frage des frühen Pharisäismus', in *Treue zur Thora: Beiträge zur Mitte des christlichjüdischen Gesprächs* (VIKJ 3), ed. P. von der Osten-Sacken. Berlin: Kirchlichen Hochschule, 1977, pp. 54–64.

Bicknell, E.J. *The First and Second Epistles to the Thessalonians* (WC). London: Methuen and Co., 1932.

Bietenhard, H. 'Hell, Abyss, Hades, Gehenna, Lower Regions', *NIDNTT* 2. Grand Rapids, Mich.: Zondervan Pub. House, ET 1976, pp. 205–10.

'Lord, Master', *NIDNTT* 2. Grand Rapids, Mich.: Zondervan Pub. House, ET 1976, pp. 508–20.

Black, M. *Romans* (NCB). London: Oliphants, 1973.

Blair, E.P. *Jesus in the Gospel of Matthew.* Nashville–New York: Abingdon Press, 1960.

Bonnard, P. *L'épître de saint Paul aux Galates*, 2nd ed. (CNT 9). Neuchâtel: Delachaux et Niestlé, 1972.

*L'épître de saint Paul aux Philippiens* (CNT 10). Neuchâtel: Delachaux et Niestlé, 1950.

*L'évangile selon saint Matthieu* (CNT 1). Neuchâtel: Delachaux et Niestlé, 1963.

Bornkamm, G. 'Das Doppelgebot der Liebe', in *Neutestamentliche Studien für Rudolf Bultmann* (BZNW 21), ed. W. Eltester. Berlin: Alfred Töpelmann, 1954, pp. 85–93.

*Das Ende des Gesetzes. Paulusstudien* (BET 16). München: Chr. Kaiser Verlag, 1952.

'Die Verzögerung der Parusie. Exegetische Bemerkungen zu zwei synoptischen Texten', in *In Memoriam Ernst Lohmeyer*, ed. W. Schmauch. Stuttgart: Evangelisches Verlagswerk, 1951, pp. 116–26.

'End-Expectation and Church in Matthew', in *Tradition and Interpretation in Matthew* (NTL), ed. G. Bornkamm *et al.* London: SCM Press, ET 1963, pp. 15–51.

*Paul.* London: Hodder and Stoughton, ET 1971.

'The Authority to "Bind" and "Loose" in the Church in Matthew's Gospel: The Problem of Sources in Matthew's Gospel', in *Jesus and Man's Hope*, vol. I, ed. D.G. Miller and D.Y. Hadidian. Pittsburgh Theological Seminary: Perspective, 1970, pp. 37–50.

'The Missionary Stance of Paul in 1 Corinthians 9 and in Acts', in *Studies in Luke–Acts*, ed. L.E. Keck and J.L. Martyn. London: S.P.C.K., 1968, pp. 194–207.

'The Risen Lord and the Earthly Jesus', in *The Future of our Religious Past*, ed. J.M. Robinson. London: SCM Press, ET 1971, pp. 203–29.

'The Stilling of the Storm in Matthew', in *Tradition and Interpretation in Matthew* (NTL), ed. G. Bornkamm *et al.* London: SCM Press, ET 1963, pp. 52–7.

Bottorff, J.F. 'The Relation of Justification and Ethics in the Pauline Epistles', *SJT* 26 (1973), 421–30.

Bowker, J. *Jesus and the Pharisees.* Cambridge University Press, 1973.

*The Targums and Rabbinic Literature. An Introduction to Jewish Interpretations of Scripture.* Cambridge University Press, 1969.

Bowman, J.W., and Tapp, R.W. *The Gospel from the Mount.* Philadelphia: Westminster Press, 1957.

Brandon, S.G.F. *The Fall of Jerusalem and the Christian Church. A Study of the Effects of the Jewish Overthrow of A.D. 70 on Christianity*, 2nd ed. London: S.P.C.K., 1957.

Branscomb, B.H. *Jesus and the Law of Moses.* London: Hodder and Stoughton, 1930.

Brauch, M.T. 'Perspectives on "God's righteousness" in recent German discussion', appendix to E.P. Sanders, *Paul and Palestinian Judaism.* London: SCM Press, 1977, pp. 523–42.

Braumann, G., and Brown, C. 'Present, Day, Maranatha, Parousia: ἡμέρα', *NIDNTT* 2. Grand Rapids, Mich.: Zondervan Pub. House, ET 1976, pp. 886–95.

Braun, H. *Spätjudisch-häretischer und frühchristlicher Radikalismus. Jesus von Nazareth und die essenische Qumransekte*, 2 vols. (BHT 24). Tübingen: J.C.B. Mohr (Paul Siebeck), 1957.

Bring, R. *Christus und das Gesetz. Die Bedeutung des Gesetzes des Alten Testaments nach Paulus und sein Glauben an Christus.* Leiden: E.J. Brill, 1969.

Brown, C. 'The Parousia and Eschatology in the NT', *NIDNTT* 2. Grand Rapids, Mich.: Zondervan Pub. House, ET 1976, pp. 901–35.

Brown, M.P., Jr. 'Matthew as ΕΙΡΗΝΟΠΟΙΟΣ', in *Studies in the History and Text of the New Testament, in honor of K. W. Clark* (Stud. and Docu. 29), ed. B.L. Daniels and M.J. Suggs. Salt Lake City: University of Utah Press, 1967, pp. 39–50.

Bruce, F.F. *1 and 2 Corinthians* (NCB). London: Oliphants, 1971.

'Paul and the Law of Moses', *BJRL* 57 (1975), 259–79.

*Paul: Apostle of the Free Spirit*. Exeter: Paternoster Press, 1977.

*The Epistle of Paul to the Romans* (TNTC). London: Tyndale Press, 1963.

Bruce, F.F., and Simpson, E.K. *Commentary on the Epistles to the Ephesians and the Colossians* (NLCNT). London: Marshall, Morgan and Scott, 1957.

Brunner, E. *The Divine Imperative: A Study in Christian Ethics*. London–Redhill: Lutterworth Press, ET 1937.

Bruppacher, H. 'Was sagte Jesus im Matthäus 5.48?' *ZNW* 58 (1967), 145.

Büchsel, F. 'παράδοσις', *TDNT* 2. Grand Rapids, Mich.: Wm B. Eerdmans Pub. Co., ET 1964, pp. 172–3.

Buck, C., and Taylor, G. *Saint Paul: A Study of the Development of his Thought*. New York: Charles Scribner's Sons, 1967.

Bultmann, R. *Jesus and the Word*. London: Ivor Nicholson and Watson, ET 1935.

*The History of the Synoptic Tradition*, 2nd ed. Oxford: Basil Blackwell, ET 1968.

*Theology of the New Testament*, 2 vols. New York: Charles Scribner's Sons, ET 1951, 1955.

Burchard, C. 'Das doppelte Liebesgebot in der frühen christlichen Überlieferung', in *Der Ruf Jesu und die Antwort der Gemeinde: Exegetische Untersuchungen Joachim Jeremias zum 70. Geburtstag gewidmet von seinen Schülern*, ed. E. Lohse *et al.* Göttingen: Vandenhoeck und Ruprecht, 1970, pp. 39–62.

Burton, E. De W. *A Critical and Exegetical Commentary on the Epistle to the Galatians* (ICC). Edinburgh: T. and T. Clark, 1921.

Bushell, G. 'Law and Christian Spirituality According to St Paul', *Aus. Bib. Rev.* 5 (1956), 99–117.

Butler, B.C. *The Originality of St Matthew: A Critique of the Two-Document Hypothesis*. Cambridge University Press, 1951.

Caird, G.B. *Paul's Letters from Prison* (NClB). Oxford University Press, 1976.

*Principalities and Powers*. Oxford: Clarendon Press, 1956.

Campenhausen, H. von. *Die Begründung kirchlicher Entscheidungen beim Apostel Paulus: Zur Grundlegung des Kirchenrechts* (SHAW). Heidelberg: Carl Winter, Universitätsverlag, 1957.

*Ecclesiastical Authority and Spiritual Power in the Church of the First Three Centuries*. London: Adam and Charles Black, ET 1969.

*The Formation of the Christian Bible*. London: Adam and Charles Black, ET 1972.

Carlston, C.E. 'Interpreting the Gospel of Matthew', *Interp.* 29 (1975), 3–12.

'The Things that Defile (Mark VII.14) and the Law in Matthew and Mark', *NTS* 15 (1968), 75–96.

Carson, H.M. *The Epistles of Paul to the Colossians and Philemon* (TNTC). London: Tyndale Press, 1960.

Catchpole, D.R. 'The Synoptic Divorce Material as a Traditio-Historical Problem', *BJRL* 57 (1974), 92–127.

Cave, S. *The Christian Way: A Study of New Testament Ethics in Relation*

*to Present Problems*. London: Nisbet and Co., 1949.
Cerfaux, L. *The Christian in the Theology of St Paul*. London: Geoffrey Chapman, ET 1967.
Chadwick, H. '"All Things to All Men" (1 Cor. IX.22)', *NTS* 1 (1955), 261–75.
Charles, R.H. *A Critical History of the Doctrine of a Future Life in Israel, in Judaism, and in Christianity*. London: Adam and Charles Black, 1913.
Clark, K.S.L. *The Gospel According to Saint Matthew*. London: Darton, Longman and Todd, 1974.
Cleland, J.T. 'The Religious Ethic of St. Paul', 2 vols. Unpublished doctoral dissertation, Union Theological Seminary (New York), 1954.
Cohn-Sherbok, D.M. 'An Analysis of Jesus' Arguments Concerning the Plucking of Grain on the Sabbath', *JSNT* 2 (1979), 31–41.
Cole, R.A. *The Epistle of Paul to the Galatians* (TNTC). London: Tyndale Press, 1965.
Conzelmann, H. *An Outline of the Theology of the New Testament*. London: SCM Press, ET 1969.
*1 Corinthians* (Hermeneia). Philadelphia: Fortress Press, ET 1975.
'συνίημι, κ.τ.λ.', *TDNT* 7. Grand Rapids, Mich.: Wm B. Eerdmans Pub. Co., ET 1971, pp. 888–96.
Cope, O.L. *Matthew: A Scribe Trained for the Kingdom of Heaven* (CBQ Monograph Series 5). Washington, D.C.: Catholic Biblical Association of America, 1976.
Corriveau, R. *The Liturgy of Life: A Study of the Ethical Thought of St. Paul in his Letters to the Early Christian Communities* (Studia 25). Bruxelles–Paris: Desclée de Brouwer, 1970.
Cranfield, C.E.B. 'St. Paul and the Law', *SJT* 17 (1964), 43–68.
*The Epistle to the Romans*, 2 vols. (ICC). Edinburgh: T. and T. Clark, 1975, 1979.
Cremer, F.G. 'Der "Heilstod" Jesu im paulinischen Verständnis von Taufe und Eucharistie', *Bib. Zeit.* n.s. 14 (1970), 227–39.
Crowther, C. 'Works, Work and Good Works', *ExT* 81 (1970), 166–71.
Cullmann, O. *Christ and Time*. London: SCM Press, ET 1951.
Cupitt, D. 'God and Morality', *Theol.* 76 (1973), 356–64.
Daniélou, J. *The Theology of Jewish Christianity*. London: Darton, Longman and Todd, ET 1964.
Daube, D. *The New Testament and Rabbinic Judaism*. University of London: Athlone Press, 1956.
Davies, P.E. 'Reward', *IDB* 4. Nashville–New York: Abingdon Press, 1962, pp. 71–4.
Davies, W.D. 'Ethics in the NT', *IDB* 2. Nashville–New York: Abingdon Press, 1962, pp. 167–76.
'Law in the NT', *IDB* 3. Nashville–New York: Abingdon Press, 1962, pp. 95–102.
'Matthew, 5, 17–18', in *Mélanges bibliques rédigés en l'honneur de André Robert* (TICP 4). Paris: Bloud et Gay, 1958, pp. 428–56.
'Paul and Jewish Christianity According to Cardinal Daniélou: A Suggestion', *Rech. Sci. Rel.* 60 (1972), 69–79.

*Paul and Rabbinic Judaism*, 3rd ed. London: S.P.C.K., 1970.
'Paul and the People of Israel', *NTS* 24 (1977), 4–39.
*The Gospel and the Land: Early Christianity and Jewish Territorial Doctrine*. Berkeley: University of California Press, 1974.
'The Moral Teaching of the Early Church', in *The Use of the Old Testament in the New and Other Essays: Studies in Honor of William Franklin Stinespring*, ed. J.M. Efird. Durham, N.C.: Duke University Press, 1972, pp. 310–32.
*The Setting of the Sermon on the Mount*. Cambridge University Press, 1964.
'Torah and Dogma: A Comment', *Harv. Theol. Rev.* 61 (1968), 87–105.
*Torah in the Messianic Age and/or the Age to Come* (JBL Monograph Series 8). Philadelphia: Society of Biblical Literature, 1952.
Delling, G. 'Der Tod Jesu in der Verkündigung des Paulus', in *Apophoreta: Festschrift für Ernst Haenchen* (BZNW 30). Berlin: Verlag Alfred Töpelmann, 1964, pp. 85–96.
'*στοιχεῖον*', *TDNT* 7. Grand Rapids, Mich.: Wm B. Eerdmans Pub. Co., ET 1971, pp. 670–87.
Derrett, J.D.M. *Law in the New Testament*. London: Darton, Longman and Todd, 1970.
Dewar, L. *An Outline of New Testament Ethics*. London: University of London Press, Hodder and Stoughton, 1949.
Dibelius, M. *Jesus: A Study of the Gospels and an Essay on 'The Motive for Social Action in the New Testament'*. London: SCM Press, ET 1949, 1963.
*Paul*, ed. W.G. Kümmel. London: Longmans, Green and Co., ET 1953.
Dimitroff, S. *Der Sinn der Forderungen Jesu in der Bergpredigt*. Sofia: Druck S.M. Staikoff, 1938.
Dobschütz, E. von. 'Matthäus als Rabbi und Katechet', *ZNW* 27 (1928), 338–48.
'The Most Important Motives for Behavior in the Life of the Early Christians', *Amer. Jour. Theol.* 15 (1911), 505–24.
Dodd, C.H. *Gospel and Law: The Relation of Faith and Ethics in Early Christianity*. Cambridge University Press, 1951.
'Matthew and Paul', in *New Testament Studies*. Manchester University Press, 1953, pp. 53–66.
*The Apostolic Preaching and Its Developments*. London: Hodder and Stoughton, 1936.
'The Beatitudes: A Form Critical Study', in *More New Testament Studies*. Manchester University Press, 1968, pp. 1–10.
*The Bible and the Greeks*. London: Hodder and Stoughton, 1935.
*The Epistle of Paul to the Romans* (MNTC). London: Collins, 1932, 1959.
'The Ethics of the New Testament', in *Moral Principles of Action: Man's Ethical Imperative*, ed. R.N. Anshen. New York–London: Harper and Bros., 1952, pp. 543–58.
'The Ethics of the Pauline Epistles', in *The Evolution of Ethics*, ed. E.H. Sneath. New Haven: Yale University Press, 1927, pp. 293–326.

'The Mind of Paul', I and II, in *New Testament Studies*. Manchester University Press, 1953, pp. 67–82, 83–128.

'The "Primitive Catechism" and the Sayings of Jesus', in *More New Testament Studies*. Manchester University Press, 1968, pp. 11–29.

Donfried, K.P. 'Justification and Last Judgement in Paul', *ZNW* 67 (1976), 90–110.

'The Allegory of the Ten Virgins (Matt 25:1–13) as a Summary of Matthean Theology', *JBL* 93 (1974), 415–28.

Doughty, D.J. 'The Presence and Future of Salvation in Corinth', *ZNW* 66 (1975), 61–90.

Drane, J.W. *Paul: Libertine or Legalist? A Study in the Theology of the Major Pauline Epistles*. London: S.P.C.K., 1975.

'Theological Diversity in the Letters of St. Paul', *Tyn. Bull.* 27 (1976), 3–26.

'Tradition, Law and Ethics in Pauline Theology', *Nov. Test.* 16 (1974), 167–78.

Drury, J. 'Midrash and Gospel', *Theol.* 77 (1974), 291–6.

*Tradition and Design in Luke's Gospel: A Study in Early Christian Historiography*. London: Darton, Longman and Todd, 1976.

Dülmen, A. van. *Die Theologie des Gesetzes bei Paulus* (SBM 5). Stuttgart: Katholisches Bibelwerk, 1968.

Duncan, G.S. *The Epistle of Paul to the Galatians* (MNTC). London: Hodder and Stoughton, 1934.

Dungan, D.L. *The Sayings of Jesus in the Churches of Paul*. Philadelphia: Fortress Press, 1971.

Dunn, J.D.G. *Baptism in the Holy Spirit* (SBT 15, 2nd ser.). London: SCM Press, 1970.

*Jesus and the Spirit* (NTL). London: SCM Press, 1975.

'The Birth of a Metaphor – Baptized in Spirit', *ExT* 89 (1978), 134–8, 173–5.

*Unity and Diversity in the New Testament*. London: SCM Press, 1977.

Dupont, J. *Les Béatitudes*, 3 vols. (EB). Paris: J. Gabalda et Cie Éditeurs, 1958, 1969, 1973.

Du Toit, A.B. 'Dikaiosyne in Röm 6. Beobachtungen zur ethischen Dimension der paulinischen Gerechtigkeitsauffassung', *ZThK* 76 (1979), 261–91.

Ebeling, G. *Word and Faith*. London: SCM Press, ET 1963.

Eissfeldt, O. '*Πληρῶσαι πᾶσαν δικαιοσύνην* in Matthäus 3.15', *ZNW* 61 (1970), 209–15.

Ellis, E.E. *Paul and His Recent Interpreters*. Grand Rapids, Mich.: Wm B. Eerdmans Pub. Co., 1961.

'II Corinthians V.1–10 in Pauline Eschatology', *NTS* 6 (1960), 211–24.

Ellison, H.L. 'Paul and the Law – "All Things to All Men"' in *Apostolic History and the Gospel*, ed. W.W. Gasque and R.P. Martin. Exeter: Paternoster Press, 1970, pp. 195–202.

Enslin, M.S. *The Ethics of Paul*. New York–London: Harper and Bros., 1930.

Ernesti, H. *Die Ethik des Apostels Paulus in ihren Grundzügen dargestellt*, 3rd ed. Göttingen: Vandenhoeck und Ruprecht's Verlag, 1880.

Esser, H.-H. 'Law, Custom, Elements: νόμος', *NIDNTT* 2. Grand Rapids, Mich.: Zondervan Pub. House, ET 1976, pp. 438–51.
'Mercy, Compassion: ἔλεος', *NIDNTT* 2. Grand Rapids, Mich.: Zondervan Pub. House, ET 1976, pp. 593–8.
Evans, C.F. *Explorations in Theology 2*. London: SCM Press, 1977.
*The Lord's Prayer*. London: S.P.C.K., 1963.
Farmer, W.R. *The Synoptic Problem: A Critical Analysis*. New York: Macmillan Co., 1964.
Farrer, A.M. 'On Dispensing with Q', in *Studies in the Gospels: Essays in Memory of R.H. Lightfoot*, ed. D.E. Nineham. Oxford: Basil Blackwell, 1955, pp. 55–86.
Fascher, E. 'Theologische Beobachtungen zu δεῖ', in *Neutestamentliche Studien für Rudolf Bultmann* (BZNW 21), ed. W. Eltester. Berlin: Alfred Töpelmann, 1954, pp. 228–54.
Faw, C.E. 'The Anomaly of Galatians', *Bib. Res.* 4 (1960), 25–38.
Fenton, J.C. *The Gospel of St Matthew*, rev. ed. (PNTC). London: SCM Press, 1977.
Feuillet, A. 'Les fondements de la morale chrétienne d'après l'Épître aux Romains', *Rev. Thom.* 70 (1970), 357–86.
'Morale ancienne et morale chrétienne d'après Mt V.17–20; Comparaison avec la doctrine de l'Épître aux Romains', *NTS* 17 (1970–1), 123–37.
Filson, F.V. *The Gospel According to St. Matthew* (BNTC). London: Adam and Charles Black, 1960.
Fitzmyer, J.A. 'The Matthean Divorce Texts and Some New Palestinian Evidence', *Theol. Stud.* 37 (1976), 197–226.
Flew, R.N. *Jesus and His Way: A Study of the Ethics of the New Testament*. London: Epworth Press, 1963.
Flückiger, F. 'Christus, des Gesetzes τέλος', *Theol. Zeit.* 11 (1955), 153–7.
Foerster, W. 'ἄξιος, κ.τ.λ.', *TDNT* 1. Grand Rapids, Mich.: Wm B. Eerdmans Pub. Co., ET 1964, pp. 379–80.
'κύριος, κ.τ.λ. (Later Judaism, NT)', *TDNT* 3. Grand Rapids, Mich.: Wm B. Eerdmans Pub. Co., ET 1965, pp. 1081–98.
Frame, J.E. *A Critical and Exegetical Commentary on the Epistles of St. Paul to the Thessalonians* (ICC). Edinburgh: T. and T. Clark, 1912.
Frankemölle, H. 'Die Makarismen (Mt 5, 1–12; Lk 6, 20–23). Motive und Umfang der redaktionellen Komposition', *Bib. Zeit.* 15 (1971), 53–75.
Franzmann, M.H. *Follow Me: Discipleship According to Saint Matthew*. St. Louis: Concordia Publishing House, 1961.
Freyne, S. *The Twelve: Disciples and Apostles. A study in the theology of the first three gospels*. London: Sheed and Ward, 1968.
Friedlander, G. *The Jewish Sources of the Sermon on the Mount*. London: George Routledge and Sons, 1911.
Fuchs, E. 'Der Anteil des Geistes am Glauben des Paulus. Ein Beitrag zum Verständnis von Römer 8', *ZThK* 72 (1975), 293–302.
Furnish, V.P. 'The Jesus–Paul Debate from Baur to Bultmann', *BJRL* 47 (1965), 342–81.

*The Love Command in the New Testament* (NTL). London: SCM Press, 1973.
*Theology and Ethics in Paul.* Nashville–New York: Abingdon Press, 1968.
Gaechter, P. *Das Matthäus-Evangelium.* Innsbruck: Tyrolia Verlag, 1963.
Gager, J.G., Jr. 'Functional Diversity in Paul's Use of End-Time Language', *JBL* 89 (1970), 325–37.
Gardner, H. *The Business of Criticism.* Oxford: Clarendon Press, 1959.
Gärtner, B. 'The Habakkuk Commentary (DSH) and the Gospel of Matthew', *Stud. Theol.* 8 (1955), 1–24.
Gaston, L. 'The Messiah of Israel as Teacher of the Gentiles', *Interp.* 29 (1975), 24–40.
Geldard, M. 'Jesus' Teaching on Divorce: thoughts on the meaning of *porneia* in Matthew 5:32 and 19:9', *Churchman* 92 (1978), 134–43.
Georgi, D. *Die Gegner des Paulus im 2. Korintherbrief* (WMANT 11). Neukirchen-Vluyn: Neukirchener Verlag, 1964.
Gerhardsson, B. 'The Hermeneutic Program in Matthew 22:37–40', in *Jews, Greeks and Christians* (SJLA 21), ed. R. Hamerton-Kelly and R. Scroggs. Leiden: E.J. Brill, 1976, pp. 129–50.
Gogarten, F. *Die Verkündigung Jesu Christi: Grundlagen und Aufgabe*, 2nd ed. (HUT 3). Tübingen: J.C.B. Mohr (Paul Siebeck), 1965.
Goodspeed, E.J. *Matthew: Apostle and Evangelist.* Philadelphia: John C. Winston Co., 1959.
Goppelt, L. *Apostolic and Post-Apostolic Times.* London: Adam and Charles Black, ET 1970.
*Christologie und Ethik: Aufsätze zum Neuen Testament.* Göttingen: Vandenhoeck und Ruprecht, 1968.
*Theologie des Neuen Testaments*, 2 vols. Göttingen: Vandenhoeck und Ruprecht, 1976.
Goudge, H.L. *The First Epistle to the Corinthians* (WC). London: Methuen and Co., 1903.
*The Second Epistle to the Corinthians* (WC). London: Methuen and Co., 1927.
Goulder, M.D. *Midrash and Lection in Matthew.* London: S.P.C.K., 1974.
'On Putting Q to the Test', *NTS* 24 (1978), 218–34.
*The Evangelists' Calendar: A Lectionary Explanation of the Development of Scripture.* London: S.P.C.K., 1978.
Grant, F.C. 'Matthew, Gospel of', *IDB* 3. Nashville–New York: Abingdon Press, 1962, pp. 303–13.
Grant, R.M. *A Historical Introduction to the New Testament.* London: Collins, 1963.
'Jewish Christianity at Antioch in the Second Century', *Rech. Sci. Rel.* 60 (1972), 97–108.
Grayston, K. 'Sermon on the Mount', *IDB* 4. Nashville–New York: Abingdon Press, 1962, pp. 279–89.
Green, H.B. 'Georg Strecker: Der Weg der Gerechtigkeit', *JTS* 15 (1964), 361–5.
*The Gospel According to Matthew* (NClB). Oxford University Press, 1975.

Greenwood, D. 'Saint Paul and Natural Law', *Bib. Theol. Bull.* 1 (1971), 262–79.
Grosheide, F.W. *Commentary on the First Epistle to the Corinthians*, 2nd ed. (NLCNT). London: Marshall, Morgan and Scott, 1954.
Grossouw, W. *In Christ: A Sketch of the Theology of St. Paul.* London: Geoffrey Chapman, ET 1959.
Grumm, M.H. 'Motivation in Paul's Epistles', *Con. Theol. Mon.* 35 (1964), 210–18.
Grundmann, W. 'ἀγαθός', *TDNT* 1. Grand Rapids, Mich.: Wm B. Eerdmans Pub. Co., ET 1964, pp. 10–18.
*Das Evangelium nach Matthäus* (THNT). Berlin: Evangelische Verlagsanstalt, 1968.
'The Teacher of Righteousness of Qumran and the Question of Justification by Faith in the Theology of the Apostle Paul', in *Paul and Qumran*, ed. J. Murphy-O'Connor. London: Geoffrey Chapman, 1968, pp. 85–114.
Guelich, R. 'The Antitheses of Matthew V.21–48: Traditional and/or Redactional?' *NTS* 22 (1976), 444–57.
Gulin, E.G. 'The Positive Meaning of the Law According to Paul', *Luth. Qtr.* 10 (1958), 115–28.
Gundry, R.H. *The Use of the Old Testament in St. Matthew's Gospel* (SNT 18). Leiden: E.J. Brill, 1967.
Gunther, J.J. *St. Paul's Opponents and their Background: A Study of Apocalyptic and Jewish Sectarian Teachings* (SNT 35). Leiden: E.J. Brill, 1973.
Günther, H. 'Die Gerechtigkeit des Himmelreiches in der Bergpredigt', *Ker.u.Dog.* 17 (1971), 113–26.
Günther, W., and Brown, C. 'Love: φιλέω', *NIDNTT* 2. Grand Rapids, Mich.: Zondervan Pub. House, ET 1976, pp. 547–51.
Günther, W., and Link, H.-G. 'Love: ἀγαπάω', *NIDNTT* 2. Grand Rapids, Mich.: Zondervan Pub. House, ET 1976, pp. 538–47.
Gustafson, J.M. 'The Relation of the Gospels to the Moral Life', in *Jesus and Man's Hope*, vol. II, ed. D.G. Miller and D.Y. Hadidian. Pittsburgh Theological Seminary: Perspective, 1971, pp. 103–17.
Gutbrod, W. 'νόμος, κ.τ.λ. (NT)', *TDNT* 4. Grand Rapids, Mich.: Wm B. Eerdmans Pub. Co., ET 1967, pp. 1059–91.
Guthrie, D. *New Testament Theology*. Leicester: Inter-Varsity Press, 1981.
Guy, H.A. *The Gospel of Matthew*. London: Macmillan and Co., 1971.
Haenchen, E. 'Matthäus 23', in *Gott und Mensch: Gesammelte Aufsätze*. Tübingen: J.C.B. Mohr (Paul Siebeck), 1965, pp. 29–54.
Hahn, F. 'Das Gesetzesverständnis im Römer- und Galaterbrief', *ZNW* 67 (1976), 29–63.
Hamerton-Kelly, R.G. 'Attitudes to the Law in Matthew's Gospel: a Discussion of Matthew 5:18', *Bib. Res.* 17 (1972), 19–32.
Hamilton, N.Q. *The Holy Spirit and Eschatology in Paul* (SJT Occasional Papers 6). Edinburgh–London: Oliver and Boyd, 1957.
Hare, D.R.A. *The Theme of Jewish Persecution of Christians in the Gospel According to St Matthew* (SNTS Monograph Series 6). Cambridge University Press, 1967.

Harrington, D.J. 'Matthean Studies Since Joachim Rohde', *Hey.Jour.* 16 (1975), 375–88.
Harris, M.J. '2 Corinthians 5:1–10: Watershed in Paul's Eschatology?' *Tyn.Bull.* 22 (1971), 32–57.
Hasler, V. *Amen: Redaktionsgeschichtliche Untersuchung zur Einführungsformel der Herrenworte 'Wahrlich ich sage euch'*. Zürich–Stuttgart: Gotthelf-Verlag, 1969.
'Das Herzstück der Bergpredigt: Zum Verständnis der Antithesen in Matth. 5, 21–48', *Theol. Zeit.* 15 (1959), 90–106.
Hauck, F. ὀφείλω, κ.τ.λ.', *TDNT* 5. Grand Rapids, Mich.: Wm B. Eerdmans Pub. Co., ET 1967, pp. 559–66.
Hebert, G. 'The Problem of the Gospel According to Matthew', *SJT* 14 (1961), 403–13.
Held, H.J. 'Matthew as Interpreter of the Miracle Stories', in *Tradition and Interpretation in Matthew* (NTL), ed. G. Bornkamm *et al.* London: SCM Press, ET 1963, pp. 165–299.
Hengel, M. *Judaism and Hellenism. Studies in their Encounter in Palestine during the Early Hellenistic Period*, 2 vols. London: SCM Press, ET 1974.
*Nachfolge und Charisma: Eine exegetisch-religionsgeschichtliche Studie zu Mt 8.21f. und Jesu Ruf in die Nachfolge* (BZNW 34). Berlin: Verlag Alfred Töpelmann, 1968.
Herbert, A.S. 'Biblical Ethics', in *A Companion to the Bible*, 2nd ed., ed. H.H. Rowley. Edinburgh: T. and T. Clark, 1963, pp. 418–35.
Héring, J. *The First Epistle of Saint Paul to the Corinthians.* London: Epworth Press, ET 1962.
*The Second Epistle of Saint Paul to the Corinthians.* London: Epworth Press, ET 1967.
Hiers, R.H. 'Eschatology and Methodology', *JBL* 85 (1966), 170–84.
Hill, D. 'ΔΙΚΑΙΟΙ as a Quasi-technical Term', *NTS* 11 (1964), 296–302.
'False Prophets and Charismatics: Structure and Interpretation in Matthew 7, 15–23', *Biblica* 57 (1976), 327–48.
*Greek Words and Hebrew Meanings: Studies in the Semantics of Soteriological Terms* (SNTS Monograph Series 5). Cambridge University Press, 1967.
'On the Use and Meaning of Hosea VI.6 in Matthew's Gospel', *NTS* 24 (1977), 107–19.
*The Gospel of Matthew* (NCB). London: Oliphants, 1972.
Himmelfarb, M. 'On Reading Matthew', *Commentary* 40 (1965), 56–65.
Hoffmann, E. 'Hope, Expectation: ἐλπίς', *NIDNTT* 2. Grand Rapids, Mich.: Zondervan Pub. House, ET 1976, pp. 238–44.
Hollenbach, B. 'Col ii.23: Which Things lead to the Fulfilment of the Flesh', *NTS* 25 (1979), 254–61.
Hooker, M.D. 'Authority on her Head: An Examination of 1 Cor. XI.10', *NTS* 10 (1964), 410–16.
Hoskyns, E., and Davey, N. *The Riddle of the New Testament*, 3rd ed. London: Faber and Faber, 1947.
Houlden, J.L. *Ethics and the New Testament.* Harmondsworth: Penguin Books, 1973.

*Patterns of Faith: A Study in the relationship between the New Testament and Christian doctrine*. London: SCM Press, 1977.
*Paul's Letters from Prison*, rev. ed. (PNTC). London: SCM Press, 1977.
'The Place of Jesus', in *What about the New Testament? Essays in Honour of Christopher Evans*, ed. M. Hooker and C. Hickling. London: SCM Press, 1975, pp. 103–15.
Howard, G.E. 'Christ the End of the Law: The Meaning of Romans 10.4ff.', *JBL* 88 (1969), 331–7.
Howard, J.K. '"... into Christ": A Study of the Pauline Concept of Baptismal Union', *ExT* 79 (1968), 147–51.
Hubbard, B.J. *The Matthean Redaction of a Primitive Apostolic Commissioning: An Exegesis of Matthew 28:16–20* (SBL Dissertation Series 19). Missoula, Mont.: SBL and Scholars' Press, 1974.
Hübner, H. 'Das ganze und das eine Gesetz: Zum Problemkreis Paulus und die Stoa', *Ker.u.Dog.* 21 (1975), 239–56.
*Das Gesetz bei Paulus: Ein Beitrag zum Werden der paulinischen Theologie*. Göttingen: Vandenhoeck und Ruprecht, 1978.
*Das Gesetz in der synoptischen Tradition. Studien zur These einer progressiven Qumranisierung und Judaisierung innerhalb der synoptischen Tradition*. Witten: Luther Verlag, 1973.
'Identitätsverlust und paulinische Theologie. Anmerkungen zum Galaterbrief,' *Ker.u.Dog.* 24 (1978), 181–93.
Hughes, P.E. *Paul's Second Epistle to the Corinthians* (NLCNT). London: Marshall, Morgan and Scott, 1961.
Hull, J.M. *Hellenistic Magic and the Synoptic Tradition* (SBT 28, 2nd ser.). London: SCM Press, 1974.
Humbert, A. 'La morale de Saint Paul: morale du plan du salut', *Mél.Sci. Rel.* 15 (1958), 5–44.
Hummel, R. *Die Auseinandersetzung zwischen Kirche und Judentum im Matthäusevangelium* (BET 33). München: Chr. Kaiser Verlag, 1963.
Hunter, A.M. *Design for Life: An Exposition of the Sermon on the Mount*, rev. ed. London: SCM Press, 1965.
*Paul and His Predecessors*, rev. ed. London: SCM Press, 1961.
Hurd, J.C., Jr. 'Pauline Chronology and Pauline Theology', in *Christian History and Interpretation: Studies Presented to John Knox*, ed. W.R. Farmer, C.F.D. Moule, and R.R. Niebuhr. Cambridge University Press, 1967, pp. 225–48.
*The Origin of I Corinthians*. London: S.P.C.K., 1965.
Jeremias, J. 'ᾅδης', *TDNT* 1. Grand Rapids, Mich.: Wm B. Eerdmans Pub. Co., ET 1964, pp. 146–9.
'κλείς', *TDNT* 3. Grand Rapids, Mich.: Wm B. Eerdmans Pub. Co., ET 1965, pp. 744–53.
*New Testament Theology. Part One: The Proclamation of Jesus* (NTL). London: SCM Press, ET 1971.
*The Parables of Jesus*, rev. ed. (NTL). London: SCM Press, ET 1963.
*The Prayers of Jesus* (SBT 6, 2nd ser.). London: SCM Press, ET 1967.
*The Sermon on the Mount*. University of London: Athlone Press, 1961.
Jessop, T.E. *Law and Love: A Study of the Christian Ethic*. London: SCM Press, 1940.

Jewett, R. *A Chronology of Paul's Life*. Philadelphia: Fortress Press, 1979.
*Paul's Anthropological Terms: A Study of Their Use in Conflict Settings* (AGJU 10). Leiden: E.J. Brill, 1971.
Joest, W. *Gesetz und Freiheit: Das Problem des Tertius usus legis bei Luther und die neutestamentliche Parainese*. Göttingen: Vandenhoeck und Ruprecht, 1951.
Johansson, N. '1 Cor. XIII and 1 Cor. XIV', *NTS* 10 (1964), 383–92.
Johnson, S.E. 'Paul and the Manual of Discipline', *Harv.Theol.Rev.* 48 (1955), 157–65.
'The Gospel According to St. Matthew', *IB* 7. Nashville–New York: Abingdon–Cokesbury Press, 1951, pp. 231–625.
Johnston, G. 'Love in the New Testament', *IDB* 3. Nashville–New York: Abingdon Press, 1962, pp. 168–78.
Jones, M. *The Epistle to the Philippians* (WC). London: Methuen and Co., 1918.
Juncker, A. *Die Ethik des Apostels Paulus*, 2 vols. Halle: Max Niemeyer, 1904, 1919.
Jüngel, E. 'Erwägungen zur Grundlegung evangelischer Ethik im Anschluss an die Theologie des Paulus', *ZThK* 63 (1966), 379ff.
*Paulus und Jesus: Eine Untersuchung zur Präzisierung der Frage nach dem Ursprung der Christologie* (HUT 2). Tübingen: J.C.B. Mohr (Paul Siebeck), 1962.
Kallas, J. 'Romans XIII.1–7: An Interpolation', *NTS* 11 (1965), 365–74.
Käsemann, E. *An die Römer* (HNT). Tübingen: J.C.B. Mohr (Paul Siebeck), 1973.
'Sentences of Holy Law in the New Testament', in *New Testament Questions of Today* (NTL). London: SCM Press, ET 1969, pp. 66–81.
'The Beginnings of Christian Theology', in *New Testament Questions of Today* (NTL). London: SCM Press, ET 1969, pp. 82–107.
' "The Righteousness of God" in Paul', in *New Testament Questions of Today* (NTL). London: SCM Press, ET 1969, pp. 168–82.
'The Spirit and the Letter', in *Perspectives on Paul* (NTL). London: SCM Press, ET 1971, pp. 138–66.
Keck, L.E. 'Justification of the Ungodly and Ethics', in *Rechtfertigung: Festschrift für Ernst Käsemann zum 70. Geburtstag*, ed. J. Friedrich, W. Pöhlmann, and P. Stuhlmacher. Tübingen: J.C.B. Mohr (Paul Siebeck); Göttingen: Vandenhoeck und Ruprecht, 1976, pp. 199–209.
'The Sermon on the Mount', in *Jesus and Man's Hope*, vol. II, ed. D.G. Miller and D.Y. Hadidian. Pittsburgh Theological Seminary: Perspective, 1971, pp. 311–22.
Kee, H.C. *Community of the New Age: Studies in Mark's Gospel* (NTL). London: SCM Press, 1977.
Kempthorne, R. 'Incest and the Body of Christ: A Study of I Corinthians VI.12–20', *NTS* 14 (1968), 568–74.
Kertelge, K. *'Rechtfertigung' bei Paulus: Studien zur Struktur und zum Bedeutungsgehalt des paulinischen Rechtfertigungsbegriffs* (NA n.s. 3). Münster: Verlag Aschendorff, 1967.
Kilpatrick, G.D. *The Origins of the Gospel According to St. Matthew.*

Oxford: Clarendon Press, 1946.
Kingsbury, J.D. 'The Verb *Akolouthein* ("To Follow") as an Index of Matthew's View of his Community', *JBL* 97 (1978), 56–73.
Kinniburgh, E. 'Hard Sayings – III (Matthew 23.33)', *Theol.* 66 (1963), 414–16.
Kittel, G. 'εἰκών (NT)', *TDNT* 2. Grand Rapids, Mich.: Wm B. Eerdmans Pub. Co., ET 1964, pp. 395–7.
Klausner, J. *From Jesus to Paul.* London: George Allen and Unwin, ET 1944.
Klijn, A.F.J. 'The Study of Jewish Christianity', *NTS* 20 (1974), 419–31.
Klostermann, E. *Das Matthäusevangelium*, 4th ed. Tübingen: J.C.B. Mohr (Paul Siebeck), 1971.
Knox, J. *Chapters in a Life of Paul.* London: Adam and Charles Black, 1954.
*Philemon among the Letters of Paul.* London: Collins, 1960.
'Romans', *IB* 9. Nashville–New York: Abingdon–Cokesbury Press, 1954, pp. 355–668.
*The Ethic of Jesus in the Teaching of the Church.* London: Epworth Press, 1961.
Knox, W.L. *St Paul and the Church of Jerusalem.* Cambridge University Press, 1925.
*St Paul and the Church of the Gentiles.* Cambridge University Press, 1939.
Kodell, J. 'The Celibacy Logion in Matthew 19:12', *Bib.Theol.Bull.* 8 (1978), 19–23.
Kraft, R.A. 'In Search of "Jewish Christianity" and its "Theology"; Problems of Definition and Methodology', *Rech.Sci.Rel.* 60 (1972), 81–92.
Kramer, W. *Christ, Lord, Son of God* (SBT 50). London: SCM Press, ET 1966.
Kretzer, A. *Die Herrschaft der Himmel und die Söhne des Reiches: Eine redaktionsgeschichtliche Untersuchung zum Basileiabegriff und Basileiaverständnis im Matthäusevangelium* (SBM 10). Echter: KBW Verlag, 1971.
Kümmel, W.G. 'Futuristic and Realized Eschatology in the Earliest Stages of Christianity', *JR* 43 (1963), 303–14.
*Introduction to the New Testament*, rev. ed. (17th). Nashville–New York: Abingdon Press, ET 1975.
'Jesus und der jüdische Traditionsgedanke', *ZNW* 33 (1934), 105–30.
*The Theology of the New Testament.* London: SCM Press, ET 1974.
Kuss, O. *Der Römerbrief*, 2 vols. 2nd ed. Regensburg: Verlag Friedrich Pustet, 1963.
Ladd, G.E. *A Theology of the New Testament.* Guildford–London: Lutterworth Press, 1975.
*Jesus and the Kingdom: The Eschatology of Biblical Realism.* London: S.P.C.K., 1966.
Lagrange, M.-J. *Évangile selon saint Matthieu*, 7th ed. (EB). Paris: Librairie Lecoffre, 1948.
Lampe, G.W.H. *God as Spirit.* Oxford: Clarendon Press, 1977.

Larsson, E. *Christus als Vorbild: Eine Untersuchung zu den paulinischen Tauf- und Eikontexten* (ASNU 23). Uppsala–Lund: C.W.K. Gleerup, 1962.
LaVerdiere, E.A., and Thompson, W.G. 'New Testament Communities in Transition: A Study of Matthew and Luke', *Theol. Stud.* 37 (1976), 567–97.
Leaney, A.R.C. 'The Experience of God in Qumran and in Paul', *BJRL* 51 (1968), 431–52.
Leenhardt, F.J. *The Epistle to the Romans*. London: Lutterworth Press, ET 1961.
Lehmann-Habeck, M. 'Das Gesetz als der gute Gotteswille für meinen Nächsten. Zur bleibenden Bedeutung des Gesetzes nach dem Matthäus-Evangelium', in *Treue zur Thora: Beiträge zur Mitte des christlichjüdischen Gesprächs* (VIKJ 3), ed. P. von der Osten-Sacken. Berlin: Kirchlichen Hochschule, 1977, pp. 47–53.
Leivestad, R. ' "The Meekness and Gentleness of Christ" II Cor. X.1', *NTS* 12 (1966), 156–64.
Léon-Dufour, X. 'Redaktionsgeschichte of Matthew and Literary Criticism', in *Jesus and Man's Hope*, vol. I, ed. D.G. Miller and D.Y. Hadidian. Pittsburgh Theological Seminary: Perspective, 1970, pp. 9–35.
Levine, E. 'The Sabbath Controversy According to Matthew', *NTS* 22 (1976), 480–3.
Lietzmann, H. *An die Korinther*, 2 vols., 3rd ed. (HNT). Tübingen: J.C.B. Mohr (Paul Siebeck), 1931.
Lightfoot, J.B. *St Paul's Epistle to the Galatians*. London: Macmillan and Co., 1865.
*St Paul's Epistle to the Philippians*. London: Macmillan and Co., 1868.
Lillie, W. *Studies in New Testament Ethics*. Edinburgh–London: Oliver and Boyd, 1961.
Lindars, B. 'Imitation of God and Imitation of Christ', *Theol.* 76 (1973), 394–402.
'Jesus and the Pharisees', in *Donum Gentilicium: New Testament Studies in Honour of David Daube*, ed. E. Bammel, C.K. Barrett, and W.D. Davies. Oxford: Clarendon Press, 1978, pp. 51–63.
Ljungmann, H.L. *Das Gesetz erfüllen*. Lund: Univ. Årsskr., 1957.
Lohmeyer, E. *Das Evangelium des Matthäus* (KEKNT). Göttingen: Vandenhoeck und Ruprecht, 1956.
' "Mir ist gegeben alle Gewalt!" Eine Exegese von Mt. 28, 16–20', in *In Memoriam Ernst Lohmeyer*, ed. W. Schmauch. Stuttgart: Evangelisches Verlagswerk, 1951, pp. 22–49.
Lohse, E. *Colossians and Philemon* (Hermeneia). Philadelphia: Fortress Press, ET 1971.
' "Ich aber sage euch" ', in *Der Ruf Jesu und die Antwort der Gemeinde: Exegetische Untersuchungen Joachim Jeremias zum 70. Geburtstag gewidmet von seinen Schülern*, ed. E. Lohse *et al.* Göttingen: Vandenhoeck und Ruprecht, 1970, pp. 189–203.
' "Wir richten das Gesetz auf!" Glaube und Thora im Römerbrief', in *Treue zur Thora. Beiträge zur Mitte des christlichjüdischen Gesprächs* (VIKJ 3), ed. P. von der Osten-Sacken. Berlin: Kirchlichen

Hochschule, 1977, pp. 65–71.
Long, E.L., Jr. *A Survey of Christian Ethics*. Oxford University Press, 1967.
Loosley, E.G. *The Challenge from the Mount*. London: Epworth Press, 1964.
Losie, L.A. 'A Note on the Interpretation of Phil 2.5', *ExT* 90 (1978), 52–4.
Luz, U. 'Die Erfüllung des Gesetzes bei Matthäus (Mt 5, 17–20)', *ZThK* 75 (1978), 398–435.
'Die Jünger im Matthäusevangelium', *ZNW* 62 (1971), 141–71.
McArthur, H.K. *Understanding the Sermon on the Mount*. London: Epworth Press, 1961.
McComiskey, T. 'Judgment: βῆμα', *NIDNTT* 2. Grand Rapids, Mich.: Zondervan Pub. House, ET 1976, pp. 369f.
McConnell, R.S. *Law and Prophecy in Matthew's Gospel: The Authority and Use of the Old Testament in the Gospel of St. Matthew* (TD 2). Basel: Friedrich Reinhardt Kommissionsverlag, 1969.
McDermott, T. 'The Four Types of Gospel', *New Blackfriars* 50 (1969), 700–8.
McEleney, N.J. 'Conversion, Circumcision and the Law', *NTS* 20 (1974), 319–41.
Macgregor, G.H.C. 'The Concept of the Wrath of God in the New Testament', *NTS* 7 (1961), 101–9.
McKenzie, J.L. 'Natural Law in the New Testament', *Bib.Res.* 9 (1964), 3–13.
'The Gospel According to Matthew', *The Jerome Biblical Commentary*, vol. II. London: Geoffrey Chapman, 1968, pp. 62–114.
McNeile, A.H. *The Gospel According to St. Matthew*. London: Macmillan and Co., 1915.
Maher, M. '"Take my Yoke upon You" (Matt. XI.29)', *NTS* 22 (1975), 97–103.
Manns, F. 'La halakah dans l'évangile de Matthieu', *Antonianum* 53 (1978), 3–22.
Manson, T.W. *Ethics and the Gospel*. London: SCM Press, 1960.
'Romans', *Peake's Commentary on the Bible*. London: Thomas Nelson and Sons, 1962, pp. 940–53.
'The Life of Jesus: A Survey of the Available Material. (4) The Gospel According to St. Matthew', *BJRL* 29 (1946), 392–428.
*The Sayings of Jesus*. London: SCM Press, 1949.
*The Teaching of Jesus*. Cambridge University Press, 1935.
Marguerat, D. 'Jésus et la Loi, selon Matthieu', *Foi et Vie* 78 (1979), 53–76.
Marshall, L.H. *The Challenge of New Testament Ethics*. London: Macmillan and Co., 1946.
Martin, B.L. 'Some reflections on the unity of the New Testament', *SR* 8 (1979), 143–52.
Martin, J.P. 'The Church in Matthew', *Interp.* 29 (1975), 41–56.
Martin, R.P. 'A Suggested Exegesis of 1 Corinthians 13:13', *ExT* 82 (1971), 119–20.

*Colossians and Philemon* (NCB). London: Oliphants, 1974.
*New Testament Foundations: A Guide for Christian Students*, 2 vols. Grand Rapids, Mich.: Wm B. Eerdmans Pub. Co., 1975, 1978.
*Philippians* (NCB). London: Oliphants, 1976.
'St. Matthew's Gospel in Recent Study', *ExT* 80 (1970), 132–6.
Marxsen, W. 'Erwägungen zur neutestamentlichen Begründung der Taufe', in *Apophoreta: Festschrift für Ernst Haenchen* (BZNW 30). Berlin: Verlag Alfred Töpelmann, 1964, 169–77.
*Introduction to the New Testament: An Approach to its Problems.* Oxford: Basil Blackwell, ET 1968.
Masson, C. *L'épître de saint Paul aux Colossiens* (CNT 10). Neuchâtel–Paris: Delachaux et Niestlé, 1950.
*Les deux épîtres de saint Paul aux Thessaloniciens* (CNT 11*a*). Neuchâtel–Paris: Delachaux et Niestlé, 1957.
Mattern, L. *Das Verständnis des Gerichtes bei Paulus* (ATANT 47). Zürich: Zwingli Verlag, 1966.
Meier, J.P. *Law and History in Matthew's Gospel: A Redactional Study of Mt. 5:17–48* (Ana.Bib. 71). Rome: Biblical Institute Press, 1976.
Menzies, A. *The Second Epistle of the Apostle Paul to the Corinthians.* London: Macmillan and Co., 1912.
Merk, O. *Handeln aus Glauben: Die Motivierungen der paulinischen Ethik* (MarTS 5). Marburg: N.G. Elwert Verlag, 1968.
Merkel, H. 'Jesus und die Pharisäer', *NTS* 14 (1967–8), 194–208.
Metzger, B.M. *A Textual Commentary on the Greek New Testament.* London–New York: United Bible Societies, 1971.
*The New Testament: its background, growth, and content.* Nashville: Abingdon Press, 1965.
Michael, J.H. *The Epistle of Paul to the Philippians* (MNTC). London: Hodder and Stoughton, 1928.
Michaelis, W. '*μιμέομαι, κ.τ.λ.*', *TDNT* 4. Grand Rapids, Mich.: Wm B. Eerdmans Pub. Co., ET 1967, pp. 659–74.
Michel, O. 'Der Abschluss des Matthäusevangeliums', *Ev.Theol.* 10 (1950), 16–26.
*Der Brief an die Römer* (KEKNT). Göttingen: Vandenhoeck und Ruprecht, 1955.
Micklem, P.A. *St Matthew* (WC). London: Methuen and Co., 1917.
Milligan, G. *St Paul's Epistles to the Thessalonians.* London: Macmillan and Co., 1908.
Minear, P.S. *Commands of Christ.* Edinburgh: Saint Andrew Press, 1972.
'False Prophecy and Hypocrisy in the Gospel of Matthew', in *Neues Testament und Kirche: Für Rudolf Schnackenburg*, ed. J. Gnilka. Freiburg: Herder, 1974.
'The Disciples and the Crowds in the Gospel of Matthew', *Ang.Theol. Rev.* supp. ser. 3 (1974), pp. 28–44.
*The Obedience of Faith: The Purposes of Paul in the Epistle to the Romans* (SBT 19, 2nd ser.). London: SCM Press, 1971.
*Mishnah.* trans. H. Danby. Oxford University Press, ET 1933.
Mitton, C.L. 'Matthew's Disservice to Jesus', *EpR* 6 (1979), 47–54.

Moffatt, J. *Love in the New Testament*. London: Hodder and Stoughton, 1929.
*The First Epistle of Paul to the Corinthians* (MNTC). London: Hodder and Stoughton, 1938.
Moloney, F.J. 'Matthew 19, 3–12 and Celibacy: A Redactional and Form Critical Study', *JSNT* 2 (1979), 42–60.
Montefiore, C.G. *Rabbinic Literature and Gospel Teachings*. London: Macmillan and Co., 1930.
*The Synoptic Gospels*, vol. II, 2nd ed. London: Macmillan and Co., 1927.
Montefiore, H. 'Thou Shalt Love the Neighbour as Thyself', *Nov.Test.* 5 (1962), 157–70.
Moore, A.L. *1 and 2 Thessalonians* (NCB). London: Thomas Nelson and Sons, 1969.
*The Parousia in the New Testament* (SNT 13). Leiden: E.J. Brill, 1966.
Moore, G.F. *Judaism in the First Centuries of the Christian Era*, 3 vols. Cambridge, Mass.: Harvard University Press, 1927.
Morgenthaler, R. *Statistik des neutestamentlichen Wortschatzes*. Zürich: Gotthelf-Verlag, 1958.
Morris, L. *The First and Second Epistles to the Thessalonians* (NLCNT). London: Marshall, Morgan and Scott, 1959.
*The First Epistle of Paul to the Corinthians* (TNTC). London: Tyndale Press, 1958.
Morton, A.Q. 'The Authorship of the Pauline Corpus', in *The New Testament in Historical and Contemporary Perspective: Essays in Memory of G.H.C. Macgregor*, ed. H. Anderson and W. Barclay. Oxford: Basil Blackwell, 1965, pp. 209ff.
Moule, C.F.D. 'Anselm Schulz: Unter dem Anspruch Gottes: das neutestamentliche Zeugnis von der Nachahmung', *JBL* 87 (1968), 364.
'"... As we forgive ...": a Note on the Distinction between Deserts and Capacity in the Understanding of Forgiveness', in *Donum Gentilicium: New Testament Studies in Honour of David Daube*, ed. E. Bammel, C.K. Barrett, and W.D. Davies. Oxford: Clarendon Press, 1978, pp. 68–77.
'Colossians and Philemon', *Peake's Commentary on the Bible*. London: Thomas Nelson and Sons, 1962, pp. 990–5.
'Commentaries on the Gospel According to St Matthew', *Theol.* 66 (1963), 140–4.
'Further Reflexions on Philippians 2:5–11', in *Apostolic History and the Gospel: Biblical and Historical Essays*, ed. W.W. Gasque and R.P. Martin. Exeter: Paternoster Press, 1970, pp. 264–76.
'Obligation in the Ethic of Paul', in *Christian History and Interpretation: Studies Presented to John Knox*, ed. W.R. Farmer, C.F.D. Moule, and R.R. Niebuhr. Cambridge University Press, 1967, pp. 389–406.
'St. Matthew's Gospel: Some Neglected Features', in *Studia Evangelica* 2 (TU 87). Berlin: Akademie-Verlag, 1964, pp. 91–9.
*The Epistles of Paul the Apostle to the Colossians and to Philemon* (CGTC). Cambridge University Press, 1957.

'The Influence of Circumstances on the Use of Eschatological Terms', *JTS* 15 (1964), 1–15.
'The Intention of the Evangelists', in *New Testament Essays: Studies in Memory of Thomas Walter Manson*, ed. A.J.B. Higgins. Manchester University Press, 1959, pp. 165–79.
*The Origin of Christology*. Cambridge University Press, 1977.
*The Phenomenon of the New Testament* (SBT 1, 2nd ser.). London: SCM Press, 1967.
Moulton, J.H. *A Grammar of New Testament Greek*, vol. III: Syntax, by N. Turner. Edinburgh: T. and T. Clark, 1963.
Mowry, L. 'Beatitudes', *IDB* 1. Nashville–New York: Abingdon Press, 1962, pp. 369–71.
Müller, J.J. *The Epistles of Paul to the Philippians and to Philemon* (NLCNT). London: Marshall, Morgan and Scott, 1955.
Munck, J. *Paul and the Salvation of Mankind*. Richmond, Va.: John Knox Press, ET 1959.
Murphy-O'Connor, J. *L'existence chrétienne selon saint Paul* (Lectio Divina 80). Paris: Cerf, 1974.
Murray, J. *Principles of Conduct: Aspects of Biblical Ethics*. London: Tyndale Press, 1957.
*The Epistle to the Romans*, 2 vols. (NLCNT). London: Marshall, Morgan and Scott, 1960, 1965.
Nauck, W. 'Das *οὖν*–paräneticum', *ZNW* 49 (1958), 134–5.
Neil, W. 'I & II Thessalonians', *Peake's Commentary on the Bible*. London: Thomas Nelson and Sons, 1962, pp. 996–1000.
*The Letter of Paul to the Galatians* (CBC). Cambridge University Press, 1967.
Neill, S. *The Interpretation of the New Testament 1861–1961*. Oxford University Press, 1964.
Nepper-Christensen, P. *Das Matthäusevangelium: Ein Judenchristliches Evangelium?* Aarhus: Universitetsforlaget, 1958.
Neugebauer, F. 'Das Paulinische "In Christo"', *NTS* 4 (1958), 124–38.
Neusner, J. 'Comparing Judaisms: E.P. Sanders, Paul and Palestinian Judaism: A Comparison of Patterns of Religion', *Hist. of Religs.* 18 (1978), 177–91.
Nieder, L. *Die Motive der religiös-sittlichen Paränese in den paulinischen Gemeindebriefen: Ein Beitrag zur paulinischen Ethik* (MünTS 12). München: Karl Zink Verlag, 1956.
Nineham, D.E. *Explorations in Theology 1*. London: SCM Press, 1977.
'The Genealogy in St. Matthew's Gospel and its Significance for the Study of the Gospels', *BJRL* 58 (1976), 421–44.
*The Gospel of St Mark*, rev. ed. (PNTC). London: SCM Press, 1977.
*The Use and Abuse of the Bible*. London: Macmillan Press, 1976.
Nygren, A. *Agape and Eros*, rev. ed. London: S.P.C.K., 1953.
*Commentary on Romans*. London: SCM Press, ET 1952.
O'Brien, P.T. *Introductory Thanksgivings in the Letters of Paul* (SNT 49). Leiden: E.J. Brill, 1977.
Ogg, G. *The Chronology of the Life of Paul*. London: Epworth Press, 1968.

O'Neill, J.C. *Paul's Letter to the Romans*, rev. ed. (PNTC). London: SCM Press, 1977.

Orr, W.F., and Walther, J.A. *1 Corinthians* (AB). Garden City, N.Y.: Doubleday and Co., 1976.

Osborn, E. *Ethical Patterns in Early Christian Thought*. Cambridge University Press, 1976.

Perrin, N. 'The Evangelist as Author: Reflections on Method in the Study and Interpretation of the Synoptic Gospels and Acts', *Bib.Res.* 17 (1972), 5–18.

*The Kingdom of God in the Teaching of Jesus* (NTL). London: SCM Press, 1963.

*The New Testament: An Introduction*. New York: Harcourt, Brace, Jovanovich, 1974.

Pesch, W. *Der Lohngedanke in der Lehre Jesu, verglichen mit der religiösen Lohnlehre des Spätjudentums* (MünTS 7). München: Karl Zink Verlag, 1955.

*Matthäus der Seelsorger* (SB 2). Stuttgart: Verlag Katholisches Bibelwerk, 1966.

Philipose, J. 'Romans 5.20: Did God have a bad motive in giving the Law?' *Bib.Trans.* 28 (1977), 445.

Pierce, C.A. *Conscience in the New Testament* (SBT 15). London: SCM Press, 1955.

Piper, J. *'Love your enemies': Jesus' love command in the synoptic gospels and in the early Christian paraenesis* (SNTS Monograph Series 38). Cambridge University Press, 1979.

Plummer, A. *A Commentary on St. Paul's Epistle to the Philippians*. London: Robert Scott, 1919.

*A Commentary on St. Paul's First Epistle to the Thessalonians*. London: Robert Scott, 1918.

*A Commentary on St. Paul's Second Epistle to the Thessalonians*. London: Robert Scott, 1918.

*A Critical and Exegetical Commentary on the Second Epistle of St Paul to the Corinthians* (ICC). Edinburgh: T. and T. Clark, 1915.

*An Exegetical Commentary on the Gospel According to S. Matthew*. London: Elliot Stock, 1909.

Pokorný, P. 'The Core of the Sermon on the Mount', in *Studia Evangelica* 6 (TU 112), ed. E.A. Livingstone. Berlin: Akademie-Verlag, 1973, pp. 429–33.

Preisker, H. *Das Ethos des Urchristentums*, 3rd ed. Gütersloh: C. Bertelsmann, 1968.

Procksch, O. 'ἁγιασμός', *TDNT* 1. Grand Rapids, Mich.: Wm B. Eerdmans Pub. Co., ET 1964, p. 113.

Przybylski, B. *Righteousness in Matthew and his world of thought* (SNTS Monograph Series 41). Cambridge University Press, 1980.

Radford, L.B. *The Epistle to the Colossians and the Epistle to Philemon* (WC). London: Methuen and Co., 1931.

Ramsey, P. *Basic Christian Ethics*. London: SCM Press, 1953.

Reese, J.M. 'How Matthew Portrays the Communication of Christ's Authority', *Bib.Theol.Bull.* 7 (1977), 139–44.

Reicke, B. 'The Law and This World According to Paul: Some thoughts concerning Gal. 4.1–11', *JBL* 70 (1951), 259–76.
Rengstorf, K.H. 'διδάσκω, διδάσκαλος, κ.τ.λ.', *TDNT* 2. Grand Rapids, Mich.: Wm B. Eerdmans Pub. Co., ET 1964, pp. 135–65.
'μανθάνω ... μαθητής, κ.τ.λ.', *TDNT* 4. Grand Rapids, Mich.: Wm B. Eerdmans Pub. Co., ET 1967, pp. 390–461.
Reumann, J. *Righteousness in the New Testament*. Philadelphia: Fortress Press, 1982.
Rey, B. 'L'homme nouveau d'après S. Paul', *Rev.Sci.Phil.Théol.* 48 (1964), 603–29.
Richardson, A. *An Introduction to the Theology of the New Testament*. London: SCM Press, 1958.
Ridderbos, H.N. *Matthew's Witness to Jesus Christ: The King and the Kingdom* (WCB 23). London: United Society for Christian Literature–Lutterworth Press, 1958.
*Paul: An Outline of His Theology*. London: S.P.C.K., ET 1975.
*The Epistle of Paul to the Churches of Galatia*, 2nd ed. (NLCNT). London: Marshall, Morgan and Scott, ET 1954.
Riegel, S.K. 'Jewish Christianity: Definitions & Terminology', *NTS* 24 (1978), 410–15.
Rigaux, B. *Témoignage de l'évangile de Matthieu* (Pour une histoire de Jésus, vol. II). Louvain: Desclée de Brouwer, 1967.
Robertson, A., and Plummer, A. *A Critical and Exegetical Commentary on the First Epistle of St Paul to the Corinthians* (ICC). Edinburgh: T. and T. Clark, 1911.
Robinson, J.A.T. *Jesus and His Coming: The Emergence of a Doctrine*. London: SCM Press, 1957.
*Redating the New Testament*. London: SCM Press, 1976.
*The Body: A Study in Pauline Theology* (SBT 5). London: SCM Press, 1952.
Robinson, J.M., and Koester, H. *Trajectories through Early Christianity*. Philadelphia: Fortress Press, 1971.
Robinson, T.H. *The Gospel of Matthew* (MNTC). London: Hodder and Stoughton, 1928.
Roetzel, C. *Judgement in the Community: A Study of the Relationship between Eschatology and Ecclesiology in Paul*. Leiden: E.J. Brill, 1972.
Rohde, J. *Rediscovering the Teaching of the Evangelists* (NTL). London: SCM Press, ET 1968.
Romaniuk, K. 'Les motifs parénétiques dans les écrits pauliniens', *Nov. Test.* 10 (1968), 191–207.
Ropes, J.H. *The Synoptic Gospels*. Cambridge, Mass.: Harvard University Press, 1934.
Ruef, J.S. *Paul's First Letter to Corinth*, rev. ed. (PNTC). London: SCM Press, 1977.
Sand, A. *Das Gesetz und die Propheten: Untersuchungen zur Theologie des Evangeliums nach Matthäus* (BU 11). Regensburg: Verlag Friedrich Pustet, 1974.
*Der Begriff 'Fleisch' in den paulinischen Hauptbriefen* (BU 2).

Regensburg: Verlag Friedrich Pustet, 1967.
'Die Polemik gegen "Gesetzlosigkeit" im Evangelium nach Matthäus und bei Paulus: Ein Beitrag zur neutestamentlichen Überlieferungsgeschichte', *Bib.Zeit.* n.s. 14 (1970), 112–25.
Sanday, W., and Headlam, A.C. *A Critical and Exegetical Commentary on the Epistle to the Romans*, 5th ed. (ICC). Edinburgh: T. and T. Clark, 1902.
Sanders, E.P. 'On the Question of Fulfilling the Law in Paul and Rabbinic Judaism', in *Donum Gentilicium: New Testament Studies in Honour of David Daube*, ed. E. Bammel, C.K. Barrett, and W.D. Davies. Oxford: Clarendon Press, 1978, pp. 103–26.
'Patterns of Religion in Paul and Rabbinic Judaism: A Holistic Method of Comparison', *Harv.Theol.Rev.* 66 (1973), 455–78.
*Paul and Palestinian Judaism: A Comparison of Patterns of Religion.* London: SCM Press, 1977.
'Paul's Attitude Toward the Jewish People', *Un.Sem.Qtr.Rev.* 33 (1978), 175–87.
Sanders, J.A. 'Torah and Christ', *Interp.* 29 (1975), 372–90.
'Torah and Paul', in *God's Christ and His People: Studies in Honour of Nils Alstrup Dahl*, ed. J. Jervell and W.A. Meeks. Oslo: Universitetsforlaget, 1977.
Sanders, J.N. 'Galatians', *Peake's Commentary on the Bible.* London: Thomas Nelson and Sons, 1962, pp. 973–9.
Sanders, J.T. *Ethics in the New Testament: Change and Development.* London: SCM Press, 1975.
'First Corinthians 13: Its Interpretation Since the First World War', *Interp.* 20 (1966), 159–87.
Sandmel, S. *A Jewish Understanding of the New Testament*, augmented ed. London: S.P.C.K., 1974.
*The First Christian Century in Judaism and Christianity: Certainties and Uncertainties.* Oxford University Press, 1969.
Schelkle, K.H. *Theologie des Neuen Testaments*, vol. III: Ethos. Düsseldorf: Patmos-Verlag, 1970.
Schlatter, D.A. von. *Der Evangelist Matthäus: Seine Sprache, sein Ziel, seine Selbständigkeit.* Stuttgart: Calwer Vereinsbuchhandlung, 1929.
Schlier, H. *Der Brief an die Galater* (KEKNT). Göttingen: Vandenhoeck und Ruprecht, 1949.
*Der Römerbrief* (HTKNT). Freiburg: Herder, 1977.
*Grundzüge einer paulinischen Theologie.* Freiburg: Herder, 1978.
*Principalities and Powers in the New Testament.* London: Thomas Nelson and Sons, ET 1961.
Schmahl, G. 'Die Antithesen der Bergpredigt: Inhalt und Eigenart ihrer Forderungen', *Tri.Theol.Zeit.* 83 (1974), 284–97.
Schnackenburg, R. *The Moral Teaching of the New Testament.* London: Burns and Oates, ET 1965.
Schneeberger, V.D. 'Charisma und Agape', *Comm.Viat.* 19 (1976), 151–6.
Schneider, E.E. 'Finis legis Christus: Röm. 10, 4', *Theol.Zeit.* 20 (1964), 410–22.
Schneider, W. 'Judgment ...: κρίμα', *NIDNTT* 2. Grand Rapids, Mich.:

Zondervan Pub. House, ET 1976, pp. 362–7.

Schniewind, J. *Das Evangelium nach Matthäus* (NTD), 12th ed. Göttingen: Vandenhoeck und Ruprecht, 1968.

Schoeps, H.J. *Paul: The Theology of the Apostle in the Light of Jewish Religious History*. London: Lutterworth Press, ET 1961.

'Von der Imitatio Dei zur Nachfolge Christi', in *Aus Frühchristlicher Zeit: Religionsgeschichtliche Untersuchungen*. Tübingen: J.C.B. Mohr (Paul Siebeck), 1950, pp. 286–301.

Schrage, W. *Die konkreten Einzelgebote in der paulinischen Paränese*. Gerd Mohn: Gütersloher Verlagshaus, 1961.

'Zur Frontstellung der paulinischen Ehebewertung in 1 Kor. 7.1–7', *ZNW* 67 (1976), 214–34.

Schrenk, G. 'δίκαιος, δικαιοσύνη, δικαίωμα', *TDNT* 2. Grand Rapids, Mich.: Wm B. Eerdmans Pub. Co., ET 1964, pp. 182–210, 221–3.

Schubert, P. 'Paul and the New Testament Ethic in the Thought of John Knox', in *Christian History and Interpretation: Studies Presented to John Knox*, ed. W.R. Farmer, C.F.D. Moule, and R.R. Niebuhr. Cambridge University Press, 1967, pp. 363–88.

Schulz, A. *Nachfolge und Nachahmen: Studien über das Verhältnis der neutestamentlichen Jüngerschaft zur urchristlichen Vorbildethik* (SANT 6). München: Kösel-Verlag, 1962.

*Unter dem Anspruch Gottes: das neutestamentliche Zeugnis von der Nachahmung*. Munich: Kösel-Verlag, 1967.

Schweizer, E. 'Christianity of the Circumcised and Judaism of the Uncircumcised – The Background of Matthew and Colossians', in *Jews, Greeks and Christians* (SJLA 21), ed. R. Hamerton-Kelly and R. Scroggs. Leiden: E.J. Brill, 1976, pp. 245–60.

'Christologie und Ethik im Kolosserbrief', in *Apophoreta: Festschrift für Ernst Haenchen* (BZNW 30). Berlin: Verlag Alfred Töpelmann, 1964, pp. 156–68.

' "Der Jude im Verborgene ..., dessen Lob nicht von Menschen, sondern von Gott kommt." Zu Röm 2, 28f und Mt 6, 1–18', in *Neues Testament und Kirche: Für Rudolf Schnackenburg*, ed. J. Gnilka. Freiburg: Herder, 1974.

'Dying and Rising with Christ', *NTS* 14 (1967), 1–14.

'Gottesgerechtigkeit und Lasterkataloge bei Paulus (inkl. Kol und Eph)', in *Rechtfertigung: Festschrift für Ernst Käsemann zum 70. Geburtstag*, ed. J. Friedrich, W. Pöhlmann, and P. Stuhlmacher. Tübingen: J.C.B. Mohr (Paul Siebeck) – Göttingen: Vandenhoeck und Ruprecht, 1976, pp. 461–77.

*Lordship and Discipleship* (SBT 28). London: SCM Press, ET 1960.

'Matth. 5, 17–20: Anmerkungen zum Gesetzesverständnis des Matthäus', in *Neotestamentica*. Zürich–Stuttgart: Zwingli Verlag, 1963, pp. 399–406.

*Matthäus und seine Gemeinde* (SB 71). Stuttgart: KBW Verlag, 1974.

'Observance of the Law and Charismatic Activity in Matthew', *NTS* 16 (1970), 213–30.

'πνεῦμα, πνευματικός, κ.τ.λ. (NT)', *TDNT* 6. Grand Rapids, Mich.: Wm B. Eerdmans Pub. Co., ET 1968, pp. 396–455.

*The Good News According to Matthew*. London: S.P.C.K., 1976.
Scott, C.A.A. *Christianity According to St Paul*. Cambridge University Press, 1927.
*New Testament Ethics: An Introduction*, 2nd ed. Cambridge University Press, 1934.
Scott, E.F. *Paul's Epistle to the Romans*. London: SCM Press, 1947.
*The Epistles of Paul to the Colossians, to Philemon and to the Ephesians* (MNTC). London: Hodder and Stoughton, 1930.
'The Ethics of the Gospels', in *The Evolution of Ethics*, ed. E.H. Sneath. New Haven: Yale University Press, 1927, pp. 267–91.
*The Spirit in the New Testament*. London: Hodder and Stoughton, 1923.
Scroggs, R. 'Paul as Rhetorician: Two Homilies in Romans 1–11', in *Jews, Greeks and Christians* (SJLA 21), ed. R. Hamerton-Kelly and R. Scroggs. Leiden: E.J. Brill, 1976, pp. 271–98.
Selwyn, E.G. 'The Authority of Christ in the New Testament', *NTS* 3 (1957), 83–92.
Shepherd, M.H. 'The Epistle of James and the Gospel of Matthew', *JBL* 75 (1956), 40–51.
Sheridan, M. 'Disciples and Discipleship in Matthew and Luke', *Bib.Theol. Bull.* 3 (1973), 235–55.
Smalley, S.S. 'The Delay of the Parousia', *JBL* 83 (1964), 41–54.
Smith, B.T.D. *The Gospel According to S. Matthew* (CGT). Cambridge University Press, 1950.
Soden, H. von. 'Die Ethik des Paulus', *ZThK* 2 (1892), 109–45.
Sommerlath, E. *Der Ursprung des neuen Lebens nach Paulus*, 2nd ed. 1927.
Sorg, T. 'Heart: καρδία', *NIDNTT* 2. Grand Rapids, Mich.: Zondervan Pub. House, ET 1976, pp. 180–4.
Spicq, C. *Agape in the New Testament*, vols. I and II. London: B. Herder Book Co., ET 1963, 1965.
' "Joseph, son mari, étant juste ..." (Mt. I, 19)', *Rev.Bib.* 71 (1964), 206–14.
*Théologie Moral du Nouveau Testament*, 2 vols. (EB). Paris: Librairie Lecoffre, 1965.
Spivey, R.A., and Smith, D.M., Jr. *Anatomy of the New Testament: A Guide to its Structure and Meaning*, 2nd ed. New York: Macmillan Pub. Co., 1974.
Stacey, W.D. *The Pauline View of Man in Relation to its Judaic and Hellenistic Background*. London: Macmillan and Co., 1956.
Stählin, G. 'ὀργή (NT)', *TDNT* 5. Grand Rapids, Mich.: Wm B. Eerdmans Pub. Co., ET 1967, pp. 419–47.
'φιλέω, κ.τ.λ.', *TDNT* 9. Grand Rapids, Mich.: Wm B. Eerdmans Pub. Co., ET 1974, pp. 113–72.
Stamm, R.T. 'The Epistle to the Galatians', *IB* 10. Nashville–New York: Abingdon–Cokesbury Press, 1962, pp. 429–593.
Stanley, D.M. ' "Become Imitators of Me": The Pauline Conception of Apostolic Tradition', *Biblica* 40 (1959), 859–77.
Staub, K. 'Die Anwendung des theologischen Kriteriums Gesetz/Evangelium auf gesellschaftliche Strukturprobleme', *Z.Ev.Eth.* 14 (1970), 270–82.

Stauffer, E. 'ἀγαπάω, ἀγάπη, ἀγαπητός', *TDNT* 1. Grand Rapids, Mich.: Wm B. Eerdmans Pub. Co., ET 1964, pp. 35–55.
Steensgaard, P. 'Erwägungen zum Problem Evangelium und Paränese bei Paulus', *Ann.Swed.Theol.Inst.* 10 (1975–6), 110–28.
Stendahl, K. 'Matthew', *Peake's Commentary on the Bible*. London: Thomas Nelson and Sons, 1962, pp. 769–98.
*Paul among Jews and Gentiles, and other Essays*. London: SCM Press, 1977.
*The School of St. Matthew and its Use of the Old Testament*, rev. ed. Philadelphia: Fortress Press, 1968.
Stern, J.B. 'Jesus' Citation of Dt 6, 5 and Lv 19, 18 in the Light of Jewish Tradition', *CBQ* 28 (1966), 312–16.
Stevenson, J. (ed.) *A New Eusebius: Documents illustrative of the history of the Church to A.D. 337*. London: S.P.C.K., 1957.
Stewart, J.S. *A Man in Christ: The Vital Elements of St. Paul's Religion*, rev. ed. London: Hodder and Stoughton, 1964.
Stock, A. 'Matthean Divorce Texts', *Bib.Theol.Bull.* 8 (1978), 24–33.
Stonehouse, N.B. *The Witness of Matthew and Mark to Christ*. London: Tyndale Press, 1944.
Strachan, R.H. *The Second Epistle of Paul to the Corinthians* (MNTC). London: Hodder and Stoughton, 1935.
Strack, H.L., and Billerbeck, P. *Kommentar zum Neuen Testament aus Talmud und Midrasch*, vols. I–III. München: C.H. Beck'sche Verlagsbuchhandlung, 1956.
Strecker, G. *Der Weg der Gerechtigkeit: Untersuchung zur Theologie des Matthäus* (FRLANT 82). Göttingen: Vandenhoeck und Ruprecht, 1962.
'Die Makarismen der Bergpredigt', *NTS* 17 (1971), 255–75.
*Handlungsorientierter Glaube: Vorstudien zu einer Ethik des Neuen Testaments*. Stuttgart–Berlin: Kreuz Verlag, 1972.
'Strukturen einer neutestamentlichen Ethik', *ZThK* 75 (1978), 117–46.
Stuhlmacher, P. 'Das Ende des Gesetzes: Über Ursprung und Ansatz der paulinischen Theologie', *ZThK* 67 (1970), 14–39.
'Das Gesetz als Thema biblischer Theologie', *ZThK* 75 (1978), 251–80.
*Gerechtigkeit Gottes bei Paulus* (FRLANT 87). Göttingen. Vandenhoeck und Ruprecht, 1965.
Stumpff, A. 'ζημία, κ.τ.λ.', *TDNT* 2. Grand Rapids, Mich.: Wm B. Eerdmans Pub. Co., ET 1964, pp. 888–92.
Styler, G.M. 'The Basis of Obligation in Paul's Christology and Ethics', in *Christ and Spirit in the New Testament*, ed. B. Lindars and S.S. Smalley. Cambridge University Press, 1973, pp. 175–87.
Suggs, M.J. *Wisdom, Christology, and Law in Matthew's Gospel*. Cambridge, Mass.: Harvard University Press, 1970.
Swete, H.B. *The Holy Spirit in the New Testament*. London: Macmillan and Co., 1909.
Synofzik, E. *Die Gerichts- und Vergeltungsaussagen bei Paulus: Eine traditionsgeschichtliche Untersuchung* (GTA 8). Göttingen: Vandenhoeck und Ruprecht, 1977.
Tagawa, K. 'People and Community in the Gospel of Matthew', *NTS*

16 (1970), 149–62.
Tannehill, R.C. *Dying and Rising with Christ* (BZNW 32). Berlin: Verlag Alfred Töpelmann, 1966.
Tasker, R.V.G. *The Gospel According to St. Matthew* (TNTC). London: Tyndale Press, 1961.
*The Second Epistle of Paul to the Corinthians* (TNTC). London: Tyndale Press, 1958.
Thomas, G.F. *Christian Ethics and Moral Philosophy*. New York: Charles Scribner's Sons, 1955.
Thompson, A.A. 'Motivation in the Ethics of Paul' (unpublished Ph.D. thesis). Cambridge, Mass.: Harvard University, 1952.
Thompson, G.H.P. *The Letters of Paul to the Ephesians, to the Colossians, and to Philemon* (CBC). Cambridge University Press, 1967.
Thompson, W.G. *Matthew's Advice to a Divided Community: Mt. 17, 22–18, 35* (Ana.Bib. 44). Rome: Biblical Institute Press, 1970.
Thornton, L.S. *The Common Life in the Body of Christ*, 4th ed. London: Dacre Press, 1963.
Thrall, M.E. *The First and Second Letters of Paul to the Corinthians* (CBC). Cambridge University Press, 1965.
'The Pauline Use of ΣΥΝΕΙΔΗΣΙΣ', *NTS* 14 (1967), 118–25.
Thurneysen, E. *The Sermon on the Mount*. London: S.P.C.K., ET 1965.
Thysman, R. 'L'Éthique de l'Imitation du Christ dans le Nouveau Testament: Situation, notations et variations du thème', *Eph.Theol.Lov.* 42 (1966), 138–75.
Tinsley, E.J. 'Imitation of Christ', in *A Dictionary of Christian Ethics*, ed. J. Macquarrie. London: SCM Press, 1967, p. 163.
*The Imitation of God in Christ* (LHD). London: SCM Press, 1960.
Trilling, W. *Das Wahre Israel: Studien zur Theologie des Matthäus-evangeliums*, 3rd ed. (SANT 10). München: Kösel-Verlag, 1964.
*The Gospel According to St. Matthew*, 2 vols. (NTSR). London: Burns and Oates, ET 1969.
Turner, H.E.W. 'The Life and Teaching of Jesus', in *A Companion to the Bible*, 2nd ed., ed. H.H. Rowley. Edinburgh: T. and T. Clark, 1963, pp. 436–94.
Tyson, J.B. ' "Works of Law" in Galatians', *JBL* 92 (1973), 423–31.
Vermes, G. *Jesus the Jew: A historian's reading of the Gospels*. London: Collins, 1973.
Via, D.O. 'The Church as the Body of Christ in the Gospel of Matthew', *SJT* 11 (1958), 271–86.
Vidler, A.R. *Christ's Strange Work: An Exposition of the Three Uses of God's Law*, rev. ed. London: SCM Press, 1963.
Vidler, A.R., and Whitehouse, W.A. (eds.) *Natural Law: A Christian Reconsideration*. London: SCM Press, 1946.
Vielhauer, P. 'Gesetzesdienst und Stoicheiadienst im Galaterbrief', in *Rechtfertigung: Festschrift für Ernst Käsemann zum 70. Geburtstag*, ed. J. Friedrich, W. Pöhlmann, and P. Stuhlmacher. Tübingen: J.C.B. Mohr (Paul Siebeck) – Göttingen: Vandenhoeck und Ruprecht, 1976, pp. 543–55.
Vincent, M.R. *A Critical and Exegetical Commentary on the Epistles to*

*the Philippians and to Philemon* (ICC). Edinburgh: T. and T. Clark, 1897.

Vögtle, A. 'Röm 13, 11–14 und die "Nah"-Erwartung', in *Rechtfertigung: Festschrift für Ernst Käsemann zum 70. Geburtstag*, ed. J. Friedrich, W. Pöhlmann, and P. Stuhlmacher. Tübingen: J.C.B. Mohr (Paul Siebeck) – Göttingen: Vandenhoeck und Ruprecht, 1976, pp. 557–73.

Walker, R. *Die Heilsgeschichte im ersten Evangelium* (FRLANT 91). Göttingen: Vandenhoeck und Ruprecht, 1967.

Warnach, V. *Agape: Die Liebe als Grundmotiv der neutestamentlichen Theologie*. Düsseldorf: Patmos-Verlag, 1951.

Watson, N.M. 'J.A. Ziesler: The Meaning of Righteousness in Paul: A Linguistic and Theological Enquiry', *NTS* 20 (1974), 217–28.

Wellhausen, J. *Das Evangelium Matthaei*, 2nd ed. Berlin: Druck und Verlag von Georg Reimer, 1914.

Wendland, H.-D. *Ethik des Neuen Testaments: Eine Einführung* (GrNT 4). Göttingen: Vandenhoeck und Ruprecht, 1970.

Westerholm, S. *Jesus and Scribal Authority* (CB: New Testament Series 10). Lund: C.W.K. Gleerup, 1978.

White, R. 'Antinomianism and Christian Ethics', *Theol.* 67 (1964), 202–7.

Whiteley, D.E.H. *Thessalonians* (NClB). Oxford University Press, 1969.

*The Theology of St. Paul*. Oxford: Basil Blackwell, 1974.

Wilckens, U. *Der Brief an die Römer*. Vol. I: Röm 1–5 (EKKNT). Cologne: Benziger Verlag, 1978.

'Statements on the Development of Paul's View of the Law', in *Paul and Paulinism: Essays in honour of C.K. Barrett*, ed. M.D. Hooker and S.G. Wilson. London: S.P.C.K., 1982, pp. 17–26.

Wilder, A.N. 'Eschatological Imagery and Earthly Circumstance', *NTS* 5 (1959), 229–45.

*Eschatology and Ethics in the Teaching of Jesus*, rev. ed. New York: Harper and Bros., 1950.

'Kerygma, Eschatology and Social Ethics', in *The Background of the New Testament and Its Eschatology*, ed. W.D. Davies and D. Daube. Cambridge University Press, 1956, pp. 509–36.

'Sermon on the Mount', *IB* 7. Nashville–New York: Abingdon Press, 1951, pp. 155–64.

Williams, C.S.C. 'I & II Corinthians', *Peake's Commentary on the Bible*. London: Thomas Nelson and Sons, 1962, pp. 954–72.

Wilson, W.E. 'The Development of Paul's Doctrine of Dying and Rising again with Christ', *ExT* 42 (1931), 562–5.

Windisch, H. 'Das Problem des paulinischen Imperativs', *ZNW* 23 (1924), 265–81.

*Der Sinn der Bergpredigt*, 2nd ed. (UNT 16). Leipzig: J.C. Hinrichs Verlag, 1937. ET: *The Meaning of the Sermon on the Mount*. Philadelphia: Westminster Press, 1951.

*Paulus und Christus: Ein biblisch-religionsgeschichtlicher Vergleich* (UNT 24). Leipzig: J.C. Hinrichs'sche Buchhandlung, 1934.

Wire, A.C. 'Pauline Theology as an Understanding of God: the Explicit and the Implicit' (Ph.D. Thesis). London: University Microfilms

International, 1974.
Yoder, J.H. *The Politics of Jesus*. Grand Rapids, Mich.: Wm B. Eerdmans Pub. Co., 1972.
Young, F.M. 'Temple Cult and Law in Early Christianity', *NTS* 19 (1973), 325–38.
Zahn, T. *Das Evangelium des Matthäus*. Leipzig: A. Deichert'sche Verlagsbuchhandlung (Georg Böhme), 1903.
Ziesler, J.A. *The Meaning of Righteousness in Paul: A Linguistic and Theological Enquiry* (SNTS Monograph Series 20). Cambridge University Press, 1972.
Zillessen, A. 'Die Begründung der sittlichen Forderungen bei Jesus und bei Paulus', *Theol.Arbeiten*, n.s. 5 (1901), 33–71.
Zimmerman, H. 'Christus Nachfolgen: Eine Studie zu den Nachfolge-Worten der synoptischen Evangelien', *Theol.u.Glaube* 53 (1963), 241–55.
Zumstein, J. *La condition du croyant dans l'Évangile selon Matthieu* (OBO 16). Göttingen: Vandenhoeck und Ruprecht, 1977.

# INDEX OF SCRIPTURE REFERENCES

## GENERAL INDEX

(*M:* Matthew  *P:* Paul  *C:* Comparison of Matthew and Paul)